The Sociology of War and Violence

War is a highly complex and dynamic form of social conflict. This new book demonstrates the importance of using sociological tools to understand the changing character of war and organised violence. The author offers an original analysis of the historical and contemporary impact that coercion and warfare have on the transformation of social life, and vice versa. Although war and violence were decisive components in the formation of modernity most analyses tend to shy away from the sociological study of the gory origins of contemporary social life. In contrast, this book brings the study of organised violence to the fore by providing a wide-ranging sociological analysis that links classical and contemporary theories with specific historical and geographical contexts. Topics covered include violence before modernity, warfare in the modern age, nationalism and war, war propaganda, battlefield solidarity, war and social stratification, gender and organised violence, and the new wars debate.

Siniša Malešević is Senior Lecturer in the School of Political Science and Sociology at the National University of Ireland, Galway. His recent books include *Identity as Ideology: Understanding Ethnicity and Nationalism* (2006), *The Sociology of Ethnicity* (2004) and a co-edited volume, *Ernest Gellner and Contemporary Social Thought* (Cambridge, 2007).

The Sociology of War and Violence

Siniša Malešević

CAMBRIDGE UNIVERSITY PRESS
Cambridge, New York, Melbourne, Madrid, Cape Town, Singapore,
São Paulo, Delhi, Mexico City

Cambridge University Press
The Edinburgh Building, Cambridge CB2 8RU, UK

Published in the United States of America by Cambridge University Press, New York

www.cambridge.org
Information on this title: www.cambridge.org/9780521731690

First published 2010
Reprinted 2012

Printed in the United Kingdom at the University Press, Cambridge

A catalogue record for this publication is available from the British Library

Library of Congress Cataloguing in Publication data
Malešević Siniša.
  The sociology of war and violence / Siniša Malešević.
    p. cm.
  Includes bibliographical references and index.
  ISBN 978-0-521-51651-8 – ISBN 978-0-521-73169-0 (pbk.)
  1. War and society. 2. Sociology, Military. 3. Violence–Social aspects. I. Title.
  HM554.M35 2010
  303.6–dc22
  2010014629

ISBN 978-0-521-51651-8 Hardback
ISBN 978-0-521-73169-0 Paperback

For my grandmother Vuka, a decorated survivor of two brutal wars, and for my two boys, Alex and Luka, with a hope that they will never experience the calamity of organised violence.

Contents

Part III   Warfare: ideas and practices

Part IV   War, violence and social divisions

Acknowledgments

I am indebted for support and suggestions to many colleagues who have either read draft chapters or heard me presenting segments of this work at various conferences and workshops: John Breuilly, Stewart Clegg, Randall Collins, Brendan Flynn, John Hutchinson, Richard Jenkins, Krishan Kumar, Michael Mann, Niall O'Dochartaigh, John Rex, Kevin Ryan, Anthony D. Smith and Gordana Uzelac. Special thanks go to Miguel Centeno, John A. Hall and Stacey Scriver for their encouragement and comments on the entire manuscript and for Stacey's invaluable help with editing. I am also grateful for the suggestions provided by the anonymous reviewers for the Cambridge University Press.

Some sections of Chapters 1 and 2 have appeared in print before in a substantially different form ('Solidary Killers and Egoistic Pacifists: Violence, War and Social Action', *Journal of Power*, 2008, 1 (2): 207–16; 'Collective Violence and Power', in S. Clegg and M. Haugaard (eds.), *Sage Handbook of Power*, London: Sage, 2009. pp. 274–90 and 'How Pacifist were the Founding Fathers?', *European Journal of Social Theory*, 2010, 13 (2)). Chapter 10 is a revised version of the paper originally published as 'The Sociology of New Wars?: Assessing the Causes and Objectives of Contemporary Violent Conflicts', *International Political Sociology*, 2008, 2(2): 97–112. I am thankful to the publishers for permitting me to draw upon these papers.

Introduction: war, violence and the social

The human relationship with violence and war is complex and paradoxical. On the one hand there is near universal condemnation of violent acts, which is reflected in the strong normative prohibitions against the physical harm of fellow humans and, as such, is underpinned by legal systems all around the world. On the other hand, our popular culture, novels, history textbooks, mass media, art, games, children's toys and many other everyday outlets are saturated with images and instruments of violence. Although no sound person would openly advocate organised killing of other human beings, there is a palpable and widespread fascination and even obsession with violence and warfare. Just skimming the popular bestsellers of the last several decades it becomes obvious that there is an almost inexhaustible hunger for books, documentaries and motion picture portrayals of violent movements and warmongering individuals.[1] Whereas it seems there can never be enough books and films on Hitler and the Nazis, the works and deeds of Gandhi and Mother Theresa draw very modest audiences. While peace and brotherly love might be the proclaimed ideals, it is war and violence that attract popular attention and fascination.

All of this could suggest that a human being is a hypocritical creature and that below the surface of civilised manners and altruistic ethics lays a dormant beast that awaits the first opportunity to inflict injury on its fellow humans. Such a view, in one or another form, has dominated much of social and political thought from the early works of Machiavelli and Hobbes to the contemporary realist and the neo-Darwinian interpretations of 'human nature'. In Machiavelli's (1997 [1532]: 65) own words: 'it may be said of men in general that they are ungrateful and fickle, dissemblers, avoiders of danger, and greedy of gain'. In a similar way, for Hobbes (1998 [1651]) our original 'state of nature' was characterised by endemic violence involving ferocious

[1] For example Gardner and Resnick's research (1996) on the 2,000 programmes broadcasted on the major US television networks between 1973 and 1993 shows that over 60 per cent featured violent action and more than 50 per cent of the programmes' leading characters were involved in violence.

struggle over gain, security and reputation – 'a war of every man against every man'.

This highly popular understanding of the human relationship to violence and war is countered by an alternative and also influential view that goes all the way back to Rousseau, Kant and Paine and is currently echoed in much of the literature that dominates such fields as conflict resolution and peace studies. This perspective starts from the proposition that human beings are essentially peaceful, reasoned, compassionate and cooperative creatures who become violent under the influence of 'social ills' such as private property, class divisions, institutionalised greed or something else. As Rousseau (2004 [1755]: 27) puts it: 'The first man who, having fenced in a piece of land, said "this is mine", and found people naive enough to believe him, that man was the true founder of civil society. From how many crimes, wars, and murders, from how many horrors and misfortunes might not any one have saved man-kind, by pulling up the stakes, or filling up the ditch, and crying to his fel-lows: Beware of listening to this impostor; you are undone if you once forget that the fruits of the earth belong to us all, and the earth itself to nobody'.

These two sharply contrasting perspectives assume that either we inhabit an egoistic universe of insecurity and violence where, as Hobbes puts it, like wolves, each man preys on those around him, or that our natural state is one of a harmonious communal life characterised by intense solidarity, altruism and peace. From the first perspective, society is the external guarantor of order that pacifies the beast within us all; from the second, modern society is responsible for corrupting the essential goodness of human nature.

Although these two contrasting standpoints have commanded much atten-tion for the past three centuries, neither provides a sociologically accurate account of the human relationship to war and violence. Rather than being an inherent biological or psychological reflex for self-preservation or an expedi-ent instrument for individual gain, much of human violence is profoundly social in character. Being social does not automatically imply an innate pro-pensity towards harmony and peace. On the contrary, it is our sociality, not individuality, which makes us both compassionate altruists and enthusiastic killers. The recent empirical research (Holmes 1985; Grossman 1996; Bourke 2000; Collins 2008) shows clearly that as individuals we are not particu-larly good at violent action, and in contrast to the popular representation, a great deal of violent individual behaviour is characterised by incompetence, messiness and is of very short duration (see Chapter 8). As Collins (2008: 14) demonstrates, the majority of serious fights involving small groups are no more than quick blusters and one-punch affairs: 'the actual gunfight at the

O.K. Corral in Tombstone, Arizona, in 1881 took less than thirty seconds' while 'the movie version took seven minutes'. In real life, rather than enjoying actual violence, human beings tend to avoid violent confrontations. In contrast to Machiavelli's and Hobbes's diagnosis, a solitary individual is unlikely to fight: when alone and weak we avoid violent altercations, we run away. The war of all against all is an empirical impossibility: as any successful violent action entails organisation and as organised action requires collective coordination, hierarchy and the delegation of tasks, all warfare is inevitably a social event.

Hence, violence is neither a result of innate aggressiveness nor of externally induced 'social ills' but is something that requires intensive social action. As human beings we are capable of, and prone to, both selfishness and solidarity. The key paradox of the Machiavelli/Hobbes vs. Rousseau/Kant debate is that since both perspectives lack the sociological eye, they misdiagnose social reality: the point is that when we act in the image of Hobbes's state of nature – as egoistic self-preservers – we do that for very Rousseauian reasons and nearly always in Rousseauian contexts. As we need others to kill so we also need others for whom to sacrifice ourselves. Our social embeddedness is the source of both our selfishness and our altruism. We fight and slaughter best when in the presence of others – to impress, to please, to conform, to hide fear, to profit, to avoid shame and for many other reasons too. And it is these very same social ties that make us equally and often simultaneously martyrs and murderers. Historical experience indicates that life becomes 'poor, nasty, brutish and short' not when we are 'solitary' but when, and because, we live in groups.

The fact that much of our relationship with violence and war is determined by our social character suggests that to understand warfare and violence we need to understand the social. In other words, without comprehensive sociological analysis there cannot be a proper explanation of violence and war. Unfortunately, it seems that a great deal of contemporary scholarship does not share this view as neither the conventional studies of war and collective violence engage significantly with sociology nor does a contemporary mainstream sociology devote much attention to the study of war and organised violence (Shaw 1984; Joas 2003; Wimmer and Min 2006). The main aim of this book is to demonstrate the intrinsic indispensability of using sociological tools to gain a full understanding of the changing character of war and violence. In particular, the book focuses on the historical and contemporary impact of coercion and warfare on the transformation of social life and vice versa. Although collective violence and war have shaped much of recorded human history and were decisive components in the formation of the modern social order, most contemporary analyses tend to shy away from the socio-logical study of the gory origins and nature of social life. However, whether we like it or not, violence is one of the central constituents of human subjectivity, and modern subjectivity in particular, since modernity as we know it would be unthinkable without organised violence.

This is not to say that human beings as such are either prone to or like violence. On the contrary it is precisely because we share a normative abhor-rence towards violent behaviour, are generally – as individuals – feeble exe-cutioners of violent acts and much of our daily life is free of violence, that we find wars and killing so fascinating. They are fascinating because, from the everyday standpoint, they are rare, difficult and strange. Our obsession is rooted in our fear and awe of something that is not common, usual and regular but extraordinary and, as such, in some respects incomprehensible. Since inflicting harm on other humans goes so much against the grain of our socialisation and is not something we ordinarily see or participate in, it becomes enthralling. Rather than being a sign of our 'essentially violent nature', the human fascination with violence and war is a good indicator that these phenomena are odd, unusual and atypical. We are curious about some-thing we do not know and rarely, if ever, experience, not with something that is ordinary and ever present. Violence attracts our attention precisely because we are not good at it and do not encounter it on a daily basis. As Moscovici (1986: 157) sardonically remarks, the image of the devil 'is so useful and so powerful precisely because you do not meet him in the street'.

However if human beings are for the most part wary of violence and bad at being violent, why is warfare so prevalent in human history and, particularly, why has it so dramatically increased in the modern age?

In an attempt to answer this question this book focuses on the role of social organisation and ideology in fostering social conditions for the mass participation of individuals in large-scale violent acts and especially in war-fare. The central argument is that, although as individuals we are neither very willing nor very capable of using violence, social organisations and the process of ideologisation can and often do aid our transformation into fer-vent and adept killing machines. The key point is that any long-lasting col-lective violence, particularly large-scale conflicts such as warfare, entails two vital ingredients: a complex, structural, organisational capacity and a potent legitimising ideology. As violence does not come naturally and automatic-ally to humans, its successful application on a mass scale, such as warfare, requires highly developed organisational mechanisms of social control and well articulated and institutionally embedded ideological doctrines capable of justifying such action. As Collins (2008: 11) puts it adeptly: 'if it were not socially well organised, wide-participation fighting would not be possible'. Instead of interpreting war and other forms of organised violence in biological, cultural, individualist or collective rationalist terms the focus shifts towards the role of organisation and ideology. More specifically, I analyse the relationship between war, violence and the social through the prism of two historical processes which I see as paramount in accounting for the dramatic rise of organised violence in modernity: the cumulative bureaucratisation of coercion and the centrifugal (mass) ideologisation.

The cumulative bureaucratisation of coercion

Max Weber (1968) provided the most potent diagnosis of modernity by emphasising the almost inescapable iron cage of rationality that gradually permeates and routinises everyday social life. The ever increasing transformation from traditional forms of social action towards those governed by instrumental and value rationality creates a social environment whereby personal ties and nepotistic relationships become slowly but steadily replaced with impersonal rules and bureaucratic regulations. Unlike traditional authority, where a leader's domination was essentially an inherited personal right, bureaucratic organisation operates through a consistent system of abstract laws. Although both the traditional and the bureaucratic forms of organisation are rigorously hierarchical, unlike its ad hoc and clientelist traditional counterpart, the typical bureaucratic administration is built around principles that insist on the rule-governed, meritocratic and transparent model of hierarchical domination. The key feature of the bureaucratic model of administration lies in its privileging of knowledge (i.e. epistemic authority) which, according to Weber, makes this form of social action much more effective and productive than any of its historical predecessors. In other words, the phenomenal historical success of the bureaucratic mode of social organisation owes a great deal to its instrumental efficiency.

Although Weber's analysis of bureaucratic rationalisation has become a staple of mainstream contemporary sociology, most analysts neglect two crucial facts. Firstly, although much social theory focuses on the economic or cultural characteristics and consequences of bureaucratic rationalisation (e.g. Lash and Urry 1987; Sklair 1991; 2002), and in particular the relationship between the bureaucracy and capitalism, the principle realm of bureaucratisation, the realm where it originated, is the military. As Weber (1968: 1152) emphasises, the central component of bureaucratic rationality is discipline and 'military discipline gives birth to all discipline' (see Chapter 1). Hence, to deal adequately with the process of bureaucratisation it is necessary to shift our attention towards the role of the organisation of coercion.

Secondly, the birth and expansion of the bureaucratic model of rational organisation has historically been wedded to institutions that were able to monopolise the use of violence. That is, there is no effective use or threat to use violence without developed social organisation. Historically speaking, it was warfare that gave birth to, and consequently depended on the existence of, large-scale social organisations (see Chapter 9). Despite popular perceptions that see the modern world as less violent than its historical precursors and bureaucratic rationalisation as something that prevents coercive action, all bureaucratisation is deeply rooted in coercive control. Since bureaucratic domination rests on the inculcation and control of discipline and remains dependent on disciplined action, it requires and demands obedience. In this sense a factory worker, a civil servant, a teacher or a nurse are, in a general sense, governed by the very same principles of bureaucratic organisation as soldiers and the police. This implies not only clearly defined hierarchies, the division of labour and meritocratic social mobility, but also the regular and regulated execution of commands, strict compliance with the rules of the respective organisation and loyalty to the organisation. Moreover, all of these organisational demands are underpinned by the legal codes that stipulate penalties for noncompliance. In other words, the organisational principles which govern most of our lives are profoundly coercive in character which is not surprising since they originated in the military sphere.

However, what is important to emphasise is that this process of bureaucratisation which in its rudimentary form emerged with the birth of warfare in the late Mesolithic era has been constantly expanding since. The coercive power of social organisations, most recently taking the dominant form of nation-states, has increased over the last 10,000 years and has dramatically intensified over that last 200 years (see Chapters 3 and 4). Not only have the modern social organisations, such as states, managed to monopolise the use of violence over huge stretches of their territory thus eventually covering most of the globe, but they have also gradually become capable of mobilising and recruiting entire societies for warfare and have spectacularly multiplied the numbers of those killed in conflicts. Whereas in the pre-modern world of the nascent bureaucratisation of coercion, killing was limited in scope, the modern bureaucratic machines are able to act swiftly and murder millions in a matter of months if not days. As Eckhardt (1992: 272) shows, while at the beginning of the high Middle Ages the casualties of all wars throughout the known world had amounted to a mere 60,000; the twentieth century alone was responsible for more than 110 million deaths caused directly by warfare. Hence, despite contextual contingencies, time-specific reversals and historical ups and downs the bureaucratisation of coercion is a cumulative historical process: it continues to increase over time as does the destructive power of social organisations. In other words, as human populations increase, develop and expand there is a greater demand for the multiplicity of services, material and symbolic goods that only large-scale social organisations can provide on a regular basis. However, as human beings grow ever more dependent on the social organisations, the organisations themselves become more powerful and continue to increase their coercive reach and depth. This is most evident in the gradual transformation of warfare which initially was limited to a narrow circle of aristocrats engaging in quasi-ritualistic skirmishes with a few casualties, and eventually became a total event involving millions of mobilised and ideologised citizens bent on the destruction of entire societies deemed to be enemies.

It is true that social organisations are not superhuman and omnipotent things that entirely determine human behaviour but are processual and dynamic entities created by and reliant on continuous human action. Nevertheless, it is precisely these dynamic, historical contingencies that have ultimately created the situation wherein human beings require, and in some ways feel comfortable with, the prevalence of social organisations around them. The cumulative bureaucratisation of coercion is a historical process that for the most part does not go against the grain of the popular doxa: although it is essentially a coercive mechanism it is not something superimposed on individuals against their will. Instead, it is a process that entails tacit and sustained support at all levels of society. It is a product of long-term human action and, as such, is much more overbearing precisely because it necessitates, and grows on, continuous ideological legitimation. To sum up, the bureaucratisation of coercion is cumulative because it is an ongoing historical process that involves the constant increase of organisational capability for destruction; it is bureaucratic since it entails ever-expanding bureaucratic rationalisation in the Weberian sense, which originated in the military sphere; and it is coercive since it involves not only the control and employment of violence and the waging of wars but it is also able to internally pacify social order by establishing the monopolistic threat on the use of violence.

Centrifugal ideologisation

Since human beings as individuals are circumspect of, and incompetent at, violence, successful warfare entails the existence of elaborate social organisations. It is the internal disciplinary effects of social organisations that make soldiers fight by inhibiting them from escaping the battlefields and it is social organisation that transforms chaotic and incoherent micro-level violence into an organised machine of macro-level destruction. However, no social organisation would be able to succeed in the long term if its actions were not popularly understood as just. This is particularly relevant for organisations that utilise violence since violent action per se is nearly universally perceived as an illegitimate form of social conduct. Hence, the cumulative bureaucratisation of coercion often goes hand in hand with the legitimizing ideology.

Since ideology is one of the most deeply contested concepts in social science, it is essential to make clear from the outset what is meant by this term. Traditionally, ideology was conceived as a rigid, closed system of ideas that governs social and political action.[2] Typically, individuals were deemed to be ideological if they expressed unquestioned loyalty to the principles set out in the doctrine they adhered to, or if they followed a particular ideological blueprint so that they acted contrary to their own self-interests. Representative examples of such rigid systems of thought include followers of closed religious sects or radical political organisations. Recent studies have questioned such understandings of ideology by emphasising the flexibility and plasticity of ideological beliefs and practices, as well as the indispensability of ideology for making sense of one's social and political reality. In a number of highly influential works Michael Billig (1988, 1995, 2002) has demonstrated that the popular reception of ideological messages is always unsystematic and riddled with contradictions. Beliefs are often anchored in shared categories and concepts of recognisable ideological traditions, and are commonly perceived not as ideological but as obvious, normal and natural, and yet these categories of thought are rarely, if ever, treated as monolithic systems of meaning. Rather, popular beliefs and practices are filled with 'ideological dilemmas' that originate in the social environment, where there are always competing hierarchies of power. Hence, when ideology confronts the complexities and contingencies of everyday life, human beings find themselves in ongoing

[2] For an extensive critique of the Marxist, functionalist and post-structuralist approaches to ideology see Malešević 2002; 2006.

'contradictions of common sense'. Michael Freeden (1996, 2003) emphasises the cognitive necessity of ideological belief and practice, in addition to its flexibility. In his view, ideology maps one's social and political world. Social facts and political events never speak for themselves and thus require a process of decoding, and it is the use of a particular ideological map that helps one understand and contextualise these facts and events. Ideology imposes coherence and provides structure to contingent actions, events and images so that the ideological narrative assists in creating socially comprehensible meaning. Hence, ideology is best conceptualised as a relatively universal and complex social process through which human actors articulate their actions and beliefs. It is a form of 'thought-action' that infuses, but does not necessarily determine, everyday social practice. Since much of the ideological content projects transcendent grand vistas of the particular (imagined) social order, it surpasses experience and as such evades testability. Most ideological discourses invoke superior knowledge claims, advanced ethical norms and collective interests, and often rely on popular affects with a view of justifying actual or potential social action. Ideology is a complex process whereby ideas and practices come together in the course of legitimising or contesting power relations (Malešević 2002; 2006).

Although some form of proto-ideological power has been around since the emergence of warfare and other forms of organised violence, the modern age is the true cradle of fully fledged ideologies and the ongoing processes of centrifugal ideologisation (see Chapters 3, 4 and 6). Whereas traditional rulers made extensive use of the legitimising potency of proto-ideologies, such as religion and mythology, to justify conquests and coercive forms of governance, it is really modernity that requires and provides a really elaborate and full justification of violent action. There are many reasons why this is so but three points stand out. Firstly, the unprecedented structural and organisational transformation of social orders brought about by modernity have, as Nairn (1977) aptly puts it, invited ordinary people into history. In other words, the bureaucratic organisation of modern states, the spread of secular, democratic and liberal ideas, the dramatic increase in levels of literacy, the expansion of cheap and affordable publishing and the press, the extension of the military draft and the gradual development of the public sphere, among others, have all fostered the emergence of a new, much more politicised citizenry. Whereas the medieval peasantry generally had neither any interest in, nor the possibility of, politically engaging in the working of the polities they inhabited, the people of the early modern world were not only receptive to new political interpretations of their reality but were also able and willing to take an active part in these political processes. Hence from then on, centrifugal (mass) ideologisation proliferates: ideologies become central for large sections of the population, meeting the popular demand to articulate the parameters of a desirable social order.

Secondly, the gradual dissemination of the Enlightenment (and later the Romanticist and other) principles that posit human reason, autonomy, toleration and peace as the central values of modernity, make the use of violence in this era less legitimate than in any previous period. What started off in the eighteenth and early nineteenth centuries as the eccentric ideas of a handful of intellectuals became universal rules safeguarded in the constitutions of nearly all modern states: rights to life, liberty, equality before the law, the preservation of peace and the prohibition of 'cruel and unusual punishment' (see Chapter 4). In principle, the modern age, like no other, has little tolerance for the use of violence against other human beings. Torture and public hangings are now popularly perceived as barbaric practices that have no place in the modern world.

Thirdly, as this historical period also saw an unprecedented expansion of mass scale violence, there was an organisational and popular demand to find a reconciliation between this violent reality and the profoundly anti-violent normative universe of the era. Since more people were killed in the twentieth century alone than in the rest of human history combined, during that century it became imperative to resolve the ontological dissonance created by the discrepancy between the reality and the stated ideals. Thus, ideology took and still takes central stage in this process of interpreting and justifying something that seems so absurd and irreconcilable. In this way, ideology becomes a cornerstone of everyday life not just for the main perpetuators of violence, such as the social organisations and their leaders, but also for the ordinary citizens who all wish to feel comfortable that their struggle has a just cause and the use of violence against the monstrous enemy is nothing more than a necessary evil (see Chapter 7).

Furthermore, as social organisations in modernity become ever larger they require and use ideological glue to tie the diverse citizenry into quasi-homogenous entities able and willing to support war and other coercive causes when necessary. To achieve this, the rulers utilise the process of ideologisation with the intention of projecting the genuine bonds of micro-level solidarity onto the ideological mass terrain of large-scale nation-states (see Chapter 6). In this sense, centrifugal ideologisation is a mass phenomenon that historically spreads from the centre of social organisations (or social movements, or both) to gradually encompass an ever wider population. It is centrifugal because it is created by the political and cultural elites, it initially originates in small circles of dedicated followers and it radiates from the centre of the ideological activity (i.e. the state, religious organisation, military institution or the social movement) towards the broader masses of population. This, however, does not presuppose that ideologisation is an exclusively one-way, top-down, process. Rather its strength and pervasiveness are dependent on mutual reinforcement: while the social organisations help disseminate and institutionalise the ideological message (through mass media, education institutions, public sphere, governmental agencies, police and military), groups in civil society and family networks buttress the normative scaffolding which ties the ideological macro-level narrative with the micro-level solidarity of face–to-face interaction.

The plan of the book

Any book that attempts to discuss war and violence from a sociological viewpoint encounters one important obstacle: on the one hand, although there is a vast literature on warfare and violence, most of it lacks any sociological grounding; on the other hand, contemporary sociology has devised potent conceptual and analytical tools for the study of social reality, but much of mainstream sociology shows little or no interest in studying warfare and organised violence. This means that since nearly all aspects of social life have been affected and shaped by violence and warfare there is a need for thorough theoretical and empirical engagement with the huge repertoire of social processes and social institutions involved in violence and warfare. However, as it is virtually impossible to deal with all aspects of these phenomena in a single book I have had to be selective in my presentation. For example, the book does not deal extensively with specific types of collective violence such as policing, revolutions, genocides or terrorism, which are the only forms of organised coercion that have received extensive attention in mainstream sociology.[3] Instead, this book focuses on the topics that are central in defining the field of the sociology of war and violence. Hence, the first part charts the theoretical foundations; the second situates the sociological study of violence and war in specific historical timeframes and geographical settings; the third and fourth explore the major thematic issues that shape the

---

[3] On revolutions see Moore 1966; Tilly 1978; Skocpol 1979; Goldstone 1991; on policing and surveillance see Giddens 1985; Dandeker 1990; Lyon 2001; on genocide see Bauman 1989; Mann 2005; on terrorism see Hafez 2006, Pape 2006 and Gambetta 2006.

relationships between war, violence and society such as nationalism, propaganda, solidarity, stratification and gender, whereas the last part looks at contemporary warfare.

The first chapter analyses the contributions of classical social thought
to the study of war and violence. It argues that contrary to the established
view, and unlike their contemporary counterparts, the classical social theorists were preoccupied with the study of war and violence and devised complex concepts and models to detect and analyse the social manifestations of
coercion. Moreover, I attempt to show that most of classical social thought
was in fact sympathetic to the 'militarist' understanding of social life. In
many respects, the classical social theorists shared the analytical, epistemological and even moral universe that understood war and violence as the key
mechanisms of social change. The structural neglect of this rich and versatile theoretical tradition is linked to the hegemony of normative 'pacifist'
re-interpretations of the classics in the aftermath of the two total wars of the
twentieth century.

In the second chapter I provide a critical survey of the contemporary sociology of war and violence. Although mainstream contemporary sociology
remains for the most part ignorant of this research topic, there are significant individual contributions that deserve appraisal. I critically assess
instrumentalist, culturalist and sociobiological explanations before devoting
considerable attention to the most fruitful paradigm in the field: organisational
materialism. I argue that the intrinsic quality of this particular research tradition is in significant part derived from its ability to revive, and indirectly
rehabilitate, the concepts, ideas and explanatory models of classical social
thought about wars and violence.

The third chapter explores the social and historical origins of war and
organised violence. I trace the development and transition of collective violence and warfare from the beginning of the Mesolithic period, through
antiquity and medieval times and all the way to early modern times. In all
of these historical periods the relationship between war, violence and the
social is analyzed through the prism of the cumulative bureaucratisation of
coercion and centrifugal ideologisation. I argue that contrary to the popular
perception, warfare is a historically novel phenomenon feeding off, and simultaneously stimulating, the growth of social organisations and ideologies.

Chapter 4 expands this argument further by looking at the paradoxical
character of modernity, which prides itself on being the most enlightened era
while at the same time witnessing more destruction and bloodshed then ever
before. This situation is defined as a form of an ontological dissonance that

entails extensive reliance on ideological justification and the proliferation of social organisations involved in this process. Hence the chapter charts the development and the dramatic expansion of the cumulative bureaucratisation of coercion and centrifugal ideologisation in the context of late eighteenth-, nineteenth- and twentieth-century warfare.

In an attempt to go beyond the historical experience of Western Europe, Chapter 5 looks at the relationship between organised violence and social development in Eastern Europe, Asia, Africa, and North and South America. The focal point is the role of warfare as a vehicle of rapid modernisation. Although I agree with the general argument that posits Europe as developing historically unique conditions for early modernisation (i.e. the 'European miracle' debate), I depart from the 'Europeanist' position in stressing the variety of non-European cases where warfare was a catalyst of intensive social change.

Since warfare and nationalism are often perceived as conceptual twins, Chapter 6 focuses on dissecting this rapport. I outline and criticise the two dominant interpretations, both of which posit a direct causal link between nationalism and war. In contrast to the naturalist theories that see strong national attachments as a primary cause of war and the formative approaches that understand nationalism as an inevitable product of warfare, I argue that there is no automatic link between the two. Instead, I articulate an alternative interpretation that problematises the nature of group solidarity in large-scale violent conflicts and that focuses on the role of centrifugal ideologisation and the cumulative bureaucratisation of coercion in fostering nationalist habitus.

Chapter 7 analyses war propaganda and the workings of micro-level solidarity on the battlefield. The aim is to dispel some commonly held views and myths about the impact of war propaganda and to assess what motivates individuals to participate in protracted large-scale violent conflicts. I argue that rather than being an all-pervasive force able to change popular opinion quickly and dramatically, much of war propaganda is a weak and parasitic force that supplements and crystallises already held views. Consequently, the most receptive audiences for propaganda are those who are far away from the battlefield. In contrast, frontline soldiers are largely ignorant of propaganda messages since their principal source of motivations is located in the micro-level solidarity of the small group bond.

Chapter 8 critically engages with the sociological research on stratification. It pinpoints the inherent neglect of the role organised coercion plays in establishing, maintaining and reproducing social hierarchies that characterises the mainstream sociological theories of stratification. I argue that since stratification originates in violence it remains wedded to the coercive mechanisms: notwithstanding its fairly recent ostensible indiscernibility, there is no social inequity which in the last instance is not underpinned by coercive organisation. In particular, the chapter explores the transformation of stratification through the prism of the cumulative bureaucratisation of coercion and centrifugal ideologisation.

Chapter 9 undertakes a similar analysis with regards to the relationship between gender and war. It attempts to unravel the riddle of women's near universal exclusion from frontline fighting. In contrast to the existing masculinist, culturalist and feminist explanations of this phenomenon I advance an interpretation that emphasises the crucial impact of social organisations and ideologies. Although there is no denying that the gendering of war is functional to the perpetuation of warfare, what is sociologically more interesting is the fact that this division is created and reinforced by the organisational and ideological apparatuses and is, as such, indispensable for initiating and maintaining warfare.

Finally, the last chapter engages with the current sociological analyses of the so-called 'new wars'. It has been suggested that these new wars erupt in the empty space that allegedly separates the coordinated machinery of global markets from the incoherent and disconnected forms of localised politics. The chapter provides a critical analysis of the sociological accounts of the new-wars paradigm with a spotlight on the purpose and causes of the recent wars. I argue that despite the development of elaborate models these analyses rest on shaky foundations and hence fail to convince. There has been no dramatic shift in the causes and objectives of contemporary violent conflict; indeed, in most respects, recent warfare follows the already established tracks that have been on the increase since the dawn of modernity: the cumulative bureaucratisation of coercion and centrifugal ideologisation.

Part I

Collective violence and sociological theory

1 War and violence in classical social thought

Introduction

Most contemporary commentators reproach the classical sociologists for ignoring the study of warfare and collective violence (Shaw 1984; Marsland 1986: 8; Giddens 1985; Scruton 1987a; 1987b; Mann 1988: 147; Joas 2003). Ashworth and Dandeker state that given the ubiquity of war and violence in human history 'it is remarkable that its study has remained largely at the periphery of sociological analysis' (1987: 1). The most common reason identified for this neglect is the foundational heritage of the Enlightenment, purportedly shared by all major social theorists, which conceptualised modernity in terms of universal rationality, economic growth, scientific progress and peace (Tiryakian 1999: 474–8; Joas 2003). Rather than being seen as a regular and structurally intrinsic feature of social life, war and violence were largely perceived as irrational, atavistic facets of the primeval era that were bound to disappear with the arrival and spread of modernity. Although there is some truth in these criticisms, the judgment is both too severe and too hasty. The apparent neglect has less to do with classical social thought itself and much more to do with developments in social and political thinking after World War II (WWII). The central premise of this chapter is that classical social thought was not, by and large, ignorant of war and violence. Instead it is the hegemony of anti-militarist social theory in the second half of the twentieth century that has cleansed sociology from the study of warfare by simultaneously ignoring its rich and versatile 'bellicose' tradition and by reinterpreting the classics in strictly 'pacifist' terms.[1] Classical social thought was actually much wider and significantly less 'pacifist' than that of the 'holy trinity', Marx, Durkheim and Weber, who were established as the principal, if not the only, representatives of the sociological canon following WWII.

---

[1] The use of quote marks for the terms such as 'pacifist' and 'bellicose' is to indicate where these terms are used in a purely descriptive rather than the standard normative sense.

In many respects the late nineteenth century and early twentieth century, the time of sociology's birth as a field of study, was dominated by 'militarist' social thought. Much of this intellectual tradition is worth revisiting, as once the trappings of normative bellicosity are removed there is a wealth of sociologically potent concepts and ideas that can help us make sense of the profoundly sociological phenomena of war and violence.

The chapter is in three parts: in the first part, Marx's, Durkheim's and Weber's understanding of war and violence is explored; in the second section the central ideas of 'bellicose' classical social thought are analysed; the final part briefly assesses the contemporary relevance of this thought – a topic which is explored further in the following chapter.

The 'holy trinity' and organised violence

Although the second half of the twentieth century saw Marx, Durkheim and Weber firmly established as the undisputed 'founding fathers' of sociology this outcome was far from inevitable. In fact when sociology took its first institutional steps at the end of the nineteenth and beginning of the twentieth century the influence of these three authors was not greater and in some cases was significantly less than those of Gabriel Tarde, Ferdinand Toennies, Werner Sombart, Lester Ward, Leopold von Wiese, Ernest Troeltsch and Ludwig Gumplowicz, to name but a few. While both Marx and Weber were recognisable names neither was seen as a sociologist, while Durkheim's influence could not compare to that of August Comte, whose ideas influenced statesmen from Turkey to Brazil, or Herbert Spencer, whose books were absolute bestsellers in Britain and the United States (Risjord 2005: 56).[2] The emergence of the 'holy trinity' as the canon of classical social thought is in great part related to the relevance of their concepts and theories in understanding the directions which the course of modernity took in the second half of the twentieth century. It is difficult, if not impossible, to dispute the originality, sophistication, complexity and applicability of their ideas and models. As Mouzelis (1995: 245–6) rightly argues, Marx, Weber and Durkheim were not imposed on the sociological community by decree but were accepted on the basis that their conceptual models, theories and analytical frameworks were nearly universally deemed to be superior to the works of others in terms of their 'cognitive potency, analytical acuity,

---

[2] As Risjord (2005: 56) points out 'Among the nineteenth century bestsellers Herbert Spencer's Social Statics (1851) trailed only the Bible and Harriet Beecher Stowe's Uncle Tom's Cabin'.

power of synthesis and imaginative reach and originality'. However their obvious merit is only part of the story, as the later eminence of the 'holy trinity' has also a sociological basis itself – the legacy of two world wars.

The distaste for war and violence on the part of the general public was shared by many post-WWII sociologists, and this helped to refocus the discipline's main research interests away from those dominating the *fin de siecle* period. Hence, instead of 'race struggle', 'group selection through violence', nationalism, polygeny, cultural and biological difference, and warfare, sociologists became preoccupied with social stratification, gender inequality, welfare, rationalisation, secularisation, urbanisation and normative systems. The developmental and progressivist models that were the order of the day in 1950s, 60s and 70s favoured a distinctly 'pacifist' sociology, and this lead to the cleansing of classical social thought of its militarist heritage. In part because Nazi war crimes and the absolute carnage brought about by war were interpreted as the direct outcome of ideas and theories fermented among the 'bellicose' intellectuals of the turn of the century, classical social thought was largely 'sanitised' of this legacy. Consequently sociology's principal focus on 'pacifist' themes such as status and class divisions, education, industrialisation, crime, bureaucracy and transformations in cultural and religious values augmented the importance of classical social theorists such as Marx, Durkheim and Weber, as they had made significant contributions in these respective areas. At the same time classical social theorists whose research interests were located elsewhere became marginalised. After several decades the 'holy trinity' had become institutionalised and canonised in introductory sociology textbooks and university lecture halls worldwide.

Nonetheless, a closer look at the late nineteenth and early twentieth centuries provides a very different picture of the sociological thought of that time. The themes and authors that dominated social and political thinking were not those that are now commonly associated with sociology. Ludwig Gumplowicz, Franz Oppenheimer, Gustav Ratzenhofer, Alexander Rustow, Lester Ward, Albion Small, William McDougall and Franco Savorgnan are names that, for the most part, escape sociology textbooks. Similarly, concepts such as 'struggle for life', *Kriegsbegeisterung* (war enthusiasm)', 'instinct of pugnacity', superstratification, syngenism and *Erobererstaat* (conquest state) have no place in the vocabulary of contemporary sociology. Nevertheless it is these authors and these and similar concepts that were prevalent during the period when sociology was taking its first institutional steps. In other words the late nineteenth and early twentieth centuries were characterised by the primacy of militarist ideas in social thought.

However, before one engages with this prolific and diverse 'militarist' tradition of social inquiry it is necessary to situate the theories of Marx, Durkheim and Weber in this historical context. Although their central theoretical interest were located elsewhere, they could not avoid the spirit of their times and had to engage with questions of violence. In addition, while they were building universal sociological grand theories of social change they had to reflect, no matter how sporadically, on the role of collective violence and war in modernity.

Durkheim: pacifism, war and solidarity

As a direct descendent of the Enlightenment tradition and its strong emphasis on the inevitability of human progress, Emile Durkheim was the most pacifist, in both an analytical and normative sense, of the 'founding fathers'. His focus was firmly on the collective mechanisms that produce and reproduce solidarity. For Durkheim, social advancement was located in complex solidarity networks of mutual interdependence which were built on normative congruence, in stark opposition to pre-modern forms of solidarity based on mere resemblance. However, in both historical epochs, pre-modern and modern, human beings are seen as predominantly norm-driven creatures. In Durkheim's evolutionary functionalism, human sociability generally tends towards accord: social life is for the most part consensual and social conflicts are the exception rather than a rule. Hence what characterises the arrival of modernity is that one form of consensus (mechanical solidarity) is transformed into another, largely superior, form (organic solidarity).

In this context there is no real place for collective violence; Durkheim thus interpreted war as an aberration, a historical relic destined to disappear. As he put it: 'here, in war, we have only something of an anomalous survival, and gradually the last traces of it are bound to be wiped out' (Durkheim 1986: 43), or again 'War during this time, except for some passing setbacks ... has become more and more intermittent and less common (Durkheim 1992: 53). In a firm evolutionary vein he argued that industrial and technological development both requires and fosters peace (Durkheim 1959: 130) and that violence belongs to the agrarian pre-modern world and has no place in the modern social order. All this would imply that Durkheim had nothing to say about warfare and violence; nevertheless, he made two valuable sociological contributions that stem directly from his theory of solidarity. Firstly in his study on suicide Durkheim (1952) successfully tested a proposition that war and suicide rates are inversely proportional, arguing that with the clear exception of altruistic suicide the outbreak of war leads regularly to significant reductions in suicide rates, because wars, particularly national wars, strengthen the social and moral integration of society. As Durkheim (1952: 208) makes clear: 'great popular wars rouse collective sentiments, stimulate partisan spirit and patriotism … and concentrating activity toward a single end … cause a stronger integration of society … As they force men to close ranks and confront the common danger, the individual thinks less of himself and more of the common cause'. As wars increase political and moral integration they have a direct impact in decreasing egoistic and anomic suicide rates on both winning and losing sides.

Secondly, the onset of World War I (WW1) with its unprecedented brutality came as a shock to Durkheim and he had to account for this historical glitch. Utilising his theory of solidarity Durkheim argued that the Great War was a temporary, pathological state, a large-scale anomic situation that led to the revival of mechanical solidarity (Durkheim 1915; Durkheim and Denis 1915). The source of this pathology was attributed to 'a German war mentality' which Durkheim (1915: 45) saw as an anomaly that destroyed the organic, evolutionary development of human civilisation: 'A state cannot maintain itself when it has humanity against it.' Although the focus of his WWI writings was a critique of German militarist 'hypertrophy of the will', he was really articulating arguments in opposition to the militarist *zeitgeist* that dominated European social and political thought. Durkheim's nominal target was Heinrich Treitschke, an intellectual representative of the German militarist mentality that posited state power as unlimited, omnipotent and beyond social norms. However, his objective was in fact much broader – the entire realist tradition of social and political thinking, from Machiavelli to Treitschke and beyond, which had attempted to decouple the state from society and its moral universe. In this intellectual tradition, as Durkheim (1915: 18) puts it, 'the State is not under the jurisdiction of the moral conscience, and should recognise no law but its own interest'. In contrast to this view Durkheim argues that the state is a moral authority *par excellence* which is simultaneously rooted in individual moral autonomy, is the product of this autonomy and is its safeguard: 'it is the State that redeems individual from the society … The fundamental duty of the State is … to persevere in calling the individual to a moral way of life' (Durkheim 1992: 69). Consequently his pacifism is not a free-floating ideal but is deeply rooted in his theory of solidarity. For Durkheim pacifism is linked to a specific organisational form – the nation-state (*patrie*) and any attempt to stop war by invoking simple internationalism is destined to fail as 'we cannot live outside of an organised society, and the highest organised society that exists is the *patrie*' while 'internationalism is so very often the pure and simple rejection of all organised society' (Durkheim 1973: 101–3). In other words to understand, and hence prevent, war one needs to understand the mechanisms of institutionalised solidarity which can never be obliterated but only transformed so that 'national *patrie*' envelops 'the European *patrie*' or the 'human *patrie*'. To sum up, for Durkheim war is inevitably linked to the workings of group solidarity, and to explain warfare and large-scale violence one has to tackle the mechanisms of human solidarity.

Marx: capitalism and revolutionary violence

If conflict and violence were relatively marginal to Durkheim's research interests, this undoubtedly was not the case with Marx and Weber. Not only were they generally posited as the originators of conflict theory in sociology (Collins 1985), but they were also influenced by the Western realist political thought that emphasised coercion and the materiality of direct human action. Although the nucleus of Marx's theory of social change is firmly located in the socio-economic foundations of modernity, he was well aware of the historical importance of violence in transforming social orders. While his principal preoccupation was with the optics of class conflict and, what he saw as the inexorable decline of capitalism, the prominence he gave to the revolutionary change of existing 'social formations' inevitably implied an interest in the mechanics of collective violence.

Marx (and even more so Engels) were well versed in military history, had great appreciation of Clausewitz's theory of warfare (Semmel 1981: 66) and clearly adopted a militarist discourse of collective struggle and revolutionary violence as essential to class conflict. However as class struggle was linked to transformation in the modes of production and their ownership, the central focus was not so much on killing or incapacitating the bourgeoisie, as in real war, but rather on appropriating and redistributing their property. The driving motive was not the extermination, but the expropriation of the expropriators. Hence the language of violence was employed either in a metaphorical sense – e.g. 'class war' or 'cheap prices as the heavy artillery of bourgeoisie' (Marx and Engels 1998: 41–2), or in the context of the extraordinary processes accelerating the inevitable arrival of a peaceful communist order. Despite an abundance of militarist rhetoric in Marx's and Engels's works, they primarily associated violence with the brief final stage of revolutionary upheaval: 'when the class struggle nears the decisive hour, the process of dissolution going on within the ruling class … assumes such a violent, glaring character' (Marx and Engels 1998: 45). And even in this situation the use of force was defined and justified in defensive terms as a reaction to an intrinsically coercive capitalist state and the brutality of the bourgeoisie. As Merleau-Ponty (1969) argues, the Marxist understanding of revolutionary violence was conceptualised (and legitimised) on the premise that its use would facilitate the elimination of all violence in the long term and in particular the dominant form that violence exhibits under capitalism – class exploitation.

Nevertheless Marx and Engels make two sociologically relevant points on the relationship between warfare, violence and the modern state. First, in a process similar to Durkheim's experience with WWI, Marx's understanding of war and violence changed during and after the short lived experiment of the Paris Commune (1871). Reflecting, in the *Civil War in France* (1871), on the failure of this 'workers' state', Marx argues that violence is an integral part of modernity and more specifically of capitalist modernity. He singles out the role of the coercive apparatuses of the modern state as being decisive in transforming any social order. The brutality with which the Paris Commune was crushed made clear to Marx that, as he put it, 'the working class cannot simply lay hold of the ready-made State machinery and wield it for its own purposes' (Marx 1988: 54). Instead the transfer of power from the bourgeoisie to the proletariat would necessitate the destruction of the existing structures of the state and its recreation under revolutionary principles. In other words, Marx detected the inherent link between the economic, political and ideological foundations of social orders in modernity. While, in his earlier work, violence is largely ephemeral, from now on it takes centre stage as Marx interprets the state primarily as a coercive apparatus of capitalism. In this context capitalism cannot be abolished without eliminating its coercive structural base – the state apparatus itself. Drake (2003: 27) succinctly summarises Marx's argument: 'Violence by the state warrants a violent response from the proletariat, provided that the revolutionary cause is thereby advanced.' In the *Civil War in France*, the new preface to the *Communist Manifesto* (1872), the *Critique of the Gotha Programme* (1875) and other works from that period Marx emphasises the importance of the violent revolutionary takeover of the state. He traces the historical development of the centralised state structure from early absolutism to bourgeois society where it acted as 'a mighty weapon in its struggles against feudalism', after which it gradually becomes an instrument of capital over labour, a force 'organised for social enslavement, or an engine of class despotism' (Marx, 1988 [1871]: 55). As Marx becomes aware of the power of the centralised nation-state in the modern era, his advice is to adopt a strategy similar to that of the bourgeoisie during the French Revolution, that is, to demolish the state machinery. However, unlike its bourgeois predecessor this new polity was to be replaced by 'a dictatorship of the proletariat' as the political, economic and ideological vanguard, while its military foundation would be the 'armed people'. In his own words: 'While the merely repressive organs of the old governmental power were to be amputated, its legitimate functions were to be wrested from an authority usurping pre-eminence over society itself, and restored to the responsible agents of society' (Marx 1988: 58). The concept of 'armed people' as the only legitimate and 'responsible agents of society' is important as it initiates a militarist doctrine of the 'proletarian militia', more fully articulated in Lenin's, Mao's and Lin Piao's theory and strategy of 'armed proletariat' and 'peasant guerrilla warfare', which were decisive for the communist takeover of state power in Russia and China.[3] Hence despite the economistic foundations of his theory Marx had to acknowledge the major role of violence in capitalist modernity, and especially the coercive power of the nation-state.

Secondly, following in the footsteps of the first 'dialectical' materialist Heraclitus, Marx and Engels saw violence as a mechanism of rapid social change. As Marx (1999: 376) puts it in *Capital*: 'Force is the midwife of every old society pregnant with a new one.' The new social order cannot be created before the old has been deposed. At the end of *The Communist Manifesto* this is bluntly and clearly stated: 'They [the Communists] openly declare that their ends can be attained only by the forcible overthrow of all existing social conditions.' However for Marxists violence and war are never *sui generis* phenomenon but are strongly linked to the specific modes of production. In Engels's (1878) rebuttal of Duhring's force theory, violence is firmly understood as being grounded in economic power. Rather than being the 'free creations of the mind of generals of genius', armies and navies, organisation, the tactics and strategy of warfare, are all 'dependent on economic pre-conditions'. More specifically: 'always and everywhere it is the economic conditions and instruments of force which help "force" to victory, and without these, force ceases to be force' (Engels 1962 [1878]: 55).

[3] Lenin did not hesitate in spelling out clearly the link between violence and Marxist thought: 'True Marxism ... was based on violence, a dictatorship of the proletariat maintained by armed troops' (Semmel 1981: 16).

In this view the historical expansion of warfare and militarism rests on scientific invention and technological development (of armaments in particular), in turn requiring enormous financial investment. Consequently capitalism is seen as the backbone of arms production, as 'money must be provided through the medium of economic production; and so once again force is conditioned by the economic order' (Engels 1962: 49). To recap, Marx was not oblivious to war and violence – he saw it as a significant generator of social transformation in history, a potent vehicle of state power in the modern era, and an important instrument of capitalist economic structure.

Weber: rationalisation through violence

If there is any doubt as to Durkheim and Marx's interest in collective violence, the same cannot be said about Weber. Grounded in part in a Nietzschean ontology, Weber's social theory strongly emphasises the coercive character of political life. Not only does Weber link power to violence and the modern state to physical force, he also views social relations through the prism of irreconcilable ultimate values. In Weber's thought violence has material and ideal origins – the inherent irrationality of *Weltanschaungen* is often decided on the battlefield while the genesis of capitalism and instrumental rationality in the West are linked in part to the multipolarity of the European militarist feudal states. It is true that Weber does not provide a theory of collective violence or war, and that his view of modernity privileges structural and value rationalisation over the destruction and irrationality of bloodshed. Nevertheless, his key concepts such as rationality, bureaucracy and cultural prestige have firm militarist origins. In this context Weber has made at least four vital contributions to the understanding of the relationship between warfare, violence and modernity.

Firstly, his study of the birth and expansion of modernity via rationalisation is firmly linked with structural violence. The development of Western rationalism, which to a large extent rests on the growth of disciplinary techniques and practices, owes a great deal to warfare. As Weber (1968: 1155) argues, 'military discipline gives birth to all discipline'. In his analysis, both technological development and economic growth require disciplined social action. Hence transformation in the field of warfare, which will eventually influence the transformation of entire social orders, was linked to changes in disciplinary ethics and practice. As Weber (1968: 1152) puts it: 'The sober and rational Puritan discipline made Cromwell's victories possible ... gunpowder and all the war techniques ... become significant only with the existence of discipline ... the varying impact of discipline on the conduct of war has had even greater effects upon the political and social order.' More specifically, military discipline with its increasing rationalisation is seen by Weber as a basis of bureaucratic organisation in modern European states. He also draws parallels between military discipline and the capitalist factory and argues that without disciplinary practices the rationalisation process would be unthinkable: 'This whole process of rationalisation, in the factory as elsewhere, and especially in the bureaucratic state machine, parallels the centralisation of the material implements of organisation in the hands of the master. Thus, discipline inexorably takes over ever larger areas as the satisfaction of political and economic needs is increasingly rationalised' (Weber 1968: 1156).

Secondly for Weber (1994: 360), the most important means of politics is violence. There is no politics which in the last instance is not rooted in the use of force, or the threat of its use, and violence is seen by Weber as the *raison d'etre* of the state's existence. Although the modern state is defined in terms of the possession of a monopoly over the legitimate use of force within a particular territory, Weber understands the state, not as a substance, but, exclusively through its violent means: 'the modern state can only be defined sociologically in terms of a specific means which is peculiar to the state, as it is to all other political associations, namely physical violence' (Weber 1994: 310). While he argues that social order rests on three pillars – legitimacy, trade and coercion – what distinguishes political life from other spheres of human activity is the use or threat of violence. As the process of rationalisation advances, the political sphere tends towards radical separation from the economic, aesthetic or religious sphere where it is, according to Weber, likely to develop its own ethics and compete with the moral universes of other spheres. It is in the context of warfare that the political sphere proves its ethical autonomy and mobilizing potency: 'War, as realised threat of force, is able to create in the modern political community pathos and feeling of community and thereby releases an unconditional community of sacrifice among the combatants. Furthermore, war releases the work of compassion and love for the needy which breaks through all the barriers of naturally given groups, and it does this as mass phenomenon.' (Weber 2004: 225). Warfare, as organised violent social activity, profoundly influences the individual and collective sense of meaning as soldiers face the constant threat of death. In this process it creates 'community until death' which transforms the ordinary individual feeling concerning the inevitability of death into a sacrifice for a specific, noble cause: 'Death in arms, *only* here in this massiveness of death, can the individual believe he *knows* that he dies "for" something' (Weber 2004: 225, his italics). In other words, despite its cataclysmic destructiveness war creates conditions for individual and collective sacrifice, thus enhancing the meaning of social life and providing dignity for 'the political body that exercises violence'.

Thirdly, his account of the rise of Western rationality is structurally traced in part to the military origins of the European feudal states and their social structure of lords, vassals and fiefs that created an anarchic environment with a multipolar power base. Unlike Marx, who understood feudalism in economic terms, Weber saw it primarily as an order based on a distinct military organisation defined by 'the ruling class which is dedicated to war or royal service and is supported by privileged land holdings' (Weber 1976: 38). Unlike patrimonialism, where warriors become the personal dependents of kings, feudalism, in its Western European form, relied on the contractual arrangements where vassalage did not imply subjugation. On the contrary, the loyalty of vassal warriors to their lords was secured by enhancing their high status, derived from an 'exalted conception of honour'. This sense of personal loyalty and warriors' honour in combination with the dominance of cavalry over infantry created a relatively unusual situation in Europe whereby multiple power autonomy would eventually help create conditions for the rationalisation of social order and the expansion of capitalism. As Weber (1968: 1078) argues: 'the peculiarity of Occidental, fully developed feudalism was largely determined by the fact that it constituted the basis of cavalry – in contrast to the plebeian … ancient Oriental fief-holding soldiers'.

Finally, for Weber, war is an important source of social change and is tightly linked to the concept of prestige since, as he puts it: 'Cultural prestige and power prestige are closely associated. Every victorious war enhances the [state's] cultural prestige' (Weber 1968: 926). Its historically early form is 'holy war' which Weber (1963: 86–7) defines as 'a war in the name of god, for the special purpose of avenging a sacrilege, which entailed putting the enemy under the ban and destroying him and all his belongings completely'. Although already present in antiquity it was only with the arrival of the monotheistic religious systems that holy war becomes prevalent through its appeal to a sense of collective superiority of status. While Judaism initiated the practice where 'the people of Yahweh, as his special community, demonstrated and exempted their god's prestige against their foes', holy war was adopted vigorously in Islam where it involved 'subjugation of unbelievers to political authority' and Christianity where 'unbelievers or heretics had only the choice between conversion and extirpation' (Weber 1963: 87). With the gradual rationalisation of social life, warfare, as with other forms of social action, becomes routinised, instrumental and bureaucratic. The general rationalisation of military practice and principles replaces the individual heroism of primitive warriors. What characterises modern armies is not the personal and emotional displays of bravery but an efficient bureaucratic machinery of war. In Weber's analysis, war as a social activity cannot escape the universal logic of rationalisation that affects all spheres of human life.

This brief overview of the 'holy trinity' clearly indicates that Marx, Durkheim and Weber were not ignorant of the sociological importance of war and violence. Whereas Durkheim's awareness of belligerence reinforced his interest in the alternative 'pacifist' mechanisms of solidarity, Weber and Marx understood violence and war as powerful devices of social change. Although the founding fathers did not develop full blown theories of collective violence and war, their contributions remain indispensable. Moreover, the nature of their analyses and their engagement and debates on these issues indicate something even more relevant – they were reflecting on the dominant, principally 'bellicose', ideas of their time. As I argue in the next section, the late nineteenth and early twentieth centuries were characterised by the prevalence of militarist ideas in social thought. Not only did war and violence constitute the *esprit de corps* of German academia (Mann 1988; 2004), but similar ideas were widespread and highly popular within leading academic circles throughout Europe and North America. It is important to revisit this 'bellicose' legacy not only to show that, contrary to the popular academic view, this was a dominant research and explanatory paradigm of its age but also to demonstrate its intrinsic relevance for contemporary sociology. As I elaborate later (and more extensively in the next chapter), although much of this legacy is forgotten, contemporary political sociology implicitly owes a great deal to the classical 'bellicose' tradition of social thought.

The bellicose tradition in classical social thought

Hans Joas (2003) has recently disputed the existence of what many have referred to as the militarist tradition in German social thought. He argues that there was little in common between individual thinkers taken to be representatives of this tradition. Although he is right that belligerence was not unique to German academia he is wrong in minimising the social impact and internal coherence of this research paradigm. Although there is evident diversity in their political views, their disciplinary interests and their country of origin, a number of influential authors in Europe and North America shared a common research focus on war, violence and state power. In addition they interpreted social and political life through a distinct 'bellicose' approach, all of considerations set them apart as representatives of a particular intellectual tradition. In other words, there is a potent militarist tradition in classical social thought which is broad and includes a variety of distinct approaches: German belligerent statism, Austro-American group struggle paradigm, German sociological libertarianism, Italian elite theory, Anglo-American evolutionary theory and the Franco-German social metaphysics of violence.

German belligerent statism

Grounded in Leopold von Ranke's historical romanticism and idealism and underpinned by the peculiar geopolitical position of Germany, and particularly Bismarck's Prussia in the nineteenth century, a number of influential German intellectuals became preoccupied with the role of power and violence in the historical processes of state creation. While Ranke's legacy imprinted an intellectual hostility upon the Enlightenment's universalism and rationalism, including its scientific methodology and causality which were firmly rejected in favour of historical uniqueness, the Prussian statists moulded their reverence of the state and their emphasis on the importance of foreign policy in understanding social relations. Although there were many influential representatives of this 'bellicose' tradition of thought, three social thinkers in particular stand out: Heinrich von Treitschke, Otto Hintze and Carl Schmitt.

Treitschke was both an academic and a prominent public figure whose ideas left their mark on several generations of German intellectuals in the late nineteenth and early twentieth centuries. For Treitschke, power is for the most part equated with the ability of the state to pursue its will. In fact, the state is defined as power: 'the State is the people legally united as an independent power' or 'the State is the public power of offence and defence' (Treitschke 1914: 9, 12). In this view the state is completely anthropomorphised, reified and essentialised as it acquires fixed and unchangeable humanlike abilities – personality, will and needs. In his own words: 'if we remember that the essence of this great collective personality is power, then it is in that case the highest moral duty of the State to safeguard its power' (Treitschke 1914: 31).

Not only is it the case that in this understanding there is no power outside of, or above the state, but also the state's *raison d'etre* is the accumulation, maintenance and utilisation of power. As he emphasises, 'Power is the principle of the State, as Faith is the principle of the Church, and Love of the family.' (Treitschke 1914: 12). In this account the state performs two essential functions: within its borders it administrates justice while outside of its borders it fights wars. As a sovereign entity its power has no limits either internally or externally as the state can declare wars or suppress rebellions when and how it pleases. Moreover 'without war there would be no State at all' as states are created exclusively through warfare (Treitschke 1914: 21). Following in part von Ranke, Treitschke argues that the very institution of the state originated through warfare, as the embryo of early statehood is to be located in the conquest of stronger tribes over the weaker ones (Aho 1975: 38).

Contrary to Enlightenment principles Treitschke (1914: 39) argues that states are not created on the basis of people's sovereignty but in fact 'against the will of the people'. It is the experience of war that moulds individuals into nation-states: 'only in war a people becomes in very deed a people' (Davis 1915: 150). And in the final instance it is the possession of the army that defines the state. As Treitschke (1914: 100) puts it succinctly: 'the State is no Academy of Arts, still less a Stock Exchange; it is power, and therefore it contradicts its own nature if it neglects the army'. As with other representatives of the Prussian historical school who were also deeply influenced by Hegelian teleology, such as Droysen and Duncker, Treitschke understands history as an ethical process: the success of a particular state, defined largely by its ability to win wars, is interpreted as an indicator of its higher morality. The state is a moral absolute that stands above individuals, that possesses omnipotent powers, and that shapes its existence through eternal conflict with other states.

Otto Hintze was a student of Treitschke, a fact that is evident in his early work, which occasionally exhibits 'a mystical belief in the state as a higher entity with a life of its own' (Gilbert 1975: 13). However, despite his strong emphasis on state power and the importance of foreign policy and warfare in the formation of modern order, Hintze developed a much more sophisticated approach to the study of power and collective violence. Unlike Treitschke's normativist militarism and glorification of state and war, Hintze begins to explicate what is essentially a historical sociology of power transformation. Tracing the historical development of the constitutional state, Hintze (1975: 181) argues that 'all state organisation was originally military organisation, organisation for war'. The roots of representative political institutions such as assemblies are to be found in the congregation of warriors, as membership in a political community was determined by one's ability to fight wars. Through extensive exploration of the structure and origin of ancient Greek and Roman political institutions, the European feudal system, the thirteenth and fourteenth century Standstaat, and the absolutist orders of the eighteenth and early nineteenth century, Hintze concludes that the two determining historical factors of state creation are the structure of social classes and the external ordering of states. Both of these factors are linked to warfare, as external and internal conflicts are regularly inversely proportional. As Hintze (1975: 183–4) points out with respect to the example of Rome: 'wherever the community was sufficiently adaptable, as in Rome, the pressure of the foreign situation forced a progressive extension of the citizenry with political rights, because greater masses of soldiers were needed. It was at heart this joint operation of external pressure and internal flexibility that enabled Rome to progress from city-state to world empire'. He identifies three dominant historical moments in the transformation of state and military power: a) the tribal and clan system, in which 'the state and the army are virtually identical units', and often underpinned by kin solidarity and a substantial degree of social equality; b) the feudal epoch, which changed the nature of warfare through a shift from non-professional mass infantry to the heavily armed professional cavalry, while a looser central authority with a multiple pyramid structure gave way to a rigid hierarchical and eventually hereditary social structure; and finally c) the age of militarism in which the expansion of warfare created habitual fiscal crises thus prompting tax and state centralisation, the development of universal military service ('a nation in arms') and a constitutional state structure defined by new egalitarian principles in which 'the division between warriors and the citizenry – the fighters and the feeders – was overcome' (Hintze 1975: 207). In this view the modern, or as he calls it, the militarist, era is even more prone to collective violence, because individuals do not fight as mercenaries or servants of a monarch but are socialised to see their nation-state as a supreme moral authority, 'a community, a corporate collective personality' worth dying for. In other words, for Hintze (1975: 199), just as for Treitschke, it was the 'power politics and balance-of-power politics' that created 'the foundations of modern Europe'.

Although Carl Schmitt was a jurist and a legal, rather than social, theorist, his theory of the political is an integral part of the belligerent statist tradition. Just like Treitschke and Hintze, Schmitt emphasises the coercive, conflict-driven and power-driven nature of social life. However, unlike the other two thinkers he understands power and the political in much broader terms than as the power of the nation-state alone. He believes that that political action historically precedes state formation but also once democratisation takes off and state and society fully develop they permeate each other and in this situation 'what had been up to that point affairs of state become thereby social matters, and, vice versa, what had been purely social matters become affairs of state' (Schmitt 1996: 22). In other words, Schmitt takes radical statism to its logical conclusion where the state and society become indistinguishable. For Schmitt the political cannot be defined only negatively – as an antithesis of the religious, the cultural or the economic – but must have its own positive definition. Echoing Treitschke's principle association between faith and church, love and family, and power and state, Schmitt (1996: 26) argues that if the realm of morality is characterised by a distinction between good and evil, economics by the profitable and the unprofitable, and aesthetics by the beautiful and the ugly, then the concept of the political also necessitates an absolute categorical distinction. In his view this ultimate distinction of the political is between friend and enemy. In other words the political is to be disassociated from the ethical and studied in its own terms: 'The political enemy need not be morally evil or aesthetically ugly; he need not appear as an economic competitor ... but he is, nevertheless, the other, the stranger; ... existentially something different and alien, so that in the extreme case conflicts with him are possible' (Schmitt 1996: 27). The two are understood by Schmitt not as symbols or metaphors but as essential and existential categories of social action. Political action is embedded in antagonisms and in the final instance politics is a form of warfare: if there is no external threat to maintain the friend–enemy distinction at the level of sovereign states this polarisation is likely to replicate itself in the domestic sphere where party politics becomes deeply antagonistic.[4] However the ultimate potency of the political is rooted in its potential virulence: 'The friend, enemy, and combat concepts receive their real meaning precisely because they refer to a real possibility of physical killing. War follows from enmity. War is the existential negation of the enemy' (Schmitt 1996: 33). Hence as power politics and conflict are cornerstones of social life one can never eradicate the friend–enemy distinction without obliterating political life itself.

Although there are obvious differences between these three thinkers they share two central propositions: coercive power is seen as central to social and

---

[4] Schmitt (1996: 34f) incorporates Clausewitz's dictum that war is the continuation of politics by other means into his friend–enemy distinction by arguing that 'war, for Clausewitz, is not merely one of many instruments, but *ultima ratio* of the friend–enemy grouping. War has its own grammar ... but politics remains its brain. It does not have its own logic'.

political life; and the state is perceived as an omnipotent and independent political force created and sustained through the use of violence.

Austro-American group struggle paradigm

While belligerent statism was distinctly structural and macro-historical most other 'bellicose' schools of thought had much more agency-centred perspectives. Although, as demonstrated later, there is a substantial diversity in the 'bellicose' tradition of classical social thought, the underlying logic of their general argument is broadly similar – social life is mostly characterised by conflict between distinct groups. In their analyses violence and war play a vital role either as the principal means of collective struggle or as social mechanisms used to acquire or maintain power.

Even though Ludwig Gumplowicz, Gustav Ratzenhofer and Lester Ward are mentioned only as marginal representatives of continental and American social Darwinism (if they are mentioned at all), their concepts and theories have little, if anything, in common with Darwinism. In fact Gumplowicz's positivist sociologism is in many respects an epistemological predecessor of Durkheim's thought as he was the first sociologist who argued that social facts have *sui generis* quality and that social life cannot be reduced to biological or psychological realities. Gumplowicz is critical of attributing a biological and organicist imagery to social processes, arguing that society is no more than an aggregate of collectivities: 'the real elements of a social process are not separate individuals but groups' (Gumplowicz 2007 [1883]: 39). In his theory groups determine individual thoughts and behaviour and as such are prone to interminable conflicts. His most important work *Der Rassenkampf* (1883) argues that groups are the key generators of social action and are held together by intensive feelings of inter-collective solidarity rooted in cultural similarity and joint action, a process he referred to as *syngenism*.[5] As a potent source of collective cohesion developed over a long historical period, syngenism fosters ethnocentric feelings, thus pitting groups against each other. In his cyclical view of history, group struggle is the foundation of social change: social life is inherently violent as one group conquers another. Syngenic divisions encouraged the formation of hordes, clans and tribes, all of which engaged in periodic raids and warfare.

---

[5] It is important to make clear that in much of the late nineteenth and early twentieth century sociological literature the term 'race' was often used as a synonym for the social group without the inherent biological and racist overtones it was to acquire later. Hence Gumplowicz's 'race struggle' really means 'group struggle'.

Gumplowicz traces the origins of family, private property and law to these violent group pillages where winning warriors would capture women, goods and exercise rights over the captives while attempting to exterminate the losing group. Moreover the origin of the state as a centralised, territorially based organisation is located in warfare. According to Gumplowicz (1899) the state emerges through a violent process whereby one group subjugates another and in so doing institutionalises slavery and direct exploitation of the conquered group. As this process intensifies smaller groups become amalgamated into a larger and better organised entity underpinned by a highly stratified division of labour. This is ideologically enhanced by the emergence of a legal system which is devised solely to reinforce the privileged position of the conquering group. For Gumplowicz this is seen as a universal phenomenon which is replicated in a more complex form in modernity as states fight wars of supremacy and conquest. The advancement of human civilisation is linked to warfare, as culture, art and science emerge through successful conquest: victories in war create an aristocratic parasitic leisure class that turns defeated warriors into workers. Despite the apparent complexity of modern societies and states, Gumplowicz argues that group struggle has operated on basically the same principles throughout history and retains its intensity today.

Gustav Ratzenhofer was a Habsburg general, military historian, sociologist and close collaborator of Gumplowicz, and he took group struggle theory a step further. Ratzenhofer also sees human life through the prism of intensive social conflict and explains state formation through violent conquest. In his view the origins of social life are to be found in the Hobbesian-like logic of 'absolute hostility'. In a similar way to Gumplowicz he focused on collective action rather than structure, as he understands sociology as 'the science of the reciprocal relationships of human beings' (Ratzenhofer 1904: 177). He also shares his mentor's positivist epistemology in arguing that sociology's central task is the discovery of universal laws that govern social life. However his general account of human development is much more developmental, teleological and optimist than Gumplowicz's. Although no social Darwinist in any strict sense, he nonetheless adopted the standard evolutionary scheme of his time to explain the gradual development of societies moving from the primitive to the advanced stages. In this context he argues that each stage of development is characterised by internal and external conflicts and that social progress and collective violence are tightly linked: 'Wars are consequence of social development' (Ratzenhofer 1904: 186). In his view the conquest state (*Erobererstaat*) that has dominated the history of human societies is destined to be replaced by a culture state (*Kulturestaat*).

Nevertheless, unlike Gumplowicz who posits tangible groups as the dominant instigators of social action, Ratzenhofer identifies collective 'interests' as key generators of social conflict. In his theory the social world is essentially a battlefield of competing group interests. These interests are active social forces that direct collective action and as such are difficult to detect, thus requiring an analytical abstraction from real life (Bentley 1926: 252–3). Ratzenhofer distinguishes a variety of group interests operating at different levels of abstraction: from 'general interest', 'national interest', 'class interest' and 'kinship interest' to 'rank interest', 'pecuniary interest' or 'creedal interest' (Ratzenhofer 1881; Small 1905: 252). What is central here is that, as interests are multiple and varied, individuals and groups are inevitably dynamic agents that can compete and conflict over different interests; thus, there is no necessary overlap between an entire group and specific interests. Nonetheless, because it is directed by irreconcilable interests, social life in this account remains wedded to conflict and violence.

Lester Ward was profoundly influenced by Gumplowicz and Ratzenhofer's theories and together with Albion Small was responsible for disseminating their ideas in the USA. In a Heraclitian manner, Ward (1913, 1914) argued that conflict is the source of all creation – physical, biological and social. He developed the concept of synergy which was understood as a cosmic principle that 'begins in collision, conflict, antagonism, and opposition, but as no motion can be lost it is transformed, and we have the milder forms of antithesis, competition' which eventually can lead to compromise and cooperation (Ward 1914: 175). In contrast to social Darwinism which understood group divisions in terms of inherent genetic qualities, Ward adopted Gumplowicz's interpretation of the origins of class divisions and the state in the violent conquest of one group over another. He argues that all larger polities have emerged through violence. Initially the conquered group maintained its intensive dislike of its conquerors, but would gradually become coercively assimilated whereby the emergence of shared 'national sentiment' would help unify the polity thus creating the nation-state. Ward saw violence and war both as the normal condition of social life and as the paramount generators of social advancement. In his view the sociological analysis of history shows that 'war has been the chief and leading condition of human progress … when races [social groups] stop struggling, progress ceases ….If peace missionaries could have their counsel prevail there might have been universal peace, nay general contentment, but there would have been no progress' (Ward 1914: 240).[6] However not all forms of collective violence are seen as beneficial to social development. Ward distinguishes between revolutionary violence, which is interpreted as detrimental since it simply destroys the long-built organic social order without being able to replace it with a better alternative, and warfare, which is in principle productive, as conquests create more complex social units. In his own words, the result of successful war is the preservation of 'all that is best in different structures thus blended, and creating a new structure which is different from and superior to any prior structures' (Ward 1914: 247). Although Ward's approach is broadly in agreement with Gumplowicz's model, he clearly departs from Gumplowicz's pessimism. Instead Ward was a firm believer in planned, state-directed social progress. In this context he created the concept of 'telic intelligence' (telesis) which unlike 'genetic intelligence', which operates unconsciously, is seen as a conscious, scientifically developed social device to effect a positive, progressive change. Hence, Ward advocated the idea of telesis by which social evolution can be directed through the use of education and science.

German sociological libertarianism

Franz Oppenheimer and Alexander Rustow were significantly influenced by the Austrian group-conflict school in their interpretations of the violent origins of the state. However while starting from similar premises concerning the intrinsically coercive history and character of the state, their conclusions were very different to those of Gumplowicz and Ratzenhofer, as they both shared an anti-statist libertarian normative universe.

Following the Austrian conflict tradition, Oppenheimer (2007 [1926]) develops a conquest theory of the state arguing that: 'the State, completely in its genesis, essentially and almost completely during the first stage of its existence, is a social institution, forced by a victorious group of men on a defeated group'. In his view the state is essentially an organisation of violence that emerges as a result of violent conflict through which the dominant group subjugates the defeated group. As such it is a hierarchical and class-based organisation that requires the continuous dominance of one group over others. However, unlike Gumplowicz, Oppenheimer distinguishes between the political means of social action which he sees as fundamentally violent

---

[6] In Ward's view war cannot be a form of social pathology simply because 'as the entire history of mankind has been characterised by incessant war, it follows that disease has been the prevailing condition and leading characteristic of human society' (Ward 1907: 298).

(e.g. robbery), and the economic means which are for the most part peaceful (e.g. labour). In this account world history is conceived as an incessant contest between the two spheres, since political means such as war – defined as organised mass robbery – has historically proven to be the more efficient mechanism of appropriating the labour of others. Oppenheimer argues that the state arises only with the appearance of nomadic tribes, as settled peasants do not make efficient warriors: 'the cause of the genesis of all states is the contrast between peasants and herdsmen, between labourers and robbers … the war-like character of the nomads is a great factor in the creation of states' (Oppenheimer 2007: 28). Whereas initially nomadic warriors act as 'bears' bent on destruction of their weaker enemy, gradually, as the institutions of the state develop, they transform into 'bee-keepers' who spare their enemies in order to live by their exploitation through tribute. In this process the state rulers also develop laws and install religious authorities both of which justify the status quo. However according to Oppenheimer the central feature of the state remains the same through time: 'States are maintained in accordance with the same principles that called them into being. The primitive state is the creation of warlike robbery; and by warlike robbery it can be preserved' (Oppenheimer 2007: 57). And the same principle applies to their more advanced counterparts: 'Conquest of land and populations is the *ratio essendi* of a territorial state; and by repeated conquest of land and populations it must grow, until … its sociological bounds are determined by contact with other states of its kind, which it cannot subjugate' (Oppenheimer 2007: 85). Nonetheless in contrast to Austrian conflict theory Oppenheimer was optimistic about the possibility of economic means overtaking political means as intensified global commerce and trade lead to 'preponderating importance over the diminishing warlike and political relations' (Oppenheimer 2007: 153).

Alexander Rustow starts from a similar proposition: the origins of the modern state system can be traced back to conquest by dominant groups. He introduces three key concepts to explain the patterns of development in world history: 'superstratification', 'high culture' and the 'culture pyramid'. Superstratification refers to a historically universal process of military conquest whereby one group invades the territory of another and establishes its control thus creating 'human social groupings that, in their inner structure, were based on bloodshed and violence' (Rustow 1980). While on the one hand this process produces hierarchical relations within society by firmly differentiating dominators and dominated, on the other hand it paradoxically fosters the development of 'high cultures'. Although high cultures emerge as a consequence of coercive specialisation, once they are fully developed, according to

Rustow (1980: 131), they are likely to open possibilities whereby 'bondage could be overcome, and independence and freedom consonant with human nature once again achieved'. This paradoxical state of historical development is conceptualised through the 'law of the culture pyramid' by which Rustow means the following: Any substantial advancement of civilisation requires large-scale organisation which can only be, and historically has been, created through the coercive means of integrating many sedentary tribes under the domination of one conquering group. Once such a complex polity with an advanced division of labour is established, it allows for the appearance of the specialised professional creative producers of culture recruited from the ruling strata now liberated from manual labour. In other words, there would be no advanced civilisations without the 'original sin' of the violent process that is superstratification. For Rustow, the rise of Western 'high culture' in the ancient Greek world was a first substantial break of the cycle of conquest and superstratification, as the Greek polis provided a balance between communal life and individual freedom through the existence of a relatively weak polity. In his analysis any attempt to strengthen the state and empower the rulers beyond the necessary minimum leads to what he terms 'feudal' order, which reintroduces superstratification at the expanse of human liberty and communal solidarity. Hence he identifies various moments in European history where 'feudal' social relations were reinitiated resulting in the loss of individual freedom, including the Reformation's attack on the church hierarchy, which lead to the sacralisation of politics as the Counter-Reformation brought about theological absolutism paving a way for authoritarian and eventually totalitarian politics. Similarly, colonial and imperial expansion on the part of European states opened the door for new periods of superstratification as slavery and territorial conquest triggered the return of feudal tendencies in the West.

Italian elite theory

While Vilfredo Pareto and Gaetano Mosca are well known as key representatives of elite theory in sociology, not much attention is paid to their analyses of violence and war. Both interpret history in terms of perpetual domination by an organised minority over a disorganised majority, and they also emphasise the indispensable role of coercion in this process. More specifically they both identify the two essential and concomitant ingredients that secure elite domination in all social and political orders – ideology and force.

In Pareto's (1935) theory of the circulation of elites, the decadence of old rulers is counterbalanced by the ascent of a new elite out of the ordinary masses thus making history 'the graveyard of aristocracies'. However, any elite, regardless of its origin, in order to acquire and stay in power has to rely on ideological hegemony ('derivations'), and, even more so, on force. Although recognising the importance of coercion for social change he distinguishes between violence and force: 'Violence … is not to be confused with force. Often enough one observes cases in which individuals and classes which have lost force in order to maintain themselves in power make themselves more and more hated because of their outbursts of random violence. The strong man strikes only when it is absolutely necessary, and then nothing stops him. 'Trajan was strong, not violent: Caligula was violent not strong' (Pareto 1973 [1902]: 79). Consequently force is seen as a backbone of successful rule both within a particular society and in relation to other societies. For Pareto, the profligacy and dissoluteness of a ruling elite inevitably leads to the violent overthrow by emerging new elites, while the inability to defend one's state is likely to result in conquest by another state. The first case is illustrated by the outcome of the French Revolution: 'The knife of the guillotine was being sharpened in the shadows when, at the end of the eighteenth century, the ruling classes in France were engrossed in developing their "sensibility". This idle and frivolous society, living like a parasite off the country, discoursed at its elegant supper parties of delivering the world from superstition and of crushing *l'Infâme*, all unsuspecting that it was itself going to be crushed' (Pareto 1973: 81). The second case is even more common as 'there is not perhaps on this globe a single foot of ground which has not been conquered by the sword at some time or other'. In this context Pareto understands colonial policy as nothing more than coercion camouflaged under the pretence of 'civilising missions' and 'humanitarian sentiments'. The scramble for Africa and control of China are accomplished and maintained by naked force and can be reversed by force alone. In Pareto's view, ideology is not to be contrasted with coercion as it is only a means of attaining force. Indirectly echoing Weber, Pareto argues that 'for right or law to have reality in a society, force is necessary' as both laws and rights originated in force, hence, 'it is by force that social institutions are established, and it is by force that they are maintained' (Pareto 1973: 80–1).

Mosca's general argument is similar as he too sees force as central to social development and to minority rule. As he puts it: 'history teaches that the class that bears the lance or holds the musket regularly forces its rule upon the class that handles the spade or pushes the shuttle' (Mosca 1939: 228). However, his theory focuses much more on the organisational and institutional mechanisms that enable the domination of an organised minority over a disorganised majority. This is particularly evident in Mosca's analysis of military action and warfare where he argues that the birth and expansion of the modern state is rooted in the processes of the gradual centralisation of power and extension of bureaucratic organisation in the two key spheres – the military (efficient control of the army) and the financial (efficient control of money). In *The Ruling Class* (1939: 222–43) he provides a comparative historical analysis of military organisations in order to show how neither the establishment of a professional army nor an all-inclusive conscript army can prevent the emergence of minority rule. The conscript model where all citizens are soldiers and where professional military organisation and 'specialists in matter of war' are lacking, is likely to produce a situation such that 'in the moment of peril there will be no soldiers at all' and the army will be easily defeated by a smaller but better organised counterpart who will then impose themselves on the conquered society. The model of the professional army creates another problem: 'In [the contemporary] bureaucratic state ... the standing army will absorb all the belligerent elements, and, being readily capable of prompt obedience to a single impulse, it will have no difficulty in dictating to the rest of society' (Mosca 1939: 228). Thus military might requires a delicate balance and power-sharing between economic, military and political ruling classes to prevent a slide into military rule. Furthermore, in both of these cases the efficiency of the army rests in part on its rigid hierarchical structure that enables the successful division of labour between a minority officer class ('usually recruited from the politically dominant ranks of society') and a majority of mostly obedient 'privates and petty officers'. Although, as Mosca points out, this distinction is highly arbitrary it nonetheless is present in all organised and successful standing armies throughout history from ancient Egypt through the time of military mandarins in China to contemporary armies. There is no military effectiveness, and hence wars cannot be won, without a strict social hierarchy. Seeing human beings as primarily conflict-driven creatures, Mosca, just as Pareto, is pessimistic about the prospect of a world without war. In his analysis conflicts never disappear but only become displaced from one sphere into another: 'there will always be conflict of interest, and the will to have one's own way by brute force ... When that organisation [of the contemporary standing army] has been dissolved or weakened, what is to prevent small organisations of the strong, the bold, the violent, from again coming to life to oppress the weak and peaceful? When war has ended on large scale, will it not be revived on a small scale in quarrels between families, classes or villages?' (Mosca 1939: 242).

Anglo-American evolutionary theory

It is truly paradoxical that the only classical tradition of social thought that gained a notable reputation for belligerence was in fact the least militarist of all. Often pejoratively referred to as social Darwinism, early sociological evolutionary theory, represented most potently in the works of Herbert Spencer and William G. Sumner, had a largely amiable view of modernity. Both Spencer and Sumner conceptualised social life in a teleological and progressivist way whereby human societies are seen as moving from primitivism and violence towards complexity, sophistication and concord.

Although Spencer coined the term 'survival of the fittest' and applied a heavy organicist and biological imagery to the social world, his understanding of evolutionary development was Lamarckian rather than Darwinian. In other words, unlike Darwin, who explained evolution through natural selection without any set direction, meaning or *telos*, Spencer firmly believed that acquired biological traits can be transmitted to offspring and that evolutionary development is destined to reach a final point, a state of perfection – an equilibrium. In Spencer's theory, social orders resemble nature as they advance from simple, undifferentiated homogeneity to complex, differentiated heterogeneity. In this context he identified two ideal types of society: the militant and the industrial. Whereas industrial society is seen as being peaceful, decentralised, economically vibrant, socially mobile and essentially based on voluntary, contractual social arrangements, its militant counterpart was the exact opposite: hierarchical, violent, centralised, authoritarian, obedient and socially immobile. Hence for Spencer war is a phenomenon of undifferentiated societies that value strong and concentrated systems of internal regulation since they regularly find themselves in conflict with neighbouring societies. In this social order, the military and society become one: 'the militant type is one in which the army is the nation mobilised while the nation is the quiescent army' (Spencer 1971 [1876]: 154). The volatile social environment with intensive conflicts reinforces discipline, faith in authority, autarky, and the hierarchical social structure of militant society as the central value becomes the ability to collectively defend it from violent attacks by outsiders. In such a society there is no place for an individual as 'its members exist for the benefit of the whole'. More specifically this is a society of compulsory co-operation where 'the social structure adopted with dealing with surrounding hostile societies is under a centralised regulating system to which all the parts are completely subject: just as in the individual organism the outer organs are completely subject to the chief nervous centre' (Spencer

1971: 159–60). Nevertheless despite his general identification of militarism with pre-modernity Spencer was well aware that the complexity of a particular social order is no guarantee of its inherent peacefulness. A much better predictor is the presence or absence of external conflict, as societies that enter protracted conflicts tend to develop a militant social structure regardless of their complex organisation.

Sumner follows Spencer in distinguishing between simple and largely homogenous pre-modern societies and the complex heterogeneous social orders of modernity. He also posits natural selection as a key generator of social change, which in the social world is identified with unconstrained autonomy of action: 'if there is real liberty, a natural selection results; but if there is social prejudice, monopoly, privilege, orthodoxy, tradition, popular delusion … selection does not occur' (Sumner 1911: 222). Summer too understands war through the biological metaphor of 'competition of life', arguing that unlike the struggle for existence which arises from the individual's instinct for survival, the competition of life is a group phenomenon that separates a 'we group' from antagonistic outsiders. In his view it is 'the competition of life' that 'makes war' (Sumner 1911: 209). In a similar way to Spencer, he envisages the emergence of militancy in the context of group polarisation. He coined the concept of ethnocentrism to explain the link between the in-group sense of innate superiority and the resulting hostility towards out-groups. However Sumner's focus here is not psychological but sociological, as he explains the phenomenon of in-group homogeneity through the intensity of out-group conflict: 'the exigencies of war with outsiders are what makes peace inside' and 'these exigencies also make government and law in the in-group' (Sumner 1906: 12). In other words war and peace are dialectically linked as internal cohesion and amity are dependent on external conflict and vice versa. More specifically the proximity and strength of the enemy directly determines the magnitude of warfare: 'The closer the neighbours, the stronger they are, the intenser is the warfare, and the intenser is the internal organisation and discipline of each' (Sumner 1906: 12). However, Sumner's theory differs from Spencer's in two respects. Firstly he argues that warfare expands and intensifies with civilisation: 'Man in the most primitive and uncivilised state known to us does not practice war all the time; he dreads it. He might rather be described as a peaceful animal. Real warfare comes with the collision of more developed societies' (Sumner 1911: 205). The practice of war is linked to the naissance of political organisation. Although conflict is a universal feature of humankind, shared with the rest of the animal world, the institution of warfare is a social product dependent on advances in civilisation. Secondly, unlike Spencer, for whom war was an almost exclusively destructive force, Sumner identifies the unintended productive consequences of warfare in human history: 'While men were fighting for glory and greed, for revenge and superstition, they were building human society. They were acquiring discipline and cohesion; they were learning cooperation, perseverance, fortitude, and patience' (Sumner 1911: 212). Not only then does war foster technological development, scientific invention and educational advancement, but 'war also develops societal organisation; it produces political institutions and classes' and builds 'larger social units and states'. In other words, for Sumner, 'war operates as rude and imperfect [natural] selection' (Sumner 1911: 222). This is not to say that Sumner advocated militarism. On the contrary he understood war as both a social and a natural phenomenon which requires human remedy: 'A statesman who proposes war as an instrumentality admits his incompetence; a politician who makes use of war as a counter in the game of parties is a criminal' (Sumner 1911: 224).

Franco-German metaphysics of violence

Perhaps the most pugnacious approach in classical social thought is represented in the works of Georges Sorel and Georg Simmel. Although these two thinkers are rarely, if ever, thought of as belonging to the same scholarly tradition, there is a great deal of similarity in their understanding of war and violence. Despite their different epistemological frameworks they both interpret violence as a social and ontological necessity. Blending the analytical and the normative they see the experience of warfare and bloodshed as powerful generators of individual and collective meaning, and as initiators of dramatic social transformation. Although their starting positions are very different, their metaphysical diagnoses of violence and society largely overlap.

For Sorel (1950 [1908]) violence is an indispensable mechanism of social change. His focus is in particular on proletarian violence, which he sees as central to the overthrow of an exploitative capitalist state. However, unlike conventional Marxism, Sorel proposes a voluntaristic and largely irrationalist model of revolutionary transformation. In his view such radical change requires both ideological and violent means: the political myth of the general strike and the intensification of class warfare. Sorel understands the idea of a general strike as a romantic, fictional, but potent, symbol, which is able to provoke proletarian action. Drawing on the Bergsonian concept of intuition Sorel perceives human beings, and hence workers, as being driven by emotions that can be channelled through the myth of a general strike. While this political myth provides ideological motivation and guidance, the principal instrument of social change is class war. He calls this process 'heroic aggressiveness' which is no different from standard warfare: 'Proletarian acts of violence … are purely and simply acts of war; they have the value of military manoeuvres and serve to mark the separation of classes' (Sorel 1950: 105). The aim is to intensify class differences, to polarise workers and bourgeoisie, to make apparent who the enemy is in order to make successful revolution possible. In other words, class war is not a metaphor but a real, bloody, violent, conflict that can be settled only by the application of force and the victory of one side over the other. In this view there is no better society without the bloodshed and violent strikes that are only episodic battlefields in social war: 'socialism could not continue to exist without an apology for violence … the strike is a phenomenon of war … the social revolution is an extension of that war in which each great strike is an episode' (Sorel 1950: 301). In Sorel, violence is associated with the moral revival and rebirth of society purified from materialistic decadence. Through the use of this revolutionary, pure and just violence, workers become sanctified. His revolutionary syndicalism is understood as a new and higher moral stage of civilisation that requires blood sacrifice. In this view violent action is inevitable, since the old, unjust and morally corrupt social order cannot be replaced through reform but solely through the use of force.

Simmel articulates a similar argument but in the wider context of total war. Although his earlier studies identify conflict as constitutive of social order and as a necessary step in transforming micro-level group dynamics, his later work advances this view much further in the context of radically transformed macro-level situations such as warfare. For Simmel (1955 [1908]) all social conflicts exhibit some universal traits, as, they act as a source of group integration, they enhance out-group boundaries by intensifying collective polarity, they strengthen in-group loyalty and they help centralise group structure. However war is more than social conflict. In his view war constitutes an 'absolute situation', a unique social event that dramatically transforms the entire society and its core values, principles and practices. Writing in the middle of WWI, Simmel (1917: 20) states: 'most of us are now living in what we might call an absolute situation. All the situations and circumstances in which we found ourselves in the past had something relative about them, deliberations between the more and the less seemed to be order of the day. None of this poses a problem now, since we are faced with an absolute decision. We no longer have the quantitative dilemma as to whether or when we must make a sacrifice or a compromise'. War heightens one's experience and recreates the meaning of life beyond everyday banality. On the one hand, war spells the end of consumerist obsession (what he termed 'mammonism' and the 'chaos of the soul') of worshipping money and commodities for their own sake, while on the other hand, it acts as a 'unifying, simplifying and concentrating force' whereby an individual life becomes subordinated to the higher goal of collective self-preservation. War offers an escape from the 'cyclical repetition of everyday life' as it provides a 'deeply moving existential experience of an ecstatic feeling of security that liberates our personality from inhibitions and opens it up to social impulses once again' (Joas 2003: 65). Despite the bloodshed and murder, war is a total event which frees one's potential, as it produces 'a form and a means for the total exaltation of life' (Watier 1991: 231). Just like Sorel, Simmel saw the violent experience of war as transforming social relations and the human soul. The context of war was perceived as 'pregnant with great possibilities', affirming collective solidarity and potentially creating new men. By sacrificing their lives soldiers enhance the meaning of the collective to which they belong. In this process the moral fabric of society becomes revitalised and a new social order is possible.

The contemporary relevance of bellicose thought

The horrifying experience of the two twentieth century total wars – the result of which was nearly 70 million human lives lost – had a profound impact on sociological theory too. Any association with the concepts and ideas that interpreted war and violence in analytically neutral or even an indirectly positive light found no place in academic life. On one hand, *fin de siecle* intellectual militarism was in part held responsible for the horrors of the two wars, and on the other hand, the 'bellicose' comprehension of social life was deemed irrelevant for understanding the social realities of post-WWII industrial society. As a result the 'bellicose' tradition of classical social thought was largely forgotten – either through outright rejection, or via socially unconscious suppression. Any attempt to seriously revisit these works was simply labelled as an attempt to rehabilitate social Darwinism, thereby invoking instant condemnation as being morally reprehensible. In consequence, much of the second half of twentieth century social thought was dominated by the 'pacifist' theories that drew upon 'non-bellicose' interpretations of Marx, Durkheim and Weber and articulated class and political inequality (neo-Marxism, conflict theory), normative system functionality (structural functionalism) or bureaucratic rationalisation (neo-Weberianism) as key themes of social life in an industrial age.

However, as the second half of the last century and the beginning of this century clearly demonstrate, collective violence and warfare have not evaporated. On the contrary, while the Cold War generated numerous third-world proxy wars between the two superpowers, its ending saw a proliferation of collective violence and warfare throughout the world, not least among the successor states of the former communist federations. As Holsti (1991) and Tilly (2003) document well, the twentieth century was by far the bloodiest century in recorded human history, with 250 new wars and over 100 million deaths. With the dramatic increase in organised terrorist violence and continuing wars in Africa, Iraq, Afghanistan and many other places, this century is not looking promising either. In other words, rather than being an aberration, violence and war remain an integral part of human social experience and as such require serious sociological engagement. Nevertheless contemporary sociology, for the most part, tends to ignore war and collective violence. Still coloured by the strong normative bias inherited from the legacy of the two world wars, much contemporary sociological research combines an intensive rejection of violence with the blatant neglect of its presence (Joas 2003).

Although there is a relatively long tradition of (mostly American) military sociology (Stouffer *et al.* 1949; Janowitz 1953; 1957; Segal 1989; Burk 1998) and since mid 1980s there has been a revival of interest in warfare by comparative political and historical sociologists (e.g. Giddens 1985; Tilly 1985; Mann 1986; 1988; Hall 1987) – which I explore extensively in the next chapter – their focus is either on the workings of military organisation or on the historical impact of warfare on state formation and less on the sociology of war and violence *per se*. As Wimmer and Min (2006: 868) rightly point out: 'sociologists have discussed war as a cause for other phenomena of interest to them, but rarely as an *explanandum* in its own right'.

Therefore, to help articulate a potent contemporary sociology of war and violence which would directly engage with these processes it is paramount to revisit classical social thought, which, as I attempt to show, provides a source of versatile sociological concepts and theories of war and violence. To make classical approaches relevant it is vital to eliminate the normative militarist baggage present in some of these theories and to read, interpret and utilise them not as ontology or ethics but as analytical sociology. That is, reconceptualising these heuristic models in a non-essentialist, non-reificatory and non-moralist discourse will allow us to develop a constructive conceptual apparatus for the sociological study of war and violence. In some respects the revitalisation of sociological interest in warfare as a catalyst of state-making that occurred in the late 1980s has indirectly rehabilitated some of the ideas developed by the classical theorists. As I demonstrate in the next chapter there are clear links and overlaps between the theories of the contemporary political and historical sociologists and those of the classical 'bellicose' tradition. Nevertheless these similarities and the direct influence of the classical theorists are almost never acknowledged and there are no serious attempts to rehabilitate the classical 'bellicose' tradition. However, if our aim is to understand and explain the continuing impact of war and collective violence on social relations and vice versa it is essential that we seriously engage with the classical works as they offer rich conceptual apparatus that requires sober scrutiny, application and further articulation. Forgotten concepts such as Gumplowicz's syngenism, Ratzenhofer's distinction between the conquest state and culture state, Rustow's superstratification, high culture and culture pyramid as well as Simmel's understanding of war as an absolute situation and Sorel's heroic aggressiveness are still highly relevant and useful starting models capable of illuminating an analytical understanding of the role violence and war play in social orders. While syngenism focuses our attention on the role of culturally framed group solidarity in mobilising and popularly justifying war actions, heroic aggressiveness points in the direction of exploring the hypothesis that violent confrontation is the basis of most moral virtues, since a willingness to endanger oneself in combat for the sake of a group is often perceived by the group members as the height of group morality. As I elaborate in more detail later (see Chapter 7), recent sociological, historical and psychological research into battlefield behaviour confirms the explanatory utility of these conceptual models as small-group solidarity – rather than strong ideological commitments or self-interest – is found to be a decisive factor in mobilising soldiers to fight. Moreover these studies clearly corroborate Gumplowitz's argument that micro-level solidarity and the syngenetic quality of social relationships are the cornerstones of joint collective action. They also empirically support the view that the cataclysmic context of war reinforces inter-group morality whereby in combat situations most soldiers come to perceive their platoons and regiments in intensive kinship-like terms.

In addition, the usefulness of the concept of war as an absolute situation that transcends and radically and utterly transforms social relations, central values and everyday life depends on having obtained sound empirical evidence of this in the context of large-scale warfare. Extensive research on social behaviour in the two world wars and the Vietnam War has already demonstrated that, contrary to popular perceptions, killing does not come 'naturally' to trained soldiers but requires intensive coercive regulation and control (Grossman 1996; Collins 2008). Moreover self-sacrifice for a close group is often preferred to killing the supposedly hated enemy. As I attempt to show later (see Chapters 6 and 7) not only are war experiences and propaganda regularly inversely proportional, as the dehumanisation of the enemy progressively increases with the distance from the battlefield, but also as the soldier's sense of sociability is dramatically intensified in this 'absolute situation' and his life hinges on the strength of small group ties then these ties become sacred and the group itself becomes greater than any of its members (Bourke 2000: 237; Collins 2008: 74).

Similarly, the theory of the historical transformation from the conquest-driven state to the culture state, whereby the refinement of civilisation is rooted in a culture pyramid which originated in the violent superstratification, needs thorough historical and theoretical examination to assess its merits. The recent research on the 'new wars' (Kaldor 2001; Bauman 2002b; Shaw 2005) shows that, as predicted by Rustow, the former colonial powers (conquest states) have become internally pacified and highly advanced (culture states) often at the expense of exporting war to the poorer parts of the word (superstratification). These studies might be interpreted as substantiating Rustow's ideas since they see new violent conflicts as predatory wars resulting from the rampant economic liberalisation that undermines already weak states in the South. The leading proponents of the 'new-wars' paradigm, such as Bauman and Kaldor, build indirectly on Rustow since they perceive globalisation as a force that leads to state failure that, eventually, creates a Machiavellian environment with armed warlords utilising identity politics to spread terror and control the remnants of state structures (Kaldor 2001; Bauman 2003). Although, as I argue in Chapter 10, this economistic interpretation overstates the historical novelty of 'new wars' it clearly opens avenues for new research that owes a great deal to the unacknowledged predecessor, Alexander Rustow.

None of this is to deny that some or even most of the concepts and theories developed by the classical theorists may be problematic or not applicable to contemporary forms of violent conflicts and wars. It may be the case that the results of more recent archaeological, historical or psychological research have made some or many of the claims made in these classical theories redundant and obsolete. Nevertheless as sociology is, for the most part, not an unambiguously cumulative discipline where it is possible to draw a simple distinction between fact and value, the 'old' concepts are not necessarily prone to academic ageing and respectful burial. As Alexander (1987) notes, in the social world there is no empirical data that is not already tainted by theory, so new empirical evidence nearly always requires significant theoretical shifts to initiate foundational paradigm changes. As a consequence, rather than discarding their predecessors as irrelevant and outdated, sociologists remain indebted to them for ideas, concepts and theories that are made afresh through the ongoing debate with contemporaries and by a constantly changing social environment. Hence, what really matters is whether the conceptual apparatuses articulated by classical 'bellicose' social thinkers still retains heuristic value for the contemporary study of war and violence. As much of mainstream sociology continues to shy away from the proper study of violence and warfare it seems reasonable to start from the already existing concepts that the classical theorists provide rather than from scratch. And as we will see in the next chapter, the fact that some of the classical ideas have been indirectly revived in recent political and historical sociology suggests that they have clear explanatory value. However, to succeed in this analytical enterprise of revisiting the classics it is important to leave our post-WWII normative biases behind and to try to understand, as the classical theorists did so well, that whether we like it or not, war and violence are not pathological aberrations but integral parts of social life.

2 The contemporary sociology of organised violence

Introduction

It might seem paradoxical to write about the contemporary sociology of war and violence since, strictly speaking, there is no such field of study. Not only are there no established specialised journals or professional organisations within sociology that focus exclusively on warfare but there are very few, if any, books and journal articles that study the relationship between social structure, agency and wars or other forms of organised violence.[1] Unlike political science, anthropology, geography, international relations, security studies and military history where warfare and violence receive extensive coverage resulting in numerous books and articles and well developed research paradigms, contemporary sociology has little to offer in this regard. This is not to say that there are no individual sociologists who study war and violence or that these topics have not been tackled by those within sociology whose research interests lie primarily elsewhere. The point is that contemporary mainstream sociology, unlike its classical predecessors, remains intractable in its near absolute ignoring of warfare. Such obdurateness has resulted in the complete marginalisation of the research field, even though its focus is one of the most important sociological phenomena that has profoundly shaped the history of human sociality: warfare. Moreover, this neglect within the discipline has created a situation where an overwhelming number of studies dealing with warfare and organised violence lack any sociological grounding. Instead of attempting to provide coherent explanatory accounts of social action during wars or how warfare impacts on the transformation of social structure, most studies provide extremely detailed descriptive narratives of individual battles, epic portrayals of actors and

[1] It is important to emphasise that although there are several associations and journals dedicated to military sociology they mostly focus on the relationship between armed forces and society and rarely engage with the study of warfare as a sociological phenomenon not reduced to military activities (cf. Ender and Gibson 2005: 250).

events or offer simplistic 'commonsense' explanations of the highly complex sociological processes involved in organised collective violence.

This chapter focuses on the exemplary, and still rare, cases where contemporary sociologists have engaged with the study of warfare and have done so in a highly creative way. The aim is to show how and why sociological analysis is indispensable in understanding war and violence. Although the lack of systematic and extensive research has stifled the proliferation of clearly articulated and versatile research paradigms it is still possible to identify several distinct sociological approaches in the study of warfare and organised violence. The first section of this chapter provides a brief critical analysis of the sociobiological, instrumentalist and culturalist interpretations of warfare and violence. The second section focuses on the research perspective within sociology which, although essentially centred on topics other than warfare (i.e. origins and transformation of the state, rise of the West, birth of modernity etc.), has elaborated the most potent and dynamic explanatory models for understanding war and violence: organisational materialism. This section and the final section of the chapter highlight the strengths and weaknesses of this approach and pinpoint the links between this perspective and classical 'bellicose' social thought. The final part of the chapter also briefly sketches an alternative sociological account that attempts to go beyond organisational materialism by emphasising the relationship between ideology and coercive bureaucratisation.

The central argument of this chapter is that the contemporary sociology of warfare and violence is most successful when it is able to build creatively on classical social thought. Although much of this classical legacy still remains unrecognised and unappreciated it clearly offers a powerful building block for the contemporary sociological study of war and violence.

The sources of violence and warfare: biology, reason or culture?

Unlike other key sociological phenomena such as class, ethnicity, gender, religion, power and education, warfare is rarely featured in sociology textbooks and when it appears there are no references to distinct sociological theories dealing with this phenomenon (Ahmad and Wilke 1973; Ender and Gibson 2005).[2] Hence, while one is informed about a variety of sociological interpretations of religion or education (e.g. Marxist, Weberian, interactionist,

[2] For example one of the few textbooks that covers warfare is the last (6th) edition of Giddens (2009), which contains a chapter entitled 'Nations, war and terrorism'. Even this is a very recent development influenced by the post 9/11 trend since the previous editions of this book had very little to say about

functionalist etc.), warfare is only perceived as a self-evident, and presumably self-explanatory, calamity that needs no sociological theorising.[3] Obviously the textbooks only reflect the dominant view in mainstream sociology, which perceives warfare either as a remnant of the past, unenlightened, eras or as a kind of temporary anomaly that requires no deeper analysis. Most of all, as argued in the previous chapter, contemporary sociology harbours a strong bias against the study of war and violence grounded in part in the legacy of the two world wars and particularly in the outright rejection of what was deemed to be its social Darwinist past. However, as already demonstrated, this past was theoretically much broader and more resourceful than this pejorative label could possibly accommodate. By branding very diverse sociological interpretations of war and violence as social Darwinism and thus delegitimising their key concepts and explanatory models, mainstream sociology has left this important area of research to other disciplines and in this way it has opened a back door for the revival and proliferation of the neo-Darwinist and quasi-Darwinist interpretations of warfare through the dominance of other disciplines. In other words by attempting to purge alleged social Darwinism from its ranks, sociology finds itself in the paradoxical situation that, since it possesses no comprehensive theory of warfare, it cannot challenge the current prevalence of the neo-Darwinist interpretations of war and violence.

Hence, before we engage with the contemporary sociological accounts of war and violence it is important to provide a brief critical assessment of what seems to be one of the dominant and certainly most popular perspectives in the study of war and violence – a current incarnation of Darwinist thought – sociobiology.

Genetic seeds of warfare?

It is truly remarkable that while mainstream sociology largely rejects its classical tradition in the study of warfare by (wrongly) assuming it to be 'tainted' by Darwinism, many of the contemporary accounts of war and violence

warfare. However, here too warfare is mostly studied in the context of contemporary events such as the Iraq War and the 'war on terror'.

[3] As Ender and Gibson's (2005) analysis of 31 introductory sociology texts shows, even in the USA where there is a long tradition of military sociology these topics remain invisible: 'In no textbook is the military institution or the peace movement treated as a significant social institution in American society similar to how religion, medicine, the family, the economy, or education might be. The military is a sociologically invisible institution to students.' This analysis also shows that topics such as warfare and organised violence receive even less attention.

unequivocally embrace the theory of evolution. In fact, one could argue that Darwinian ideas have never been as influential and as popular as they are today. While at the end of nineteenth century these ideas were very trendy among intellectuals and a small section of the highly literate middle classes, today the mass media, internet, blockbuster films and affordable books have made the central tenets of evolutionary theory accessible to much wider audiences. The availability of sociobiological literature coupled with the institutional weakening of religious authority, the continuous rise in the prestige of science and the increasing spread of neo-liberal ethics of individual competition have all contributed to the popularity of biological interpretations of social phenomena. Hence, it is important to engage analytically with the contemporary version of this research paradigm, sociobiology, and in particular the way it explains war and violence.

Sociobiology starts from the proposition that much of social behaviour has biological roots and is the product of long periods of evolution. In this sense human action is seen as being governed by the same genetic principles as those that direct the behaviour of lizards or butterflies. The central idea is that animals (including humans) are more likely to behave in a way that has proven to be evolutionarily advantageous for the particular species. By focusing on the evolutionary origins of life forms, sociobiologists argue that social behaviour is, for the most part, the result of natural selection whereby an organism is driven towards self reproduction. Taking a gene as an elementary, and optimal, unit of natural selection, sociobiologists argue that social actions can be explained with reference to genetic reproduction. In Dawkins's words (1989: 2) 'we, and all other animals, are machines created by our genes'. However, unlike classical Darwinism, which focused on individual selection, sociobiologists aim to extend the biological principles of natural selection to the collective level. Hence, the focal point shifts towards the principles of kin selection and the idea of 'inclusive fitness'. Starting with the early works of Wilson (1975, 1978) then to more contemporary research (Dawkins 1986; 1989; Van den Berghe 1995; Van der Dennen 1999), sociobiologists interpret social behaviour through the concept of inclusive fitness arguing that when organisms cannot reproduce directly they will do so indirectly through their genetically closest kin.[4] The concept of inclusive fitness is utilised to explain altruistic behaviour; it is argued that siblings favour each other over their first or second cousins since they share significantly more

---

[4] E.O. Wilson (1975: 586) defines inclusive fitness as 'the sum of an individual's own fitness plus all its influence on fitness in its relatives other than direct descendants; hence the total effect of kin selection with reference to an individual'.

genes (i.e. half for siblings vs. one eighth for first cousins and one sixteenth for second cousins).

Even though sociobiologists recognise the impact culture and environment have on human life, they still perceive culture as secondary to nature: 'There is no denying the importance of culture, but culture is a superstructure that builds on a biological substratum. Culture grows out of biological evolution; it does not wipe the biological slate clean and start from scratch' (Van den Berghe 1981: 6).

Following the central precepts of evolutionary theory, a number of scholars have developed a comprehensive sociobiological explanation of warfare. From the early works of Tinbergen (1951), Dart (1953), Lorenz (1966) and Eibl-Eibesfeldt (1971) to more sophisticated contemporary works (Shaw and Wang 1989; Van Hooff 1990; Van der Dennen 1995; Ridley 1997; Eibl-Eibesfeldt and Salter 1998), war and violence are understood through the prism of natural selection. Whereas early ethologists such as Lorenz wrote about 'fighting instincts' and 'natural aggressive drives', contemporary sociobiologists invoke genes as the principal agents of violent conflict.[5] However the core argument is constant: human violence is just an extension of animal behaviour, which includes aggressive competition over resources or territory with the aim of maximising one's reproductive success.

The founder of modern sociobiology, E. O. Wilson, was particularly influential in propagating the image of human beings as innately aggressive and war-prone creatures. In his view humans, just as other animals, have genetically ingrained aggressive dispositions that have evolved over millions of years. Consequently the institution of war is essentially nothing more than an extension of this pugnacious disposition: 'Throughout history, warfare, representing only the most organised technique of aggression, has been endemic to every form of society, from hunter-gatherer bands to industrial states' (Wilson 1978: 101). In this view there is no distinction between individual aggression and organised violence: all violence is reduced to aggressive impulses whether it involves sexual domination, defence of one's territory, predatory aggression in hunting, enforcement of hierarchies within a social group or 'disciplinary aggression' employed to maintain the social order in a large-scale society. For Wilson (1978: 148–54), aggression has a strong genetic and hereditary underpinning since it evolved as an array of multifaceted responses of the endocrine and nervous systems and is regulated through

---

[5] Lorenz (1966: 3) sees warfare as a form of aggression rooted in 'the fighting instinct [of] beast and man which is directed against members of the same species'.

hormonal processes. More specifically, aggressive behaviour is linked to high levels of testosterone and low levels of estrogen, which leads Wilson to conclude that 'males are characteristically aggressive, especially toward one another' while genetically 'girls are predisposed to be intimately sociable and less physically venturesome' (Wilson 1978: 125–30). Thus, simply put, in this view, warfare is a form of aggression moulded by the rules of natural selection whereby men risk their lives to improve the reproductive potential of their own genes or those of their closest kin (which involves protection of their potential mates – women).

Although there is a variety of distinct positions within sociobiology there is a general understanding that warfare, as other forms of animal aggression, is universal and for the most part is a product of biological processes. As the title of the book by Shaw and Wang (1989) suggests, sociobiologists argue that there are 'genetic seeds of warfare'. While contemporary sociobiology has made some advances towards being less deterministic, the central neo-Darwinist principles which strongly tie warfare and organised violence to the biology of aggression remain unchanged. To illustrate the problems with such a perspective let us focus more intensively on one of the most comprehensive recent sociobiological interpretations of war and violence – Azar Gat's *War in Human Civilisation* (2006).

Gat offers an empirically rich and historically sweeping survey of warfare that utilises the standard arguments of evolutionary theory and maps the macro-level transformation of organised violence from the time of hunter-gatherers to early twenty-first century conflicts. Gat's central aim is to demonstrate that warfare is a universal phenomenon characterising all known societies and that, contrary to what most social scientists believe, war is not unique to the human species. For Gat, war is a form of collective aggression, and to explain its workings it is essential to understand the universal biological principles that underpin its dynamics. In this view, unlike sex and food, both of which are biologically driven ends that sustain an organism's survival, aggression is a mere means, an 'innate but optional tactic' employed by life forms to secure their existence. One of Gat's central arguments is that 'the interconnected competition over resources and reproduction is the *root* cause of conflict and fighting in humans, as in all other animal species' (Gat 2006: 87). The origins of aggression are explained by reference to the genetic make-up of organisms whereby individual action is motivated by self-reproduction. When direct genetic reproduction is not possible, the tendency is to reproduce indirectly through kinship relations, and close kin are selected over distant or non-kin. In this process of 'blind natural selection' aggression is used to acquire as many potential mates as possible (to maximise one's reproductive potential), the result of which is the indirect exclusion or direct elimination of rival males. Gat recognises the importance of culture to account for the dramatic social development and immense technological change characterising the last ten thousand years, but, as with all sociobiologists, he views cultural development as operating along pre-set biological tracks. Although the development of agriculture, and later industrial civilisation, has in some ways uncoupled the original link between 'ends and adaptive behavioural means', Gat detects the same biological principles of aggression and domination at work, even within contemporary Western societies, where violence has greatly diminished. In other words Gat argues that 'it is the evolution-shaped proximate mechanisms – the web of desire – that dominate human behaviour, even where much of their original adaptive rationale has weakened' (Gat 2006: 672).

The principal problem with the sociobiological arguments is not that they are necessarily untrue, but that they are usually insufficient in explaining social action. While it makes little sense to dispute our common genetic origin with other animals and our biological foundation (so apparent in our basic needs to eat, drink, sleep and procreate) the point is that human sociality has evolved to such levels of complexity that it now involves distinct layers of social action not found in the rest of the animal kingdom. In other words sociobiology ignores the unintended products of human action such as social structure, culture and ideology but also institutions and social organisations, which have acquired a substantial autonomy and are able to generate new social dynamics. It is no coincidence that sociobiological arguments seem most convincing when applied to the world of early humans and falter when dealing with the agrarian and industrial worlds. The ever-expanding cultural and political dynamics of later historical eras illustrate only too well the extent to which human life has been transformed with the emergence of civilisation. Hence, the key issue here is that biological explanations of social phenomena are usually not entirely mistaken, but rather that they are insufficient to account for social and cultural development. We can agree that humans share a great deal with their animal counterparts, but the point is to explain the ways in which humans and animals differ. It is like comparing diamonds and graphite by focusing on their identical chemical composition (i.e. both being allotropes of carbon). This would miss the fact that it is not chemical composition but a distinctive structural quality (not to mention social worth and cultural significance) that makes one exceptional and the other ordinary.

This general explanatory weakness is most visible in Wilson's and Gat's conceptual understandings of war. By reducing warfare to aggression, fighting and killing they miss its social origin, function and structure. Unlike aggression, which is a psychological response, war is a social phenomenon that requires organised social action, collective intentionality, the systematic use of weapons, sophisticated linguistic coordination and ritualism. In many ways, as will be argued and illustrated in this book, war is the exact opposite of aggression. War is a social mechanism that constrains biological and psychological reflexes as it necessitates the organised use of physical force for specific political purposes. To understand war one has to decouple it from 'intraspecific killing' and other violent action, as what is distinct about warfare is its sociological character – its organisational structure and ideological justification. The dramatic increase in the human capability to fight large-scale wars (evidenced in the total wars of the twentieth century) has little to do with 'natural aggression' and 'webs of desire', and a great deal to do with distinctly human constructions such as social organisations, political institutions, the modern nation-state, ideological doctrines and geopolitics. Instead of treating wars in a voluntarist fashion as products of 'human desire that underlie the human motivational system in general – only by violent means' (Gat 2006: 668), war has to be studied as a complex and highly contingent set of events and processes which require the mobilisation of power, human beings, resources, and technologies of production and communication, all of which adds up to processes and events which dramatically interrupt routine social life and generate new social dynamics. War is a social, not a biological, fact.

Furthermore while sociobiologists are persuasive when they empirically debunk the old Rousseauian myth of the noble or peaceful savage and place human development in a larger evolutionary context, their general argument ultimately fails in its attempt to encompass the totality of human history. While the central premises of evolutionary theory usually have much more resonance in discussions about very early periods of human development they seem unable to convince when the modern world is discussed. For example when Wilson and Gat focus on the agrarian and industrial eras to demonstrate continuity of natural selection they often conflate real and symbolic kinship, relying on metaphoric and figurative language to resuscitate the sociobiological argument (see in particular Gat 2006: 416, 432). If kin selection is to be a plausible explanatory model, then it cannot shift between the real and the symbolic – if it cannot be proven as real, than it is not kinship at all. Similarly their essentialist epistemology, which operates with a homogenous and bounded concept of a group, reduces gender, ethnicity and nationhood to quasi-biological attributes. As I elaborate later (see Chapters 6 and 9) since sociobiology reifies culture and sexuality it is able to explain neither the relationship between gender and war nor the development of group cohesion and nationalism in times of violent conflicts.

Homo economicus and the violent conflict

When warfare and violence are not reduced to biology they are often seen through the prism of economic rationality. Economistic theories of warfare have a long tradition in social science from Montesquieu, Adam Smith, Richard Cobden and Norman Angel to the neo-Marxist, globalist and rational choice models of recent times. Despite the obvious diversity of positions all economistic theories of collective violence presume that the social order is heavily shaped by the logic of economic rationality and in particular by individual and collective interests. The earlier proponents of this utilitarian approach argued that the expansion of free trade would make wars obsolete as the peaceful exchange of goods and services would ultimately prove beneficial to all sides, thus making the deployment of violence irrational. As Angel put it in 1909: 'the only feasible policy in our day for a conqueror to pursue is to leave the wealth of a territory in the possession of its occupants; it is a fallacy, an illusion, to regard a nation as increasing its wealth when it increases territory' (Angel 2007: 139).[6] Even though early Marxism turned this interpretation on its head by arguing that capitalism and territorial expansion are fully compatible as imperial conquest provides new markets and new resources, this view too reduces warfare and violence to economics. In Lenin's formulation, the imperial scrabble for Africa and WWI are just examples of another, higher, state of capitalism: 'The more capitalism is developed, the more the need for raw materials is felt, the more bitter competition becomes, the more feverishly the hunt for raw materials proceeds throughout the whole world, the more desperate becomes the struggle for the acquisition of colonies' (Lenin 1939: 82).

Contemporary versions of these views are more sophisticated and better grounded in evidence-based research, but they still retain the strong emphasis on the role of economic reasoning as the principal cause of warfare. Two contemporary approaches dominate much of academic discussion: the

---

[6] It is a tragicomic twist of history that Angel wrote and published this extremely popular book (*The Great Illusion*), a book that interprets war as a vestige of dark, long-gone, past eras, and fiercely advocates trade as a bulwark against violence, on the eve of the most vicious war ever fought.

globalisation theory and the rational choice models of social action. Whereas the globalisation theorists centre their attention on the macro-structural transformations which allegedly have changed the character of organised violence in the late twentieth and early twenty-first centuries, the rational choice theorists focus on the micro level: how individual rationality shapes collective action in war situations.

The theorists of globalisation such as Bauman (1998, 2002a, 2002b, 2006), Sassen (2006) and Kaldor (2001, 2004, 2007) interpret current social, political and economic conditions as historically exceptional. They share a view that the character of the global, neo-liberal, economy has changed to such an extent that its power overrides that of most individual nation-states. The dramatic advancement of technology is perceived as providing new modes of communication and transport that erode the conventional forms of social organisation and 'annul temporal/spatial distances'. Sassen (2006: 1) states that globalisation 'consists of an enormous variety of micro-processes that begin to denationalise what had been constructed as national – whether policies, capital, political subjectivities, urban spaces, temporal frames, or any other of a variety of dynamics and domains'. More specifically the emphasis is on the deeply stratified nature of this change whereby globalisation is understood as a force that generates new forms of inequality. In Bauman's (1998: 18) words: 'rather than homogenising the human condition, the technological annulment of temporal/spatial distances tends to polarise it'. In this context the argument is that organised violence has changed too. Clearly echoing C. Wright Mills (1958), Bauman and Kaldor claim that warfare has now become an instrument of economic policy: as neo-liberal globalisation advances, it corrodes the political power of most individual states, with multinational corporations reaping profits on the ruins of collapsing polities. At the same time military power is gradually devolved to private contractors who are able to quickly multiply their earnings through the overcharging for their services. Hence they understand all contemporary warfare as linked to globalisation: while 'neo-imperial' wars such as that in Iraq in 2003 are seen through the prism of struggle for material resources (e.g. oil), the many civil wars in the failing, non-Western, states are perceived to be a direct consequence of the ruthless search for profit.

The essential problem with this view is that, just as its Marxist predecessors, it reduces the inherent complexity of violent action to the simple business of profit maximisation. Although the proponents of this approach might be right in arguing that globalisation in its neo-liberal form is more likely to generate greater social inequalities, this in itself does not tell us much about the character of violence and warfare. Not only does this economistic argument overstate the supposed novelty of global trade but it also wrongly downplays the role of nation-states' political and military strength. While there is no denying that the infrastructural and despotic powers of some states have been weakened significantly in recent years and that some states, such as Somalia and the Democratic Republic of Congo, have virtually ceased to be single organised entities, this is not historically unique, nor is there any substantial evidence that this process is directly caused by the greed of the multinational corporations (Hirst and Thompson 1999; Hall 2000; Newman 2004). As I argue later (see Chapter 10) many of the central claims made by the theorists of globalisation (and in particular their concept of the 'new wars') are built on overblown generalisations and factually incorrect data. Although ever-increasing new technologies and the changing character of the global economy have had a significant impact on contemporary warfare, they remain secondary to the old forces of geopolitics, ideology and bureaucratic power.

Rational choice theories focus more on the actions and choices made by individuals in violent conflicts. Starting from the assumption that human beings are predominately rational and self-interested creatures, this approach analyses the dynamics of individual and collective decision-making. Although there is a substantial diversity among rational-choice models, they all perceive individuals as utility maximisers who choose the best action according to a stable set of, mostly universal, preferences. Even though a person's actions are usually restricted by experience and social norms, it is argued that much of human behaviour can be explained and predicted by looking at the instrumental rationality of individuals (Elster 1985; Hechter 1995; Boudon 2003).

When applied to the study of war this model focuses on the motivation of individuals in participating in violent behaviour (Fearon 1995; Wintrobe 2006; Laitin 1995; 2000; 2007). Warfare and violence are explored in reference to one's economic gains and losses. Laitin (2007: 22) puts it bluntly: 'If there is an economic motive for civil war … it is in the expectation of collecting the revenues that ownership of the state avails.' The key argument is that the use of violence is risky and is, in economic terms, a costly strategy often resulting in outcomes that are not beneficial to either party involved in the conflict. Hence, the attention of researchers has centred on the rationale behind the deployment of violence in inter-group action. For example, Fearon (1994, 1995), Weingast (1998) and Walter (2002) analyse the role of trust in the context of civil wars. Since a war environment generates individual insecurity it becomes paramount for actors involved to know who can be trusted. The wars are difficult to stop as neither side is willing to trust their opponents' nominal commitment to disarm. Such difficult choices are studied in reference to game theory problems such as the prisoner's dilemma or the chicken game, both of which demonstrate how individual rationality often results in collective irrationality. In the multi-ethnic context of the newly established independent states, such as those in the post-colonial or post-communist environment, a problem of 'credible commitment' (Fearon 1994) may arise, whereby the minority group may doubt the dominant group's commitment to ensuring full representation and protection. As a result individuals from the minority group might decide that it is more rational to secede rather than to wait and see whether their rights will be respected. Furthermore, rational-choice theorists argue that once warfare intensifies it is difficult to acquire reliable information so 'information asymmetry' and media monopolies have a direct impact on the decisions of individuals to fight or not. So, if individuals in a group are bombarded with messages that the enemy is unlikely to stop fighting until it annihilates the entire group, most individuals from that group will act rationally by opting to fight such an enemy (Weingast 1998); thus, in all of these studies primacy is given to the actor's instrumental rationality and economic opportunities, with violence being interpreted as an (often unintended) outcome of rational decision-making.

Although utilitarian models have been applied widely to the study of violence there is still a lack of comprehensive sociological accounts of warfare written from this perspective. The most thorough of such models is Stathis Kalyvas's work on the dynamics of civil wars. While this approach is developed in a number of recent publications (Kalyvas 2003; 2005; 2007; 2008) it is most fully articulated in his book *The Logic of Violence in Civil War* (2006). Since this book represents a milestone in the rationalist tradition of sociological research on war, it is of paramount importance to critically engage with its arguments so as to demonstrate the inherent weaknesses of the utilitarian approach.

In contrast to the popular views and journalistic depictions that understand and portray warfare as a product of irrationality, collective madness and chaos, Kalyvas sets out to show that collective violence has a logical structure. His focus in particular is on the selective use of violence in civil wars, where he argues that violence is produced as the animosities of local actors intersect with the strategies and motives of political elites. In other words, local actors map their own private grievances onto the larger political narratives articulated by centrally based elites. Civil wars then are not to be understood as events where every segment of political life becomes politicised. Instead, they create situations in which politics itself becomes privatised: neighbours are denounced to authorities in order to settle personal scores. In fact, Kalyvas maintains that civil wars are best understood by looking at the micro-cosmic level – local cleavages and struggles – rather than the official macro-ideological frameworks which are generally used to articulate the meaning of the conflict both internally and externally.

Although violence as a strategic device is often used by different groups and individuals, it cannot be reduced to a simple matrix of individual rationality whereby actors seek to maximise opportunities or optimise outcomes. Instead, violent action is a dynamic, complex, interactive process that defies the Hobbesian image of war of all against all. In Kalyvas's view, rather than violence being something which is intrinsic to human nature, it takes place precisely because people have an aversion to it. Contrary to popular opinion, the course of a civil war is not marked by continuous violence between opposing groups; rather it is used most often by local leaders to control the activities of their own groups. As Kalyvas demonstrates, most atrocities happen when one social actor either has near-hegemonic status or when none of several actors is in full control of a particular territory. The degree and scope of brutality in civil war atrocities is comparable to the ruthlessness of gang violence, with both operating on the basis of similar principles. Violence serves as a deterrent: a graphic reminder of the controlling actor's ability to monitor, and capacity to sanction, disobedience. In a situation where an actor manages to achieve full control, or in a situation where a territory is not controlled at all, then there is no need (or possibility in the latter case) for excessive brutality.

Kalyvas's approach rightly challenges many commonsense views of collective violence. Drawing on extensive empirical research and utilising both quantitative and qualitative data analysis and a variety of primary and secondary studies of violence and civil war, Kalyvas is able to dispel many myths that surround the character of civil war: in terms of scope, levels of atrocity, internal rationality and the relationship between the micro- and macro-worlds. His analysis of the micro-dynamics of the Greek civil war is particularly outstanding. However, despite Kalyvas's occasional criticism of the strategic models of explanation, his argument remains firmly grounded in an overly rationalist and instrumentalist epistemology which conceptualises human beings as *homines economici* in pursuit of rational interests. Kalyvas frames violence quite narrowly – either actors are utilitarian or are driven by irrational cultural doctrines. This strategy ultimately leads to a reduction of complexity, so that war situations become a single-variable calculus of whether actors make the choice to inform on their neighbours or not: 'most individuals participate in the production of violence indirectly, via denunciation' (Kalyvas 2006: 336). The weakness here is that social action is always richer, more complex and messier than this formula allows for. Not only is it the case that utilitarian models lean towards *ex post facto* types of explanation and tautological reasoning, but their overly voluntaristic and intentionalist view of social action tends to thwart any serious analysis of the asymmetrical nature of how individual choices are made (Malešević 2004: 94–110).

Furthermore, by examining ideological action as an either/or singular phenomenon rather than a multilayered process, Kalyvas, just as Hechter (1995), Laitin (2007) and other utilitarians, ignores contemporary developments in the study of ideology. It is somewhat surprising, given Kalyvas's clear ability to demystify clichéd views on violence, that he accepts what amounts to a redundant understanding of ideology. Ideology is not a form of social pathology but a multifaceted social process through which individual and social actors articulate their beliefs and behaviours. Rather than assuming 'ideological irrationality' as given, it is paramount to understand that ideology is a form of 'thought-action' that penetrates most of social and political practice and which is conveyed through the distinct conjunctural arrangements of a particular social order (Freeden 1996; 2003; Malešević 2006). People do not take an ideology on board as a complete and closed system of ideas, but rather take it on in a piecemeal and unsystematic fashion, riddled with contradictions (Billig *et al*. 1988).

A further question follows from the way the adoption of the strict utilitarian epistemology forces rational-choice models towards ahistorical analyses, which lack the important distinction between modern and pre-modern forms of collective violence. For example neither Kalyvas (2006: 116, 121) nor Hechter (1995) make a distinction between wars fought in agrarian social orders such as the Peloponnesian War (431–404 BCE) and the Thirty Years War (1618–1648) and those of modern age such as the American Civil War (1861–5) and the Spanish Civil War (1936–9). Although there is no doubt that many aspects of human behaviour are universal and trans-historical, the character of violent conflict has changed significantly with the development of complex bureaucratic institutions and the increased organisational potential of modernity. Not only is it the case that in the modern age the combination of technology, science and industry make violence a much more potent means of wielding state power, but the development and expansion of ideological mobilisation also transforms warfare from the privilege of a few noblemen into a mass phenomenon. As I argue later (see Chapter 4) modern wars are quintessentially different from their pre-modern counterparts, as mass-scale violence entails complex organisation, technological development, centralised authority and advanced mechanisms of ideological persuasion, all of which are products of modernity. It is only in the modern era that non-external violence is completely delegitimised; wherein 'internal pacification' is substituted with the cumulative bureaucratisation of coercion and centrifugal forms of ideologisation (see Chapters 3 and 4).

The cultural foundations of war and violence

While in biological and utilitarian theories of war and violence the spotlight is on (genetic or economic) interests, the focal point for the culturalist approaches are social meanings and values. From Spengler (1991[1918]) and Toynbee's (1950) early works on the rise and fall of civilisations to the more recent studies of Huntington (1993, 1996), cultural explanations of violence have gained a great deal of popularity. Whether they accentuate differences in religious beliefs, cultural practices or civilisational clashes, nearly all of these perspectives perceive human beings as essentially norm-driven creatures. Both war and violence are conceptualised as the product of culture: while some approaches stress the irreconcilable struggles of different worldviews or theological doctrines as a source of violent action (e.g. the idea of jihad, the Christian Crusades etc.), others focus on symbolism, ritualism and signification as the key features of warfare. In particular, there is a long established tradition within military history that attempts to explain various aspects of warfare by invoking cultural and civilisational parameters. For example, since the Greco-Persian wars (499–448 BCE), the European and later North American historians have adopted a syntagma 'the Western way of war' to distinguish the Western from the non-Western forms of warmaking. According to this highly popular view – perpetuated in one form or another from the Greek, Roman and Medieval European periods to contemporary times – the two models of fighting are the exact opposites: whereas 'Oriental' warfare is supposedly characterised by ambushes, missile throwing from a distance and avoidance of close combat, the 'Western way of war' is exemplified by direct face-to-face battle to death. Highly influential military historians, such as Hanson (1989, 2001) and Keegan (1994), argue that this cultural divide originated in the historical specificity of the ancient Greek city-states and as such was a decisive factor in the eventual rise of Western rationality. They argue that the unique position of the free city-states allowed for the development of the pitched battle between two heavy infantries. This, in turn, gave birth to the legal system to provide the platform for formal declarations of war and peace negotiations, and gradually transformed warfare from disorganised skirmishes and hero worship of commanders towards the collective enterprise of disciplined armies engaged in a single decisive contest.[7] In this sense, for Keegan (1994: 387), culture is 'a prime determinant of the nature of warfare'.[8]

Although such crude forms of cultural determinism have been proven conceptually flawed and factually inaccurate (Lynn 2003; Sidebottom 2004),[9] more subtle culturalist arguments have found a great deal of resonance within sociology. For example, historical sociologists such as Mosse (1991), Winter (1995), A. D. Smith (1999) and Hutchinson (2005), draw directly or indirectly on Durkheimian theories of solidarity and religion to explain the role collective memories, myths and commemoration play in making the war experience socially meaningful. Both Mosse and Winter have explored the character of collective remembrance in the wake of modern wars. Mosse (1991) traces the origin of what he calls 'the myth of the war experience' from the Napoleonic wars to WWI by emphasising how war was glorified and sanctified by military cemeteries, monuments and war memorials. In addition, this mythology was perpetuated and reinforced through banal artefacts of everyday life such as postcards, military toys and souvenirs. His focus is in particular on the heroic myths of the Great War, which became a sacred totem for national worship not only for the side that won it but even more for the side that lost it. According to Mosse, this lionisation of the fallen dead helped transform popular perceptions of war, with violence and loss of life in the name of a nation becoming gradually acceptable among the general public. The myth of the war experience bestowed a particular social meaning on the idea of mass sacrifice for the national cause.

In a similar vain, Anthony D. Smith and John Hutchinson analyse the links between the practice of commemorating past wars and the processes of nation-formation. More specifically, Smith (1991, 1999, 2003) explores the historical alteration of the notion of a 'chosen people', whereby this religious idea, grounded in 'the covenant with God', has gradually acquired

[7] Hanson (1989) identifies the Battles of Marathon and Gaugamela and the Siege of Ten as prime examples of successful Western victories over 'Oriental' armies.
[8] Keegan's cultural determinism is well illustrated by the contrast he makes between the armies of Darius and Alexander: 'The death of Darius at the hands of his entourage, who hoped that by leaving his body to be found by Alexander they might save their own skins, perfectly epitomises the cultural clash between expediency and honour in these two different ethics of warmaking' (Keegan 1994: 390).
[9] I provide a brief critical analysis of this position in Chapter 6.

an officially secular national connotation. However, for Smith, the strength of this notion is retained only because it maintains a quasi-religious aura since 'only religion, with its powerful symbolism and collective ritual, could inspire such fervour' (Smith 2003: vii). What is crucial here is that the feeling that you are a chosen people implies a sense of collective superiority (the existence of sacred communion protected by God) only on the premise that a specific moral obligation is fulfilled. While in the pre-secular era this is a covenant with a deity, in the modern age this deity is a nation itself. Hence, in an unambiguously neo-Durkheimian argument Smith points to the 'glorious dead' as those who invoke a sense of normative commitment. National commemorations such as Armistice Day represent 'a reflexive act of national self-worship' through which the 'nation is revealed as a sacred communion of the people, a union of the prematurely dead, the living and the yet unborn, its "true self" lodged in the innate virtue of the Unknown Warrior and symbolised by the empty tomb' (Smith 2003: 249).

This Durkheimian understanding of social action is also evident in the recent work on collective trauma following mass killings during war. Cultural sociologists such as Jeffrey Alexander (2003, 2004), Bernhard Giesen (1998, 2004) and Neil Smelser (2004) study the social construction of meanings as shaped after traumatic events. Nevertheless, as Alexander points out there is no simple causal relationship between horrifying events (e.g. the bombing of Dresden or the Holocaust) and traumatic collective experience. Rather, collective trauma is a socially mediated attribution that may or may not relate to the actual event. For Alexander (2004: 10), 'only if the patterned meanings of the collectivity are abruptly dislodged is traumatic status attributed to an event. It is the meanings that provide the sense of shock and fear, not the events in themselves'. Giesen (2004) looks at the changing character of collective trauma in post-war Germany through the competing narratives of collective victimisation and guilt. In particular, he analyses the collective trauma of the perpetuators of the Holocaust and the rituals of remembrance through which this trauma is discursively mediated and eventually unravelled.

Although there is variety of culturalist approaches to the study of war and violence, a very small minority of them have a strong sociological basis. Since Philip Smith's (1991, 1994, 2005, 2008) approach represents the most well articulated sociological attempt to explain violent action through the cultural parameters, let us focus more extensively on his work.

In contrast to the Hobbesian epistemology of biological or economic instrumentalism, Philip Smith understands social action largely in

Rousseauian terms. He even makes this explicit: 'we come to understand collective violence as a cultural act underpinned to a greater or lesser extent by what Jean-Jacques Rousseau called the popular will' (Smith 2005: 224). Combining neo-Durkheimian structural analysis with hermeneutics and the study of narrative formation, Smith argues that the most important features of warfare are to be found in its cultural foundations. In his own words: 'war is not just about culture, but it is all about culture' (Smith 2005: 4, 212). Despite the contextual specifics of warfare, Smith contends that all war – or more specifically, all war discourses – exhibit similar patterns couched in particular narrative structures. For Smith, human beings are primarily cultural creatures and, as the structural properties of culture are universal, so the discourses and codes of war narratives are 'always a case of new wine in old bottles' (Smith 2005: 35). One of the central aims of his project is to decode the cultural logic of different narratives that are articulated in the process of justifying a specific military action. By focusing on the empirical cases of the Suez Crisis of 1956, the Gulf War of 1991 and the War in Iraq of 2003, Smith (2005) attempts to demonstrate how different social actors provide often irreconcilable portrayals of the same violent conflict. He compares and contrasts the ways in which the US, British, French and Spanish media, as well as political elites, publicly narrate the same violent historical events by espousing very different binary codes. While for one audience certain political actions are framed and conceptualised through the 'discourse of liberty', for others they belong to the 'discourse of repression'. For example, before the Suez crisis, for the US public, Nasser was a charismatic liberator, while for the French and British publics he was no more than a ruthless thug. Or again, throughout the Iran–Iraq War Saddam Hussein was a brave and progressive leader, while the two Gulf wars transformed him – in the US public arena at least – into a ravenous monster.

In Smith's view (1994, 2005) all wars require coherent and believable narratives, and all narratives are built on disparate binary codes that separate the sacred from the profane, good from evil, and the rational from the irrational. These binary codes are usually interwoven into a larger narrative structure that attempts to articulate a particular conflict through one of the following four cultural genres: mundane, tragic, romantic and apocalyptic. Among these it is apocalyptic narratives that are 'the most efficient at generating and legitimating massive society-wide sacrifice', and as such are 'the only narrative form that can sustain war as culturally acceptable' (Smith 2005: 27). Although political elites are important in this process they cannot impose a particular war narrative that is not 'couched in terms of the shared codes of civil society'. Smith concludes that as cultural patterns shape individual and social action, so war can never be explained without understanding its narrative structure.

There are three major problems with Smith's argument and with the general culturalist approaches to warfare. First, although neo-Durkheimians are correct in arguing that cultural background, shared (public) perceptions and narrative configurations of violent conflict are important in understanding the logic of particular wars they cannot explain either the origin or the persistence of violent action. While the neo-Durkheimian position is not as culturally determinist as its predecessors it still unduly overemphasises the role of culture at the expense of other social factors, thus being unable to comprehend the full complexity of war situations. Rather than being solely, or even primarily, a discourse, narrative or cultural code, war is first and foremost a material event that involves organised physical destruction, killing and dying. While we can agree that any given violent conflict requires collective interpretation, public articulation and cultural coding, none of these is either sufficient or necessary in initiating and prosecuting a war. Smith's (2005: 208) steadfast culturalism rests on a questionable view that sees 'the image of the enemy and the narrative inflation of the precipitating crisis [as something] that leads to war'. Cultural codes certainly make the war effort smoother, more plausible, and no doubt even meaningful, but they do not in themselves create war. Although storytelling is an important part of social life, life itself is much more than storytelling. Despite his attempts to distance himself from an idealist epistemology, Philip Smith's understanding of social action in general, and warfare in particular, just as Alexander's or Anthony Smith's, is deeply wedded to the Rousseauian and Durkheimian image of humans as essentially norm-governed creatures.[10] What we see in his writing is a inflexible culturalism and structural functionalism combined in a view of human action as being conditioned by Parsonian 'general value patterns'. There is little or no room for individual and collective interests, political motives or internal social conflicts.

Arguing that 'social life can be treated like a text', P. Smith (2005: 36) reduces the materiality of human life to a set of symbols, codes and genres. Such a research strategy cannot really help us to explain why and how some individuals resist the dominant interpretation of the reality of war while others blindly accept it, or why those most exposed to images of the enemy's

---

[10] For a more comprehensive critique of Anthony D. Smith's epistemology see Malešević (2006: 109–135); while his response to my criticism is given in Smith (2009: 122–130).

cruelty such as soldiers at the frontline are often the least resentful towards the enemy (Holmes 1985; Bourke 2000).

A second problem is Smith's inability to fully verify this neo-Durkheimian theoretical model through his selection of case studies. Not only do his case studies demonstrate the multilayered character of each war, where cultural codes and narratives are but a segment of a much larger phenomenon and processes, but more importantly, even here it is apparent that geopolitical, material and other factors often appear more prominent than cultural genres. Rather than being a causal force, cultural coding is a supplement (an important one) to politically initiated social actions. For example, when writing about the Suez crisis Smith is forced to recognise implicitly that geopolitics was decisive in determining the direction of respective cultural codings. As the 'Suez Canal was of greater strategic importance to Britain than to the United States' (Smith 2005: 74), it seems logical that this would be reflected in the differing narrative articulations of this conflict in these two countries. Similarly, when discussing the US media's ignorance of the Halabja poison gas attack of 1988 and its sudden and dramatic media re-appearance before the 2003 Iraq war, Smith tells us more about the media's dependence on the actions of political elites than about commonly shared cultural narratives.

Finally, nearly all culturalists deduce violence from culture: while for Spengler, Huntington and many military historians it is the intrinsic incompatibility and irreconcilability of the values of civilisations that leads to warfare, for more sophisticated neo-Durkheimians such as Alexander, Giesen and the two Smiths, violence is a by-product of mismatched solidarities. However, what remains unexplored in this tradition of research is the alternative hypothesis: that culture itself is a product of violence. Although culturalists such as Rene Girard (1977) and Georges Bataille (1986) link the foundation of human culture to the origin of sacrifice, whereby culture (and in particular religion) emerges as a social mechanism for controlling violence, they do not explain culture as directly emanating from violence. Instead, in a Durkheimian fashion they see culture through the opposing categories of sacredness and profanity, with rites of victimisation acting as the cultural barrier to the proliferation of violence. For Girard the scapegoat mechanism by which the group removes internal conflict through violent action directed at an arbitrarily selected victim is the social device that keeps violence in check and that preserves the social order. However, such a view wrongly presumes that human beings are intrinsically violent and that without the structures of culture and civilisation there would be a war of all against all. With Girard, Durkheimianism reaches its full circle: although it starts with a rejection of Hobbes and an appreciation of Rousseau it ends up with a quasi-Hobbesian diagnosis of collective violence. Hence, as I elaborate later, (see Chapters 6 and 7) there is a need for an alternative interpretation of the relationship between culture and violence which focuses on the role of social organisation and ideology.

Organisational materialism: war, violence and the state

Despite insightful contributions made from sociobiological, instrumentalist and culturalist perspectives, there is only one research tradition in contemporary sociology that has engaged with warfare and organised violence in a systematic and comprehensive way: organisational materialism.[11] Even though the focal point of this approach is the origins of states, social power, and the birth and expansion of modernity, organisational materialists have had to devote substantial attention to the study of war and violence, since this perspective treats coercion as one of the central explanatory variables. Nevertheless, what remains unrecognised and unappreciated is the fact that contemporary organisational materialism owes a great deal to classical 'bellicose' social thought. Although most contemporary sociologists of violence and war such as Michael Mann, Randall Collins, Charles Tilly, Anthony Giddens, John A. Hall and Gianfranco Poggi, rarely, if ever, invoke classical militarists as their predecessors, it is possible to demonstrate the unbroken intellectual continuity between the two research traditions. Moreover, it is this continuity with classical 'bellicose' social thought that has fostered the synergetic creativity which characterises organisational materialism. However, this classical legacy is generally ignored. Instead, if any link to intellectual predecessors is made, then it is nearly always to Max Weber as a founding father of both the comparative historical method and the originator of a macro-level social theory which goes beyond narrow economism and culturalism, and thus places coercion at its heart.

In this context nearly all contemporary organisational materialists uphold Weber's definitions of power and state – both of which underline the coercive nature of these social entities. However, although Weber emphasised the forceful, almost zero-sum, character of power relations, and describes

---

[11] In some respects Raymond Aron (1958; 1966) is a clear precursor of organisational materialism and one of the few mainstream post-WWII sociologists who takes the study of war seriously. However as his focus is more on the sociological and philosophical understanding of international relations his work is beyond the scope of this book.

the state in terms of the monopoly of physical force, he did not provide a fully fledged sociological theory of either state or collective violence and war. Weber did develop a highly influential typology of power stratification which forms a backbone for some of the contemporary theories; nevertheless, as already outlined (see Chapter 1), there is too little analysis to provide a full blown theory of collective violence, war and the state in the way it is invoked by the leading theorists of organisational materialism. Rather, Weber's emphasis on the role of violence was in part a reflection of his time: Weber shared the *esprit de corps* of German academia which was heavily influenced by militarist thought. In some respects, Weber provided a morally acceptable face to the 'bellicose' tradition: lending to it his impeccable intellectual credentials through which the key arguments of the militarist tradition were kept alive and revived in the contemporary context, and with little or no apparent consequences. It seems it is much safer and morally responsible to be an intellectual descendent of Weber, than of Treitschke or the repulsive 'Social Darwinists'. However, it is the emphasis of Treitschke, Gumplowicz, Rustow, Oppenheimer, Hintze and Schmitt on the military origins of the state, the view of state power as autonomous and omnipotent, the decisive role of warfare in historical transformations, and the conflictual nature of human sociability that lie at the heart of contemporary organisational materialism. Despite his Nietzschean invocation concerning the will and glory of the state's power prestige, Weber (1968: 910–11) largely ignores the broader geopolitical context in which states emerge and operate. Although he defines state power in terms of territoriality and a monopoly of violence, he does not explore the exogenous context in which they occur. However, the modern state does not appear or function in a geopolitical vacuum, and its very existence is premised on mutual recognition of other such states. And it is from this very Treitschkeian and Gumplowiczian, rather than Weberian, angle that contemporary organisational materialism develops. Hence, if we examine closely their arguments, it is possible to see that there is a direct link between contemporary historical sociologists that espouse organisational materialism and the classical militarist tradition of social thought.

Charles Tilly's (1975, 1985, 1992b) entire life was devoted to the task of explicating the relationship between the birth and expansion of state power and the use of large-scale violence. Although he defines power in relational terms by insisting on its 'incessantly negotiated character', his focus is firmly on the conflictual and asymmetrical dimension of power relations: 'Power is an analyst's summary of transactions among persons and social sites: we can reasonably say X has power over Y if, in the course of a stream of interaction between

X and Y, 1) a little action from X typically elicits a large response from Y, and 2) their interaction delivers disproportionate benefit to X' (Tilly 1999: 344). More specifically, his focal point is what he sees as a dominant form of power in modernity – the power of the nation-state. Although throughout human history enormous power was often concentrated in the hands of a few individual despots, tyrants and emperors, it was the arrival of modernity that for the first time provided structural and organisational capabilities not only for the concentration of, but also for a monopoly over, coercive power channelled through the institutions of the nation-state. To explain the gradual emergence and eventual dominance of this form of power Tilly traces its historical origins to seventeenth century Europe where the sheer cost of prolonged military campaigns on the part of European monarchs led to the rapid centralisation, territorialisation and bureaucratisation of rule. In other words, directly echoing Gumplowicz, Ratzenhofer, Oppenheimer and Hintze, Tilly (1985: 170–2) argues that 'war makes states', or more precisely, that 'war making, extraction, and capital accumulation interacted to shape European state making'. As do Treitschke and Mosca, Tilly (1992b: 1) analyses states primarily as 'coercion-wielding organisations' which possess ultimate power over a particular territory. In early modernity warfare proved to be the most efficient mechanism of social control, state expansion, capital accumulation and the extraction of resources. As a consequence, modernity was witness to the proliferation of mass-scale violence as wars gained in intensity and brutality, with the twentieth century – with its 250 wars, causing over 100 million deaths – by far the bloodiest in recorded history (Tilly 2003: 55).

Following in footsteps of Ratzenhofer, Treitschke and Hintze, Tilly sees war-making as the most important state activity, through which state power acquired unprecedented autonomy and external geopolitical strength, while it simultaneously pacified its domestic realm. The monopoly over the legitimate use of violence within a particular territory develops as a direct outcome of intensification of inter-state warfare. There is a clear link with Ratzenhofer and Rustow here as they too highlighted the fact that the centralised and territorial nature of the modern state owes a great deal to the original 'sin' of violence and warfare. In many respects, Tilly's (1985) concept of the state as a giant political racquet that eventually brings about internal pacification resembles Ratzenhofer's distinction between the 'conquest state' and 'culture state' and Rustow's law of culture pyramid that links the birth and advancement of civilisation to military domination. Hence, when Tilly (1992a: 191) argues that 'we owe today's pacific social democracy to yesterday's rapacious military state' he just restates the central ideas developed by the thinkers of the Austro-American group struggle paradigm and German sociological libertarianism.

Furthermore, the Schmittian distinction between friend and enemy emerges fully only in the context of modern state-building, as enmity becomes displaced outside of the borders of a nation-state and as private violence is largely eradicated through severe policing and social delegitimisation. War and preparations for war are potent generators of dramatic social change, the offshoot of which is the development of both an extensive state apparatus as well as a vibrant civil society. Through warfare the state advanced its fiscal administration, courts and other legal institutions, regional administration and financial infrastructure while more widespread mobilisation of the people, including universal conscription, led towards the steady extension of various political and social rights to a wider population, thus enhancing civil society. To sum up, for Tilly, just as for many of the thinkers of the classical 'bellicose' tradition, the concentration and monopolisation of power in the institutions of the modern nation-state were direct products of extensive war-making.

Although Michael Mann (1986, 1993) has been nearly universally regarded as a neo-Weberian sociologist,[12] his theory of state power owes as much to classical militarist tradition as it does to Weber. Like Tilly, Mann moves the focus of sociology from society to state, as state autonomy and its geopolitical environment largely determine the conditions of existence of a particular society. Instead of the unitary and inflexible notion of society that dominates much of social science, Mann (1986: 2) prefers to speak of 'multiple overlapping and intersecting power networks'. In other words, in a Treitschkeian and Oppenheimerian vein, but with much more in the way of reflexivity, and much less in the way of teleology, Mann positions social power and state expansion at the centre of societal change. A social world is ordered first and foremost as a conglomerate of intertwined power networks. More specifically, social power is analysed along the axes of four central and interrelated sources: political, economic, military and ideological power. Although they are treated as autonomous institutional and organisational forms, Mann (1986: 2) also contends that they are 'overlapping networks of social interaction' that 'offer alternative organisational means of social control'.

Unlike Weber, though much like Hintze, Mann separates political and military power, thereby treating militarism as a distinct organisational capacity. By military power he means 'the social organisation of concentrated lethal

---

[12] For example see most chapters in Hall and Schroeder 2006.

violence' (Mann 2006: 351). Even though states have originated and developed their organisational might primarily through warfare, state power is not to be reduced to its military capabilities. While the primary function of states throughout history was to fight wars and balance geopolitical arrangements, and though this is still a potent generator of state activity and its authority, historically the administrative and military modes of control have rarely acted as one indivisible entity. As a result the modern nation-state is a forceful war-making machine; but this is not its only source of strength. In other words, the omnipotence of a nation-state in modernity is derived from its military might, economic control of material resources and ideological legitimacy. However, most of all its institutional supremacy is rooted in its territorialised organisational potency. For Mann (1993: 9, 2006: 352), just as for Gumplowicz, Ratzenhofer, Treitschke and Schmitt, and again very unlike Weber, 'political power means state power'. The ascendancy of the political arises from the state's monopolistic, centralised and institutionalised control over a particular territory. The steady rise of this administrative power of state is linked to the historical process that Mann (1986: 112–14) calls 'social caging' whereby rulers have gradually imposed restrictions on individual freedoms in exchange for economic resources and political and military protection, in this way simultaneously generating mechanisms of social stratification and triggering the long-term process of institutional and administrative centralisation. In early historical periods social caging was fostered by the artificial irrigation of agriculture in enclosed river-valley civilisations, but in the early modern era this process reinforced the tight administration of nation-states which eventually created an institutional shell for the arrival of democracy (see Chapter 3).

While there is no denying that the concept of social caging is Mann's own illuminating creation there are clear similarities between this idea and Rustow's concepts of 'cultural pyramid', 'superstratification' and 'high culture'. Both Rustow and Mann emphasise that the emergence of civilisation requires large-scale organisation which in turn entails coercive means of integration. Furthermore, in a profoundly Hintzean way Mann (1988) argues that citizenship rights were historically shaped by the interests of economic, political and military elites who controlled the state, whereby the extension of civil and political rights was directly linked to deep fiscal crises of the state and the introduction of universal conscription. The democratisation of the state in modernity, including the extension of the universal franchise and welfare reforms, was in many respects a direct outcome of the mass mobilisation for warfare. In a nutshell, Mann's (1986, 1993) analytical models that emphasise the decisive impact of warfare on nation-state creation were in many respects anticipated by both the Austro-American group struggle tradition and German sociological libertarians' conquest thesis. Although these two approaches are more agency-centred than Mann's (or Tilly's) structural models, they too locate the origins and expansion of the modern state in warfare.

Even though Gianfranco Poggi is nominally considered as one of the most Weberian of all contemporary political sociologists, and regards himself as such (Poggi 2001: 12–14), his account of coercive power and violent action is really much closer to the classical 'bellicose' tradition than it is to Weber, while his understanding of the origins of state power is distinctively Gumplowiczian and Hintzean. Even though he follows Weber's tripartite division between political, economic and ideological power, for the most part, his interpretation of social power overemphasises the coercive character of domination and as such is only partially Weberian. Unlike Weber, who stresses the administrative and juridical foundations of state power and attributes great importance to the contents of various religious doctrines and especially to the distinctive form of rationalisation that emerged in medieval Christian Europe, Poggi concentrates almost exclusively on the violent sources of social power, and, whereas Weber writes about political power in general terms, including its various modalities (domination, legitimacy, authority, status, coercion etc.), for Poggi (2001: 30), political power is constituted and exercised exclusively in reference to coercive actions: 'What qualifies the power … as political is the fact that it rests ultimately upon, and intrinsically … refers to, the superior's ability to sanction coercively the subordinate's failure to comply with commands.' In other words, political power cannot be properly defined without reference to organised violence. Or as he recently put it, and in very stark terms: '[ancient Greeks] did not subscribe to my own bloody-minded identification of politics with violence' (Poggi 2006: 137). While for Weber violence is by and large just a means of politics, for Poggi violence is its essence. In a way that is reminiscent of Treitschke and Ward, Poggi (2001: 31) writes about 'the harsh material basis of primordial political experience' and echoing Sorel and Schmitt, argues that political power is anthropologically grounded in a capacity to inflict physical pain, suffering and death and so, in the last instance, politics is unthinkable without violence.[13] In this

---

[13] In a rare direct reference to Schmitt in his early work on state formation Poggi (1978: 5–13) acknowledges the ontological importance of Schmitt's account of politics: 'Much as one might discount Schmitt's view as demonic or fascist, history has repeatedly born him out. Once the dangerousness and the ultimate disorderliness of social life are recognized, their implications remain utterly amoral and-today more than ever utterly frightening'.

view all forms of political power, including 'even discursively generated laws', ultimately require coercive sanctioning. In other words, the ability to command obedience presupposes the threat of violence. The development of technology expands the capability of human beings to kill and injure other humans both in terms of scope (the fiercest tiger can only kill a handful of animals with his teeth and claws in one go, while by detonating a nuclear bomb a single human can annihilate millions) and form (e.g. devising a variety of strategies and methods for slaughter). This expansion of violence directly affects political power, as in Poggi's account the two are intrinsically connected, thus simultaneously extending the range and modes of political domination. With the birth of modern state structures, political power, being rooted in the monopolistic and legitimate control of violence, multiplies exponentially. The fact that rulers in modern nation-states (in the West) are institutionally constrained in their use of violence while pursuing political goals does not mean that violence disappears with modernity. Instead, as Poggi (2001: 53) argues 'the political system's superior capacity to use violence as a means of enforcement is assumed and kept in the background by institutionalisation ... [and] such settled social circumstances are in turn the product of wanton and brutal violence, however occasionally exercised'. Adopting Hintzean and Oppenheimerian analysis Poggi (2004: 99) understands the modern state-making process through the prism of evolving warfare: 'From the beginning, the modern state was shaped by the fact of being essentially intended for war-making, and primarily concerned with establishing and maintaining its military might.' With his accentuation of violence as a central feature of both social power and state building, Poggi's account remains inextricably wedded to the classical militarist tradition of social thought.

Randall Collins is almost unique among contemporary organisational materialists in his attempt to reconcile the macro- and micro-levels of analysis as he integrates the large-scale structural historical study of state formation and geopolitical changes with face-to-face interactional exploration of social conflict.[14] Situating conflict at the heart of social relations, Collins (1975, 1986, 1999) explains social action with reference to technological change, available resources, shared experiences of privilege, communication and cooperational networks and collective subjective perceptions,

---

[14] In his more recent work Collins (2004, 2008) shifts his attention to the micro-interactional level of conflict which attempts to integrate the key tenets of organisational materialism with the neo-Goffmanian and neo-Durkheimian analysis of micro-foundations of violence. For a sympathetic criticism of this position see Malešević 2008a: 212–14.

but most of all, to status struggle. Adopting a Paretian/Machiavellian angle (though with a Weberian twist), Collins tells us that 'Life is basically a struggle for status in which no one can afford to be oblivious to the power of others around him and everyone uses what resources are available to have others aid him in putting on the best possible face under the circumstances' (Collins 1975: 60). Nevertheless his understanding of political and state power is fully in tune with Tilly, Mann and Poggi, and thus with classical militarist thought, in the way he interprets politics almost exclusively through the prism of violence. Echoing Tretschke and Oppenheimer even more so than Weber, Collins (1975: 352) defines the state through its unimpeded capacity to pursue its will by relying on the means of coercion: 'The state is, above all, the army and the police, and if these groups did not have weapons we would not have a state in the classical sense.' In this account, political power relates to warfare, while coercive threats and politics more generally, as with Schmitt, are chiefly about force and the organisation of violence.

Like Mosca and Pareto, Collins (1974, 1989) emphasises the importance of organised force in the birth and expansion of modern bureaucratic institutions. According to Collins (1975: 351–3), in pre-modern social orders private violence and politics are more or less identical, while the modern nation-state monopolises its means ('the state consists of those people who have the guns or other weapons and are prepared to use them') which leads to a situation where 'much politics does not involve actual violence [anymore] but consists of manoeuvring around the organisation that controls the violence'. Hence, in the modern age the dominant form of political power becomes state power. The might of a particular state is determined by its ability to secure high prestige both internally (through the penetration and successful mobilisation of civil society groups) and externally (by raising and maintaining its geopolitical standing). Drawing on Weber directly and on Hintze indirectly, Collins (1981, 1986, 1999) argues that the state's geopolitical status is grounded in the military experience of its population whereby war victories raise the prestige of state rulers and enhance the power and legitimacy of the state, whereas military defeats do the opposite. War is seen as a catalyst of social and political change in history and a prime mover of state formation. To fully grasp the political power of the state one has to understand the military and other coercive apparatuses of a particular social order. The fact that modern liberal democracy allows more voice, dissent, popular representation and consequently power-sharing is far from being a reliable indicator of a relentless march forward. Instead this historical contingency is deeply rooted in the coercive structure of its social order. It is the relatively balanced dispersal of resources – coercive and otherwise – among well organised and independent social groups able to mobilise different interests that has created a distinctly multi-polar social and political environment.

As is evident from this brief analysis, despite their almost exclusive identification and self-identification with the Weberian approach, the leading contemporary organisational materialists are deeply grounded in classical militarist social thought. However, because they are profoundly wary of the ethical implications of building on this highly contested tradition, there is little direct reference to the works of Gumplowicz, Ratzenhofer, Treitschke, Hintze, Schmitt, Sorel and others. This is perhaps a form of internalised concealment which is largely unnecessary as these thinkers successfully de-essentialise, historically contextualise and remove the normative proto-fascist baggage from classical militarism, thus providing much more sophisticated and explanatory potent accounts of the role violence and war play in social life. What, in the works of the classical militarists, starts as teleology, ontology and in some cases, such as Treitschke, Schmitt, Sorel and Simmel, even an apology for violence and the omnipotence of state power, ends up in the writings of Mann, Tilly, Collins and Poggi as a refined epistemology of social conflict and a highly persuasive historical sociology of domination. In this way, by drawing on classical 'bellicose' thought, contemporary organisational materialism has managed to seriously undermine the hegemony of the instrumentalist, culturalist and biological theories of social change by shifting the explanatory emphasis from the control of the means of production, individual rationality, genetics and culture towards something far more important in understanding social world – the control of the means of destruction. As Collins, Poggi, Mann and Tilly convincingly argue and empirically prove, one cannot explain the transformation and continual importance of social power without reference to violence and one cannot understand the origins of state formation and the current, almost indisputable, institutionalised supremacy of the nation-state system in the world, without intense engagement with the coercive nature of social life. However, although these contemporary accounts are highly convincing in underlining and analysing the intrinsically coercive character of politics and social life, they nonetheless seem less convincing when addressing the popular legitimisation of violence. In other words, whereas these theoretical models extensively, and for the most part adequately, elucidate social and organisational power, there seems to be too little explanatory space for an understanding of ideological power.

From coercion to ideology

Despite the hopes and aspirations of the Enlightenment that the new era would bring about a world without violence, where conflicting interests and values would be accommodated through rational argumentation, dialogue and debate, modernity has turned out to be the most violent epoch in recorded history. Underpinned by grand vistas of an ideal social order, well equipped with the latest scientific and technological discoveries, and highly adept in mobilising an enormous popular base, modern, democratising, constitutional states have proved to be incomparably vicious and much more efficient as war machines than any of their despotic and non-egalitarian predecessors. Notwithstanding the cruelty of pre-modern rulers, no tyrant of agrarian civilisation could match the brutal efficiency of mass slaughter in concentration camps or the scope and speed of carnage caused by machine guns, aerial bombardment or nerve gas. There is no historical equivalent in terms of numbers to all the revolutions, total wars and genocides of modernity. Yet it is this era more than any previous epoch that proclaims the emancipation and liberation of the human subject as its central and core value. As direct heirs of the Enlightenment, modern constitutional orders, including both rulers and citizens, embrace ideas of reason, justice, liberty, equality and humanity as self evident principles on which all social life should rest.[15]

This situation – whereby modernity is normatively built on principles that glorify reason and human life and despise violence, while at the same time it has witnessed more bloodshed and mass killing than any other epoch – may seem to be a puzzling paradox. However if one engages with the form, content and structure of ideological power in the modern age then this particular outcome seems less mysterious. Although Poggi, Mann, Collins and Tilly adroitly explain why modernity was born out of and structurally remains reliant on violence, for the most part they provide no answer to the question: Why modern self-reflexive beings, socialised in an environment that abhors the sacrifice of human life, nonetheless tolerate and often tacitly support murder on a massive scale? To answer this question properly one needs to take ideological power much more seriously than organisational materialists have done.

Although Mann, Poggi, Collins and Tilly all acknowledge the importance of collective values and beliefs, they nevertheless still essentially treat ideology

---

[15] For example, as stated in the preamble to the American Constitution: 'We hold these truths to be self-evident, that all men are created equal, that they are endowed, by their Creator, with certain unalienable Rights, that among these are Life, Liberty and the pursuit of Happiness.'

either as a second-order reality or almost exclusively reduce ideological power to religious doctrines. Thus, for example, Poggi (2001) identifies ideological or normative power as one of the 'three basic power forms' together with political and economic power. He sees it as important, but 'of derivative nature', and associates it almost exclusively with religion. In his own words 'religious power [is seen] as a prime and indeed primordial manifestation of ideological/normative power' (Poggi 2001: 71). Similarly, Collins (1975: 369, 371) does not see much difference between traditional religions and modern secular ideologies: 'secular ideologies operate in most respects like religious ones', or 'modern ideologies are variants of the same basic set of conditions, new forms appropriate to modern conditions of the same appeals for moral solidarity and for obedience to the organisation stretching beyond individuals that make up the social essence of religion'. Tilly (1985, 2003) devotes even less attention to ideology, seeing it as an epiphenomenon shaped by political, military and economic forces. It is only in the work of Mann (1986, 1993) that ideological power receives more attention, as he identifies ideology as one of the four central pillars of social power and conducts extensive historical analysis of worldwide ideological transformations.

By ideological power Mann (2005: 30) understands 'the mobilisation of values, norms, and rituals in human societies that surpasses experience and science alike, and so contains contestable elements'. He distinguishes between its transcendent and immanent forms, whereby transcendent ideologies largely correspond to autonomous and universalist doctrines capable of generating a large-scale support base by transcending existing institutions and projecting 'sacred' authority. Immanent ideologies refer to more dependent sets of beliefs and values that serve to strengthen the solidarity of existing power networks and organisations. However, even here ideology is perceived, in both of its forms, as a weak force and rarely, if ever, figures as key *explanandum*. Not only does Mann argue that pre-modern ideological doctrines 'had no general role of any significance, only world-historical moments' (Mann 1986: 371), and that the impact of ideas generated in the French Revolution on the European states was much smaller than generally assumed, but more importantly, he argues that the power of ideology, and religion in particular, since the nineteenth century, was and is by and large in decline.[16] In addition, Mann adopts a very instrumentalist understanding of ideology which focuses almost entirely on the function and means of ideological movements,

---

[16] In recent writings Mann (2006: 345) has acknowledged this problem and now seems to accept that late modernity has been and still is highly ideological.

and thus has little to say about the ends and contents of ideological messages (J. M. Hobson 2004; Gorski 2006).

This apparent neglect of ideology among contemporary organisational materialists was not shared by their militarist predecessors. Gumplowicz, Oppppenheimer, Rustow, Mosca, Pareto, Treitschke, Schmitt and Hintze were well aware that the successful proliferation and institutionalisation of collective violence requires potent mechanisms of justification. Moreover, they properly understood that the collapse of the old monotheistic universe of traditional order and its replacement by competing doctrines of universalist and egalitarian principles of modernity opened up the possibility for much fiercer bloodshed. In a post-Nietzschean world of mortal deity there are no moral absolutes. To echo Dostoyevsky's Ivan Karamazov – once God is dead everything is permissible. As Schmitt (1996: 54) argues, ideas such as humanity, justice, progress and civilisation are especially potent ideological devices as they allow one side in a conflict 'to usurp a universal concept against its military opponent' and treat him not as a disliked though nonetheless respected adversary, but rather as something outside the norms of humanity, that is, as a monster; and monsters have no place in the world of humans – they unconditionally deserve annihilation. As President Truman put it in justifying his decision to drop atomic bombs on Japan: 'When you have to deal with a beast, you have to treat him as a beast. It is most regrettable but nevertheless true' (Alperovitz 1995: 563). Consequently wars have 'decreased in number and frequency' but have 'proportionally increased in ferocity' (Schmitt 1996: 35).

Although some classical militarists, such as Treitschke, Schmitt and Simmel, often approach ideological power more from a normative, prescriptive position rather than an explanatory one – glorifying as they do omnipotent state power, militarist ethics, rigid nationalism and overt or covert racism – they also demonstrate that one cannot easily separate violence from ideology. To fully understand the proliferation of violence in modernity one has to study its ideological underpinnings. In other words, any successful attempt to draw on the classical militarist tradition requires engagement with both the organisationally coercive and the ideological nature of power. To succeed, power requires legitimation, and coercive power even more so.

The accounts of ideology presented in the works of contemporary historical sociologists suffer from two pronounced weaknesses. Firstly there is a degree of conceptual confusion whereby ideology is treated either too widely, when used as a synonym for culture (e.g. Mann 1986; 1993; 2006), or too narrowly and historically inaccurately when reduced to traditional religious doctrines

(Collins 1975; Mann 1986; Poggi 2001). As I have argued elsewhere (Malešević 2002: 58–61), although in modernity religious doctrines often acquire ideological attributes and can act as fully fledged ideologies, pre-modern religions lacked the institutional and organisational resources to function like modern ideologies do. Not only did they operate in a context where there was no mass public literacy, standardised vernacular languages, state sponsored public education systems and print capitalism (Anderson 1983), but traditional religions also lacked sophisticated mechanisms for the dissemination of information and a bureaucratic organisational structure, all of which are essential for ideological power. As they appeal to reason and offer a rational explanation of social reality, normative ideologies require a fully formed literate public. Ideologies were born in a post-Enlightenment secular environment where what had formerly been a largely undisputed religious (Christian) monopoly was suddenly substituted by ideological pluralism. In this new historical context religious doctrines found themselves competing with the secular *Weltenschauungen*. Unlike pre-modern religious doctrines modern ideologies are often underpinned by the authority of science, humanist and other secular ethics and collective interests that are grounded in principles that stand in stark opposition to theological world-views. Unlike religions, ideologies are deeply rooted in earth and not heaven. As Gouldner (1976) points out, the mass appeal of ideologies in our age comes only with the creation of a modern human subject who 'must be more interested in the news from this world than in the tidings from another'. Against the promise of an afterlife, ideologies articulate competing blueprints for the transformation of the existing social reality. Liberalism, socialism, anarchism, scientific racism and many other ideologies offer secular blueprints and political grand vistas of social change capable of mobilising millions of individuals. Since the time of Machiavelli we know that secularised politics, unconstrained by religious ethics, is able to do both to generate mass popular appeal and to be extremely ruthless in the implementation of its ideological goals. In this context ideologies appear as a much more potent generator of social action than traditional religions could ever be.

And this leads us to the second problem of the contemporary historical sociologists – their perception of ideology as a weak explanatory force. As Mann (2006: 346–7) puts it bluntly 'ideas can't do anything unless they are organised'. But this view can just as easily be turned on its head, as all organisations are built and run on particular ideas and without ideas organisations cannot do anything. This is not to say that human actions are ultimately governed by ideas and values rather than material or political interests – the general mistake of all idealist epistemologies – but that the apparent success of coercive power in the modern age cannot be adequately explained without understanding the justificatory power of modern ideologies. In other words, ideological power is not the only, and not necessarily the primary, generator of social action, but its social significance lies in its legitimising capacity. When ends are perceived as ultimate truths, underpinned by unquestioned scientific authority and the ethical certainties of humanism, then all means become valid. In this context the question of the use of violence is often transformed into a question of mere efficiency. A decision to drop a uranium-235 20,000 ton nuclear warhead on a large urban congregation, which will inevitably kill hundreds of thousands of human beings, becomes a matter of precision and effectiveness. The first words of captain William Sterling Parsons after dropping a bomb on Hiroshima reveal this only too well: 'Results clear cut successful in all respects. Visible effects greater than any test. Conditions normal in airplane following delivery' (Truman papers 1945: 7). Similarly, implementing a blueprint of the racially pure society entails the use of gas chambers as the most rational means for speedy, functional and efficient disposal of 'human waste'. In the same vein, establishing an ideal classless social order may necessitate the rapid and total extermination of kulaks and other 'leeches' and 'vampires' that suck the blood of 'our proletarian people' and so on. Modern ideological doctrines with their inclusive, universalist rhetoric of collective solidarity provide the most potent, but also the most uncompromising, social mechanism of group mobilisation, able to justify the most extreme forms of violence (Malešević 2006). As possessors of ultimate secular truths, liberated from the curbs of sanctimonious virtue and equipped with the institutional structures and mass armaments of the modern state, ideologies appear simultaneously as powerful mobilisers of collective action and as legitimisers of that action. However, as violence goes against the grain of ordinary human socialisation, so it requires compelling devices of social justification. Although modern self-reflecting men and women are socialised to revere human life much more than any of their predecessors, they also possess more powerful narratives for the justification of mass slaughter – that is, ideological doctrines. In other words, violence feeds off ideological doctrines that are capable of reconciling inclusion with exclusion, fairness with discrimination, equity with bigotry, and universalist humanist ethical principles with the mass slaughter of other human beings. Couched in the language of justice, equality and fraternity and underpinned by a monopoly on 'truth', modern ideological narratives are adept at legitimising and squaring what initially might seem impossible: to guillotine thousands of

French revolutionaries in the name of human liberty, to send millions of Soviet workers to gulags while advocating proletarian egalitarianism, to drop nuclear bombs on hundreds of thousands of Japanese civilians in the name of liberal democracy, or to kill thousands of fellow Muslims while preaching the universal brotherhood of *umma* as in contemporary Afghanistan, Pakistan or Iraq. While an individual human life is sacred in principle, no price is too high when ideological goals are at stake: killing hundreds of thousands of human beings becomes 'regrettable' but acceptable when 'safeguarding democracy', 'attaining or fighting communism', 'establishing our own sovereign and independent nation', 'creating an ethnically or racially pure society' or setting up a Sharia-based, pan-Islamic caliphate. In ideological doctrines, collective violence finds a potent social and institutional mechanism for both the social mobilisation and ethical justification of political and coercive action. The dramatic increase of structural violence in the modern era is deeply connected to modernity's organisational and ideological sophistication. Once buttressed by compelling ideology there is no limit to coercive power.

Conclusion

Despite being perceived as an abomination in the modern age, violence was and remains an indispensable ingredient of social and political life. Although modern states have managed to successfully monopolise it, thus making it virtually invisible, they have not eradicated violent action. On the contrary, the enormous power that nation-states have acquired in modernity, becoming the pre-eminent political actors within their societies as well as in the international geopolitical arena, is essentially derived from this largely unchallenged monopoly on the control of violence. As Collins puts it so aptly, the state is 'above all the army and the police'. Stated more bluntly, violence and social power are inherently linked as there is no power which in the last instance is not grounded in the manipulation and control of violence. However, the relationship between the two is not one-sided whereby coercion exists only as a means of political power. Instead, once unleashed, collective violence becomes its own master, operating on its own tracks and creating new social realities. This is most evident in modern warfare where, on the one hand the use of systematic violence radically transforms social institutions and human relations thus generating new social and political orders, while on the other hand it dramatically expands the scale of human sacrifice and bloodshed. It is only in the wake of two devastating total wars and a couple of brutal revolutions that the liberal, democratic, constitutional, welfare-inclusive social order has emerged. Regardless of its distaste for violence, sociology cannot afford to ignore the other, vicious, face of the modern Janus. Although classical militarist thought and organisational materialism have both revitalised scholarly interest in the relationships between war, violence and human sociability, there is still a need for greater analytical engagement with the ideological and organisational processes through which coercion becomes legitimised and institutionalised. However, before we tackle the ongoing processes of bureaucratisation and ideologisation of violence it is vital to first chart the social origins of war and coercion.

Part II

War in time and space

War and violence before modernity

Introduction

Popular representations of violence and war tend to emphasise their ubiquity and inevitability. From elementary school history textbooks to Hollywood blockbusters warfare is depicted as an inherent and primeval phenomenon originating even before the arrival of the human species. In the indicative words of one commentator war is described 'as old as, or older than, humanity itself' (Low 1993: 13). Nevertheless, neither violence nor war came naturally to human beings. As several decades of research on killing, dying and other violent actions demonstrate, our species is neither good at, nor psychologically comfortable with, the use of violence (Holmes 1985; Grossman 1996; Bourke 2000; Collins 2008). Not only do human beings generally tend to avoid violent conflicts (most micro-level fights are no more than blustering), but the Hobbesian image of war of all against all is an empirical impossibility (Collins 2008). Despite the popular perception that violence is usually chaotic, contagious and generally spontaneous, much violent action entails a substantial degree of organisation. Furthermore, rather than being a primordial and intrinsic feature of human existence, the institution of warfare arrived fairly late on the historical stage. This, however, is not incidental since to conduct war requires organisational and ideological sophistication both of which emerge only with the development of civilisation.

This chapter explores the social origins of war and violence. It charts a historical transformation from the disorganised forms of coercion prevalent at the dawn of human history to the early forms of warfare in antiquity, more complex modes of organised violence in medieval times and the transition towards rationalised types of warfare that provided an impetus for the arrival of early modernity. The central argument focuses on the indispensable role of social organisation and proto-ideology in stimulating the growth of organised violence which ultimately spawned the seeds of the modern social orders under which we now live. In particular the chapter focuses on the two ongoing and complementary processes that constitute modernity and which can be traced all the way back to pre-antiquity: the cumulative bureaucratisation of coercion and centrifugal ideologisation.

Collective violence before warfare

Despite its near universality war is, historically speaking, a very late development. If one discounts the neo-Darwinian views that conflate warfare with aggression and feuding, most social scientists and archaeologists agree that there were no structural conditions for war before the end of the Palaeolithic and beginning of the Mesolithic. Although there is pronounced disagreement on the precise origins of warfare most would concur with the view that warfare emerged somewhere in the last 10,000 years of human development (Ferrill 1985: 18–26; Keegan 1994: 118–26; Kagan 1995: 4; ; Herwig *et al.* 2003: 1–8; Otterbein 2004: 11).[1] To place this date in the larger historical context one can say that for more than 99 per cent of its existence Homo sapiens had no experience of warfare. Before the Mesolithic era humans largely lived in very small, isolated, non-sedentary, bands of hunter-gatherers, tribes and other kinship-related groups that rarely exceeded 500 people (Mann 1986: 43).[2] As Cartmill (1993) shows, while Australopithecus was unable to produce tools or weapons and spent much of its life in fear of the larger carnivores for whom it was a desirable prey, its descendent Homo erectus was a scavenger, not a hunter, who required no weaponry of any kind. The use of rudimentary weapons such as clubs and spears became widespread after about 35,000 BCE but their use remained almost exclusively confined to the hunting and killing of animals in general. Although there is some scant archaeological indication of group-induced violence before this period, as Ferrill (1985: 16) points out, there is no conclusive evidence 'until the final stages of the Palaeolithic Age' that 'prehistoric tools or hunting weapons were used against man at all'.

---

[1] Some archaeologists single out the ancient burial site, Jebel Sahaba in Sudan, dated between 12,000 and 14,000 years ago as the oldest recorded evidence of large-scale inter-group violence, since nearly half of the fifty-nine skeletons found show evidence of violent death. However this is far from being a conclusive find since it is not clear what was the cause of these deaths (feuding, ritual executions or something else) (Fry 2007: 53).

[2] As Mann (1986: 43) emphasizes: 'Direct face-to-face communication among human beings may have practical upper limits. Above about 500 persons and we lose our ability to communicate! Gatherer-hunters are not literate and are dependent on face-to-face communication. They cannot use roles as shorthand communication, for they have virtually no means of specialisation beyond sex and age.'

It is only with key technological developments such as the invention of more complex weaponry (the bow, the mace, the sling and the dagger), the development of strategy and tactics, the deployment of columns and lines of men and the build-up of larger defensive fortifications that one can start talking about serious inter-group violent conflicts that resemble wars (Reid 1976; Ferrill 1985). What is sociologically interesting is that these military and technological advancements arrived on the historical stage at the very time when human beings were starting to replace their hunter–gatherer lifestyle with a sedentary agricultural lifestyle. In other words, it is no accident that large-scale collective violence emerged with the Neolithic revolution whereby nomadic bands and tribes were gradually replaced by permanent human settlements involving the domestication of plants and animals, expansion of farming techniques and radically transformed diets (with a reliance on vegetables and cultivated grain). All these changes had direct economic and sociological implications. Improved and stable diets allowed for a dramatic increase in the world human population which at the end of Palaeolithic totalled no more than 2–3 million while by the beginning of the Bronze Age it amounted to possibly 100 million (Keegan 1994: 125; Guilaine and Zammit 2005: 31). The availability of food surpluses was essential in accelerating large-scale trade and in developing the concept of land ownership both of which were instrumental in forging and expanding the institutions of social stratification. The end of the Stone Age also saw the beginning of a nascent social hierarchy, with the slow appearance of political and religious elites. All of these developments converged in a major structural change, a change that was indispensable for the appearance of warfare as a social institution – the birth and expansion of social organisation. This development would prove crucial later in history as the cumulative expansion of organised coercion, together with the onset of ideologisation, would mould the character of modern life as we know it.

However, saying that war is a relatively recent invention does not automatically imply subscribing to a view of prehistorical humans as innately peaceful creatures. The Rousseauian image of the 'noble savage' which was in one way or another reproduced from the early Enlightenment through the Romantic period and dominated most of twentieth-century social science, has been largely discredited by many studies, and most persuasively by well documented anthropological and archaeological writers such as Keeley (1996), Otterbein (2004) and Guilaine and Zammit (2005). They clearly show that early humans were occasionally violent and prone to murder. As Otterbein (2004: 18) indicates: 'hunter-gatherer bands are not internally peaceful. Homicide rates are high, and frequent executions of killers and witches occur'. However, although warfare requires killing and destruction, war is much more than random murders, feuding and belligerence. What Keeley, Otterbein and Guilaine and Zammit show is not that warfare was prevalent before civilisation but only that there was murderous violence before antiquity. Many sociobiologists and other authors who insist on the ubiquity of war are prone to conflate individual homicides or nearly any violent deaths with warfare. For example, in his attempt to justify his claim for the existence of 'prehistorical war', Keeley (1996) occasionally mixes individual cases of violent murder with non-violent deaths through disease and starvation, by presuming that most mass burials are automatically products of war, as shown by Fry (2007: 54). In other words, although killing is integral to war, mere homicide does not constitute war.

First and foremost war is a social institution that involves organisation, ritualism, group mobilisation, social hierarchy and many other sociological prerequisites that early humans clearly lacked. In addition, the population densities in prehistoric times were too low and distances too high to allow for raiding parties larger than 30 to 40 men. The archaeological evidence shows that the first settlements were not fortified, and were often built in areas that could not be properly defended from attack. There is no evidence of human burials before the Middle Palaeolithic (Guilaine and Zammit 2005: 41) and hence no skeletal remains that would indicate the presence of rampant homicide, let alone warfare. Simply put, prehistoric humans were probably no different to later humans in their motives, interests and affects. What was different were the structural conditions – the non-existence of technology, literacy, social stratification and most of all the social organisation that would allow early humans to form larger and coherent social networks able to sustain protracted violent conflicts. Hence popular concepts such as 'primitive war' of 'prehistoric warfare' are undoubtedly misnomers, since the social institution of warfare only came into being with the birth of civilisation.

War and violence in antiquity

There is little dispute among archaeologists that the Neolithic revolution brought about agriculture, permanent settlements and major technological discoveries. However, there is pronounced disagreement on whether the invention of, and mass reliance on, agriculture has directly influenced the birth of urban life as claimed first by Childe (1950) and many others, or if it was the other way around – that agriculture only 'helped to stabilise patterns that were already in the making' (Mellaart 1975: 277). Whichever came first it is clear that there was what Weber would call 'elective affinity' between the birth of agriculture and settled life. However, what is crucial here is that both agriculture and urban living emerged in the context of military revolution – through fortification and weaponry production. As Ferrill (1985: 28) puts it, 'the massive fortifications of various types led to, indeed required, the discovery of agriculture and the domestication of animals'. The walled settlement of Jericho (c. 8000 BCE) and the fortifications of Çatalhöyük (c. 6500 BCE) in Anatolia are often invoked as examples of the first 'militarised' architecture indicating the presence of and need for defensive structures that would repel potential violent invaders.[3] Although these early settlements suggest the possibility of warlike activities, one still has to wait until about 3000 BCE to find reliable evidence for the existence of warfare as a fully fledged social institution.[4] As Eckhardt's (1990, 1992) detailed statistical studies confirm, there was little, if any, warfare before the origin of civilisation. Thus, it is the early Bronze Age that is both the cradle of civilisation and the cradle of war. It is here that one encounters large-scale violence operating as a politically motivated organised social practice.

The great river valleys provided impetus for the emergence of the first civilisations in southern Mesopotamia (Sumer), ancient Egypt, Indus Valley (Harappan) and ancient China. Although Wittfogel's (1957) concept of the hydraulic-bureaucratic society clearly and wildly overstates the case, as the level of centralisation and bureaucratisation was still rudimentary, there is a lot of truth in his stress on the importance of major rivers that supplied almost limitless water for irrigation. As the provision of regular irrigation requires functioning systems of control, co-ordination and the division of labour, it acted as one of the key mechanisms that gave birth to social organisation and political and religious bureaucracy, underpinned by embryonic proto-ideological doctrines. The availability of storable food provided further impetus towards establishing long-term settlements – city-states – which became densely populated and hence provided a large-scale labour force and contributed further to economic, political, religious and military specialisation and the development

---

[3] It is important to note that there is an ongoing debate on whether these early walls should be interpreted in military terms as fortifications or as a simple device for flood control (see Bar-Yosef 1986; Otterbein 2004).

[4] Despite many important organisational developments such as elaborate religious practices, trade networks, sophisticated architecture and potent new weaponry the populace of these two settlements was still lacking some crucial ingredients of durable social organisation: writing, social hierarchy, a significant population density and rudimentary elements of statehood (Ferrill 1985: 24–31; Mann 1986: 41; Keegan 1994: 124–5).

of social stratification (see Chapter 8). Although the overwhelming majority of the population were peasants, regular access to stored food created a situation whereby some peasants could also act as soldiers when the need arose. Most of all, the operation of bureaucratic organisation necessitated reliable record-keeping, which eventually generated the practice of writing.

Obviously this was not a simple, evolutionary, one-way, march forward, but a highly contingent set of processes and events that involved periodic reversals, historical ups and downs and 'hybrid' models of social organisa-tion. However, what is most important here is the steady rise of administra-tive, organisational power which in time became a key component of early statehood. Mann (1986: 42–4, 112–14) articulates this historical development by using the metaphor of the social cage. Social caging came about as a grad-ual process through which the population at large acquired military pro-tection, economic and material resources and a sense of security and safety while simultaneously trading off their individual liberty and political control. This long-term process also enhanced social stratification and administra-tive centralisation by creating institutional power often monopolised by vari-ous political or military and religious elites. In other words, civilisation was born through the imposition of external constraint, since an organised polity proved to be militarily and economically superior to loose 'tribal' kinship networks typical before the formation of city-states. Institutional innovation, complex administrative capacity, cultural advancement and technological progress were all born through coercion.

What was also important for the long-term success of this process was a degree of societal solidarity enhanced by shared religious tradition. Emphasising cultural similarity of in-groups, Gumplowicz (2007 [1883]) referred to this process as syngenism. Although he was right that shared values and practices did matter, he was mistaken in his belief that these were somehow inborn collective sentiments. The key paradox of social caging is the fact that, as the process of state formation develops, it inevitably tends towards the creation of hierarchies and sharper social stratification hence diluting the egalitarian basis of potential cultural resemblance. Nevertheless, it is in the interest of the rulers to maintain or recreate this sense of shared values and practices. While in the modern age, this supposed cultural unity is achieved most efficiently through the operative ideology of nationalism (see Chapter 6), the key social device for in-group cohesion in the pre-modern world was religion. In Sumer, ancient Egypt, Shang China, Mesoamerica and other early civilisations the gradual development of a polity's organisational power went hand in hand with the proliferation of elaborate belief systems centred around the emperor who was depicted and perceived either as a god or the deity's only legitimate representative on earth. Although the historical evidence is largely lacking on how ordinary peasants understood these religious doctrines it seems from the scant archaeological findings that most shared the belief in the divine origins of their rulers (Insoll 1996; Andren and Crozier 1998; A. D. Smith 1986; 2003). The political power of rulers was enhanced as much by military victories as by these shared beliefs in serving the real divine authority.

As indicated in Chapter 1, much of classical sociological theory subscribed to the conquest thesis to explain the emergence of early states. Gumplowicz, Ratzenhofer and Oppenheimer among others held the view that state formation is directly linked to violent subordination and territorial expansion of one group over another. In this view the institution of the state owes its existence to warfare. The typical example is Akkadian Mesopotamia. Starting with the first-known emperor in history, Sargon, who, as the inscription in a temple at Nippur states, won thirty-four military campaigns and destroyed all his enemies and 'as chief of the gods' permitted no rivals (McNeill 1982 : 2), the Akkadian dynasty used warfare as a principal means of state expansion and as such created a large empire that was in existence for nearly two centuries. Most of the preserved historical documents from Mesopotamia and other early civilisations are records of various military undertakings and wars which can easily create the impression that the pre-modern world was nothing more than a giant battlefield. However, this would be a gross oversimplification. Although coercive power was an important constituent of everyday life, on both macro-structural and micro-interactional levels, it is difficult to argue that people in antiquity were more violent and war prone than in other historical epochs. For example, despite the total religious and political power of pharaohs, which was regularly depicted through militaristic imagery of successful warlords, ancient Egypt, for most of its early history (Old and Middle Kingdoms), was a stable, orderly and in some respects peaceful empire. As Mann (1986: 109) and Keegan (1994: 130) note, for nearly seven hundred years one finds little collective violence: only 'few traces of internal militarism, repression of popular revolts, slavery, or legally enforced statuses' and 'indifference to external threat'. What made the Mesopotamian Empire more violent than the Egypt of the Old Kingdom was a different geopolitical context that had direct impact on the proliferation of city-state warfare. Egypt's geographical location (the River Nile and surrounding desert) prevented the emergence of alternative power networks (e.g. tribes, towns, independent lords, etc.) that sprung up quickly in the marches, among the rain-watered agriculturalists and pastoralists of Mesopotamia (Mann 1986: 78–102, 108–13; Keegan 1994: 130–3).

Contemporary historical sociologists are more careful than their predecessors when making the link between warfare and state creation. Rather than positing a universal law they tend to qualify this link by pointing out cases where warfare did not play a pivotal role. Although war was rarely the only social mechanism of state formation it was, nevertheless, often the central catalyst of this process. The classical sociology of the group struggle paradigm was mistaken in its belief that conquest was the beginning of this process as, for conquest to happen, a substantial degree of social organisation and centralisation had already to be in place. The conquest thesis is more persuasive at the later stage when organised and centralised entities proved themselves more efficient at fighting wars than less organised or disorganised networks based on kinship. However, what is paramount here is that even in cases where war does not appear to be an important generator of state formation, as in ancient Egypt or Andean America, coercion still remains essential in the process of polity development. In both of these two cases, corvée labour was the principal means of forcing peasant masses to work on large-scale state projects such as temples, roads, quarries and canals. The enormous scale of these public works is still highly visible in the remnants of their architecture – the great pyramids and the 15,000 kilometers of paved roads built by Incas. As McNeill (1982: 5) rightly argues: 'large-scale public action in antiquity was always achieved by means of command'. These early forms of organised coercion coupled with rudimentary proto-ideology, as will be demonstrated later, were to become indispensable for social development, since they initiated the two long-term historical processes that have ultimately shaped modern life: the cumulative bureaucratisation of coercion and centrifugal ideologisation.

The gradual expansion of coercive power, whether directly through war successes or indirectly through large-scale public works, was simultaneously driven by and a driving force of social organisation. The key obstacle to further expansion in antiquity was the availability of food. To maintain and feed a standing army the rulers had to embark on periodic raids of neighbouring societies, hence utilising warfare as a form of organised robbery. A lack of food and water, as well as the ruler's absence from the capital city, could limit the extent of military expansion as there was no certainty that food would be available or that the ruler would stay in power if absent for more than three months (McNeill 1982: 8). It is interesting that social analysts in antiquity interpreted war largely in terms of profit-making and plundering. Both Plato and Aristotle understood warfare in economistic terms. In *The Republic* war is viewed as *pleonexia* – a desire for more territory, goods and power (Plato 1996; Frank 2007: 443). In *Politics* the art of war is described as 'a natural art of acquisition' (Aristotle 2004: 14)

Military historians emphasise the technological changes which are seen as decisive in transforming the character of warfare in antiquity, among which the most important were the introduction of bronze weaponry, the invention and spread of war chariots, the composite bow and, later, the proliferation of iron weapons. Whereas these technological changes had a direct impact on how wars were fought, they also had profound implications on the patterns of social stratification in societies affected by these changes. As bronze was scarce and the labour involved in its extraction and production, as well as the production of chariots, was expensive, these high-status items were available only to a very small proportion of the population. In consequence, societies that relied heavily on their use became rigidly stratified and hierarchical with a clearly differentiated warrior caste – highly skilled soldiers who, through the monopoly they had over skills, weapons and military vehicles, imposed themselves on the rest of the society. Most social orders of the Bronze Age, from Sumer to China and India, followed this pattern. In contrast, the discovery of iron, which is easily obtainable and cheap to manufacture on a large scale (and easy to maintain – one iron blade could last lifetimes, whereas bronze was quite weak and prone to breakage), led to the breakdown of social hierarchies and a general change of social order.

It is no historical accident that the ideas of political democracy and participatory citizenship were born in a society that relied on self-armed and self-equipped farmers – ancient Greece. Although much of the historical depictions of this world stress the urban character of Greek city-states (*polees*), with the image of town squares (*agoras*) acting as spaces for public deliberations, democratic politics and trade, more than 80 per cent of its population were small country-based landholders (Hanson 1989: 6). The famous Greek hoplite phalanx, a heavy infantry, were citizen militias armed with iron-based spears, swords and shields and composed almost solely of farmers. They were constituted as a close-packed heavy armoured infantry trained to fight at close quarters. There were no formal army ranks as 'military posts were as elective as civilian' (Wheeler 1991: 150–4; Keegan 1994: 246). The military superiority of the phalanx came primarily from its organisational structure, as the phalanx formation kept soldiers in line, hence not allowing the possibility of escape from the battlefield. The focus was on pushing forward and breaking the enemy's front line rather than on mass killing. The broken phalanx and fleeing enemies were rarely chased and war casualties were generally very low, rarely exceeding 15 per cent (Hanson 1989: 3–10; Keegan 1994: 251; Sidebottom 2004: 35–43). The key strength of the phalanx was its shock potential, as one side would push forward attempting to break the line of the other side with the pressure of massed ranks and files. When an enemy phalanx broke down, this created shock and panic and a chaotic retreat, which became an indicator that a battle had been won (Ferrill 1985: 103–4). As Hanson (1989: 4) summarises: 'Greek hoplite battles were struggles between small landholders who by mutual consent sought to limit warfare to a single, brief, nightmarish occasion'.

Despite the prevalent images of the ancient Greek world as brimful of warfare, with Sparta as the epitome of omnipotent militarism, the scale of collective violence was rather miniscule when compared to the wars of the modern era. The territories and populations of Greek city-states were tiny, with the combined occupying territory of the largest among them, Athens and Sparta, only slightly larger than contemporary Cyprus and having less than two thirds of Cyprus's current population. Hence, armies were fairly small and war casualties mainly low. In general, wars in the ancient Greek world tended to be limited and formalised. Even the pinnacle of military history of the ancient Greek world – the long and exhausting Peloponnesian War (431–404 BCE) was not characterised by large armies and big battlefields, but had only two or three significant land battles (Sidebottom 2004: xi). Although the Peloponnesian War was a watershed in Greek history as it ruined the economy, devastated a large part of the countryside, destroyed major cities and brought significant human casualties, the scale of devastation was still very small when compared to wars of modernity. For example, the total casualties of 27 years of war on the Athenian side amounted to 5,470 hoplites and 12,600 thetes (manual workers) (Strauss 1987). Similarly, despite fighting numerous wars and conquering much of the known world of his time, in all of his military campaigns Alexander the Great 'lost only seven hundred men to the sword'. While his enemies had much greater casualties 'almost all of this occurred *after* the battle ... when the enemy soldiers had turned their backs and began to run' (Grossman 1996: 13; see also Picq 2006).

Popular contemporary images of ancient warfare are often based on the profoundly inaccurate war narratives produced by the winning side. For example, the famous battle of Megiddo (fifteenth century BCE) fought between the Egyptian army of Pharaoh Thutmose III and a Canaanite coalition of forces led by King Kadesh I, was depicted by contemporaries as involving millions of men and hundreds of thousands of charioteers. In fact as historical record shows the battle was 'nothing but a rout, with 83 deaths and 340 prisoners taken' (Eckhardt 1992: 30).

Even Sparta was not a particularly violent society. It was an unusually militarist social order that became infamous for its rigid ascetic and merciless lifestyle that originated in the unscrupulous and rigorous military training and education (*agoge*) of very young healthy male children. However, this militaristic education was restricted to 'ethnic' Spartans (Spartiates) – a quite small elite warrior caste that at the peak of its power consisted of only 8,000 and never numbered more than 10,000. As Spartan citizenship was strictly linked to military upbringing, the number of citizens (only Spartiate males) was always decreasing (because of war deaths) so that by Aristotle's times (384–322 BCE) there were less than 1,000 (Forrest 1963; Cartledge 1979). The rest of Spartan society (more than 90 per cent of its population) was composed of the free non-citizens *perioikoi/perioeci* and *skiritai* (traders and dwellers living on the outskirts of Sparta), *neodamodes* (freed serfs), *trophimoi* (foreigners who underwent Spartan education) and, by far the most numerous, *helots*, that is, state-owned serfs who regularly outnumbered Spartans ten to one on the most important battlefields (Kagan 1995: 19).[5] In other words, Spartan militarism was directly linked to the system of helotage. The Spartiates acted as a permanently armed and vigilant master caste, because they were dependent on the labour and military capacity of helots and others but were overwhelmingly outnumbered by them.

It is ironic that much of European military tradition has modelled itself on the supposed ancient Greek heroism reflected in the so called 'Western way of war' while military successes in ancient Greece had very little if anything to do with personal acts of bravery.[6] Rather than stimulating heroism, the hoplite phalanxes were invented and deployed as an organisational mechanism to prevent soldiers escaping the battlefield. When the Spartan soldier's mother proclaims to her son that he can return from the battlefield only with his shield or on it, she is not invoking a sense of personal courage but appealing to the soldier's collective responsibility, solidarity and (proto-Durkheimian) group morality. The convex shield (hoplon) was the essential building block of the phalanx, since 'the phalanx in motion tended to slip to its right' thus

---

[5] Herodotus (1985: IX, 28–9) writes about helots outnumbering Spartans seven to one during the Battle of Plataea in 479 BCE. Xenophon (2009, Hellenica, III, 3) writing about fourth century BCE about an *agora* gathering identifies only 40 Spartans in a crowd of 4,000.

[6] The unfortunate phrase 'Western way of war' stands for an open front-line battle fought through courageous and direct confrontation with the enemy, which is opposed to the 'non-European' mode of fighting through the use of ambush or hit-and-run actions. For a good critique of the supposed origins of the 'Western way of war' in ancient Greece and Rome see Sidebottom (2004).

making every soldier protected by his neighbour's shield (Keegan 1994: 248). Hence, loosing or deliberately dropping one's shield made an entire phalanx vulnerable to attack. The social importance of the shield was also reinforced in Greek proto-ideology. As Ferrill (1985: 103) points out: 'Greek poetry of the archaic age is filled with the ethics of the new tactics – hold your place in the line, dig in, die fighting. Nothing was more disgraceful than to throw down the shield and run.'

The decisive importance of social organisation and proto-ideology for the structural expansion of violence is perhaps most clearly visible in the world's first fully fledged territorial empire – ancient Rome. The unprecedented strength, longevity and political and cultural influence of the Roman Empire were deeply rooted in its military might. For most of its existence ancient Rome was more of an army than a state. As Mann (1986: 295) rightly argues, the legion was the epicentre of Roman power. Although the legion was quint-essentially a military institution it was much more than that: 'its ability to mobilise economic, political, and, for a time ideological commitments was the main reason for its unparalleled success'. Not only was the army a potent machine of territorial conquest throughout the Mediterranean area and further abroad, but it was also an instrument of economic, political and proto-ideological expansion. The fact that legions were disciplined and highly organised to fight but could also build roads, canals, bridges, aqueducts, dams and walls as they occupied distant territories meant that, like no previous empire, Rome was able to keep hold on occupied land, to generate economic growth and to extract this wealth for further expansion. Although the origin of the legion can be traced back to the Greek phalanx, its structure and organisational sophistication set it completely apart from the hoplite model. The legion was on the one hand highly regulated, professional and organised, while on the other hand operationally very flexible. The division of centuries into cohorts with a unified command structure meant that they were easier to control and adaptable to changing battlefield conditions, as cohorts could be detached and act autonomously, or alternatively more cohorts could be added to fight prolonged and more demanding battles. Furthermore, the unit commanders of centuries, centurions, were long-serving professional officers, the first of their kind in history, making the Roman army a well organised, disciplined and structured force. In this sense, as Keegan (1994: 267) emphasises: 'no army before that of the Roman republic ... achieved its level of legally and bureaucratically regulated recruitment, organisation, command and supply'. Unlike Greek hoplites the legionaries became paid soldiers (the daily stipend was introduced in the third century BCE), which helped detach them from the land and turned them into a professional army able to fight far away from home (Santosuosso 2001: 15). To put it bluntly, the strength of the Roman state was located in its military and the strength of the military was located in its historically unprecedented social organisation.

When one takes into account that the entire bureaucratic apparatus of this enormous polity, comprising at its peak 70 million people and stretching over 3 million square kilometres, amounted to no more than 300–400 civil servants (Mann 1986: 266, 274) it is easier to comprehend the importance of the military and its organisational structure for the state's existence. The Roman state is perhaps in some respects the most palpable historical example that confirms some of the key tenets of the group-struggle paradigm. This was a typical Ratzenhofer's (1904) *Erobererstaat* (the conquest state) that relied on coercion to subjugate its weaker neighbours, turning some of them into slaves and others into loyal obedient citizens. It is estimated that up to 40 per cent of the population inhabiting the Apennine Peninsula in the first century BCE were slaves (Hopkins 1978: 102). While early Roman expansion resembled Oppenheimer's (2007) 'bears' who crushed their enemies with their potent military might, the established empire preferred the 'bee-keeper's model of domination through assimilation and economic exploitation. Rustow's (1980) model of the culture pyramid can account well for the Roman case, as super-stratification was used to coerce the weaker enemy, to acquire slaves and to establish the relations of group domination. Furthermore, the organisational capacity and extra wealth generated through military might was decisive in creating and maintaining groups of people who could specialise in non-manual, mostly discursive, labour: senators, generals, poets and other patricians.

However there are also problems with these classical theories as they are unable to account for the fact that, rather than enslaving entire groups of people, Roman armies tended towards accommodating and gradually assimilating the elites of defeated enemies. In fact, the success of running such a huge empire was based in part on ruling through the local elites who, upon surrender, would become an integral part of the Roman administrative structure. The likelihood of keeping their privileges, or even of further promotion, depended heavily on the degree of their cultural, proto-ideological, assimilation. The Roman Empire devoted a great deal of energy and resources to the Romanisation of its citizens: 'this conscious policy involved teaching language and literacy, building theatres and amphitheatres, and loosely integrating local cults into Roman ones' (Mann 1986: 269). In other words social organisation and proto-ideology were the cornerstones of Roman military and political hegemony.

War and violence in the medieval era

One of the principal strengths of the Roman Empire, its reliance on the local elites to govern its conquered provinces (*foederati*), proved also to be one of its chief weaknesses once the empire started crumbling. The exhausting Persian campaign of 363 CE, the disastrous defeat in the Gothic war at the battle of Adrianople of 378, which was often described as the most terrible defeat of the Roman army since Cannae of 216 BCE (Oman 1968: 4), and dramatic economic decline all contributed to its fall. However, all the attempts to reunite the eastern and western halves of the empire were ultimately undermined by the gradual 'barbarisation' of the western polity's institutional cornerstone – its army. Once large units of 'barbarian federates' were incorporated 'not as the auxiliaries of old had done in units raised and officered by imperial officials, but as allies under their own leaders' (Keegan 1994: 288) then the Roman army and with it the empire itself became de-Romanised in both an organisational and proto-ideological sense.[7] With less and less Romanisation there was no cohesive force to preserve the loyalty of the disparate conglomerates of tribal formations who were invading the territory of the western Roman Empire.

Furthermore, in military terms, the battle of Adrianople was also a sign of new times, as heavy cavalry proved to be a much more potent war machine than fading Roman infantry. As Oman (1968: 6) puts it: 'with this victory 'the Goth' became the ultimate 'arbiter of war, the lineal ancestor of all the knights of the Middle Ages, the inaugurator of that ascendancy of the horsemen which was to endure for a thousand years'. Although cavalry was not a new invention, dating all the way back to Assyrian horsemen of 600 BCE and reappearing on the historical stage on many occasions, the inability to fully control horses generally reduced its use to marginal roles such as herding the infantry together. With the clear exception of nomadic tribal warriors from Attila and Genghis Khan to Tamerlane, most armies of settled populations had to wait for the invention of saddles and stirrups to develop heavy cavalry as a serious instrument of warfare.[8]

The durability of the eastern half of the Roman Empire, later to be known as Byzantium, originated in great part in its ability to develop an alternative

---

[7] As Keegan (1994: 280–1) puts it: 'The "Roman" armies of Constantius and Aetius were Teutonic in composition, carried Teutonic weapons, lost all semblance of legionary drill, and even adopted the German warcry, the *baritus*.'

[8] It seems that the stirrup was invented in India and was adopted in China in the fifth century. It came into general use in Western Europe in the eighth century (Howard 1976: 2; Keegan 1994: 285).

model of social organisation and proto-ideology. No only did the Byzantine state adopt cavalry as the main means of warfare, but it also introduced sweeping changes in military and administrative organisation. Unlike its western counterpart, the Byzantine Empire was much more centralised, with the emperor acting as an absolute ruler sanctified by the divine origin theory. Court-based civil administration substantially increased at the end of the eighth century, as church officials, *sakellarios*, acted as chief administrators of the state. The importance of the military was highly discernible with the formation of the new regional system of themes or *themata* under Emperor Constans II. These distinct administrative and military units were run by the military governors, *strategos*, and in this way emphasised the military character of the state's bureaucracy. Although in terms used by Weber (1968: 1013), this was a patrimonial form of administration, with the authority vested in the will of individuals and the emperor, rather than in offices, it was still a fairly efficient and complex model of administrative organisation for its time. It had compartmentalised offices and divisions of responsibility and was even instrumental in creating the first ever foreign-intelligence-gathering agency – the Bureau of Barbarians (Antonucci 1993). The social significance of this administration was particularly evident in the eighth and ninth centuries when the civil service became so central that it represented the direct path to aristocratic status (Angold 2001; Neville 2004; Mango 2005).

The empire's reform of the military helped create an efficient and disciplined army and navy. For nearly five centuries (seventh to eleventh) its military was the most powerful and best organised in the world (Dupuy and Dupuy 1986: 214). While the city of Constantinople was protected by impenetrable walls (until the eleventh century), the empire also boasted a strong economy, thriving peasantry and an efficient system of taxation which all contributed towards establishing a potent and successful military machine. Nevertheless, the themata system contained the seeds of its own destruction as it encouraged the growth of an aristocracy that would eventually dominate the military and destabilise the central government. Once the themata system collapsed (in eleventh century), the empire was forced to rely ever more on professional paid troops, *tagmata*, many of which were foreign mercenaries and were not as reliable as soldiers of the early Byzantium.

In addition to its organisational might and military power, the Byzantine Empire was the first polity to fully institutionalise Christianity as its normative, that is state-sponsored, proto-ideology. Justinian I (527–565 CE) was particularly instrumental in this respect as his reforms codified and implemented Roman law through the empire, restored ecclesiastical and hence political unity within the state and, most of all, placed the orthodox Christian doctrine at the heart of the Byzantine Empire. These legislative reforms regulated nearly all aspects of everyday life and were associated exclusively with Christian teachings (e.g. conversion, baptism, administration of the sacraments, monastic life etc.). Orthodox Christianity was not just an official state religion but it deeply penetrated and guided the everyday life of the ordinary population. Not only did most Byzantine cities resemble fortified religious communities under ecclesiastical rule, with monastic life prevalent and highly valued, but also, in the popular perception, there was little qualitative distinction between the Imperial Court and the Heavenly Kingdom. As Mango (2005: 151, 219) emphasises 'the Byzantines imagined God and the Heavenly Kingdom as a vastly enlarged replica of the imperial court at Constantinople ... Just as the universe is ruled monarchically by God, so mankind is governed by the Roman emperor'. The central focus was not on earthly life, but on the immanent doom to be followed by the second coming of Christ and the afterlife. In popular understanding, the proto-ideological complexity of the religious message was largely ignored. Instead, the popular focus was on the veneration of icons, that is, simplified images of favourite saints, the Virgin Mary and Christ.

The small kingdoms that emerged from the ruins of the western Roman Empire initially lacked much of the institutional and proto-ideological power that characterised the early Byzantine Empire. After several centuries of destructive in-fighting between the royal houses and mass conversions to Christianity, the Carolingian dynasty managed to establish itself as the dominant political and military force in the western part of the continent. The coronation of Charlemagne, by Pope Leo III in 800, bestowing on him the title of *Imperator Romanorum* ('Emperor of the Romans'), was a symbolic watershed that signified the end of geopolitical chaos in the west and the emergence of a new power able to challenge Byzantium both militarily and proto-ideologically. The Carolingian system of rule relied heavily on the combination of the Germanic war-band tradition of personal attachment and mutual loyalty between the warrior chief and his close associates (*Gefolgschaft*) and the Roman practice of the *precarium*: in order to provide for the resources that warriors required in times of peace (when there was little opportunity for pillage), the king would reward top warriors through the lease of land. In this way the military service of vassals was linked to land tenure granted by the lord and the relative permanence of this relationship was sanctified by the Church's doctrine of fealty (Poggi 1978: 18–30; Keegan 1994: 284–5).

This long-term arrangement was a backbone of feudalism which, although an anarchic and weak system of rule with overlapping and crisscrossing layers of authority, eventually proved to be the most fertile structural environment for the dramatic social change that was to transform Europe and consequently the rest of the world for ever. As Weber (1968) was already well aware, the birth of institutional rationality and bureaucratic organisation that was to come later owed a great deal to the military character of feudalism. Feudal kingdoms were built on the military contract between the ruler and his vassals. What ultimately set the Byzantine Empire apart from Western Europe was the feudal system of vassalage. Being highly centralised and patrimonial, Byzantium initially was much more economically and militarily successful than the chaotic world of the tribal confederations that emerged in the west. However, the multi-polar power structure of the smaller western kingdoms proved in time more beneficial for the gradual rationalisation of social life and the expansion of contractual arrangements in trade, banking, civil relations and political life. The key difference here was the relationship between the rulers and their top warriors: while in the patrimonial world of the Byzantine Empire the aristocracy always remained reliant on the emperor, western feudal anarchy created a condition of mutual inter-dependence between the lord and his vassals. The fact that no king, prince, count or bishop had enough power to establish absolute domination over the other rulers meant that the structural autonomy of different political actors, which would eventually help create both modern nation-states and civil society, was rooted not in the strength but in the weakness of this social order. Furthermore, as vassals were not subjects of kings' whims, but highly independent social agents, the rulers had to secure their loyalty through both material (land tenure) and ideational (status hierarchy) means. While the rulers could not fight successful wars nor protect their realm without the military assistance of their vassals, the vassals required the rulers' protection, grants of land and social recognition. To complicate things further, the feudal order consisted of multiple overlapping networks of authority whereby the vassal would pledge allegiance to a variety of kings, counts and bishops while they themselves were likely to make competing political claims over the same stretches of territory (Beeler 1971; Herwig *et al.* 2003).

The fact that feudalism was first and foremost a military order was clearly visible in the patterns of social stratification whereby a small number of heavily armoured mounted knights completely dominated the rest of the population, consisting of serfs and the a stratum of urban artisans. Social rank was not determined by the degree of individual liberty or personal wealth but by

whether one was or was not a knight (Hintze 1975). Knighthood was a way
of life that on the one hand implied extensive and expensive military training, costly weaponry and equipment, and the possession of quality horses,
while on the other hand it indicated a social distinction sanctioned by the
kings and the ceremonies of the Church; it also had an ethos of chivalry that
glorified the virtues of courage, honour and courtesy. As McNeill (1982: 20)
points out, the reliance on heavy armoured cavalry 'constituted a reprise of
the impact of chariotry on social and political structures some eighteen hundred years earlier' as 'superior force came to rest in the hands of a few elab-
orately equipped and trained individuals' thus allowing for the conversion of
the monopoly of violence into the political, economic and cultural domination of knights.

Even though Christianity played a similar role in the West as it did in
Byzantium, acting as a dominant normative proto-ideology, the differing geopolitical contexts of the two regions made its social role very different. While in
the Byzantine Empire religion largely overlapped with the polity, thus directly
reinforcing it and creating a monopolistic situation, the small and anarchic
western kingdoms, in their attempt to dominate one another, were forced also
to struggle for the legitimacy that could be provided only by the Church. As
Sombart (1913) and Hall (1985) convincingly argue, the failure to establish a
large and unified empire in the western part of the European continent and
the relatively permanent state of warfare between these small polities, with the
Church acting as an independent power broker, proved indispensable in generating the large-scale social transformation and eventual modernisation of
the European continent. While the fact these polities shared the same normative universe (the proto-ideology of Christianity) prevented these small-scale
conflicts and wars from escalation, their regular and frequent occurrence provided an impetus to gradual social change in the economy, politics and technology as monarchs ultimately had to negotiate with the emerging domestic
civil society. Weber (1968) made it clear that only Western European cities
gained full autonomy including their own governments, financial and banking
structures and armies. In this way, constant military pressure was paramount
in forcing feudal rulers to co-operate with their own nascent civil societies. In
other words, military competition between small polities that were all part of
the larger proto-ideological universe was instrumental in fostering contractual relationships within these societies which would later prove to be crucial
for the birth of the modern nation-state.

Although feudal Europe was almost constantly at war, a great majority of
these wars were small-scale, characterised by low casualties and few proper

battles. As the knights represented the core of all medieval forces, armies were quite small and expensive while direct battles were generally avoided whenever possible making regular warfare no more than plundering expeditions.[9] Despite the popular perception of the Crusades as involving huge armies and many battle casualties, the largest army ever gathered in defence of Jerusalem (in 1183) had less than 15,000 soldiers (Beeler 1971: 249–50) and an overwhelming majority of deaths occurred on the way to the Holy Land from exhaustion, disease, malnutrition and hunger or were the result of the indiscriminate killing of civilians and prisoners. For example 80 per cent of those who embarked on the First Crusade between 1096–7 did not survive (Tyerman 2004: 147). The total number of soldiers involved in the First Crusade was around 12,000 of whom less than 1,300 were knights; the famous siege of Antioch in 1097 pitched a Christian army of less than 3,000 against a slightly larger Muslim force (Herwig *et al.* 2003: 164). Most of the feudal battles were decided after one decisive assault 'with one side signalling defeat by fleeing to the safety of a castle' (Herwig *et al.* 2003: 146). After the initial joint onslaught, battles would quickly deteriorate into one-on-one fights between the knights. As the focus was on personal honour and one's reputation 'there existed no common sense of discipline, for in feudal Europe the very spirit of the hereditary warrior class militated against this' (Herwig *et al.* 2003: 148). One of the key features of feudal wars was that more soldiers died during the retreats than in the battles, as retreats were highly chaotic and archers and infantry were no longer protected by a line of pikes (Mann 1986). As Eckhardt (1992: 85) shows 'war-related deaths in ancient times were probably no more than 1 per cent of those occurring since 1945'.

The fact that medieval armies were undisciplined and, as such, fairly inefficient on the battlefield is directly linked to the institutional weaknesses of the feudal kingdoms they represented. The comically small size of the civil service and the tiny income from revenues of Henry II (1154–89), who is considered as one of more powerful kings of his time, illustrate this quite well. His total year's revenue of around £22,000 and handful of court officials indicate that the size of his bureaucracy exceeded only slightly that of the households of the chief barons and clerics and his budget 'was smaller that that of the Archbishop of Canterbury' (Mann 1986: 418). What is sociologically

---

[9] As Herwig *et al.* (2003: 146) illustrate: 'The complete knight was a costly creature. With at least three mounts, a knee-length shirt, mail coif, metal-plate armor, helmet, lance, sword, silk pennon, tent, beasts of burden to haul and to carry kitchen, kettles, victuals, and wines – this medieval "battleship" cost the equivalent of fifteen mares or twenty oxen, equal the plow teams of ten peasant families. Put differently, it required the revenues of at least 300 to 450 acres of fertile land to launch and sustain a knightly career.'

interesting here is the clear link between the lack of social organisation and low numbers of soldier causalities in medieval warfare. While the potent military organisation of the Roman Empire was able to maintain and keep mobile large-scale armies thus forcing individuals to fight and die in great numbers, the feudal world had no structural mechanisms to impose discipline on its soldiers. The fact that medieval battles were rare, short and not particularly deadly, had less to do with knightly values of chivalry and gentlemanly treatment of their fellow noblemen but had, rather, a direct structural cause – the lack of effective social organisation that could coerce soldiers to attack other soldiers.

Popular representations of medieval times, misleadingly called the Dark Ages, suggest a world of ubiquitous violence. The images of crucified prisoners, women burned alive as witches, enemy soldiers boiled to death and the invention and application of elaborate techniques of torture such as thumbscrews, impalement, hanging upside down, scalping, roasting alive and castration are all firmly associated with this period of European history. Although the medieval moral universe tolerated more excessive forms of violence than later day epochs, the grisly character of these violent actions tends to conceal two important facts. Firstly, these practices were not used as frequently as one is led to believe. The use of torture was largely confined to judicial and ecclesiastical inquiries and trials, as it was deemed a legitimate way to obtain confessions and testimonies from the suspects. For example, the most notorious institution associated with torture, the Spanish Inquisition, used these gruesome methods quite sparingly with only 2 per cent of prisoners being subjected to prolonged torture, preferring incarceration or other forms of punishment instead (Peters 1989; Monter 2003). Furthermore, despite the perception that violence was predominantly a public affair, with the carnivalesque communal executions of heretics and prisoners, most macabre forms of torture and killing were committed inside the walls of castles, and far away from the eyes of the general public. In many cases, expulsion from the village or town was preferred to corporal punishment, and proved to be a more efficient form of penalty or social deterrent.

Secondly, the horrible character of these violent actions hides the low intensity of their killing efficiency. That is, the spectacular, morbid nature of these acts of cruelty has little, if anything, to do with the numbers of people killed. Rather than being a social device for mass slaughter, medieval violence was a symbolic means of reinforcing the existing hierarchical social structure of these societies, some of the stratified ever to have existed. As Collins (1974: 422) puts it: 'torture and humiliation are above all forms of communication usable as threats and supports for claims of complete domination ... Mutilation and other public punishments are above all violence to one's social image, and hence are pre-eminently usable for upholding inter-group stratification'.

In other words the medieval world was not particularly good at large-scale brutality. When it comes to war casualties and all-encompassing structural violence, the Dark Ages were not so dark when compared either to its Roman predecessors or particularly to its modern progeny. If military efficiency is to be understood as a structural ability to mobilise large groups of people to kill and die in fulfilling a particular political/military goal, than its realisation is dependent on two central ingredients – an all-embracing ideology and sophisticated social organisation. With the partial exception of the early Byzantine Empire, this historical period of European history clearly was in possession of only one of these two – the common proto-ideology of Christianity.[10]

The institutional seeds of early modernity: war, violence and the birth of discipline

When Michael Roberts (1955) referred to the array of technological, strategic and tactical changes introduced in the late sixteenth century as a military revolution he unwittingly initiated an ongoing debate on when exactly European military development went through an unprecedented transformation that set it apart from the rest of the world. Although there is still a pronounced disagreement among historians about whether this striking social change was revolutionary or evolutionary, whether it happened earlier (Ayton and Price 1995; Eltis 1995) or later (Parker 1976; Black 1991), most would concur with the view that 'advances in technology during the later Middle Ages resulted in new weapons which gradually modified all aspects of war between 1450 and 1700' (Childs 2005: 20). The adoption of gunpowder (discovered in China in the seventh or eighth century), the invention and mass use of the cannon in siege and naval artillery, the gradual spread of early handguns such as the harquebus and matchlock musket, the development of the multi-decked galleons, the creation of virtually impregnable fortifications and so many other technological innovations have all dramatically transformed the nature of warfare. Most importantly, the relatively low production costs

---

[10] And even this common proto-ideological doctrine could never overcome either the insurmountable institutional division between the eastern Orthodox and western Catholic Churches nor its essentially stratifying character (i.e. the aristocratic elite vs. peasantry).

of easy-to-operate handguns had a profound effect on the social structure of the military, and the social orders as a whole, since nearly anyone could now learn how to load and fire the handgun.[11] As Childs (2005: 24) puts it succinctly: 'This was the essence of military change: a numerous infantry armed with cheap, crude, gunpowder weapons replaced exclusive and expansive cavalry: cantonal recruitment, conscription, and the age of mass armies beckoned. Between 1550 and 1700, battles were largely decided by missile fire seeking to disorder the enemy prior to the decisive advance.'

Although focused on technological advancements in weaponry, fortifications and other material spheres, the concept of a military revolution also encompassed the creation of new military doctrines, the development of linear tactics, improvements in control and logistics and perhaps most importantly, a substantial increase in the size of European armies. Parker (1996: 24) points out: 'Charles VIII of France had invaded Italy in 1494 with 18,000 men, but Francis I attacked in 1525 with 32,000 and Henry II captured Metz in 1552 with 36,000. By the 1630s, the armed forces maintained by the leading European states totalled perhaps 150,000 each and, by the end of the century, there were almost 400,000 French soldiers (and almost as many again ranged against them).' The size of armies in the sixteenth century went up more by than 50 per cent (Sorokin 1957: 340) and between 1500 and 1700 in most instances the increase was tenfold (Wright 1965: 655; Parker 1996: 1).

While Roberts's model of military revolution was beneficial in highlighting the extraordinary character of the technological changes that underpinned European warfare it clearly and unduly overemphasised the role of technology over those of social organisation and proto-ideology. What is crucial to stress here is that, in many respects, technological innovations went hand in hand with organisational and doctrinal changes. It is no coincidence that the principal initiators of these military changes were the deeply religious protestant generals Maurice of Nassau, Gustavus Adolphus and Oliver Cromwell. The unparalleled successes of their armies were rooted in their novel use of technological and strategic advancements as much as in their religiously inspired military doctrines and their novel social organisation. Although the early form of the warrior-monk can be traced all the way back to the military orders of the Templar, Teutonic and Hospitaller Knights of the First

---

[11] However it is important to note that the introduction of handguns in the fourteenth and fifteenth centuries was a rather gradual process. Handguns were often in competition with crossbows and soldiers armed with handguns only gradually augmented the battalions of pikemen which had dominated most European armies since the early fourteenth century (Mann 1986: 453; Keegan 1994: 328–9).

Crusades, Reformation Protestantism was a watershed in creating a model religious warrior. As Aho (1979) convincingly argues, by rigidly separating the sacred from the profane and upholding the view that the natural world is utterly profane, the Calvinist, Baptist and Lutheran military commanders successfully legitimised the scientific and rationalist pursuit of warfare. By understanding religion and political institutions as having mutually opposed purposes (i.e. an individual experience of faith vs. the inherently sinful material world), early Protestantism helped to free political life, and hence also military action, from any moral and spiritual obligations. With the expansion of the Protestant Reformation, politics – being by definition the realm of sin and immorality – acquires all the Machiavellian features, as the rigid separation of the two realms allows for the use of all means available at the disposal of the state to pursue its political goals. In this respect, the utilisation of violence becomes the most rational tool of state politics.

In addition, since Protestantism interprets political institutions as God's creation it sees a pious believer as one that fully submits to the authority of the state, even when the state takes a tyrannical form. As Luther (1974: 103) puts it: 'war and killing along with all the things that accompany wartime and martial law have been instituted by God … The hand that wields the sword and kills with it is not man's hand but God's'. With its radical asceticism and the doctrine of predestination, Calvinism goes a step further – perceiving politics and war as nothing more than a mere tool which can be used when implementing God's will. If personal wealth can be interpreted as a sign of being chosen, as in the Weberian (1930) interpretation of the elective affinity between Protestantism and capitalism, than victories in wars are no different: 'since the divine will is inscrutable and can only be deciphered *de facto*, this means that policy is right, morality and practically, which works. Might makes it right' (Walzer 1965: 38; Aho 1979: 108). Bearing in mind that Luther's published sermons sold over 300,000 copies between 1517 and 1520 and that Calvinist works were equally popular, it seems that these ideas had strong resonance among Protestant soldiers (Taylor 2003: 97).

Adopting this novel military ethics while simultaneously pursuing practical political and military aims, the Protestant generals proved exceptionally successful on the battlefield. Sharing Protestant proto-ideology with their soldiers, the military commanders built powerful armies driven in large part by religious zeal. Cromwell's New Model Army was composed of full-time professional soldiers devoted to Puritan ideals, who often sang psalms before battle and saw their enemies as representing the devil's warriors on earth. The armies of Maurice of Nassau, Gustavus Adolphus and Cromwell were highly motivated by a righteous sense of executing God's will and by 'divine hatred' of their ungodly enemies. As the soldiers understood themselves only as a means through which God's wrath was manifested on the wicked, their martial enthusiasm, as well as their cruelty towards the enemy, had no limits.

Nevertheless, regardless of how forceful the Protestant proto-ideology was, it was not enough in itself to secure military victories. What proved even more important was an attempt to revive Roman military organisational practices (McNeill 1991). With the partial exception of early Byzantium, the end of the Roman Empire largely meant the end of disciplined armies for the next thousand years of European history. Protestant military commanders planted the institutional seeds of military social organisation that eventually gave birth to the modern bureaucratic nation-state.

After reading Vegetius's Roman military manual *Epitoma rei militaris*, Maurice of Nassau reorganised his armies into smaller, better coordinated and more flexible units. Battle lines on the Roman model were reintroduced but as this involved intensive drilling there was a need for disciplined professionals who would be able both to fight and labour. Relying on mercenaries, who were able to perform both of these tasks, secured also the further centralisation of military organisations (Mann 1986: 454). Maurice introduced intensive drilling and the systematic training of soldiers, as well as strict rules of military behaviour (including rules on the treatment of civilians). The focus was on military discipline, flexibility on the battlefield, centralisation of authority, practical and adept leadership and unquestioned obedience to the military commander. Order and discipline were achieved by a variety of means but most of all by the codified regulation of military practice. Gustavus Adolphus instituted Articles of War ('The Swedish Discipline' of 1625) that strictly defined the rules of behaviour for soldiers: plundering and outrage were punishable by death; morning and evening prayer were compulsory for every regiment and deriding 'divine service' entailed a death sentence; no duelling was allowed; no 'loose' women were allowed in the camp; there was a separate court-martial for each regiment and, most importantly, any cowardly behaviour of a unit on the battlefield entailed collective punishment. Drawing on the Roman example, Article V of the code ordered the following: 'The punishment of death (loss of head and hand, or hanging) is decreed to every tenth man by lot if a regiment runs away during a battle. The other nine are to serve without their banner, lie outside the quarters, and have to clean out the camp, until they have wiped out their disgrace by a bold deed' (Fletcher 1890: 299–300). Here again, just as in the Greek and Roman cases, one can see how social organisation, an external mechanism of social control, is a backbone of military might. Once the institutional and ideological devices that prevent soldiers from running away are found, success on the battlefield is much closer.

The extensive development of social organisation was also visible in the ever increasing professionalisation and bureaucratisation of the military sphere. The first military academies were established in this period – starting with Sedan (1606), Siegen (1617) and Kassel (1618) – where warfare was studied through the prism of the latest discoveries in science, technology and mathematics. The spotlight was on the practical use of science: the ability to calculate the accuracy of artillery fire, to successfully construct fortifications, bridges, canals, to work out optimal regiment and camp sizes, to estimate the range of battlefield supplies and so on. The first military manuals and drill books were produced and widely circulated among the new officer corps and soldiers, some of which relied on illustrations rather than texts, such as the first modern drill book – *Arms Drill with Arquebus, Musket and Pike* (1607) (McNeill 1991; Childs 2005: 20). These musketry drill manuals proved important in inculcating modernist, rationalist and disciplinary techniques of thinking and acting on the wider scale as they taught soldiers inductive thought, causality and logic, and how to prioritise and allocate tasks. As Keegan (1994: 342) stresses, these booklets were the equivalents of industrial safety manuals of later eras as they 'divide the sequence into numerous precise actions – forty-seven in Maurice of Orange's drill book of 1607 – from the moment when the musketeer takes up his weapon to that when he pulls the trigger'.

These practices stand in stark opposition to the medieval times in which the prevailing ethics were firmly resistant to most forms of military innovation. For example, for decades the early forms of gun (harquebus, musket, etc.) were rejected on religious grounds: 'The gun was … regarded as an instrument of the devil, imported from eastern infidels like the Turks and Chinese, and developed by magicians, a 'cowardly' weapon which killed from afar' (Taylor 2003: 83).

Following another Roman example, Gustavus Adolphus was the first military commander to introduce uniforms, thus on the one hand preventing soldiers from switching sides in times of danger and on the other hand making military activity a much more standardised and bureaucratic service – a soldier as a state employee with defined rights and responsibilities. The centrality of bureaucratic organisation was also evident in the gradual adoption of the practice of having written orders with clearly and logically defined roles for commanders, regiment leaders, and administrative personnel and in the setting up of a regular system of army salaries which were paid directly from the state treasury. Adolphus was also instrumental in developing sophisticated training techniques (including the first modern use of closed areas for training and drilling during peacetime) and a reliable system of supply and logistics: his armies were 'clothed, sheltered, and fed from magazines, all of which were run by specially trained commissary staffs' (Aho 1979: 114). Furthermore, he invented military conscription. Although most armies of this era consisted of mercenaries and volunteers, Sweden also relied on a complex system of partial conscription (*indelningsverket;*) from 1620 to 1682 (Childs 2005: 32). This was a first and significant institutional step towards transforming officers and soldiers from contracted professionals into full-time state employees.

As a consequence of major technological changes, the expansion of bureaucratic organisation and proto-ideological commitments, wars became more protracted and destructive with a substantial increase in human casualties. The more intensive and accurate use of artillery and the introduction of new battle tactics, together with the religious flux of populations and novel social organisation, had a profound impact on the number of war casualties. The most destructive event of this era, the Thirty Years War (1618–1648), was characterised by a very high proportion of deaths in battle. For example, the Swedish lost 50 per cent of their troops at the battle of Nordlingen (1634) while 60 per cent of Saxon and Holy Roman Empire troops were killed at the Battle of Wittstock (1636) (Lee 1991: 53).[12] As a result of the pillage, destruction, famine and disease brought by the armies, there was a significant population decline in the territories directly affected by war: the Holy Roman Empire went from 21 million in 1618 to 13.5 million in 1648; the population of Bohemia declined from 3 million to 800,000 (Lee 1991: 55). However the excesses of the Thirty Years War were more an exception than the rule as warfare in this period of time was still governed by ritualistic practices that prevented the deliberate slaughter of enemy soldiers, let alone civilians. While the new technology such as heavy artillery and firearms provided a means of mass extermination of enemy combatants the ideological conditions were still not ripe

---

[12] While deaths in battle have dramatically increased when compared to the medieval era, the absolute figures still remain relatively small when contrasted with modern warfare. For example the actual number of soldiers killed (hidden behind these percentages) in these two large-scale battles was around 5,000. Until the modern era most war casualties were caused by disease rather than battlefield action. As Jones (1987: 36) illustrates: 'A typhus epidemic killed 17,000 of the 20,000 men lost by the Spanish army besieging Granada in 1490 … Eleven Frenchmen died of deprivation and exposure between Moscow and the Beresina for every one who died in combat'.

for justification of such actions, which did not come until the arrival of the modern age. In the words of Childs (2005: 37): 'Killing was not the main purpose. European warfare was concerned with capturing territory not people; enemy soldiers were simply pawns in the greater game, not ends in themselves.'

Continuous warfare required large standing armies, now consisting almost exclusively of less expensive infantry than costly cavalry, which were a heavy burden on state finances. To facilitate effective co-ordination of troops, and their transport, accommodation, training, supply and sustenance, military administration had to become more integrated, centralised and geographically unified, reflecting similar trends occurring at the level of the state itself. As Childs (2005: 34) observes: 'Whilst on campaign, the armies of the sixteenth century and the Thirty Years War had tended to pillage or gather contributions: the better-organised and … disciplined national forces of the later seventeenth century usually paid for some of their supplies'. The increasing state centralisation was paralleled by the state's ability to collect higher taxes, which were nearly all used for military purposes. A large proportion of the state's revenues was spent on war chests. For example, France allocated 74 per cent of its total revenues to the military (army and navy) during the Nine Years War while England spent 75 per cent of its revenue on this conflict and on the War of the Spanish Succession; Russia's military spending between 1679 and 1725 amounted to between 60 and 95 per cent of the total state revenue (Childs 2005: 33). As military organisation was expanding, so was the state and its bureaucratic apparatus as well. What started off as a handful of court officials responsible for tax collection and communication with the army commanders, was to end up as the massive state and military organisational machine of the modern era. As Tilly (1975) and Giddens (1985) demonstrate convincingly, warfare and preparation for war were the most important reason for the development of the state. However, this had little to do with the calculated acts of individual monarchs and military leaders and more with the contingencies of European history: 'The growth of the state was less the result of conscious power aggrandisement than of desperate searches for temporary expedients to stave off financial disaster. The sources of that threat were less the deliberate actions of a rival power than the unintended consequences of European economic and military activity as a whole' (Mann 1986: 434). In their constant efforts to finance the costly wars (and the conquest of newly discovered overseas lands), the rulers were forced to centralise authority, and this would ultimately break the power dualism that characterised late feudalism and the polity of estates epoch (*Ständestaat*), thus moving towards absolutist rule. The absolutist model of rule was crucial in the process of state formation as on the one hand, it, was responsible for articulating the state as a 'pre-eminent bordered power container' (Giddens 1985: 291) able to monopolise and legitimise the use of violence within its territory, and, on the other hand, it unwittingly created a public sphere in its pursuit of legitimacy. As Poggi (1978: 83) argues: 'The very existence of a public realm was largely the consequence of the absolutist state's policy of bypassing the *Stände* and addressing directly the generality of its subjects through its laws, its taxation, its uniform and pervasive administration, its increasing appeal to patriotism.' It was the context of warfare that created absolutism and it was the absolutist state that opened up the door to modernity.

Hence, what is distinct about this period of European history is the ever-increasing institutional and organisational rationalisation of military and, consequently, all social conduct. As Weber (1968: 1155) rightly argues, military discipline was the cornerstone of all other practices of social regulation. The expansion of rationalisation that was to gradually and eventually dominate most organisations of the modern age was rooted in the ideas and practices of individual, collective and institutional self-restraint linked in part to ideals of ascetic Protestant proto-ideology and in part to military compulsion. To succeed in the protracted wars of the seventeenth and eighteenth century it was not enough to rely on the zeal of the new Protestant proto-ideology. The military commanders had also to draw on the organisational experience of the Roman legions. It was only the creative synergy of these organisational and proto-ideological mechanisms that delivered victories on the battlefield. More importantly, the ultimate result of this decisive social change was a rebirth of discipline in a new organisational guise. Once fully developed and articulated, the bureaucratic mechanisms used to control soldiers easily found their application in the civilian sphere – the civil service, industry, education, communication and many other areas. In other words, it was the combination of this organisational and proto-ideological military transformation that gave birth to modernity.

Conclusion

What stands out in this socio-historical narrative that starts with prehistory and culminates in early modernity is the fact that the general increase in collective violence is deeply linked with the development of social organisation and ideology. As archaeological and contemporary social science records show, human beings, left to their own individual devices, are generally incapable of violence and unwilling to kill and die. For 99 per cent of our unrecorded history we fought no wars, and even today, on the rare occasions when people act individually, removed from organisational and ideological power, most prefer flight over fight. It is the institutional trappings of the networks of organisations and ideological doctrines that make us act more violently. To put it differently, by giving up some of their liberty to social organisations, people were able to fend off incessant hunger, improve their lifestyles and secure protection but all at the expense of increased exposure to violence. Hence, as the classical sociologists were well aware, civilisations are both cradles of cultural and economic advancement as well as the sources of utmost destruction: rather than being an inherent feature of our biology, warfare is a creation of intensive social development. Social progress is a double-edged sword since much of human advancement has gone hand in hand with the proliferation of war and violence. The two key processes in this narrative are the cumulative bureaucratisation of coercion and centrifugal ideologisation both of which intensify with the arrival of modernity. So let us explore the historical context in which they transpire.

4 Organised violence and modernity

Introduction

When attempting to delegitimise one's political opponents' actions it has become standard practice to refer to them as barbaric and medieval. Most recently such political labelling was widespread in the characterisation of the Wars of Yugoslav Succession as barbarism grounded in 'ancient hatreds' (Kaplan 1993) and depictions of the Taliban as 'medieval vandals' whose actions represent 'a regression into medieval barbarism' (Singh 2001). Such descriptions are rooted in the almost universal views that, not only is the modern age morally superior to the medieval times, but also, that we live in a substantially less violent world than our medieval counterparts. Although it is true that modernity in general dispenses with macabre displays of torture and public mutilations, this does not mean that in the modern era violent action is on the decrease. On the contrary, with modernity violence and warfare are proliferating at unprecedented levels. The total tally of twentieth century deaths caused by organised violence constitutes nearly 75 per cent of all war deaths for the last 5,000 years (Eckhardt 1992: 273). In other words, in 100 years modern human beings have managed to kill twenty-two times more people than our predecessors were able to do in 4,900 years. In comparison to this staggering figure the human casualties for the thousand years of the medieval period (500–1500) amount to only 1.6 per cent of all war deaths (Eckhardt 1992: 273). Hence the question is: How and why are popular perceptions so obviously distorted? How is it possible that we portray medieval times as barbaric and our own as the epitome of refinement and social advancement? To answer these questions it is necessary to look at the roles of social organisation and ideology in the modern era.

This chapter explores the paradoxical character of modernity and in particular its relationship with war and violence. Following the previous chapter it argues that to understand the ontological dissonance found at the heart of the modern age it is necessary to explore the two processes that shape this relationship: the cumulative bureaucratisation of coercion and centrifugal ideologisation.

Modernity and violence: an ontological dissonance?

The philosophy of the Enlightenment, with its firm and uncompromising belief in individual autonomy, reason and progress, was a progenitor of many novel ideas. However, what particularly stood out was the notion, previously rarely contemplated, that violence and warfare were not inevitable and natural conditions but a product of human action and, as such, something preventable. Once this idea gradually spread beyond the narrow circle of intellectuals from the nineteenth century onwards it became a universal norm for the majority of humankind. The contemporary world prides itself on loathing all forms of violence against fellow human beings and derides warfare as an inhumane and barbaric throwback from the past, unenlightened, ages. The tendency is to look at the 'Dark Ages' and other historical epochs as brutal and callous while perceiving modernity, for the most part, as an age of growing tolerance, dialogue and peaceful resolution of conflicts. No serious political party, organisation or movement, not even (most of) the extremist groups on the far right or far left, openly advocate killing or call for unprovoked war. Yet it is this very age that has seen more bloodshed than any previous epoch in recorded history. The birth of modernity saw a dramatic increase in the human casualties of warfare, with levels in the twentieth century reaching a pinnacle. As described in the previous chapter, levels of war deaths started to increase around the time of the Thirty Years War (1618–48) and substantially burgeoned in the eighteenth century. However, the nineteenth century saw a dramatic increase in war deaths while the twentieth century established itself as nothing short of a century of death. As Holsti (1991) and Tilly (2003) document well, with over 100 million direct casualties and up to 200 million total deaths caused by war-induced starvation, disease, malnutrition, long-term wounds, rebellions and exhaustion, this century easily surpasses all previous recorded times in the number of human casualties. In addition, Mann (2001a) estimates that up to 120 million people perished as a result of genocide and the coercive policies of ethnic cleansing. Moreover, according to the statistical analyses of William Eckhardt (1990, 1992: 272–3), there was a dramatic cumulative increase in war casualties in the last thousand years: while in the combined tenth and eleventh centuries there were only 60,000 war casualties; in the twelfth and thirteenth centuries this figure rises to 539,000;

in the fourteenth and fifteenth the numbers increase to 1,379,000; and in the sixteenth and seventeenth the number of deaths jumps to 7,781,000. However, the last two centuries outstrip everything seen before as the loss of human life escalates to more than 19 million in the nineteenth century and 111 million in the twentieth century. Put simply, this means that the modern era (the last three centuries) accounts for 90 per cent of all war casualties from the beginning of proper warfare in 3000 BCE to the present day.

The modern era is also responsible for the invention and perfection of many mass-slaughter devices from the guillotine and machine gun to nerve gas and nuclear bombs. Concentration camps, gas chambers, electric chairs and elaborate torturing techniques were all masterminded in this era.

Although there were episodes of mass slaughter throughout human history, what is distinct about the modern age is that mass extermination becomes systematic, organised and prolific on a scale unseen before, and paradoxically, is happening at the very same time that human life is nominally most valued. In other words, there is an inherent discrepancy between a normative universe that cherishes human life and scorns war and violence while simultaneously practising killing at an exceptional and unprecedented rate. Unlike Festinger's (1957) cognitive dissonance, this is really an ontological dissonance that demands an answer to the question: How is it possible to abhor the killing of human beings while concurrently tolerating and even implicitly supporting such killing on an enormous scale? It is important to emphasise that this is not (only) a moral, but primarily a sociological question that demands a sociological answer. Although there is no simple solution to this puzzle, most of the answer is to be found in the specific structural interplay between the organisational and ideological powers that have emerged with modernity. The ever-increasing social organisation of violence, and the proliferation of modern ideologies, is the backbone of this ontological dissonance.

The cumulative bureaucratisation of coercion

The principal ideals of the French and American Revolutions such as liberty, equality, fraternity and the pursuit of happiness seem so obvious and uncontroversial today that it is often forgotten that their near-universal acceptance owes less to their logical and ethical appeal and more to the bayonets and cannons of the French and American armies. Not only were these values of

the Enlightenment originally instituted through violent revolutionary uprisings, thus making them immediately contradictory, but their aftermath was
even more brutal, as the revolutionaries took it upon themselves to impose
these ideas on the rest of the world through warfare. While from 1792 the new
French Republic embarked on an almost uninterrupted twenty years of warfare, including the merciless crushing of its domestic counter-revolutionary
movements in the Vendée and Brittany, the new American Republic relied
heavily on coercion and war in its territorial conquest of the North American
continent. Many of the French revolutionaries saw war as inevitable, arguing
that if revolution did not continue to expand outside the borders of France it
would inevitably be destroyed. As the National Assembly's Girondin deputy
Vergniaud put it: 'Our revolution has spread the most acute alarm to all the
crowned heads of Europe; it has shown how the despotism which supports
them can be destroyed. The despots hate our Constitution because it makes
men free and because they want to reign over slaves' (Forrest 2005: 59). In
this context the 'right to bear arms' became interpreted as another right of
a free citizen, thus fostering conditions for the creation of the new citizen
army.

The central legacy of the French Republic was a mass army established
on the principle of putting all fit males at the disposal of the Republic (the
levée en masse decree of 1793) which created a military of 983,000 men
(Keegan 1994: 352). Although the newly recruited officers and soldiers
were initially driven by revolutionary ideals their long-term compliance
was secured through the unprecedented potential of social mobility and
new organisational mechanisms. As Lynn (1990: 168–9) shows, in less than
five years the structure of the officer corps had changed beyond recognition: while in 1789, 90 per cent of officers were noblemen, by 1794 they constituted only 3 per cent of all officers. The military success of these armies
was rooted in part in the sheer numbers of soldiers, in part in the rationalism of the meritocratic principles upon which they were built (hence
opening up the possibility of rapid social promotion to talented individuals
of humble background), and most of all on the potent social organisation
created by the new French state.[1] The *levée en masse* was not only based
on popular commitment to revolutionary ideas but was also a coercive

---

[1] Napoleon quickly realised the significance of meritocracy for military success and rewarded soldiers
through decorations and political posts: 'Of 38,000 men promoted to the Legion of Honour between
1802 and 1814, all but around 4,000 were soldiers. Similarly, it was from the ranks of the military that
were drawn the Marshals of France, who stood at the very apex of the Napoleonic elite. They were
chosen on merit … from all social backgrounds' (Forrest 2005: 63).

mechanism that relied on local quotas which had to be met and which were generally and reluctantly filled by lot (Forrest 2005: 64). The extraordinary victories of the revolutionary armies during the Napoleonic wars had less to do with the charismatic authority and intuitive military genius of Napoleon and much more to do with his own and the state's ability to recruit and co-ordinate huge numbers of soldiers. The ferocious administrative machine of the French state was able to monitor, police, repress and severely punish unwilling recruits and potential deserters. As Forrest (2005: 65) notes: 'Visits by gendarmes, routine punishments for mayors, and the billeting of troops on recalcitrant parents were all essential parts of the recruitment process.' In this way Napoleon's armies became by far the largest military forces the world had ever known, amounting to a staggering two million soldiers between 1800 and 1814. The true skill was to turn this relatively amorphous mass of people into an efficient war machine and this is where Napoleon was at his best. Some organisational improvements had already been made at the time of the rule of the Directory: the establishment of permanent general staff; highly trained professional officers; battalions that were co-ordinated and grouped into larger units (brigades, divisions and corps) by which supplies were drawn from a wider area, and units that remained flexible on the battlefield. Although Napoleon's contribution to the development of tactics in battle was minimal, he was a master of organisation, being able to swiftly deploy, redeploy and co-ordinate large armies on the battlefield. The new organisational model, which was eventually adopted by most European militaries for the next 150 years, combined a centralised supreme command with a highly decentralised and adaptable regiment structure (Howard 1976: 83).

As armies are first and foremost bureaucratic machines, the organisational breakdown is a key to winning battles. As Collins (1989: 366) rightly argues: 'It is social organisation, rather than physical bodies and physical equipment, that is the object of the manoeuvrings of combat. Armies fight, not in order to kill soldiers, incapacitate weapons, and take ground, but to destroy the ability to resist. Organisation is both the weapon and the target of war.' Where Napoleonic army command was particularly strong was its ability to group huge numbers of soldiers in one spot and then inflict a rapid and decisive breakdown of the enemy's organisational structure: the French armies 'learned to break quickly, reforming in columns so as to concentrate large numbers of troops in a single area of the battlefield. Throughout the Napoleonic period the quick interchange of line and column remained a central aspect of French soldiering, with columns used to intimidate and bludgeon the enemy's forces or to provide surprise assaults from the flanks' (Forrest 2005: 69).[2]

Similarly, the secret of Prussian military capability throughout the nineteenth century, whereby such a small state was able to mobilise greater and more efficient troops than its much larger neighbours, lay firmly in its organisational might.[3] Prussia relied on a conscript army that was divided into corps and divisions organised on a territorial basis and armed and equipped as self-sufficient units. Compulsory short-term military service had been in place since 1814 but was tightly re-organised under William I in 1858 and by 1866 every citizen was liable for service of three years with the colours, four years of reserve and five years in the *Landwehr* (French 2005: 78). All military undertakings were initiated, planned, governed and carefully co-ordinated by the Prussian general staff, who 'made war a matter of scientific calculation, administrative planning, and professional expertise' (Howard 1976: 101). The invention and introduction of the railway and telegraph meant the end of the stockpiling of food and supplies close to the front lines, thus allowing for greater mobility of soldiers, better top-down communication of orders and more protracted battles. The fact that Prussia built its railway system around existing and potential front lines was just another indicator that not only was this 'not so much a State which possessed an army as an army which possessed a State' (Howard 1991: 52), but also that its military efficiency was deeply rooted in its ability to utilise new technologies to further enhance its organisational supremacy. It is this organisational superiority – its ability to mobilise and strike much rapidly than its opponents – that secured victory in the Franco-Prussian war of 1870. The strict discipline of the Prussian soldiers was rooted in the specific ethic of service, Prussianism (*Preussentum*), 'rendered and exacted in a precisely defined hierarchy, an ethic strengthened by a Protestantism' (Howard 1991: 52), but was also enforced through rigorous drill, fear and obedience, as is unambiguously stated by Frederick II: 'A soldier must fear his officer more than his enemy' (Andreski 1968: 188).[4] The clear outcome of this war indicated that the time of small, long-service professional armies was over and the Prussian system of short-service well trained

---

2 Napoleon was well aware of the centrality of organisation. In his own words: 'Strategic plans are like sieges; concentrate your fire against a single point. Once the breach is made, the balance is shattered and all the rest becomes useless' (Howard 1976: 83).

3 For example although it had a population half that of Austria, Prussia could mobilise 245,000 soldiers in the 1866 war while Austria could not muster more than 320,000 (French 2005: 77).

4 A similar attitude was expressed by Trotsky, which perhaps in part can account for the later success of the Red Army in the Russian Civil War (1917–23): 'A soldier must be faced with the choice between a probable death if he advances and certain death if he retreats' (Andreski 1968: 188).

conscript armies, supported by reservists and governed by an expert general staff, became a norm for all continental militaries. The switch to compulsory military service with large standing armies required further expansion and bureaucratisation of the state as it now became the principal organising force responsible for the maintenance of armies (including feeding, arming, paying, clothing, housing, training and supplying troops). As a consequence, military spending increased enormously: in the period of 1874–96 Germany increased defence spending by 79 per cent, Russia by 75 per cent, Britain by 47 per cent and France by 43 per cent (French 2005: 82).

To finance such costly armies the states had to develop more extensive and better penetrating fiscal systems capable of enforcing taxation at source which also implied a necessary increase in the size of the state administration. While the early nineteenth century was characterised by prolonged warfare and, as such, state finances were shaped by constantly increasing military demands, the long European peace after 1870 stabilised military expenditure but at very high rates. The modern bureaucratic nation-state emerged as a contingent and, in some respects, even residual outcome of these intensive and expensive war-making processes. In Tilly's (1985: 172) words: 'power holders' pursuit of war involved them willy-nilly in the extraction of resources for war making from the populations over which they had control and in the promotion of capital accumulation by those who could help them borrow and buy. War making, extraction, and capital accumulation interacted to shape European state making'. The increasing size of the military apparatus meant also a continuous increase in the size and scope of the state's bureaucratic machine: the greater the cost of military spending the larger was 'the organisational residue', as illustrated so well in the Prussian case. As states grew institutionally, organisationally and infrastructurally and acquired military might in this process, they were able to monopolise the use of violence within their own borders. Hence, the Weberian (1968: 54) definition of the state that links administrative rule with a monopoly on the legitimate use of physical force within marked territory is really a description of the modern nation-state – a polity sufficiently bureaucratised, infrastructurally potent enough and coercively strong enough to enforce its laws within its boundaries.

The emergence of such a bounded powerful entity also owes a great deal to technological and organisational changes that are sometimes referred to as the 'second military revolution' (Hirst 2001: 7) or 'revolution in military affairs' (Herwig et al. 2003: 412). Even though advancements in technology had continued throughout the seventeenth, eighteenth and early nineteenth century, the second half of the nineteenth century represented a spectacular breakthrough that would change warfare for good. With the discovery and mass production of steamships, electric field telegraphs, railways, automatic weapons, machine guns, high explosives, canned foods and barbed wire, warfare had entered a new, industrial, phase. What is particularly distinct about this period is the intensified structural fusion of science, technology, industry and bureaucratic administration. Once the utility of a specific scientific discovery became apparent both the state and big corporations had interests in its mass production and such success would often provoke a chain reaction as one discovery led to another. The invention of the steam engine dramatically transformed the nature of transport on land and sea, as new steamships and trains proved much faster, more reliable and, eventually, cheaper as a means for transporting troops to the front lines. In fact, the ability to move troops relatively quickly to a state border created the concept of the 'front' by ending long and exhausting marches, ad hoc skirmishes and open-field battles (Giddens 1985: 224).

While the railway boom trebled the speed of movement, increased carrying capacity and allowed for quick replacement of wounded and sick soldiers by fresh contingents, steamships utterly transformed intercontinental commerce and trade, which were the backbone of military might. The rapid improvements in means of transport required technological innovations in communications to co-ordinate the movements of regiments. As telegraph cables were laid close to the fronts and, later, crossed the intercontinental divides (from 1870s to Asia and America), the European imperial powers were able to control the movements of their fleets and armies around the globe. In this way the telegraph also served as a means of further military command centralisation as it 'made possible strategic, and thus political, direction and greatly reduced the scope of local military control' (Hirst 2001: 27). The later invention and mass application of radio communications during WWI made this centralisation even more stringent. With the mass proliferation of newspapers, increased public literacy and the presence of journalists at the fronts, the general public was able, for the first time in history, to immediately follow the events from the battlefields. For example, the detailed depiction of the Crimean War of 1854–5 in newspaper reports (Howard 1976: 98–9) provoked a great deal of interest among the British public thus opening up a debate on its merits and involving civil society in military affairs.[5]

[5] However these scientific and technological changes were not inevitable and have often come across substantial resistance. For example, as the British fleet already reigned supreme many admirals were reluctant to embrace these changes. An 1828 British Admiralty memorandum reads: 'Their Lordships feel it is their bounded duty to discourage to the utmost of their ability the employment of steam vessels, as they consider that the introduction of steam is calculated to strike a fatal blow at the naval supremacy of the Empire' (Lewis 1957: 224; McNeill 1982: 226).

The radical transformation of transport and communication was matched by revolutionary changes in weapons manufacture. The key development was the application of industrial mass-production techniques of standardisation and inter-changeability of parts in weaponry making. The discovery and widespread adoption of the Minie bullet and rifle, able to fire accurately up to 1,000 metres, extended the killing zone of the front lines from 100 to 500 metres and also gave impetus to further military discoveries (Hirst 2001: 28). The 'Bessemer' and 'American' systems of manufacture relied on semi-automatic machines to cut the component parts for weapons to prescribed shapes which permitted an exceptionally fast production rate: 'Whereas in the late 1840s it would have taken Nikolaus von Dreyse thirty years of arti-san production to equip the 320,000 men of the Prussian army with his new "needle-gun", Antoine Alphonese Chassepot after 1866 was able in four years to produce one million of his famous breechloaders for the French army' (Herwig *et al.* 2003: 413). The same industrial techniques and technologies of the assembly line, mechanisation, standardisation, precise measuring and strict division of labour were used for both the military and civilian sec-tors: this system of industrial efficiency was applied equally to Colt revolv-ers, Singer sewing machines and McCormick agricultural machinery (Hirst 2001: 28). However, it is crucial to emphasise that these industrial techniques originated, and were developed first and foremost, for military purposes. As Weber (1968) rightly noticed, it was the rationalisation and bureaucratisa-tion of the military sphere that gave birth to the administrative power of modern nation-states. What started off as a new disciplinary ethics ended as the structural rationalisation of the entire social order. From the second half of the nineteenth century onwards, science, technology, administrative organisation and the military power of nation-states became so integrated and interdependent that now it is almost unthinkable that they could operate independently.

This change was also visible in the transformation of armies and soldiers into state employees. The new military wanted to discard extravagant and mostly ritualistic features of warfare such as brightly coloured clothing, the individual warrior ethos, personal displays of heroism and character of trad-itional battle with it duels, all of which operated at the expense of martial effi-ciency and bureaucratic discipline. Instead of triumphant individual acts of bravery and fraternisation with the crowd, the focus moved to the anonymity of uniformed soldiers who are stationed in the barracks far away from civil-ians. As Giddens (1985: 230) emphasises, on the one hand: 'within the army as an organisation, the uniform has the same implications of disciplinary power as in carceral settings of other types [prisons, hospitals, police service, schools, etc], helping strip individuals of those traits that might interfere with routinised patterns of obedience'. On the other hand, the uniform separates civilians from the military indicating who is 'a specialist purveyor of the means of violence'. The professionalisation of the military that started in the seventeenth century with the first military academies and properly trained officers, reached its pinnacle in the late nineteenth and early twentieth century. From now on the military is run by highly specialised professionals that undergo long institutionalised training, that are separated from the rest of society, have a fixed system of promotion based on skill and experience, follow a consistent system of abstract rules, obey an impersonal hierarchical order where authority is derived from one's position in the hierarchy, are separated from the ownership of the means of production and whose professional relationships are regulated by written technical rules. In other words the modern military is the epitome of Weberian bureaucracy.

Once this process of the cumulative bureaucratisation of coercion took full form, the militaries and states that did not adapt quickly found themselves loosing wars and paying dearly in human lives. For example, in the American Civil War the attacks of the Confederate troops at Malvern Hill in 1862 and Gettysburg in 1863 ended in mass slaughter, as their frontal assault charges were met by the Minie rifles of the Union's mass armies. At Malvern Hill, General Lee lost 5,000 soldiers in two hours, while at Gettysburg, General Pickett sacrificed 7,500 men in less than an hour. Similarly, in the Crimean War, the Russian General Menshikov led a charge in 1854 at Inkerman against British infantry armed with rifles, losing 12,000 soldiers in a day of fighting (Hirst 2001: 28; Herwig *et al.* 2003: 415). Further improvements in armaments such as the invention and mass production of breech-loading cannon, the machine gun and the discovery of smokeless high explosives (lyddite, cordite, melinite), able to combust quickly and increase the range of all weapons to an unprecedented extent, made the battlefield exceptionally deadly (Howard 1976: 103). The machine gun was a potent symbol of the new industrial era – a mass-produced and highly efficient industrial weapon created for mass slaughter. Its quintessential modernity was emphasised by its alienating and dehumanising character: it is a weapon fired from a distance, often by an invisible anonymous soldier, at other numerous, also anonymous, soldiers. It is a weapon that epitomises the structural inequality of the machine against an individual human being as one soldier can kill thousands of others. The focus is on industrial efficiency, with quantity of death surpassing quality of fight. The machine gun breaks down all the traditional military codes of fairness, empathy with fellow soldiers, heroism on the battlefield and the duel-like face-to-face character of pre-modern fights. It is a perfect symbol of instrumental rationality taken to its logical conclusion, an instrument best suited for Clausewitz's absolute war, a weapon that dispenses with any emotional or value rational features of warfare. The machine gun is a true embodiment of the bureaucratisation of coercion in the modern age.

Unlike their traditional counterparts, modern social orders firmly separate warfare from other forms of collective violence: injuring or murdering your fellow citizen is an atrocious and severely punishable offence while slaughtering large numbers of the enemy soldiers in times of war is a sign of exceptional heroism. The cumulative bureaucratisation of coercion is a historical process that ultimately led to a clear and institutional separation between the external and internal forms of violence. While in the pre-modern context the organisational powers of polities were quite limited in their ability to control large areas that were nominally under their rule, with the rise of infrastructural powers modern states were in a position to police almost every stretch of their territory. As a consequence, it neither made much sense for traditional rulers to differentiate peasant rebellions, banditry, piracy, marauders, and local uprisings from the military challenges set by various noblemen, free cities or all-out warfare, nor had they any organisational means to do so. In contrast, modern nation-states, having acquired a near-universal monopoly on the legitimate use of violence, were able to fully monitor and police their territories, thus making certain and obvious what is external and what is internal violence. In this way, as Giddens (1985: 188) rightly points out, states have managed to pacify their domestic political and social arenas by transferring 'the sanctioning capacities of the state from the manifest use of violence to the pervasive use of administrative power in sustaining its rule'. However, the internal pacification that involves criminalisation of all violence except that legitimised by the state meant also the externalisation of violence to the borders of nation-states. In other words, despite the popular opinion that sees modern social orders as less violent when compared to the 'Dark Ages', modernity is in fact structurally much more violent than any previous epoch, not least because it possesses significantly more potent organisational means for violence. However, most of this violence has been external, rather than internal: warfare and conquests, instead of criminal homicides or violent rebellions against the state. As Wimmer and Min (2006) demonstrate empirically through their quantitative analysis of 484 wars fought in the last two centuries, most modern wars have resulted from the institutional transformation of polities – either through the incorporation of smaller political entities into empires during the nineteenth century or via the establishment and spread of nation-states across the world in the twentieth century. Since modern warfare is linked to competing projects of state building, most violence is destined to remain on the outside of states' borders. Hence violence does not disappear with the progression of modern order, it mutates and transforms into violence directed outwards. As political and social beings humans are prone to discords and conflicts, and when human action is institutionally stifled by an omnipotent nation-state and simultaneously channelled towards its borders it is bound to adapt to these alternative institutional outlets and manifest itself elsewhere. The modern nation-state does not erase violence; it only fosters its transformation through its externalisation.

Bureaucratising coercion means also making it more rationalised and less emotional. Collins (1974) argues that most collective violence in the modern age is a form of callousness – cruelty without passion. Unlike the traditional world where torture and mutilation were used to establish and reinforce individual and group position within the social hierarchy, to imprint the sign of one's domination and social status on the resisting other, and was inevitably accompanied by emotional engagement and some degree of empathy between the human beings involved, modern violence is much more depersonalised. An individual is subjected to violence as his or her actions represent an obstacle to fulfilling a particular objective. The formality and impersonality of the modern army allows for maximal callousness: the regulated delegation of tasks and responsibilities, the hierarchical and segmented organisational structure of its bureaucratic machine and personal detachment from its victims, create an ideal situation for emotionless cruelty. As Collins (1974: 433) puts it: 'bureaucratic violence is the psychological opposite of the ceremonial ferocity of patrimonial society; however painful and terrifying the consequences, they are epiphenomenal to the more general policy being carried out'. In the bureaucratic world, violence is nothing more than a rational (or in a given context most rational) means to an end. As modern warfare relies ever more on remote control technology (e.g. the use of high-altitude bombing, gas chambers, long-distance missile fire), it is able to depersonalise violence and distance human contact thus making callous cruelty rampant. However it is important to bear in mind that the bureaucratisation of coercion, and war in particular, involves two different formational layers: objective rationalisation at the institutional level and the subjective rationalisation of individual purveyors of violence (Martin 2005). The two processes are undoubtedly linked and have a direct impact on each other as subjective disciplining of individual human conduct ultimately requires the rational-isation of the institutional apparatus of the modern state and vice versa. This chapter has so far engaged with the institutional bureaucratisation of coer-cion but it is also essential to analyse the other side of the coin – changing subjective perceptions, ideas, values and practices in the context of war and violence. In other words it is paramount to tackle the process of the ideolo-gisation of violence.

The centrifugal ideologisation of coercion

The simplest and most persuasive argument that can be used against the view that human beings are naturally predisposed to war and violence is the fact that most violent actions require intricate and sophisticated processes of col-lective motivation. As Andreski (1968: 187) puts it: 'In every warlike polity (which means in an overwhelming majority of political formations of any kind) there are elaborate social arrangements which stimulate martial ardour by playing upon vanity, fear of contempt, sexual desire, filial and fraternal attachment, loyalty to the group and other sentiments. It seems reasonable to suppose that if there was an innate propensity to war-making, such stimu-lation would be unnecessary. If human beings were in fact endowed with an innate proclivity for war, it would not be necessary to indoctrinate them with warlike virtues; and the mere fact that in so many societies past and present so much time has been devoted to such an indoctrination proves that there is no instinct for war.'

In addition to this essential prerequisite of motivation, without which individuals and groups are unlikely to participate in collective violence, what is an even more important prerequisite of nearly all violent actions is the need for justification. As killing of other human beings goes so much against the grain of moral universes in the great majority of social orders, it neces-sitates potent and believable social mechanisms of justification. While, as discussed in the previous chapters, the pre-modern world found these justi-ficatory mechanisms in proto-ideologies, that is in religious doctrines, myth-ology or imperial ideals, modernity has given birth to more powerful devices of social validation – the secular and secularising ideologies. As explained in the introductory chapter, ideology is understood here in wider terms as a universal social process through which individual and collective agents articulate their beliefs, values, ideas and actions. Since the contents of ideo-logical messages, for the most part, transcend human experience, as they invoke grand vistas of collective authority, they are difficult if not impossible to test. Ideologies act as powerful mobilisers and legitimisers of social action since they are able to appeal effectively to superior moral norms, group interests and affects or advanced knowledge claims. With the Enlightenment, Romanticism and other intellectual and social movements on the one hand, and the French and American Revolutions and the Napoleonic Wars on the other, shaking the foundations of religious authority in Europe, a space was created for the proliferation of new secular doctrines. As religiously underpinned principles of the divine origins of rulers were evaporating so were the institutional and doctrinal bases of the religions themselves. Having now to compete with alternative systems of meaning that were gaining significant popular support and to legitimise their teachings and practice, religions were forced to re-articulate their doctrines in the new ideological, and inevitably secularising, discourses. The new post-Enlightenment and post-revolutionary age created an environment of intensive proliferation of ideologies with an abundance of novel doctrines struggling for the hearts and minds of citizens: from Jacobinism, socialism, Josephism, mercantilism, Jansenism, liberalism, to conservatism and many others. The key ideological transformation happened on the popular level where, for the first time, state authority was not perceived as the property of dynastic rulers, but gained legitimacy through dedication to abstract principles such as liberty, justice, equality, fraternity or nationhood. Once peasants and the urban poor started conceiving of themselves as being of equal moral worth to their former superiors – bishops, aristocrats and bourgeoisie – the age of ideology was truly born. In this context I introduce the concept of centrifugal (mass-scale) ideologisation; that is, a significantly wider proliferation of ideological discourses that radiate from the centre of a particular social organisation (e.g. the state, social movement, religious institution, the military etc.) but also have strong popular resonances.

The immediate aftermath of the French Revolution, the early 1790s, was particularly characterised by the ideological zeal of both officers and ordinary soldiers who responded to the battle-cry of *patrie en danger*. Revolutionary élan and the belief that one is fighting for the utter survival of the only just and therefore rational and morally superior state in the world against the forces of darkness spurred thousands of recruits to take up arms. The importance of ideology was evident in the fact that soldiers regularly sang political anthems that glorified the revolution, with three thousand revolutionary songs written between 1789 and 1799 (Taylor 2003: 152), wore explicitly republican uniforms, hyped the leaders of the revolution and enthusiastically cheered anti-royalist rallying calls. More vitally, the military was well aware of the significance of ideological commitments. The Committee of Public Safety launched and distributed 29,000 copies of its own journal to military units in one day (Taylor 2003: 152) while 'Minister of War, Bouchotte encouraged the troops to read the most radical political opinions of the day, distributing newspapers to the armies at public expense. Even the newspapers of Marat and Hebert were sent out to the garrisons in the north and the east; all in all, some 1,800,000 copies of Hebert's *Rere Duchesne* were purchased by the War Ministry for the education of the troops' (Forrest 2005: 61).[6] Furthermore, as the ideals of the French Revolution spread throughout Europe many ordinary soldiers sympathised with these ideas and were reluctant to fight the republican armies. For example, many recruits in the Netherlands and northern Italy quickly switched sides for ideological reasons (Keegan 1994: 352). On the other side, monarchist and clerical anti-revolutionary forces relied on the peasantry in the Vendée and Brittany to fight the republican armies. This ideological dissent quickly demonstrated the actual limits of the Enlightenment's high principles of toleration, as the rebels were ruthlessly crushed with 160,000 out of 800,000 inhabitants killed (Townshend 2005: 179).

The context of protracted and vicious warfare with huge human casualties, underpinned by an uncompromising conflict of values, created a Manichean ideological environment where war had to be won regardless of the number of dead. This adamant zeal is perfectly illustrated by Saint-Just's call to annihilate everything that opposed the Republic and Carnot's proclamation that: 'War is a violent condition: one should make it *á l'outrance* or go home. We must exterminate, exterminate to the bitter end!' (Howard 1976: 81). This unprecedented extremism was not an aberration of revolutionary ideals, but directly stemmed from the core principles of the ideological doctrine that was perceived as an absolute truth. As the Enlightenment's central goal was the establishment of a better, more rational and more just society, any opposition to this project could only be interpreted as irrational, deliberately unjust and ultimately evil and there could never be a dialogue or compromise with evil; evil must be crushed. As Bauman (1987, 1991) argues, this was an engineering aspiration bent on creating an orderly totality. The key idea was to articulate a blueprint of an ideal social order and then implement this perfect design regardless of the human costs. Revolutionaries were driven by belief in the existence of a universal, singular truth which, once found, would guarantee

---

[6] The American Revolution also stimulated dissemination of the new republican vision of social order. For example Richard Price's book *On Civil Liberty* sold 200,000 copies (Taylor 2003: 138).

the road to happiness for all. In their view the Enlightenment intellectuals were in possession of the cognitive, ethical and esthetical powers which could finally distinguish knowledge from superstition, ethical principles from unethical ones, or beauty from kitsch, and they saw themselves as the ultimate guardians of these fundamental certainties. Anybody who obstructed the implementation of these rationally conceived grand vistas of perfect social order had simply to be removed as obstacles. In this sense, guardians of the Enlightenment acted as diligent gardeners focused on eradicating all the 'mucky weeds' that might ruin the perfect image of a new social order (Gellner 1983; Bauman 1989). As modernity has no patience with ambiguities of any kind the secular progressive Republic could not tolerate the existence of the monarchist and priestly peasants in the Vendée.

With the further rise of science and new social and political theories, the second half of the nineteenth and the beginning of the twentieth century saw an increased impact of ideology on warfare. Although the period between 1870 and 1914 was often referred as the long peace, this hides the fact that European powers were waging imperial wars on other continents and crushing class and regional rebellions at home. As Halperin (2004: 120) documents, in this period European states fought thirty-four wars outside Europe, twelve within European borders and were involved in extremely violent domestic 'class warfare': 'Violent conflict was a fundamental dimension of Europe's industrial expansion in the nineteenth and early twentieth centuries: interstate and cross-border wars; ethnic and nationalist; religious and ideological conflicts; riots, insurrections, rebellions, revolutions, uprisings, violent strikes, and demonstrations; coups, assassinations, brutal repression, and terrorism were characteristic of European societies until 1945'.

Although traditional interpretations of colonialism from J.A. Hobson and Lenin to the world system model of Wallerstein overwhelmingly focused on the economic benefits of imperial powers, it seems that in many respects late nineteenth century European imperialism was more of a political, ideological and military, than economic, phenomenon. As Porch (2005: 94) argues and documents well: 'imperialism moved forward, not as a result of commerce or political pressure from London, Paris, Berlin, St. Petersburg, or even Washington, but mainly because men on the periphery, many of whom were soldiers, pressed to expand the boundaries of empire, often without orders, even against orders'.

The ever-increasing popularity of Darwinist interpretations of social life combined with the imperial doctrine of *mission civilisatrice* provided the key ideological glue for imperial expansion. Both of these value systems were grounded deeply in the Enlightenment heritage: while the civilising mission was all about transforming primitive and uncivilised indigenous rustics into proper civilised human beings on the model of their colonial masters, social Darwinism emphasised the inevitability and the violent character of this process, as those who do not adapt were destined to perish. As the extremely popular British social Darwinist, Benjamin Kidd whose book *Social Evolution* (1894: 46) was published in numerous editions, puts it: 'the winning societies gradually extinguish their competitors, the weaker peoples disappear before the stronger, and the subordination or exclusion of the least efficient is still the prevailing feature of advancing humanity'. Whereas early imperial conquests required little explanation and no justification, the second half of the nineteenth century was different in the sense that colonial occupation required an ideological legitimisation. The universally shared assumption of the cultural superiority of the European colonisers was now reinforced by the scientific/biological discourses that validated this unequal relationship and by the imperial ethics of obligation towards the inferior subjects of their rule (aptly summarised in Kipling's *White Man's Burden*). The imperial rule was perceived as the only rational and just policy 'to open up the dark places of the world, as they were seen, to the light ... while conservatives justified the imperial mission in terms of upholding law and order, the liberals saw it as preparing peoples who were still *in statu pupillari* for eventual self-rule' (Howard 1991: 26–7). Most of all, imperialism remained a military project, as empires were won, extended and defended through warfare and in this sense 'the military virtues were thus considered part of the essence of an Imperial Race' (Howard 1991: 63).

As mutinies, rebellions and wars spread throughout the colonies, the imperial powers were forced to switch from indirect rule through the trading companies to direct administrative rule backed up by a stronger military presence that extensively relied on indigenous recruitment. For example, in this period the British Empire was involved in conflicts in India (1857 Mutiny), South Africa (Boer and Zulu Wars), Egypt and the Ashanti region of Ghana. Many rebellions were mercilessly crushed, with the German massacre of Hereros and Namaqua (South West Africa) in 1904–7 qualifying as the first ideologically driven genocide of the modern era.

The successes and failures of imperial militarism and geopolitical competition had direct implications at home in Europe as well. The beginning of the twentieth century saw the urban middle classes, as well as the cultural and political elites of the major imperial powers, disenchanted with liberal and pacifist ideas and openly supporting the idea of war. Although in Germany militarism had a longer (Prussian) tradition and wider following among the middle classes and intellectuals; Britain, France and other states were also heavily infused with similar ideas that glorified war. While German writers and generals such as Bernhardi, Moltke and Goltz saw war as a Christian virtue that develops nobility of spirit, courage and self-sacrifice or as a means through which nations transact their business, British intellectuals such as Kidd, Low and Pearson among others argued that war is a precondition of progress and as such is righteous, necessary and inevitable. As J. A. Cramb put it: 'War is the supreme act in the life of the State, and it is the motives which impel, the ideal which is pursued, that determine the greatness or insignificance of that act' (quoted by Howard 1991: 75; French 2005: 83).

However, it is important to emphasise that militarism was a phenomenon associated largely with some social groups and classes rather than involving all. As Mann (1993) demonstrates, since the peasantry and manual workers of most European states had not achieved full citizenship rights by 1914 they did not perceive the nation-states as 'theirs' in the same way the middle classes, intellectuals or state bureaucrats did, and were either indifferent or passively opposed to the increasing glorification of warfare. This was more the case in the eastern half of the continent where the peasantry dominated numerically without having any proper civil rights and the middle classes were tiny and, for the most part, politically insignificant. In contrast, the political and military establishments, state careerists, cultural elites and much of the middle classes in the western half of the continent conceptualised the world in hard geopolitical terms and strongly identified with their nation-states. In other words, although it was a very powerful new ideology, nationalism, and particularly aggressive, jingoistic nationalism, was still confined to the minority of European populations, nevertheless, as the key institutional mechanisms for dissemination of nationalist messages, such as the state administration, educational institutions, publishing presses and mass media, were mostly in the hands of militarists, the veneration of the nation-state as a sacred object of self-sacrifice became the principal social value. The study of the classics, the cult of heroism and manliness, and an absence of the horrors of warfare in Europe for more than forty years, were all instrumental in forging the sense that the nation-state is a divine and eternal entity whose honour and prestige are unquestioned and if attacked requires the ultimate heroic sacrifice. To a large extent this view was shared also by many leading politicians and guided policy recommendations; as Stone (1983) shows, the correspondence and the diplomatic and private documentation of 'high politics', were preoccupied with the issues of state prestige, national strategy and status.

In the early twentieth century, as the geopolitical balance of power drastically changed with the creation and expansion of the new German Empire, which had the most vibrant economy in Europe and was swiftly catching up with Britain, tensions, mutual fears and conflicting aspirations among European powers were emerging to the point of no return. WWI was in part fuelled by objective geopolitical, military and ideological differences and in part by subjective perceptions of the other side's true intentions. As with all large-scale historical events, it was a result of many unintended consequences and contingently provoked chain reactions. There was a clear discrepancy between an autocratic Germany ruled by a militarist dynasty and dominated by the landed aristocracy (Junkers) at the top of a largely agrarian society, and an economically and politically liberal, industrialised and urbanised Britain that ultimately relied on its naval supremacy and the benefits of free trade for its position as the centre of the wealthiest and most powerful empire in the world. For stagnant semi-feudal Austro-Hungary beset by rising inter-ethnic conflicts, absolutist, impoverished, highly conservative and undeveloped Russia and economically and imperially fading France whose peasant smallholders prevented proper reform, the war meant a postponement of the inevitable social transformation.

Although everybody expected a short, intense conflict with a clear and decisive outcome, the result was a long, protracted, inconclusive war, by far the bloodiest Europe had yet witnessed. Despite the speedy mobilisation and advancement that modern technology afforded to the German troops, the fact that the French armies managed to hold their ground in the first two years of war in the face of enormous losses meant that the conflict degenerated into a horrific war of attrition with huge human casualties and little military success. Although ordinary soldiers became quickly disenchanted with war, often empathising with the soldiers in the enemy trenches and finding ways to avoid shooting directly at each other (Ashworth 1968; 1980), the military organisation made certain that the killing ratios remained high.[7] The scale of military mobilisation was historically unparalleled, with Germany and France having 4 million men by 1914, of which 2 million French and 1.7 million German soldiers fought each other on the Western Front (Howard 2002: 20). In addition Austro-Hungary had 1.3 million soldiers at its disposal whereas Russia mobilised 3.4 million. Since Britain had no conscription

---

[7] Ashworth (1968: 411) points out: 'The Live and Let Live principle was an informal and collective agreement between front-line soldiers of opposing armies to inhibit offensive activity to a level mutually defined as tolerable. This understanding was tacit and covert; it was expressed in activity or nonactivity rather than in verbal terms. The norm was supported by the system of sanctions.'

until 1916 it had to rely on volunteers; Lord Kitchener's campaign managed to recruit 2.5 million volunteers (Herwig *et al.* 2003: 484). As such a huge number of men were sent to the fronts it was necessary for the rest of society to undergo a similar process of re-organisation and mobilisation for the war cause. The mass production of arms and military supplies required mass factories and mass labour, continuous technological developments and efficient mass transport which all depended on the productive apparatus of industrialism. This also included reliance on the mass communication systems, mass propaganda and centralised organisation able to co-ordinate these complex and large social systems.

WWI was an industrial war but it was also the first total war involving and demanding the vast mobilisation of entire societies for the war cause. This was the first large-scale violent conflict that could rely on the most advanced organisational, technological and ideological means to unite the military and civilian sectors by breaking the distinction between combatants and non-combatants, between those at the front lines of battles and those supporting them in the rear, and eventually between the public and private spheres. Contributing to the war effort became a central objective for all members of society regardless of their individual wills. The state's powers dramatically increased as it took over control of the economy, and political and social life. This stifled the struggle between capital and labour. The state projected an ideological image of a unified, trans-class, trans-gender, trans-age, solidary nation confronting a ferocious adversary. What initially started off as a geopolitical conflict for the balance of power was transformed into an ideological struggle for the preservation of the human soul. While British and French media depicted Germany as ruthless and savage in its militarism and bent on destroying all civilisational advancements, the German propaganda machine interpreted the war in terms of a fight 'for a unique *Kultur* against Slavic barbarism on the one hand, and on the other, the frivolity and decadence of French civilisation and the British shopkeeper's materialism of the Anglo-Saxons' (Howard 2002: 40). As the war escalated and human casualties increased to unprecedented levels, the ideological conflict became fiercer. The enormity of the death toll created a sense of moral responsibility for sacrifice which could only be redeemed by ultimate victory on the battlefield, as peace without victory would make this sacrifice meaningless. The war intensified the already ongoing processes of centrifugal ideologisation with nationalism now becoming a dominant discursive framework for the majority of the population. The scale and intensity of war generated the cult of the fallen soldier which romanticised and glorified death on the battlefield as a sacred public event of courage and national importance and a 'prelude to their resurrection', which was contrasted with an ordinary, even cowardly, profane private death of insignificance. Military cemeteries became places of pilgrimage as the celebration of the war dead aimed to 'make an inherently unpalatable past [and present] acceptable, important not just for the purpose of consolation but above all for the justification of the nation in whose name the war had been fought' (Mosse 1991: 7). The final result was 13 million dead and over 20 million wounded (Herwig *et al.* 2003: 511). Not only had four years of horrendous, destructive war not brought the solutions to its causes, but, instead, its outcome created new structural problems that eventually led to another total war.

WWII remains by far the largest and most violent conflict ever fought on this planet, resulting in 55 million dead (Overy 2005: 138). It relied on highly developed infrastructural powers of states which were able to penetrate all social layers and mobilise entire societies for war at an extent and speed unseen before. As Overy (2005: 154) documents: 'The major combatants mobilised between a half and two-thirds of their industrial work-force, and devoted up to three-quarters of their national product to waging war.' One cause of the war was the fierce scientific and technological competition that dramatically accelerated the rate of scientific discovery and the mass application of new technologies in weaponry production and consequently in other spheres of life as well. It was also a huge macro-level conflict that required an extremely powerful and sophisticated social organisation able to co-ordinate and integrate different sectors of society and state into a well-oiled military machine. To mobilise and control all the human and material resources the states introduced largely coercive military command planning in the economy. Most of all, this was a war of uncompromising ideological projects which pitted national socialism, scientific racism and fascism against liberal polyarchy and state socialism. Whereas Nazi Germany and its allies were bent on creating a Reich that would last a thousand years where the Aryans would rule and Slavs would provide slave labour and Jews and many others would be exterminated, the Soviet Union's ambition was to demonstrate the superiority of the workers' state which would eventually bring about the collapse of global capitalism and the proliferation of communist revolutions worldwide. The handful of Western polyarchies, led by Britain, the USA and the remnants of the French Empire, were primarily interested in the liberalisation of trade and moderate expansion of liberal principles, all of which favoured a peaceful international arena and were, as the appeasement policies of 1930s and the so-called 'phoney war' of 1940 clearly demonstrate, reluctant to fight.[8] However, once the violence was unleashed there was little moderation on either side.

While the ferocity of violence in the WWI was exceptional (many taboos were broken, such as the deliberate destruction of civilian economic targets (e.g. commercial vessels etc.)), WWII left virtually no taboos unbroken. Entire cities were carpet-bombed and no significant distinction was made between the military and civilians if thought to be on the enemy side. However, WWII will always be remembered by the German state's policy of the systematic destruction of entire groups of people: Jews, Slavs, Romanies, homosexuals and the disabled. What separates genocide from traditional massacres and mass killings is its ideological and organisational modernity. It is a process whereby the modern state's monopoly of violence is employed in implementing a particular blueprint of an ideal social order which, in the case of Nazi Germany, meant an ethnically, physically and heterosexually pure society. The speed, efficiency and management of the 'Final Solution' was rooted in the advanced division of labour, hierarchical delegation of tasks and instrumental rationality – all hallmarks of modern social organisation. As Bauman (1989: 8) argues, the Holocaust was achieved through the imposition of dull bureaucratic routine where discipline was substituted for moral responsibility, as concentration camps operated on the same principle as the modern factory system: 'Rather than producing goods, the raw material was human beings and the end product was death, so many units per day marked carefully on the manager's production charts. The chimneys, the very symbol of the modern factory system, poured forth acrid smoke produced by burning human flesh. The brilliantly organised railroad grid of modern Europe carried a new kind of raw material to the factories.'

The centrality of sophisticated organisation was visible from the start of the war when the German blitzkrieg in some respects repeated Napoleon's strategy of speedy, efficient co-ordination and grouping of overwhelming force on one point of attack which was aimed at demoralising the opponent by breaking its social organisation. Through the combination of armour and aircraft with the rapid deployment of large-scale infantry and impeccable

---

[8] Halperin (2004: 200–31) convincingly argues that the politics of appeasement was deeply grounded in the Allies' fear of the Soviet Union since as late as 1940 the British Establishment focused on the class dimension and perceived the Soviet Union as a far greater threat to the UK than Nazi Germany. Lloyd George and conservative public opinion saw Nazi Germany as a 'bulwark against Bolshevism'. In Lloyd George's own words: 'In a very short time, perhaps in a year or two, the Conservative elements in this country will be looking to Germany as the bulwark against Communism in Europe … Do not let us be in a hurry to condemn Germany. We shall be welcoming Germany as our friend' (Halperin 2004: 222).

radio communications, the German armies were able to conquer huge swathes of the European continent. German Air Force General Milch explained the mystery of blitzkrieg: 'The real secret is speed – speed of attack through speed of communication' (Welchman 1982: 20). Novel technological inventions such as smaller and better radio communication, a new generation of weapons including large tanks and large-calibre mobile artillery, centimetric radar, fast monoplane fighter aircraft and pre-packed mass-produced food, all changed the character of warfare. The wartime arms race would eventually produce remarkably sophisticated technological breakthroughs such as rocket jet propulsion, complex weapons systems and nuclear weapons.

However, it is important to note that despite its organisational superiority Germany started the war with a much weaker economic base than its foes. For example, the Allied powers were in possession of 'at least twice the manufacturing strength, three times the "war potential", and three times the national income of the Axis powers, even when French shares are added to Germany's total' (Goldsmith 1946; Halperin 2004: 225). As war progressed, this structural weakness became more pronounced and Germany's military industry started to lag behind dramatically. By 1942 the Allies were producing twice as many tons of steel, four times as many aircraft and tanks and seven times as many machine guns and artillery pieces as their opponents (Herwig *et al.* 2003: 512). At the same time, the overstretching of forces, the significant losses on the Eastern Front and the severity of the climatic conditions forced the German state, in 1943, to revert to the traditional technology of earlier wars, including a heavy reliance on horse power: 'During 1942 German industry turned out only 59,000 trucks for an army of 8 million men, but the same year 400,000 horses were sent to the Eastern Front' (Overy 2005: 146). The great irony of WWII is that the German Reich was defeated largely by the very forces that Nazi ideology deemed to be subhuman and inferior in every respect – 'the Slavic hordes of the East', since the German military machine was broken on the Eastern Front. The large-scale battles of Stalingrad, Kursk, Moscow and Leningrad exhausted and severely depleted German armies; the Red Army 'destroyed some 607 divisions of German and allied forces between 1941 and 1945. Two-thirds of German tank losses were inflicted on the Eastern Front' (Overy 2005: 148).

The direct outcome of WWII was the emergence of the two ideologically opposed superpowers which were to dominate the globe for the next forty-five years. However, what is central in their historically sudden and dramatic rise was the military machines built to achieve victory in WWII. The American distance from the theatres of both world wars spared its cities from destruction, while war mobilisation of the American economy helped increase industrial output spectacularly so that living standards rose by an average of 75 per cent per person (Overy 2005: 156). Not only did the war experience help integrate the USA into the world economy, but it also forced it to transform, expand and modernise its military; by 1944 the US Army was the most modern army in the world. On the other side, despite enormous human losses and the scale of devastation of its urban and rural areas, the Soviet Union managed to recover quickly. By militarising its economy and, eventually, most other spheres of social life, the Soviet state demonstrated how far a successful combination of modern authoritarian social organisation and modern ideological monopoly can go. The clear legacy of the two total wars was a further increase in the organisational and ideological powers of modern states.

War and violence between ideology and social organisation

Although most pre-modern polities generated political power from military might and occasionally from proto-ideological validation, modern social orders are different in the sense that they, unlike their predecessors, are able both to enforce their coercive power on every stretch of their territory and to ideologically mobilise and legitimise this power. Whereas the traditional rulers had no organisational means to control large swathes of territory and had to rely on the support of local notables, modern nation-states are bureaucratic machines capable of monopolising all essential means of violence within their borders. Similarly, while pre-modern power-holders ruled over hierarchically segmented and culturally diverse illiterate peasants devoid of any sense of universal equality, modern nation-states derive legitimacy from the popularly shared belief that its inhabitants are all members of the same, principally egalitarian and, in key respects, culturally homogenous, nation. The historical transformation from the pre-modern to modern forms of rule owes a great deal to the two processes explored in this chapter – the cumulative bureaucratisation and centrifugal ideologisation of coercion. As I have tried to show in this and the previous chapters, these two processes were historically contingent, gradual and slow to emerge but once the institutional seeds of ideational and organisational power were planted, they grew exponentially to create the modern, infrastructurally, ideologically and coercively powerful nation-state. As states developed and were strengthened by internally monopolising violence and increasing ideological accord, they helped foster a sense, shared by most modern individuals, that modernity is much less violent than its historical predecessors. As the borders of nation-states became the boundaries of distinct, internally pacified, societies, any comparison with the pre-modern world seemed destined to pinpoint a sharp decline in everyday violence. After all, we do not crucify heretics, bend bodies on the wheel or boil people alive in our town squares. However, it is important to take into account that with domestic pacification violence has not vanished, it has only been transformed – mostly through externalisation into warfare. The birth of the modern age saw the rampant intensification of external collective violence – from the upheavals of the French and American Revolutions, the Napoleonic wars and colonial massacres to the total wars of the twentieth century.

What is distinct in this development is the fact that the enormous scale of human sacrifice in the nineteenth and twentieth century wars has not dented the structures of social cohesion in modern nation-states. On the contrary, the magnitude of the death toll has substantially increased one form of internal collective solidarity which in the process acquired firm ideological underpinning – nationalism (see Chapter 6). The internally shared perception that 'our' nation is morally and ideologically right and that 'our' actions are universally justifiable combined with the power of modern social organisation, able to put and hold millions of people in the war machine, has created an environment that fosters the emergence of ontological dissonance.

To reconcile the modern view that all human beings are of equal moral worth, and that human life is precious, with the everyday practice of mass extermination, a person has to deny humanity to his or her enemy. In the pre-modern world there was no structural need to depict your enemy as less than human: not only because this was a profoundly hierarchical world where everybody knew his or her place and where peasants were perceived and saw themselves as an inferior species when compared to nobility or town dwellers, but also because most wars were fought between warrior nobles engaged in ritualistic exercises involving mutual respect. Hence, by declaring universal equality, the modern age also opens the door wide for unimaginable cruelty, as any slide to protracted warfare creates conditions for the dehumanisation of the enemy. In this way, nominal equality in times of war proves to be a major disadvantage, since in order to delegitimise the actions of the adversary one has to demonstrate his or her illegibility for membership of the human race. In other words, for mass killings to happen, it is necessary to overcome ingrained values, inculcated through the long-term processes of primary and secondary socialisation, which cherish and treasure human life. To do so successfully, the nation-states and individuals themselves have to portray and understand their enemies as monsters and animals who have no regard for human moral principles and whose actions prove their intrinsic inhumanity. In order to exempt them from universal ethical standards, the Nazi state had, paradoxically, to depict Jews both as subhuman and super-human. To make a small, politically insignificant and largely invisible seg-ment of German society look dangerous, threatening and highly discernible it was essential to conceptualise Jews both as animals (parasites, vermin, etc.) and as exceptionally skilful plotters who were able to mastermind the takeover of the entire world (Judeo-Bolshevik conspiracy). The fact that most Jews were so assimilated and integrated in the German society was taken as a further proof of their (superhuman and subhuman) devious, canny and un-human nature. Similarly, one of the first twentieth century genocides, the mass killings of Armenians in 1915, was orchestrated and executed not by an authoritarian, backward and decaying empire but by the modernising, secular and Westernised Young Turks movement, bent on creating a modern culturally homogenous nation-state. To implement this ideological blueprint they had to represent the ordinary Armenian peasantry as a treacherous fifth column endangering the very existence of the modern Turkish state. They too became understood as subhuman and superhuman at the same time.

It is no historical accident that genocide is a phenomenon of modern times, as any attempt to systematically annihilate entire groups of people on the basis of their cultural difference requires the existence of both modern social organisation and modern ideology. Although contemporary humans are prone to think of their lives as being less constrained by external controls and substantially freer than those of their historical predecessors, the general increase in the organisational and ideological powers of the modern states indicates otherwise.

The key principle of any social organisation is hierarchy. Bureaucracy would not be able to function if it was not clear who gives orders to whom and if incompliance was not punished. A bureaucratic hierarchy is premised upon the relationship of the dominating and the submissive; hence follow-ing orders automatically implies the presence of external constraints and a willing obedience. In other words, the hierarchical relationships of the pre-modern world, whereby one is submissive to king or a despot, are replaced with another and much more efficient form of submission – institutional obedience channelled through organisational supremacy. As hierarchy is now seen as justified (a further sign of increasing ideological power in mod-ernity) since the compliance is derived from institutional rules and regula-tions, rather than from the vacillating human will, it acquires much more structural potency. However, the fact that bureaucratic hierarchy is more legitimate and more efficient than patrimonial systems of rule, neither makes it more pleasant nor its outcomes less violent. On the contrary, precisely because the modern bureaucratic machine has nearly universal validation, organisational strength and efficiency, it is more likely to generate large-scale systematic murder. Modern bureaucracy is not only better at achieving the submission of huge groups of people but it is also better at breaking the bonds of micro-level intra-group solidarity, as the institutional compartmentalisation of responsibility dissolves the common moral universe and makes social agency invisible. It is in this sense that the 'Eichmann syndrome' in which the individual's sense of ethical responsibility is eliminated through bureaucratic diligence and the strict following of orders is truly possible only in the modern age of advanced social organisation. The instrumental rationality of administrative apparatus thus transforms morality into institutional efficiency.

Similarly, the military bureaucratic machine applies the same principles of efficiency and productivity as a modern factory and is valued accordingly. Caputo (1977: 160) illustrates this well in the context of the Vietnam War: 'the measures of a unit's performance in Vietnam were not the distances it had advanced or the number of victories it had won, but the number of enemy soldiers it had killed (the body count) and the proportion between that number and the number of its own dead (the kill ratio)'. Hence if the number of killed Vietcong significantly surpassed the number of dead American soldiers, the organisational rationality would imply an absolute military success. In times of war this instrumental rationality is wedded with value rationality, that is, ideology, as a society that finds itself in the condition of total war has an overarching goal and values associated with this goal – a commonly shared *telos* of wining the war. While in peacetime there is no common ultimate purpose, as social and individual agents pursue their own aims, in wartime values and interests bring organisational and ideological power to the forefront: the actions of an entire society are to be governed by a single purpose. The enormous killing fields of modern battlefields, the efficiency of mass extermination through genocidal policies and the unparalleled kill ratios of twentieth century warfare all demonstrate that when it comes to successful mass murder the contemporary nation-state has no historical equivalent. No other political entity has had such potent organisational means at its disposal to coerce individuals to pursue a single military purpose, and has been able to rely on the most sophisticated mechanisms to ideologically justify such a goal.

Conclusion

There is something profoundly disturbing in modernity's relationship with war and violence. Although our age, like none before, nominally despises any use of violence, it has also generated more bloodshed and destruction than all previous historical periods combined. This is not to say that modern individuals are more violent than their pre-modern predecessors per se; on the contrary, it is precisely because contemporary humans do not tolerate individual acts of violence that they invoke the authority of an external, coercive, arbiter – the nation-state. However, the very fact that we surrender our individual or group right to violence to the monopolistic social organisation in exchange for long-term security creates a situation where such organisations gradually accumulate more coercive power which ultimately can be, and is used, against us and other human beings. In other words, the large-scale social organisations, such as the nation-states, become simultaneously realms of individual liberty and of collective imprisonment: to free ourselves from domestic robbers and individual murderers we either become state-sponsored killers ourselves (through military conscription in war) or we directly or indirectly justify such killings (through ideological legitimisation). Hence, by attempting to circumvent perpetual ontological dissonance, modern humans find themselves in a paradoxical situation in which they reinforce the very sources of this dissonance: ideologies and social organisations. To delegitimise killing and destruction caused by social organisations coated in ideological discourses, modern humans invoke further ideologies and demand action on behalf of other organisations. Even though they are both products of human action and can be transformed, or possibly even eradicated, by human action, social organisations and ideologies remain overpowering precisely because, once set in motion, there is little possibility of breaking this vicious circle.

Although the historical origins of this structural trap go all the way back to the states of Mesopotamia and Egypt, it is on the European continent that the cumulative bureaucratisation of coercion and centrifugal ideologisation have developed as fully fledged and highly discernible processes. To understand why this is so, it is paramount to explore the role war and violence have played in the social development of other continents.

5 The social geographies of warfare

Introduction

The dramatic economic rise of the European states in the last few centuries and their nearly absolute global political dominance in the nineteenth and early twentieth centuries has often been referred to as 'the European miracle' (Jones 1987). Although historical sociologists generally agree that after lagging behind for a long period of time Europe suddenly surged ahead of Asia and other continents, there is no agreement as to when, how and why this happened. There are basically two contrasting views of this development which, for the sake of simplicity, can be termed 'Europeanist' and 'non-Europeanist'. Europeanists (Hall 1985; Mann 1986; Jones 1987; Gellner 1988a) argue that the fundamental breakthrough to modernity emerged only in pre-industrial Western Europe and was deeply rooted in the continent's unique geographical, demographic, ecological and geopolitical position. In contrast, non-Europeanists (Pomeranz 2000; Goldstone 2002; Hobson 2004; Darwin 2008) see this rise as occurring much later (nineteenth century) and link it primarily to the birth of the industrial revolution, the incidental availability of cheap and abundant coal reserves in Britain and the acquisition of essential resources from the New World colonies. Europeanists stress the internal sources of this transformation, such as the relatively unique multipolar system of competitive states that encouraged the growth of civil society and hence limited rulers' despotic powers. In contrast non-Europeanists attribute more importance to external causes such as the exploitative character of European imperialism and colonialism.

What is of particular interest in this debate is the contrasting interpretations of the role warfare and military power played in the rise of European dominance. While most non-Europeanists understand warfare through the prism of its economic irrationality and destructiveness while deducing military might from economic supremacy, some Europeanists (Hall 1985; 1987; Mann 1986; 1988; 2007) emphasise the autonomy of geopolitics and focus on military competition as a driving force of European modernisation. In other words, for the non-Europeanists warfare is nothing more than a mechanism of territorial conquest whereby European empires waged wars to acquire resources for expanding capitalist and industrialist economies, while for Europeanists warfare can have both destructive and constructive outcomes. They argue that whereas in Imperial China, India and the Islamic world, warfare was parasitic and highly damaging, pre-industrial European wars played essentially a productive role in the birth of modernity. The contention is that, unlike other early civilisations, European military competition, under the common normative roof of Christianity, prevented mutual extermination while simultaneously allowing for the expansion of autonomous economic and political institutions.

The general argument of this chapter, which also follows the thread of the last two chapters (3 and 4), is closer to the original Europeanist proposition that modernity owes a great deal to the pre-industrial dynamics of warfare in Europe. However, it differs from the Europeanists account in three ways. Firstly, it emphasises that warfare was the catalyst of modernisation outside of Western Europe too. This is most clearly evident from the cases of the Ottoman Empire, Imperial Russia and Japan and the rise of the USA. Secondly, it aims to bring together some claims of the Europeanists and non-Europeanists in attempting to show under which structural conditions the outcome of warfare is likely to be socially destructive or productive. Finally, it attempts to go beyond the instances of 'continental determinism' and 'cultural essentialism' that hard notions of 'West' and 'East' regularly imply. Following the discussion from the previous two chapters that focused predominantly on the Western European experience, the idea here is to compare and contrast developments in Western Europe with the rest of the 'old' and 'new' world.

The old world

Any large-scale historical and geographical comparison encounters the problem of what the unit of analysis should be. The standard practice is to opt for one of the following categories: civilisations, continents, nations, states, societies or regions. However all of these are highly suspect, ambiguous and problematic. The concept of civilisation implies a degree of bounded homogeneity and territorial closure that has no empirical equivalent, as cultures are highly dynamic, malleable and overlapping entities, and it is nearly impossible to delineate precisely the ending of one and beginning of another civilisation in either space or time. Using continents as parameters of one's analysis is equally troubling as this suggests a form of geographical determinism which would imply that inhabitants of the same continent somehow are predisposed towards an identical course of action by the mere fact of populating the same continent. Similarly, using a region as a unit of analysis just replicates this problem on a smaller scale as the division into regions also implies the inhabitants' homogeneity and similarity while such divisions are often arbitrary, changeable and provisional. Finally writing about nations, states or nation-states encounters the problem of the intrinsic modernity of these concepts, and hence inapplicability before the modern era, as pre-modern polities clearly lacked the cultural homogeneity and territorial boundness that characterises modern nation-states. Finally, adopting the term society is just as problematic since pre-modern social orders were composed of highly stratified and hierarchically organised social layers which did not constitute 'society' in any sociological meaningful sense. In addition, the modern use of society as something that is confined to the borders of a particular nation-state is equally flawed as it presumes social homogeneity, where there are multiple crisscrossing horizontal and vertical social networks. Thus for example, writing about India in 354 BCE and India today might wrongly suggest that this is the same political and cultural entity while in fact there is very little in common between the two. Treating India as a separate and stand-alone civilisation, sub-continent, nation-state, region or society is bound to project a static trans-historical image of a geographical and social entity that has experienced tremendous transformation throughout history. Although it is quite difficult to avoid this problem of categorical equivalency altogether,[1] it is paramount to circumvent culturally and politically essentialist categories (such as 'West' and 'East', 'European civilisation' and 'Islamic world'), to try to work within time-specific categories of analysis (e.g. empire, city-state) and adopt less essentialist universal concepts such as 'social and political orders', 'collectivities' or 'polities'.[2]

The aim of conceptual clarity is not to be over pedantic with the categories and terms used but primarily to avoid projecting contemporary concepts and modes of thinking into the past. What is distinct about most pre-industrial

---

[1] As much of the academic literature is written in this discourse I too will have to make reference and use such categories as 'continents', 'regions' or 'states' but will try to avoid essentialist language that would imply homogeneity where there often was none.

[2] For persuasive critiques of the reificatory and essentialist use of concepts such as 'nations' or 'societies' see Billig 1995 and Jenkins 2002.

polities is that even when they were framed in intensive civilisational and proto-ideological colours, such as Confucianism in Ming China or Sunni Islam in the Ottoman Empire, there was little if any cross-class or cross-status cultural unity between the inhabitants of these empires. As John A. Hall (1985: 30) rightly argues, these were 'capstone governments' where the elite sat atop a huge peasantry unable to penetrate deep into the social structure of their empires. The two groups had little in common: 'the elite sometimes did not even bother itself with the magical rubbish that the masses believed, and such "tolerance" characterised much of Chinese and Roman imperial history; in other cases, such as those of Latin Christendom and Islam, there remained a massive difference between the "Great" tradition of the educated elite and the "Little" tradition of peasants and pastoralists'. The conspicuous feature of nearly all agrarian empires is the non-existence of a shared normative universe, that is, the non-existence of a unitary 'society', 'nation' or 'civilisation'.

China

Although for hundreds of years much of the old world shared these structural capstone features, the emergence of a multipolar system of independent polities within the Latin Christendom at the end of twelfth century created an institutional seed that was decisive for their eventual political dominance over the rest of the world. However, there was nothing inevitable in this development and a closer look at the twelfth-century world gives a picture of economically and technologically much more advanced polities in Asia than in Europe. Not only was the Chinese Empire home to major discoveries such as the water-driven spinning machine for hemp, the astronomical clock, the compass, gunpowder, the crossbow, the iron plough, the cast-iron cannon, the wheelbarrow and paper, among others, but it was also a pioneer of urbanisation, as for nearly two thousand years it had more cities with over 10,000 inhabitants than any other part of the world (Jones 1987: 165). Furthermore, Imperial China had excellent preconditions to make an early leap towards the industrial era, as its technology, the scale of production (with textiles in particular), the scale of commercial exchange and development of credit 'revealed a pre-industrial economy at least as dynamic as contemporary Europe's (McNeill 1982: 24–62; Darwin 2008: 13).

Once the nomadic Mongol invaders were repelled and the north and western borders secured, the emperors presided over a stable and economically potent and thriving polity that was 'within a hair's breadth of industrialising in the fourteenth century' (Jones 1987: 160). Such a prosperous empire could afford to dispatch large fleets of maritime explorers as far as east Africa, Jedah and Kamchatka. Under the command of the eunuch admiral Cheng Ho seven armadas of junks consisting of 62 vessels carrying 37,000 soldiers embarked on world exploration in the early fifteenth century – so much earlier, and on a much larger scale, than any of the early European voyages of discovery. The Chinese Empire was also a substantial military power created by military might and heavily dependent on the existence of its armies to fight recurrent invaders from the north and west. In the eleventh century the Chinese Empire had by far the largest army and navy in the world, consisting of nearly a million soldiers and 52,000 sailors that manned hundreds of large ships. To finance such a huge army and navy the Sung dynasty in the 1060s spent 80 per cent of the government's income on the military (McNeill 1982: 40–2).

However, as military strength is also dependent on the social organisation's capability to feed, cloth and arm huge number of soldiers, the central weakness of the Imperial order was its inability to successfully extract taxation to pay the sizable military costs. In the pre-modern world, where infrastructural powers of polities are weak and undeveloped, tax collection can only be undertaken indirectly via local dignitaries. Although the Chinese Empire had an elaborate bureaucratic machine – with the mandarin system of civil service, built on Confucian principles, in place – this organisation was too complex, too restrictive and too expensive to provide rulers with a reliable social mechanism of tax extraction. To become a member of this select scholar-gentry class, one had to undergo extremely difficult civil service exams that could not be passed without many years of training. Consequently, as Hall (1988: 21) rightly argues 'there was never enough mandarins to form an efficient governing class. The first Ming emperor in 1371 sought to have as few as 5,488 mandarins in government service, and by the sixteenth century there were still only about 20,400 in the empire as a whole'. To use Mann's (1986) terminology, despite extensive despotic powers Chinese emperors lacked infrastructural powers to penetrate deep into the rural areas of their empire. As Jones (1987: 208–9) illustrates: 'the emperor … may have been immensely elevated as a being, but once he had issued a hunting-licence to a provincial governor, and received his 'present', that, for most important purposes, was that. His role was liturgical, providing ceremonial that the elite had been conditioned to expect and which in their eyes legitimated the system. His function was as broker'. As a result, emperors never managed to control the entire empire and the chronic fiscal crisis meant that, at critical moments of invasions from the northern and western frontiers, tax money was often withheld by the mandarins. Furthermore, Confucian proto-ideology was highly distrustful of the military: soldiers were equally despised and feared as the 'barbarian' invaders.[3] The mandarins adopted a similar policy of divide and rule for their own military commanders and 'barbarian' chieftains living on the borders of the empire: 'pacifying undependable elements by assigning goods, titles and ritual roles to military leaders, was the recipe of the Sung officials followed, whether within or beyond China's frontiers' (McNeill 1982: 35). The Confucian proto-ideology made a clear distinction between *wen* (literate culture) and *wu* (military force) whereby *wen* was highly prized over *wu* (Herwig *et al.* 2003: 204).

In addition, the constant court intrigues and conflicts between mandarins and court officials (eunuchs) undermined the stability of the empire. Crucially, these conflicts were responsible for an unprecedented reversal of development and a withdrawal from the external world. The Ming court's decision in 1480 to abandon maritime exploration and naval military presence, the demolition of the astronomical clock (built in 1090), the discarding of various technological inventions such as the spinning machine and large ships, and the banning all trade by sea saw Imperial China reverting to the traditional inward-looking agrarian model that moved in the opposite direction to that of Europe. The power struggle between mandarins and eunuchs and the major military defeat in 1428 in Annam (Vietnam) significantly contributed to this policy of reversal (Jones 1987: 204; Hall 1988). Although this land-centred 'coastal defence but no battles at sea' policy was also in part a reflection of the geopolitical changes resulting from periodic invasions and the Empire's later inability to maintain and organise large armies, it is still not completely clear why this same policy was continued under the Manchu rulers when the Great Wall was completed and the western borders were secured. Even though the Ch'ing–Manchu era brought more stability, economic development and a significant increase in land cultivation, the result of which was a dramatic increase in the size of population by threefold between the beginning and end of eighteenth century (Adshead 1995: 253), the empire remained deeply conservative and hostile towards the implementation of scientific and technological inventions and averse to the development of naval power.

Part of the explanation for this reluctance lies in the hegemonic position of the minority Manchu elite which was segregated by marriage and residence

---

[3] The typical attitude of mandarins clearly expressed by Wang An-Shih in 11th century was that 'the educated men of the land regarded the carrying of arms as a disgrace' (McNeill 1982: 40).

from the Han majority. In this sense, Gumplowicz and Ratzenhofer's conquest thesis as well as Rustow's 'law of cultural pyramid' prove highly applicable, as the conquering Manchu rulers (totalling less than 5 million) were primarily interested in cementing their power over more than 400 million Han peasantry (Jones 1987; Darwin 2008: 131–2). In this process the Confucian proto-ideology, built on ideas that glorified obedience to authority and respect for social conventions,[4] refined and elaborated through the institution of the mandarinate, successfully legitimised the existing power asymmetry between the Manchu elite and the Han majority. Establishing their supremacy through military conquest in the 1600s – and killing in this process 25 million people or 17 per cent of China's population (Jones 1987: 36) – Ch'ing rulers built their empire as a predatory system of domination and were not particularly interested in the outside world. In consequence, most of the wars fought on this territory were highly destructive civil uprisings, local wars, invasions and perpetual conflicts over the dynastic succession, which usually proved detrimental to economic and political development. As an inward-looking empire, China lacked a European-style multipolar system of competing states and despite its economic stability and ability to feed its vast population, the empire remained unable and unwilling to make a transition towards the industrial age. Despite the initially high levels of urbanisation, its cities had no autonomy, foreign trade was banned for most of the fourteenth, fifteenth and sixteenth century, and there was no system of civil policing nor defined or demarcated frontiers to the north and west. Rather than emerging as a state institution, the military remained a private possession of the rulers: 'the emperor kept an army primarily to protect his own interests, such as defending the Grand Canal which was his monopoly right, the route by which his assigned tribute grain reached the court of Peking' (Jones 1987: 207). And finally, the economic stability lulled the empire into a 'high-level-equilibrium trap' which reinforced cultural, political and economic conservatism thus preventing social change (Darwin 2008: 201).[5]

---

[4] As Hall (1985: 39) explains: 'The key notion [of Confucianism] is that of Chun-tzu, the stoical notion that stresses that one's duties, especially towards the family, should be performed in a courteous, gentlemanly fashion … [It] placed a much greater stress on the need for the observation of ritual, by the emperor and throughout society, in the belief that this could create just order. Only in so far as the emperor behaved towards his subjects as father would harmony prevail.'

[5] When Lord Macartney visited Chinese Emperor Ch'ien-lung in 1793 aiming to establish diplomatic relations and trade links with Britain he brought new technological devices and inventions as gifts to impress the emperor but the emperor rejected the gifts as useless toys with the comment that 'I set no value on objects strange and ingenious and have no use for your country's manufacturers' (Darwin 2008: 201).

India

Most wars fought on the territories of Imperial China were destructive, and hence detrimental to social progress; however, the historical experience of the Indian subcontinent really shows how far the destructive potential of warfare can go. The fact that the Indian subcontinent was home to diverse polities of various sizes and strength, and that the north and south were united into a single entity only on three occasions in its long history,[6] might suggest a similar favourable structural precondition for the emergence of the multipolar system of competing states that characterised the Western European transition to modernity. Nevertheless, not only did the chronic instability of its kingdoms prevent the development of such a system of polities, India's proto-ideological structure actually compounded the harm done by the existence of this organisational diversity. The division of social structure along the caste system (*varna*), whereby social order is hierarchically organised according to one's caste affiliation, proved a most important generator of structural instability that made Indian warfare especially destructive.

The caste system was rooted in the Vedic teachings that distinguishes between the four principal castes (*jatis*) that are derived from the occupational specialisation, social and dietary rules and strict endogamic principles established to firmly separate the groups: the Brahmans (priests and teachers), the Ksatriyas (warriors and rulers), the Vaisyas (farmers, merchants and artisans) and the Sudras (labourers and servants). The rest of population – the untouchables (*Dalits*) – were not part of the original Varna system and as such were deemed ritually impure as any contact with them was taboo and considered to be polluting. Although the rules governing the conduct and behaviour of castes were severe and clear-cut in principle, their actual workings in practice were more complex and messier; as with the proliferation of new professions, local sub-groups of castes tended constantly to multiply (Hall 1985: 61). While the traditional caste hierarchy was not as rigid as it later became (under Mughal and British rule), allowing a degree of upward and downward mobility over time, its strict division of social roles was central in preventing a transition to modernity.

The key issue that made warfare chronic and highly destructive was the institutional separation of power and authority. The caste division between the Brahmans and Ksatriyas meant that while kings had nearly absolute

---

[6] These three unifications include Asoka's reign in the third century BCE, the Mughal Empire in the sixteenth century and British rule from the eighteenth to the mid-twentieth century.

despotic power over their domains, they lacked the authority that rested with the priestly caste of the Brahmans. Since the Hindu proto-ideology clearly distinguishes between *dharma* as a universal order of values and norms and *artha* as the realm of interest, advantage and force, the kings remained dependent on the Brahmans' authority. As Hall (1985: 63) emphasises: 'His Brahman adviser and religious specialist, the *purohita*, has a monopoly on the crucial legitimating authority, the king possessing merely political power. Power is disconnected from authority, and held inferior to it.' This split between political and ideological power created a situation whereby the rulers could not act as law-makers and were unable to build up lasting social orders, which require sanctified authority. The Brahmans had no interest in everyday political life and, following Hinduist teachings, were inwardly focused on achieving personal transcendence rather than being involved in social life, and their lack of connection with politics created an anarchic and unstable political environment. As a consequence of this structural rift the constant lack of legitimacy made kingly rule weak and temporary, as it was regularly challenged by other would-be rulers. This context made rulers predatory, self-interested and opened the door for perpetual and destructive warfare. Knowing that their rule would be short-lived, kings had no interest in building state institutions or fostering economic development but were chiefly interested in preserving or expanding their personal rule through warfare. Hence, the warring polities were never perceived by their inhabitants as their states, but solely as the personal possessions of individual kings; and, the peasantry was not loyal to the state but to a particular king. Furthermore, Hinduism's hierarchical message, its anti-social doctrine of individual escapism and its compromise with local beliefs made it quite weak as a potential mobilising proto-ideology able to surpass the world of warring petty kingdoms. Most peasants remained indifferent to, or suspicious of, political institutions: their attitude to political power is adequately illustrated in the Punjabi proverb – 'never stand behind a horse or before an official' (Jones 1987: 199) and the paintings and accounts of kingly wars that 'picture peasants continuing to plough in the sight of the battlefield' (Hall 1985: 76).

The Mughal conquest of the sixteenth century broke this incessant cycle of destructive wars by uniting and pacifying much of India under its control. The Mughal Empire brought more prosperity, promoted trade, developed agriculture and made India 'the world's greatest centre of textile production, exporting cotton cloth to the Middle East, West Africa and Europe' (Darwin 2008: 144). The empire rested on the powerful and disciplined military which was centred in north India and was composed of professional soldiers including European artillerymen and five hundred war elephants. Under Emperor Akbar (1556–1605) the army consisted of 100,000 soldiers (Herwig *et al.* 2003: 186). The empire devised a highly efficient revenue system that was able to collect in cash one half of the value of agricultural production, and this covered the costs of the large military (Darwin 2008: 85).

However, the Mughal rulers secured their dominance by using the traditional caste system to their own advantage: 'All that a conqueror had to do was to establish his rule in the capital city and go on ruling as those before him had done … This society had brought to near perfection a mode of self-government which needed the least supervision from central power. The caste had a cell-like structure' (Karve 1961: 106). The improved economic development firmly rested on the Mughal's military dominance over the large swathes of Indian peasantry. In this sense, prosperity was almost exclusively confined to the small parasitic warrior elite that enjoyed relatively luxurious lifestyles including large and extravagant castles, water-gardens, harems, expensive wardrobes, jewellery, vast menageries and numerous servants. In most respects, just as in the Chinese case under the Manchus, the Mughal rule corroborates Gumplowicz's and Rustow's conquest thesis. This empire too was built and sustained through military conquest whereby a tiny, predominantly Muslim, warrior elite of non-producers subjugated and lived off the work of millions of chiefly Hindu peasant producers.[7] In this process they were transformed into a leisurely proto-class that became famous for the architecture, advanced science, poetry, literature and a cosmopolitan and glitzy court. However, the parasitic and despotic nature of this rule was not conducive to long-term economic development as its relative wealth was wasted on the personal pleasures of a small minority who demanded absolute obedience and who treated warfare as a sport. Lord (1972: 138) illustrates this point with the example of Maharajah Gaekwar of Baroda: 'When the maharajah yawned all present must snap their fingers to discourage flies'. Although the Mughal Empire was in its early years the most prosperous part of the Islamic realm, its wealth was still relatively small when compared to some European states. For example, even at its peak the income per capita of the entire Mughal Empire was similar to that of Elizabethan England, while in mid-eighteenth century it amounted to only two-thirds of England's income

---

[7] It is important to emphasise that early Mughal rule under Emperor Akbar in the late sixteenth century favoured toleration of all religions and employed Hindus as clerks and even elite soldiers (*rajputs*) while the late seventeenth century under Emperor Aurangzeb saw a shift in the empire's policy towards religious exclusivity with an intention of creating an Islamic empire (Hodgson 1974: 105; Hall 1985: 106). As Darwin (2008: 86) points out: 'Akbar rejected the classical Islamic distinction between the Muslim faithful (the umma) and the unbelievers.'

(Maddison 1971). The huge proto-class discrepancies, the rising animosity towards the Hindus, the rulers' excesses and their periodic waging of wars of conquest provoked rebellions and put serious strains on the empire. Finally, the financial exhaustion culminated with the prolonged war in Afghanistan and Aurangzeb's twenty-five-year attempt to quash the Maratha rebellion which ultimately led to the breakdown of the empire (Jones 1987: 201).[8]

Although British rule was a stabilising force that united the Indian subcontinent for the third time in its history and brought some economic development, its policy of divide-and-rule left a problematic legacy that eventually led to bloody conflicts and wars of separation between India, Pakistan and Bangladesh. Not only was the British Empire responsible for reinforcing and in many respects institutionalising caste divisions (formalised in the census), and creating conditions that in time led to antagonisms between Muslims and Hindus, but the entire imperial order was devised exclusively for the economic and geopolitical benefit of Britain. As Darwin (2008: 16) argues, this was 'a pattern of rule through which the products and revenues of colonial regions could be diverted at will to imperial purposes. Once their Raj was in place, the British taxed Indians to pay for the military power – a sepoy army – that they needed in Asia'.

The Ottoman Empire

Although 'Europeanist' arguments about the inherent destructiveness of warfare outside Western Europe are quite convincing when looking at the empires of China and India this argument requires serious qualification when one examines the cases of the Ottoman, Russian and Japanese Empires. What is distinct about these three cases is that they demonstrate the importance of warfare as a generator of modernisation and development outside Western Europe and in this way question some of the propositions made by the Europeanists.

The Ottoman Empire was not only created through warfare but was largely sustained by wars and continuous conquest. It owed its existence to a warrior proto-class that took its Islamic proto-ideology and the doctrine of holy war or jihad (articulated in the militarist *ghazi* tradition) extremely seriously. It relatively quickly spread its power over three continents.[9] However,

---

[8] The Maratha rebellion of the late seventeenth century was the struggle of an emerging Hindu gentry whose aim was to 'share Mughal sovereignty and revenues in ways that reflected the rising importance of new landholding groups' (Darwin 2008: 148).

[9] At the peak of its power, under Suleiman the Magnificent, the Ottoman Empire reached from the gates of Vienna over the straits of Gibraltar and North Africa, down both sides of the Red Sea to the shores of the Caspian Sea and the Persian Gulf (Montgomery 1968: 142).

military success requires a balance between ideology and social organisation: the secret of the fast expansion of the Ottoman Empire was the right combination of Islamic proto-ideology and efficient organisational capacity that transformed a small Seljuk tribal grouping into a powerful and lasting world empire that occupied 'an area greater than the Roman empire' (Jones 1987: 175). Although nomadic invasions and large-scale conquests were fairly common throughout history – with Tamerlane and Genghis Khan being the most prominent cases – the Ottoman conquest was unique in two ways.

First, unlike the traditional nomadic armies that possessed no coherent and over-arching proto-ideology and as a result were short-lived as the death of the ruler would often lead to the collapse of tribal unity and gradual absorption of former invaders through intermarriage (Hall 1985: 87), the Ottomans were in possession of their own monotheistic doctrine around which the stable and durable cultural and political foundations of the empire were built.[10]

Second, the empire had a powerful social organisation that was able to maintain a highly organised military machine which by 1528 already included a large standing army of 87,000 soldiers (Inalcik 1994: 88) and was also responsible for the invention of an effective system of recruitment of elite forces through the institution of *devshirme*. This institution of a professional slave army and civil service proved exceptionally efficient, as, on the one hand, it balanced the rulers' dependence on their aristocracy, and on the other hand, it created loyal, highly skilled, disciplined and extremely well motivated elite soldiers and bureaucrats whose very existence and meaning of life was tightly linked to that of the Empire. Since Janissary soldiers mostly consisted of Muslim converts recruited as children from Christian parents and were kept separate in professional training from the rest of society, they had no other loyalties except for the empire. In other words, the *devshirme* system combined a strong proto-ideology with effective, largely merit-based, organisation that eradicated all local and kinship ties making the Janissary model, in some respects, a close resemblance of Weberian bureaucratic organisation. As most important soldiers and clerks came from this meritocratic mode of organisation and constituted the educated 'Osmali' ruling elite (*askeri*), the early Ottoman Empire could rely on a much more competent social organisation than any part of still semi-feudal Western Europe. Hence the unprecedented speed of military expansion was no accident, but had deep

---

[10] For an instructive comparison of Muhammad's and Genghis Khan's legacies and the importance proto-ideology plays in empire building see Khazanov (1993).

sociological roots: highly developed mechanisms of the bureaucratisation and proto-ideologisation of coercion.

Despite the lack of a multipolar state system, the Ottoman Empire's military competition with European polities and other neighbouring empires acted as an important catalyst of social development. The early Ottoman Empire was organisationally innovative and open to change. It adopted the *timar* and *millet* systems of administration: while the first secured revenues through the local notables who also provided military service to the empire, the second preserved inter-religious reconciliation by granting substantial communal autonomy to the empire's diverse religious and ethnic groups (Darwin 2008: 76). It built large cities, universities and libraries; it made medical advances and technological inventions such as the automated flour mill and complex lighthouses (Jones 1987: 175). It also developed skilful diplomacy capable of playing European powers against each other. Most of all, it created a powerful military organisation that seemed invincible in its territorial expansion into Europe, Africa and the Middle East. The Ottoman Empire case clearly indicates that the Europeanist argument about the structurally ingrained detrimental nature of warfare outside Western Europe requires revision as most of the wars fought in the early and mid years of the Ottoman expansion proved highly beneficial to its development. It is true that Ottoman cities had no real autonomy, its urban population remained relatively small and there were no preconditions for the creation of independent civil society.[11] However, this lack of liberty does not automatically imply economic stagnation and inflexible traditionalism. On the contrary, the Ottoman Empire case demonstrates the alternative route of early modernisation that combined militarism with meritocracy and used warfare as a principal means of development through expansion. The fact that the Ottoman state was a predatory empire and a 'plunder machine' that depended on war victories and the strategy 'to make war for no longer than three years' until its 'triumphs and acquisitions would answer the expenses' (Jones 1987: 185) just indicates that there is no single road to social development. Since the Ottoman Empire was created first and foremost as a military machine, as long as the empire was expanding it proved highly successful and the wars it fought were beneficial to its development. Its later decline and eventual demise were not the result of its structural failures, lack of freedom or non existence of civil society but they came primarily from its accomplishments;

[11] Despite its modest levels of urbanisation it is important to note that the Empire's capital Constantinople was a huge city that grew from 100,000 in 1453 to over half a million (and possible 800, 000) in 1600 making it by far the largest city on the European continent (Jones 1987: 178).

it was success that brought stagnation. Just as in Imperial China, economic sufficiency combined, in this case, with military might led to the 'high-level-equilibrium-trap'. It is no accident that the empire's downfall was initiated by its most successful ruler, Suleiman the Magnificent, and at the very pinnacle of its power, as it was he who started the transformation of the meritocratic *devshirme* system into a nepotistic and clientelistic network around the ruling elite. By permitting the sale of offices, accumulation of wealth by the top civil servants and exemptions from taxes for the Janissaries, he broke the backbone of the Ottoman's meritocratic militarism. Hence, the gradual decline of the Ottoman Empire had little to do with its structural inability to compete with the advancing European states or other external factors. Its downfall was rooted in internal causes and, most of all, in the system's overwhelming success that brought an unwillingness to change. Consequently, stagnation-bred conservatism which in turn brought decline and, in later years, saw the Ottoman Empire become the 'sick man of Europe', constantly lagging behind European developments.

Russia

The Russian Empire is another case where warfare, militarisation and territorial conquest proved essential for social development and early modernisation. Although the Russian experience is often neglected in accounts of the 'the rise of the West', its own imperial expansion was central to this story as the Western European domination of Eurasia 'was really achieved in a fractious involuntary partnership with Russia' (Darwin 2008: 21). Like that of the Ottoman Empire, the rise of the Russian Empire was spectacular, as it transformed itself from a tiny tributary state of the Mongol Golden Horde in late fifteenth century (Muscovy) into the largest state in the world and a global empire in the nineteenth and twentieth centuries. Much of this transformation had a distinctly militarist origin as, just with the Ottoman expansion, warfare was a central mechanism of societal advancement. However, unlike the Ottoman Empire which, once it reached its military peak, underwent a dramatic and irreversible decline, the Russian Empire experienced cycles of rise and fall without ever reaching a point of no return.

There is a lot of irony in the fact that Russia's early rise owes a great deal to the introduction of the institution that was later to become, in the eyes of Western observers, a symbol of the empire's backwardness and inability to modernise – serfdom. The institution of serfdom has a military origin as its introduction bonded the peasantry to the nobility, which in turn provided military service to the rulers. In order to create an empire, the old military system of *boy*ar retinues had to be abandoned in favour of the new model (*pomestia*) which centralised landholding and linked it to military obligation (Darwin 2008: 65–73). To finance new wars of expansion and to secure their loyalty, it was paramount that the nobility was able to enforce taxation and service over their territorial domains and this was achieved through the introduction of the institution of serfdom. As a result of this change the small Grand Duchy of Muscovy became relatively quickly a large Russian Empire – a polity able to muster over 100,000 soldiers by the end of seventeenth century (Hellie 1971) and conquer vast territories of north and south Asia. As Letiche and Dmytryshyn (1985: xlvii) show, the land area of the Russian Empire increased dramatically between the seventeenth and eighteenth centuries: from 2.1 to 5.9 million square miles.

Nevertheless, it is important to stress that the greatest period of the empire's economic prosperity and cultural and social advancement, under Peter the Great, was also the period of intensive warfare and immense territorial expansion of the empire. Combining effective social organisation with imperial and Russian Orthodox proto-ideology, Peter the Great was able to create a new meritocratic standing army that introduced the bureaucratic model called the Table of Ranks, and proved to be a highly efficient war machine. The empire became more centralised as the tsar tightened its control over the aristocracy and the Church. While the nobility's military service and loyalty was rewarded through land grants in the areas of conquest, the Orthodox Church acquired state-sponsored prestige as it reformed the image of its Greek Byzantine equivalent to accommodate the proto-ideological ambitions of the rising empire. The territorial conquest tripled the empire's revenues, productive capacity was doubled and new state factories and arsenals were built to supply the large armies (Blanchard 1989: 218). The central feature of Peter's Russia was an emphasis on discipline and efficient social organisation which was underpinned by the coherent proto-ideological project, and at the heart of this project was the military expansion of the new empire. In some respects, just as the Ottoman Empire did, Imperial Russia acted as a predatory state that fuelled its economic prosperity through territorial conquest. In other words, warfare proved highly beneficial to the state's development.

The second wave of modernisation, that of the 1860s under Tsar Alexander II, was also linked to warfare. As with Peter the Great's intention, the reforming drive was primarily motivated by military and imperial reasons: it came as a direct outcome of Russia's defeat in the Crimean War (1853–1856). To catch up with developments in Western Europe, the rulers embarked on an intensive process of industrialisation, economic and political liberalisation, and agrarian and military reform. Hence, the institution of serfdom was abolished (in 1861), literacy rates were substantially increased, the legal system was transformed in line with Western European models, censorship laws were reformed, cultural life was liberated and the universities gained autonomy. The speedy industrialisation brought major improvements. New extensive railroads were built, exports rose dramatically, agricultural reform made Ukraine a substantial producer of wheat and industrial output surged sharply. For example, coal production in the 1890s was fifty times greater than in the 1860s; the output of steel saw an unprecedented increase of two thousand times in the same period (Darwin 2008: 322).

However, what is often neglected in this progressivist narrative of modernisation is its inherent link with war aims. Just as with the first wave of modernisation, this second wave was combined with a massive imperial expansion in north east and central Asia. The two largest industrial projects of the time – the Trans-Caspian (1880–1888) and Trans-Siberian (1891–1904) railways – were built principally to accommodate military and imperial expansion. Underpinned by its own version of the civilising mission that saw the vast 'Asiatic' interior as its 'natural' ground for colonisation, Imperial Russia was able to utilise technological and organisational modernisation for successful territorial conquest. It is no coincidence that this particular period was a witness to both intensive economic development and a large-scale occupation. In twenty years, between 1864 and 1884, the Russian Empire waged wars of conquest throughout central Asia and in this process swallowed up the principalities of Kokand, Bokhara, Khiva, Turkmenia and Merv (Clodfelter 1992: 368–9). It also completed its conquest of north-east Asia by colonising the technologically and organisationally inferior indigenous population which was quickly overrun by millions of Russian settlers.[12] Finally, the military reform allowed the Empire to wage a new war against the Ottomans (Russo-Turkish War 1877–1878). By successfully combining efficient military organisation and the newly emerging ideological power of nationalism, Imperial Russia was able to mobilise over 900,000 soldiers and decisively defeat the armies of the Ottoman Empire (Clodfelter 1992: 331). All these military successes helped raise the empire's prestige thus reinforcing its imperial aspirations. Nevertheless, the war victories also opened up an

---

[12] As Darwin (2008: 322) points out: 'By 1914, more than 5 million Russians had crossed the Urals into Siberia, and thousands more had settled in the Muslim khanates in Russian Central Asia.'

ideological rift between those who saw Russia as essentially a European state and advocated further modernisation along these lines ('the Westernisers') and those who were emboldened by its swift expansion in Asia and attributed to Russia the messianic role of the 'Third Rome' whose principal aim was to spread the Orthodox faith, achieve 'spiritual unity' with the huge Russian peasantry and dominate most of Eurasia ('Slavophiles'). The unexpected and shocking defeat in the Russo-Japanese war 1904–1905 demonstrated the limits of both these visions but also was a potent indicator of the sudden and dramatic rise of another emerging military power – Japan.

Japan

The history of Japan is closely linked with the military and warfare. Its geographical location, an island at the edge of the Pacific Ocean, meant that, until the technological advancements of recent times, its eastern, southern and northern borders required little or no protection while its relationship with only one major power, inward-looking China, determined its security on the western borders. As a consequence of this geopolitical stability, Japan has experienced much less inter-state warfare than most other large polities. However, paradoxically, it also developed the most militarist social structure of all in which social change remained heavily dependent on transformations in its military organisation. The main reason for this outcome was the proliferation of civil warfare that reached its peak in the anarchy of warring fiefdoms throughout the fifteenth and sixteenth centuries. Until this period, and particularly from the eleventh and twelfth centuries onward, Japan was ruled by the military establishment on top of which was a *shogun* (generalissimo) and which included the large warrior proto-class, the samurai, who, in alliance with feudal lords, dominated the rest of society. The absolute pre-eminence of the military was discernible from the extremely hierarchical, ritualistic and formalist ethic (later to be reinforced with Confucianism) that penetrated the entire society; this ethic glorified status, honour and obedience to authority as its central principles.

The collapse of the shogun system of rule that came with the rise of *daimyo* local lords at the end of fifteenth century led to the disintegration of central authority and a protracted period of civil warfare between competing clans. This series of events proved central for the transformation of Japan, as intensive warfare brought about 'military revolution similar to that going on in the West' (Herwig *et al.* 2003: 208), with the introduction of cannons and firearms, infrastructural developments and a substantial increase in the size of armies. For example, the warlord Hideyoshi, who would eventually unify Japan under single central rule in 1590, 'was able to put armies of 250,000 men and more by ordering his daimyo to conscript set numbers of peasants and townsmen' (Herwig *et al.* 2003: 209). Even more importantly, intensive fighting between different warlords, in many respects not dissimilar to the European multipolar system of competing states, served indirectly as a catalyst of development, as the end of long warfare brought economic and political stability that lasted for nearly 250 years. The civil strife forced competing clans to modernise technologically but also to mobilise different segments of society that traditionally would not take part in wars. Although, unlike Western Europe, this dependency on broader sectors of the population did not necessarily result in the increase of liberties or in the birth of civil society, it nevertheless created an unusual situation whereby Japan achieved something for which Europe would have to wait for several more centuries – the internal pacification of the entire polity. The Tokugawa rule was not just a period of Japan's seclusion from the rest of the world (*sakoku* policy) it was also an era of intensive state centralisation and disarmament. Starting as soon as 1588 with Shogun Hideyoshi's order for the 'sword hunt' and Shogun Ieyasu's proclamation in 1603 which forbade the use of firearms throughout the realm, the entire country was disarmed by 1630: 'the Shimbara Christian rebellion of 1637 was the last time that firearms were seriously used in Japan for two centuries' (Keegan 1994: 40–6; Herwig *et al.* 2003: 212)[13,14]. In this way Japan became the first polity where the central government achieved near absolute monopoly on the legitimate use of violence. As a result of this pacification and the simultaneous policy of isolation, Japan was in a position to develop a mercantilist self-sufficiency and autarkic economy that was not dependent on external trade and imports and was successful in providing economic growth. In other words, seclusion did not mean economic stagnation. On the contrary, during the seventeenth and early eighteenth century Japan was politically stable and economically prosperous, experiencing a rapid growth of population, regional economic specialisation (textiles, metalwork, publishing, ceramics), high levels of internal trade and intensive

[13] The use of swords was banned on the pretext of building a giant iron Buddha. As the Hideyoshi order states: 'The people of the various provinces are strictly forbidden to have in their possession any swords, short swords, bows, spears, firearms or other type of arms. The possession of unnecessary implements [of war] makes difficult the collection of taxes and dues and tends to foment uprisings … Swords and short swords thus collected will not be wasted. They shall be used as nails and bolts in the construction of the Great Image of Buddha' (Herwig *et al.* 2003: 212).

[14] The shogun Ieyasu also centralised the manufacture of weapons and the government became the only authorised purchaser of weaponry (Keegan 1994: 43).

urbanisation.[15] For example, the total population of Japan increased from 12 million in 1600 to 31 million by 1721 with its capital Edo reaching 1 million inhabitants. At the beginning of the eighteenth century, Edo was twice the size of London (Totman 1993: 140). As daimyo and samurai settled in the castle towns with their families most cities resembled military garrisons, since a large section of their population was composed of members of this hereditary warrior proto-class. As Darwin (2008: 135) points out: 'By 1700 half of Edo's 1 million people were samurai retainers living in the great clan compounds that made up nearly three-quarters of the city area.' In other words, the state's monopolisation of violence made sure that the military remained the privileged proto-class and the core institution of the social order.

The policy of seclusion also proved instrumental in avoiding contact, and hence the possibility of conflicts and wars, with its neighbours and the European powers. Although Japan had no navy, its formidable military might indicated that by the early nineteenth century it was still invulnerable to external attacks. However, despite its rigorous enforcement of isolationism, Tokugawa Japan remained open to Chinese cultural and economic influence, as Confucian proto-ideology was favoured and sponsored by the state and Chinese merchants and artisans were allowed to settle and establish their 'Chinatowns'. In addition, Japanese rulers permitted Dutch trading ships restricted access to the port of Nagasaki which served a 'narrow gateway and a listening post where the *bakufu* [the Tokugawa government] collected information from visiting ships (whose captains were required to write "news reports" for transmission to Edo') (Darwin 2008: 135). Thus, even though Japan was not open to the world, its rulers were kept informed about developments in the rest of the world. The fact that once it became apparent that the *sakoku* policy was no longer sustainable (as Japan started to lag seriously behind), the rulers were able to implement a swift transition is a reliable indicator of the society's organisational adaptability. Despite Japan's inherent conservatism, its early experience of modernisation, state centralisation, traditionally high literacy rates and well developed social (military) organisation proved essential for the speedy shift to modernity accomplished under the Meiji restoration. The second wave of modernisation that started in the 1870s saw Japan making an extraordinarily fast transition, the epicentre of which was military reform: the creation of a strong navy, the introduction of universal military service and the mass production of modern

---

[15] As Jansen (1992: 16) shows, in 1600 Japan was the largest producer of silver in the world – it was responsible for the production of one third of the world's silver.

weaponry. All of these changes required retirement of the huge samurai proto-class (over 1 million), the abolition of vassalage and implementation of bureaucratic modes of organisation. The result of this speedy transition, reinforced by technological advancements, organisational supremacy and the strength of the modern ideology of nationalism, was the demolition of Russia's Baltic fleet at the battle of Tshushima (1905) and a decisive victory over the Russian Empire in the 1904–1905 war. This astonishing achievement clearly demonstrates not only the speed and scale of Japan's transformation, but even more importantly it shows that the transition to modernity had much deeper and more varied roots than most Europeans were willing to admit. All of this goes against the grain of the Europeanist argument which posits European intra-state warfare as unique in creating the conditions for early modernisation. The Japanese case demonstrates another example of the non-Western European situation where prolonged inter-clan and regional warfare led eventually towards state centralisation and even to the unprecedented monopolisation of violence. Just as with Russia and the Ottoman Empire, this was an alternative route to modernity that, too, owed a great deal to war and militarisation.

The new world

Sub-Saharan Africa

Although Africa is geographically an integral segment of the 'Old World' the fact that its sub-Saharan part remained largely unexplored and isolated from the rest of the world until the early nineteenth century makes its structural features, including warfare, more congruent with those of the 'New World'.[16] The central feature of contemporary sub-Saharan Africa is the infrastructural weakness of its state systems which is a direct legacy of colonial rule and to some extent also a result of pre-colonial developments. In most respects, the African case is the proto-type of the Europeanist argument, as comparison with pre-modern Europe indicates clear-cut differences that had a profound impact on the different structural outcomes of warfare on the two continents.

Unlike early Western Europe, which had a high population density and consequent scarcity and high value of land, sparsely inhabited Africa had

---

[16] As the chapter unfolds it will become clear that in terms of inter-state warfare and state weaknesses sub-Saharan Africa shares a great deal in common with South America and other post-colonial regions.

an abundance of land and a chronic shortage of people (Herbst 2000). As a result, while the European aristocracy were highly motivated to fight over territory, African rulers were more interested in acquisition of scarce labour. Hence, the patterns of social development on the two continents proceeded in different directions. As the protracted warfare in Europe became enormously costly, the rulers were eventually forced to negotiate, co-operate and grant substantial autonomy and liberties to the commoners in exchange for a continuous supply of revenue and soldiers. The direct outcome of this dependency was the development and expansion of bureaucracy, stable fiscal institutions, permanent military structures, a gradual increase in cultural homogeneity and the emergence of clearly defined state borders. Thus the result was the birth of the nation-state.

In contrast, African rulers' focus on people instead of territory led, on the one hand, to the clear regulation of property rights over people, where acquisition of slaves (through warfare and periodic raids) became the principal sources of domination. On the other hand, the absence of mutually exclusive territorial claims made state-building a rare and underdeveloped practice. The absence of permanent, visible and clearly defined large-scale external threats meant that the institutions of statehood such as administrative centralisation, fiscal organisation, unified military structures and cross-class cultural solidarity had not arisen before the colonial era. In addition, with a few notable exceptions such as the settler colonies in Rhodesia, South Africa and Kenya, the colonial powers simply utilised the existing tribal and clan-based channels to extract the natural wealth and rule the colonies, rather than developing stable state institutions. The intensification of the slave trade in the eighteenth and early nineteenth centuries caused further depopulation, as more than 10 million people were enslaved and transported across the Atlantic (Curtin 1969). The drawing of improvised and largely arbitrary borders along the lines of colonial territorial possessions contributed additionally to the establishment of the weak polities that were to emerge in the post-colonial period.

Herbst (1990, 2000) argues that this historical lack of state development and the fact that the states rarely had to fight for their survival helps explain Africa's failure to fully modernise. More specifically, unlike Western Europe, which developed through frequent and protracted inter-state warfare, the majority of wars fought in sub-Saharan Africa were civil conflicts and other intra-state conflicts which proved destructive and detrimental to economic and political development. Instead of fighting external enemies and in this process strengthening their polities, the African wars remained internal, polarising and damaging to the process of state-building. While the rise of Western Europe saw inter-state warfare obliterating many weaker polities and reducing the number of states from close to 1000 polities in the fourteenth century to around 500 in sixteenth century and to 25 at the beginning of twentieth century (Russell 1972: 244; Tilly 1975: 15), the African colonial experience was responsible for the emergence of many new states. However, the new states did not emerged as a result of conflict and violent struggle with their neighbours but were granted nominal statehood as a result of decolonisation. Hence, unlike the European model of state-building through competitive violence, the African colonial legacy protected the existence of many weak and militarily unsustainable polities. This policy was institutionally reinforced by the declaration of the Organisation for African Unity in 1963 which states that 'any change in the inherited colonial boundaries [would be regarded] illegitimate' (Herbst 1990: 124).

However, despite this general trend there are historical exceptions which indicate that alternative developments could happen in pre-colonial Africa. For example, the Sokoto Caliphate and Zululand of the early nineteenth century were powerful empires built on substantial military might and created through protracted warfare. While the Sokoto Caliphate under the rule of Usman dan Fodio (1754–1817) relied on powerful cavalry and the proto-ideological strength of Islam to establish the largest empire in Africa (stretching from Burkina Faso to Cameroon), the Zulu Kingdom under Shaka (1787–1828) controlled an area of over 15,000 square miles incorporating 250,000 people and 50,000 warriors (Morris 1965; Smaldone 1977). Military victories and the constant presence of external threat were not only essential in establishing the Sokoto Caliphate as a centralised and well organised political authority able to control much of its territory, collect taxes and recruit soldiers, but were also instrumental in bringing economic prosperity and artistic advancement to the region (Smaldone 1977). The dramatic and speedy expansion of the Zulu empire throughout southern Africa in the early nineteenth century had an enormous impact on the entire region causing demographic turmoil and large scale migrations (*Mfecane*). Shaka's empire was built on an exceptionally well organised military machine that instituted a distinct form of conscription – age cohort regiments (*ibutho*), where every man had to serve until they reached 40 years of age. The strict separation of the military from civilians (e.g. banning marriage until retirement, and solders living in secluded military barracks) and the constant drill, forced marches, well organised logistics and the developed regiment culture (each regiment having distinct names and insignia) made the Zulu army a model of military professionalism and discipline.

In addition, the introduction of new weaponry such as a short stabbing spear with long sword-like spearhead (*iklwa*), large, heavy shields, a new attacking formation (buffalo-horns model), new close-order tactics and reliance on fast moving surprise attacks and ambushes, all revolutionised the nature of warfare in pre-colonial Africa (Keegan 1994: 28–32). As Morris (1965: 17) argues, Shaka's military inventions changed the character of African warfare from 'a ritualised exchange of taunts with minimal loss of life into a true method of subjugation by wholesale slaughter'. Hence, to sum up, the inherent weakness of the states in sub-Saharan Africa is not linked exclusively to internal causes as their military development was also clogged by the speed and scale of the European colonial expansion.

Latin America

The colonial legacy was also central in the relationship between warfare and social development in Latin America. The arbitrary character of borders, a central contributor to the instability of African states, was equally present in South and Central America. The lack of cultural homogeneity, deep proto-class and status divisions, and the stringent polarisation between the white and *criollo* populations of the imperial centres and the natives living in the periphery of South and Central America, have clear counterparts in the European colonies of Africa and Asia. However, there are also important differences. Firstly, the processes of European colonisation, as well as later decolonisation, were much slower and more protracted in Latin America than elsewhere. The conquering Spanish and Portuguese Empires treated their territorial possessions in Latin America as integral and indivisible parts of the larger empires with little distinction made between the colonies and the mainland. Consequently, 'the wars of independence produced fragments of empire, but not new states. There was little economic or political logic to the frontiers as institutionalised in the 1820s ... the new countries were essentially mini-empires with all the weaknesses of such political entities' (Centeno 2002: 25). Secondly, the cultural and linguistic similarity of the 'white' and Creole-dominated metropolitan centres had a detrimental effect on the processes of state- and nation-building whereby the Bolivarian nationalist movement of the early nineteenth century had no distinguishable cultural foundations but was articulated as a continent-wide social movement. This is best illustrated by the fact that Bolivar is regarded as a father of the nation in most of Latin America (i.e. eleven nations share the same national hero) and 'every city except Montevideo and Asuncion has a major statue to the Libertador, Simon

Bolivar' (Centeno 2002: 213). However, this much longer period of independence than was experienced in Africa did not materialise in greater state stability. On the contrary, the post-independence era was characterised by the use of excessive force and militarism that still colours the image of South and Central America as regions beset by war and violence.

Nevertheless, despite the popular image of South and Central American states as violence-prone and repressive, they are distinctly weak and the region has experienced much less inter-state warfare than any other inhabited continent. The crucial feature of collective violence in Latin America is that it has tended to occur within, rather than between, states. As Miguel Centeno (2002: 35) argues: 'Latin America has experienced low levels of militarisation, the organisation and mobilisation of human and material resources for potential use in warfare. Latin Americans *have* frequently tried to kill one other, but they have generally not attempted to organise their societies with such a goal in mind.' In other words, and as in the African case, the lack of protracted inter-state warfare and the prevalence of intra-state violence proved detrimental to the political, economic and social development of the Latin American polities. Rather than strengthening the administrative and military power of the state, the great majority of wars fought in the region were harmful to the processes of state- and nation-building. Civil wars, local and regional rebellions, coups and revolutionary upheavals have fractured political authority and largely destroyed civilian administration. The relatively isolated geographical location of the region which could have brought geopolitical stability, as in the case of Japan, was in fact detrimental, as the lack of an external enemy inside and outside of the continent helped foster internal instability in the already weak states. Unlike early Western Europe, where the multipolar system, via inter-state warfare, was an 'organic' development and as such could act as a generator of economic and political development, the division of Latin America into states was an artificial, colonial creation that failed to bequeath to the states the organisational and ideological capacity to wage wars with their neighbours. Although South and Central American states were prone to border disputes, very few of these resulted in all-out wars. As Gochman and Maoz (1990) show, only 5 per cent of Latin American states' militarised disputes, between 1816 and 1976, evolved into war, whereas, in the European case the same statistic is a staggering 62 per cent.

More specifically, the region was 'not geared toward the logistical and cultural transformations required by international conflict. Conversely, domestic conflict often reflected the inability of the nascent states to impose their control over the relevant societies' (Centeno 2002: 65). Since their independence in the 1820s most Latin American polities were more like city-states in charge of mini-empires than the European-style nation-states. Their armies were, and largely remain, very small, funded by minuscule defence budgets, and have a long history of low professionalism and lack of discipline. The weak states were generally incapable of extracting revenue which could pay for a larger military and police apparatus, and conversely the lack of a large-scale coercive force was a chief obstacle in enforcing universal taxation. Incessant divisions between the top clergy, large landowners and politicians also contributed to the states' fiscal weaknesses. For example 'while the Chilean armies were marching on Lima, Peruvian finance minister Quimper suggested a small tax on capital to pay the troops in the field. These measures were defeated' (Centeno 2002: 157).

The key structural problem was the institutional discrepancy between political and military power, since historically most armies were rarely controlled by the central political authority. Instead, military force remained autonomous and thus able to switch sides easily and fight on behalf of those who were willing to pay more. In principle, most armies were no more than regionally oriented militias under the control of local *caudillos* resentful towards the central authorities. Even Bolivar's popular revolutionary upheaval had difficulty attracting potential soldiers. The first stage of his struggle (1812–1813) could rely on no more than 500 men while his opponents, the royalists, had fewer than 900 soldiers. By the time of his victorious Peruvian campaign Bolivar was in charge of 2,100 men (Centeno 2002: 226). The traditionally low participation in armed forces was also linked to the political elite's distrust of the (for the most part autonomous) military and the fact that most armies were composed of 'non-whites' who were often feared more than any external threat. Consequently, Latin American states were among the last to introduce universal conscription, with most countries having no proper military draft until the end of the nineteenth and beginning of the twentieth century.

To sum up, the character of warfare in Latin America shares a great deal with sub-Saharan Africa and other post-colonial polities. The central feature here is the predominance of internal, limited conflicts over inter-state wars, a feature which in the long term obstructs social development and makes the process of building states and nations more difficult.

North America

The case of North America clearly demonstrates that the colonial legacy by itself does not determine the direction of a region's social and political development. Although the USA and Canada were the direct products of what was an essentially British colonial expansion, and originated through protracted violent processes, most of the wars fought on their territories had an ultimately beneficial effect on the building of nations and states. This is not to say that many of these wars were benign, resulting in little destruction and low human casualties. On the contrary, from the early Indian wars, through the war of 1812, the Mexican-American War to the US Civil War, the North-American continent was a witness to enormous bloodshed and large-scale ethnic cleansing. The settlers' inexhaustible hunger for land, fully sanctioned by the colonial and later the new state authorities (especially the USA), caused the systematic slaughter of millions of native Americans over a number of years. Underpinned by their own version of the civilising mission and blatant racism, the rulers of North-American polities fostered genocidal policies that saw natives as 'savages' to be either assimilated or exterminated. For example, the Horseshoe Bend massacre of Creeks in 1814, through which the USA acquired the large territories that are today Alabama and Georgia, made General Andrew Jackson famous and eventually helped him get elected as the seventh US president. The defeat and almost total annihilation of Creeks in this war was depicted by Jackson in the following words: 'they have disappeared from the face of the Earth ... We have seen the ravens and the vultures preying upon the carcasses of the unburied slain. Our vengeance has been glutted' (Anderson and Cayton 2005: 232–3). Similarly, in his inaugural address as a first governor of California, Peter Burnett openly declared in 1849 that 'a war of extermination will continue to be waged between the two races until the Indian race becomes extinct' (Hurtado 1988: 134). As a direct consequence of this policy, in less than twelve years (in the period 1848–1860) the native American population of California declined from 150,000 to 31,000 whereas the settler population increased from 25,00 to 350,000 (Mann 2005: 89). Even when the genocidal project was almost completed at the end of nineteenth century the general attitude had not changed significantly. This is well illustrated by the words of the later Nobel Peace Prize winner, President Roosevelt, who saw this mass extermination as a noble war 'ultimately beneficial as it was inevitable' arguing that 'I don't go so far as to think that the only good Indians are dead Indians, but I believe nine out of ten are, and I shouldn't inquire too closely into the case of the tenth' (Stannard 1992: 245).

The Northwest Ordinance in 1789, which allowed for the westward expansion of the US beyond the original thirteen colonies, was a document that simultaneously allowed and justified indefinite territorial conquest of the entire North-American continent, which was defined as an 'empty frontier'. However, it was the victorious war of 1812 that proved a pivotal moment in US history as it represented a 'movement from [George] Washington's preference for orderly growth and negotiation, backed by the selective use of force ... to the aggressive claims of Jacksonian Democrats in the 1840s which gave birth to the idea that 'it was the "manifest destiny" of the United States to acquire all of North America' (Anderson and Cayton 2005: 223). As the early attempts to conquer Canada (1775 and 1812) were relative failures, the focus of US military expansion moved to the south. This gradual switch towards the imperial mode of expansion was most clearly visible in the Mexican-American War of 1846–1848 that followed the 1845 US annexation of Texas. The result of this war was a further territorial expansion through which more than half of Mexico was absorbed into the USA (California, Nevada, Arizona, New Mexico, Utah and Colorado). Nevertheless, victory in the Mexican War and the dramatic acquisition of territory in the south had seriously dented the fine balance between the political elites in the North and South. The Southern elites, including the large plantation owners, heavily dependent on slave labour, were interested in further territorial conquest as well as in the introduction of slavery into the newly acquired territories. As Mississippi senator Albert Gallatin Brown declared: 'I want Cuba ... I want Tamaulipas, Potosi, and one or two other Mexican states; and I want them all for the same reason – for the planting or spreading of slavery' (Genovese 1965: 257–8). In contrast, Northern elites, who had no links to the slave economy, were worried that the federal government was already in the hands of the slave-owning Southerners. Eventually, the escalation of these conflicts lead to the first modern industrialised war, the American Civil War (1861–1865), which involved more than 3 million soldiers and over 600,000 dead (Clodfelter 1992: 528). The enormous scale of the loss of human life was largely rooted in the clash of modern technology and pre-modern tactics. As the new, long-range, fast-firing and more accurate industrial weaponry confronted the traditional mass infantry assaults, thousands of soldiers were massacred by machine guns firing from fortified strongholds. Despite the unprecedented human casualties and the devastation that the Civil War brought, its outcome was not a weakened state, as was the case with most civil warfare in Africa and Latin America. Instead, the direct consequence of the Northern victory was the strengthening of the federal government and an exceptional increase in the organisational powers of the state. In fact, the Civil War was a 'second American revolution': 'the federal government developed into a source of power capable of intervening directly in the lives of citizens in the states, overriding at will the authority that the first Revolutionary Settlement had reserved to local jurisdictions'. The war outcome allowed the creation of a 'national banking system and a national currency, [to] raise tariffs, allocate federal resources in support of public education, and provide for such internal improvements as transcontinental railroads' (Anderson and Cayton 2005: 301). Moreover, rather than operating as a force of division and polarisation, the Civil War was institutionally articulated, and still acts as a symbol of unity in the American public memory. Hence, instead of delaying further development, the Civil War was a prime catalyst of state- and nation-building, as its direct outcome was a dramatic increase in the bureaucratic and ideological might of the American state. Furthermore, as the military victory in the Civil War was articulated in moral terms (defeating the wickedness of slavery) it also reinforced the larger American meta-narrative that underpins the dominant normative ideology which sees the USA as the beacon of human freedom. This ideological absolutism, resting on the idea of ethical and political exceptionalism, allows, and even obliges, coercive action in the name of universal liberty. The early conquest of North America, the Spanish–American War and other semi-colonial ventures, together with the wars of the twentieth and twenty-first centuries, rested on this view that military conquest is nothing more than an American collective sacrifice in the name of the moral and political advancement of humanity.

In other words, precisely because warfare in North America was far from benign, it set the foundations for the emergence of institutionally strong polities. In this way, the North-American experience is perhaps the most serious challenge to the Europeanist argument as it firmly demonstrates that the lack of substantial multipolarity and the presence of civil wars are not necessarily obstacles to political and economic development. The rise of the USA as a global superpower is historically and decisively rooted in warfare and violence. Constant military engagement – from the ethnic cleansing of the native population, through the eighteenth – and nineteenth-century wars of continental domination to the Civil War and the two world wars, was crucial in the development of the supreme organisational and ideological scaffolding around which its military, political and economic power has grown.

Conclusion

The emergence of the modern bureaucratic constitutional nation-state, able to fully control its borders, reflect the interests and values of its citizenry and promote economic growth was, in many ways, an exceptional and miraculous development. Although some substantial ingredients in this development may have come from Asia or elsewhere (Hobson 2004), there is no doubt that the birth of modernity was primarily a European miracle. Nevertheless, what is central, and is so often omitted, in this story of the sudden rise of Western Europe, and eventually the rest of the world, is the deeply violent character of its origins. As evident from the previous two chapters, the cumulative bureaucratisation of coercion and centrifugal ideologisation were the cornerstones of modernity. The early rise of Europe owed a great deal to the constant warfare which forced rulers to devolve powers and liberties, to build administrative apparatuses, fiscal systems, military machines and representative institutions. In this sense, protracted warfare has proved a generator of intensive social development. However, not all of Europe benefited from warfare: many political entities have been swallowed by the larger and more predatory states, some regions were devastated beyond repair and some remained trapped in the vicious circle of unending and destructive violence.

This uneven impact of warfare is even more pronounced outside of the European continent. Rather than being an exclusive phenomenon associated with the rise of the West, wars and organised violence have had different effects in different polities around the globe. While Imperial China, India, Sub-Saharan Africa, Latin America and much of post-colonial Asia fit the picture, painted by the Europeanists, of destructive intra-state conflicts hampering social change and development, the history of the Ottoman Empire, Japan, Russia and most of all the USA constitute clear-cut cases where the utilisation of organised violence was the central prerequisite of intensive modernisation. Although early, pre-modern, Europe was an initial catalyst of this coercive transformation, once the genie had left the lamp there was no turning back and Western Europe had no monopoly on the link between warfare and social development. Nevertheless, what stands out in this relationship between warfare and intense social advancement is the continuous impact of social organisation and ideology: while there is no guarantee that well organised and ideologically well infused military machines will ultimately bring about economic growth and cultural progress, it is almost certain that disorganised and ideologically incoherent coercive apparatuses will regularly prove destructive not only to social development but also to the very existence of their polities. However, to better understand the dynamics of these two crucial social processes – the cumulative bureaucratisation of coercion and centrifugal ideologisation – it is necessary to analyse how they work internally. Hence, the following chapters will explore nationalism, propaganda, stratification, solidarity and gender in the context of these two processes.

Part III

Warfare: ideas and practices

6   Nationalism and war

Introduction

The commonly shared view is that warfare invariably and radically transforms established patterns of group homogeneity and solidarity. It is generally assumed that the outbreak of war sharpens group boundaries across the lines of conflict, thus enhancing in-group solidarity and homogeneity vis-à-vis the threatening out-groups. More specifically, protracted violent conflicts are regularly seen as a forcing ground of intensive national attachments. Although there is disagreement on whether war and violence precede, and thus produce, strong national bonds, or whether warfare itself is a direct outcome of intensified nationalist feelings, there is virtually no disagreement that the eruption of war almost instinctively increases in-group solidarity and national homogeneity. The main aim of this chapter is to challenge this perceived link between warfare, macro-level solidarity and group homogeneity. In contrast to this, I argue that national homogenisation and the alleged large-scale group solidarity, witnessed at times of war and in the context of violent conflicts, are neither automatic and inevitable nor directly tied to warfare itself. Rather than being a cause or a direct product of war, the ostensible macro-level solidarity and group homogeneity exhibited in times of violent conflicts originate outside of these conflicts. In other words, instead of being an automatic social response, homogenisation is a complex process that requires a great deal of long-term institutional work. In-group solidarity is not something that 'just happens' and naturally occurs in times of war. It is a contested and messy process. For macro-level cohesion and national homogenisation to exist, it is paramount that the two key structural pillars are in place and fully functioning before the outbreak of violence: centrifugal ideologisation and the cumulative bureaucratisation of coercion.

The first part of the chapter provides a critical analysis of the two dominant types of explanations linking warfare and group homogeneity, while the second part elaborates an alternative interpretation.

Warfare and group homogeneity

The naturalist fallacy

Although the relationship between warfare and group cohesion has been the object of analysis across a variety of disciplines, including psychology, political science, anthropology, military history and sociology, two interpretations of this link predominate: a naturalist and a formative view.[1] Interestingly enough both of these research paradigms draw directly or indirectly on classical bellicose social thought.

The naturalist view has its predecessors in the Austro-American group struggle paradigm, particularly in the works of Gumplowicz (1899), Ratzenhofer (1904), Ward (1914) and McDougall (1915). Taking groups as the elementary units of social action, they interpreted violent conflicts as the collective strategy for domination by one group over another. In Gumplowicz's (1899) view warfare arises from the *syngenic* quality of group composition which involves cultural similarity and joint social action. Syngenism is understood as a root cause of inter-group violence, with strong ethnocentric feelings provoking hostility with other groups. Similarly, McDougall (1915) argued that group aggression is based on the 'instinct of pungency' which fosters out-group violence while reinforcing in-group cohesion. Although, as I have argued earlier (Chapters 1 and 3) much of this tradition is worth revisiting since it opens new avenues for research on war and sociality, the Austro-American group struggle paradigm remains wedded to a very narrow and unreflective view of cultural difference.

Hence it comes as no surprise that the recent articulation of this view has reappeared in a biological and culturally historical disguise. Rather than borrowing from the rest of the heuristically rich conceptual and explanatory apparatuses that the classical 'bellicose' tradition provides, contemporary sociobiological literature draws on the weakest part of the classical tradition in order to link warfare with an organism's genetic make-up and the individual's need to reproduce. For example, Eibl-Eibesfeldt (1979), Shaw and Wang (1989), Van den Berghe (1981, 1995) and Gat (2006) argue that warfare emerges in the context of competition for scarce resources and is essentially a behavioural strategy for maximising genetic survival. The in-group favouritism is postulated as a universal feature of all species whereby ethnic

---

[1] It is worth noting that, unlike contemporary sociology, which shows little interest in this topic, much of classical social thought was in fact preoccupied with the study of this relationship (see Chapter 1).

and national attachments are seen as the direct extension of kinship. In this view warfare and group solidarity have genetic foundations, with ethnocentrism and strong national bonds based on biological principles of 'inclusive fitness' and kin selection. For sociobiologists, war is a form of aggression and, as such, only a means for the efficient acquisition of resources and for procreation through elimination of non-kin rivals. In a nutshell, warfare is the outcome of kin-based group competition whereby the intensity of cultural and biological homogeneity and social solidarity ultimately leads to violent confrontation.

There is an alternative, culturalist–historicist, version of this argument which is highly popular among military historians. While the central propositions of this perspective are similar, in the sense that they too derive collective violence and war from a given group's substance, they differ slightly in stressing a cultural rather than a biological basis to warfare. In this way they share much with the early group struggle paradigm: they too emphasise the unproblematic and inherent cultural similarity of groups and perceive warfare as being deeply rooted in the cultural foundations of particular societies. For example, the leading military historian John Keegan (1994: 12) understands war as 'an expression of culture, often a determinant of cultural forms, in some societies the culture itself'. In contrast to Clausewitz's famous dictum that war is a continuation of politics by other (military) means, Keegan (1994: 46) argues that war is 'the perpetuation of a culture by its own means'. Consequently, using this interpretative frame, he explains recent wars in the Balkans and the Caucasus as 'ancient in origin', akin to 'primitive war', and 'fed by passions and rancours that do not yield to rational measures of persuasion or control; they are apolitical, to a degree for which Clausewitz made little allowance' (Keegan 1994: 58). In a similar vein WWI is regularly interpreted as being caused by 'the rising nationalism' of Germany and the national aspirations of Slavic peoples under Habsburg rule (Lee 1988; Bourne 2005).

By extrapolating the emergence of warfare from the biological and cultural characteristics of groups, the naturalist explanation suffers from four pronounced epistemological weaknesses. Firstly, it takes for granted something that requires an explanation: group solidarity. Instead of analysing when and how group solidarity and national homogeneity are created or recreated, it simply presumes that the mere fact of sharing similar cultural or biological markers will somehow automatically translate into effective collective action. However, since Weber's early works (1968), sociologists have become aware that cultural or biological resemblance by itself is no reliable predictor of joint collective action and even less of violent action. This is especially the case with national markers, as for nations to materialise one has to mobilise individuals by politicising common cultural symbols (Breuilly 1993; Brubaker 1996; Malešević 2006). Since there is an abundance of cultural symbols and practices to draw upon, the process through which a category affiliation is transformed into a conscious political organisation (e.g. nation) is always based on relatively arbitrary decisions and actions. The presumption that nations are social actors by default is based on a mistaken view that conflates groups and categories. However, unlike categories, which are taxonomic collections of entities, a group is a 'mutually interacting, mutually recognising, mutually oriented, effectively communicating, bounded collectivity with a sense of solidarity, corporate identity, and capacity for concentrated action' (Brubaker 2004: 12).

Secondly, by treating groups as inherently homogenous, clearly bounded and stable entities, naturalists cannot escape the essentialist and reifying implications of their analyses. In this discourse, groups acquire individual attributes and personality traits such as will, emotions and intentions. Moreover, the naturalist researchers imply that they can know what these traits are. So, for example, when Keegan (1994: 192) writes about the Greco-Persian wars of the fifth century BCE he states that 'the Greeks took pride in their freedom and despised the subjects of Xerxes and Darius for their lack of it [but] their hatred of Persia was at root nationalistic'. Or when discussing Mongol invasions under Genghis Khan he describes Mongol warfare as 'an extension of the primitive urge to vengeance on an enormous scale' (1994: 204). Or when referring to post Ottoman Empire military developments he writes of the Turks as an 'intelligent and resourceful warrior race' (1994: 391). This strategy of attributing individual character traits to large ethnic and national collectivities while also psychologising them in the process (i.e. despising and hating Greeks; intelligent 'warrior race' of Turks; the irrational peoples of the Balkans; and the primitive and vengeance-prone Mongols) is a sign of an extremely feeble analysis.[2] Not only is it highly unlikely that hundreds of thousands of individuals who nominally belong to a particular ethnic and national collectivity will share the same personality traits, but it is also practically impossible to empirically verify such sweeping claims. Furthermore, statements like these firmly reify and simplify group membership: instead of analysing complex, contradictory and fluid processes that characterise group formation, the naturalists simply take groups as unproblematic cultural givens that act in exactly the same way as

---

[2] The crude ethnocentrism of this discourse hardly needs pointing out.

individuals do. This primordialist view clings to a profoundly unsociological model of social action, which rather than studying the actual mechanisms of ethnic group socialisation and group formation, operates with virtually unfalsifiable notions of ineffability, apriority and simple affectivity (Eller and Coughlan 1993).

Thirdly, the naturalists make no distinction between war and psychological responses such as hostility, aggression, desire, anger, fear or even martial practices such as fighting and killing. Although all of these are often integral to warfare they do not constitute warfare, just as sex is integral to marriage but marriage cannot be reduced to sexual practice. War, as with marriage, is first and foremost a social institution that reflects social structure and involves not only the actors taking part, but also connects with wider social networks and in the process legitimises and is legitimised by political and ideological authorities. The technological sophistication of modern warfare, which relies on long-distance missiles, air power and science, is a good indicator that it is possible to wage efficient wars without any need to resort to people's physical strength, aggressive impulses, or any other emotional motivation for that matter. In fact, the success of warfare depends on institutional and instrumental rationality, which requires the taming of human wrath and physical aggression. War is the product of neither biology nor psychology. It is a social institution that utilises military force and coercion for political purposes and rests on two central pillars, social organisation and ideology, neither of which can rely exclusively on emotional or biological responses. The simple voluntaristic view of warfare as an extension of a personal feud on a grand scale ignores its organisational complexity, its situational contingency, its relative historical novelty and its social embeddedness (see Chapters 3 and 4).

Finally, the naturalists simply assume that violence is inevitably linked with cultural or biological difference. For example Van den Berghe (1995: 365) argues that ethno-national animosity, hostility and racism 'can be expected to arise whenever variance in inherited physical appearance is greater between than within groups'. In this view the mere presence of biological and cultural markers leads inevitably to conflict and ultimately to violence. However, bearing in mind that ethnic conflicts and nationalist warfare are statistically rare (Fearon and Laitin 1996; Brubaker and Laitin 1998; Laitin 2007),[3] while cultural and biological diversity among human beings is nearly

---

[3] Laitin (2007: 4–5) illustrates this well in the case of Africa, which is ordinarily perceived as the epicentre of ethnic conflicts and wars: 'the percentage of neighbouring ethnic groups that experienced violent communal incidents was infinitesimal – for any randomly chosen but neighbouring pair of ethnic groups, on average only 5 in 10,000 had a recorded violent conflict in any year'.

universal, it seems readily apparent that there is no causality between the presence of cultural differences and violent action. If speaking different languages, performing dissimilar rituals or worshiping mutually incompatible deities would automatically lead to violent confrontation, then warfare would be a permanent feature of nearly all societies at all times. Similarly, deducing cultural homogeneity and solidarity from biologically defined notions of common descent, and interpreting ethnic and national bonds through the prism of kinship, is as limiting as it is reductionist. Ethnicity and nationess are dynamic social relationships and not static, primordial and fixed group properties. Moreover, the idea of common descent among huge collectivities such as ethnic groups and nations cannot be other but symbolic and fictitious. While some naturalists such as Gat (2006) and Van den Berghe (1981) agree that in the modern age of nation-states common descent can be mythical and manipulated, they still maintain that much of group identification is based on biological descent. Nevertheless, switching from the real to the metaphorical concept of common descent is simply a sign of weak argumentation. The naturalists cannot have it both ways: either common descent is real and fully grounded in biology or it is not real at all, and thus group cohesion must be explained as a product of social and cultural processes. To sum up, the naturalist argument that collective solidarity and cultural homogeneity in themselves are the principal cause of warfare is completely unfounded.

The formative canard

Although the naturalist view remains highly popular outside of academia, most social analysts, and sociologists in particular, subscribe to what can be called the formative, that is, the inverse, relationship of the two: rather than being a cause of war, group solidarity and homogeneity are the product of war and inter-group violence. Here too classical 'bellicose' social thought remains indispensable. Since Simmel's and Sumner's early studies on the impact of conflict on group formation, most approaches start from the proposition that violent confrontation and war enhance in-group homogenisation, reinforce collective solidarity and even create groups. Breaking with the traditional mould, Simmel (1955: 13–17) switched the focus of attention from the destructive towards the integrative qualities of inter-group conflict. Not only did he interpret conflict as a positive kind of sociation that creates group unity, but also saw conflict as an intensive form of social interaction, an active process that mobilises individuals and is motivated by the desire to 'resolve divergent dualism; it is a way of achieving some kind of unity'.[4] More specifically, he links the emergence of national solidarity exclusively to the presence of an external threat: 'Essentially, France owes the consciousness of its national unity only to its fight against the English, and only the Moorish war made the Spanish regions into one people.' Similarly Sumner (1906: 12) emphasised the importance of external hostility for in-group unity: 'the exigencies of war with outsiders are what makes peace inside' and it is these exigencies that 'also make government and law in the in-group'.

Most contemporary formative approaches build on these assumptions: national bonds are not the sources but the outcome of violent conflicts. Although they all share this principal proposition the three leading formative perspectives provide different explanations of its social relevance. Neo-Durkheimians such as Antony D. Smith (1981, 1999, 2003), Hutchinson (2005, 2007) and Marvin and Ingle (1999) focus on the role of 'blood sacrifice' in the construction of nations as sacred communions of citizens. In this view, external conflicts and wars sharpen group boundaries and harden stereotypes and self-images which help to foster ethnic group identities and, in the long term, forge national consciousness. As Antony D. Smith (1981: 379) puts it: 'the historic consciousness that is so essential a part of the definition of what we mean by the term "ethnic community", is very often a product of warfare'. Since ethnic groups and nations are conceptualised in this approach as moral communities, the neo-Durkheimians focus primarily on the institutionalisation and reproduction of cultural meanings and memories associated with war sacrifices. Marvin and Ingle (1999) see nationalism as a civil religion espoused through the sacred flag and argue that the very existence of the nation is dependent on the periodic 'totem sacrifice' of its youth, as warfare is a means through which nations are re-energised and group solidarity is achieved. For Antony D. Smith (2003) and Hutchinson (2007), war heroism articulated in commemorations and monuments for the 'glorious dead' establish ethical parameters that determine future actions as they bind posterity in moral obligation to dead heroes.

In contrast, realists such as Jervis (1978) and Posen (1993) and neo-Weberians such as Tilly (1985, 1992b) and Mann (1993, 2005), argue that rather than stemming from shared moral values, national solidarity and cultural homogeneity are direct products of coercive state apparatuses. It is the anarchical character of the international state system that often leads to the

[4] Simmel put it as follows: 'the [group] boundary is not a spatial fact with sociological consequences but a sociological fact that is formed spatially' (quoted in Frisby 1984: 127).

mutual distrust of nation-states as they aim to preserve autonomy by increasing their security. Paradoxically, any substantial attempt by a state to enhance its security (e.g. increasing its military capabilities) is often interpreted by other nation-states as a direct threat triggering an arms race. Hence the initial aim to enhance security ultimately results in weakened security, as the proliferation of armaments and military spending eventually becomes exhausting and leads to less rather than more security. In this context, nationalism is the product of a 'security dilemma', as its mobilising potential improves the military capabilities of warring sides. As Posen (1993: 122) puts it: 'States or stateless groups, drifting into competition for whatever reason, will quickly turn to the reinforcement of national identity because of its potency as a military resource.' For Tilly (1985) and Mann (1986), this ever-present military competition among nation-states, coupled with protracted warfare, have fostered capital accumulation, state expansion, improved fiscal, financial and territorial organisation, administrative and legal penetration, while simultaneously mobilising popular support around the idea of the defence of the homeland. In other words, large-scale group solidarity and strong nationalist bonds are understood as by-products of competition between states: in order to mobilise their populations for wars, rulers had on the one hand to concede wide-ranging citizenship and political rights, thus extending the realm of civil society, while on the other hand their investment in the institutional mechanisms of primary and secondary socialisation (e.g. education systems, military conscription and mass media) made sure that nationalism became a dominant ideology encompassing both state and civil society.

The third formative approach is less concerned with the structural and historical contexts of how ethnic and national bonds are forged, and is more interested in universal, trans-historical motives and behaviour among the social actors involved. The rational-actor models (Banton 1983; Fearon 1995; Hechter 1995; Wintrobe 2006; Laitin 2007) explain the intensity of ethnic and national group solidarity under conditions of violent inter-group conflict with reference to the instrumental goals of individual agents. In this view, ethnicity and nationhood do not have a *sui generis* quality but operate according to the same rules of group formation as all other sociological phenomena. Starting from the proposition that human agents are utility maximisers governed by the principles of instrumental rationality, this approach argues that collective ethnic or national group action is most likely to emerge in situations where individuals can manipulate their cultural similarity for their individual benefit. In other words, ethnic and national wars generate an 'imperfect market condition' where individual instrumental rationality is situationally transformed into enhanced group solidarity and as rational individuals make informed choices to amplify or downplay their cultural markers for the purpose of self-benefit, they invariably and circuitously produce ethnic or national group solidarity and cultural homogeneity. Hechter (1995: 54) illustrates this argument by using the example of the Bosnian War of 1992–1995: 'it is not difficult to interpret events in Bosnia as the by-product of a cool, calculating land-grab by Serbs and Croats against their weaker Muslim victims, for grabbing land, like other forms of looting, is profitable in the absence of effective state authority'. In a similar vein, Laitin (2007: 22) explains the rational calculation behind secessionist movements: 'civil war is profitable for potential insurgents, in that they can both survive and enjoy some probability of winning the state'. In a nutshell, collective solidarity and homogeneity are direct corollaries of interest-driven individual action: intense nationalist feelings are a consequence of an extraordinary situation where violent confrontation encourages a structural overlap between an individual and in-group interests.

While there is no doubt that the formative accounts are a substantial improvement on the naturalist interpretations of the sources of group cohesion in times of war, they too have a number of epistemological flaws. Firstly, much of the formative explanations simply presume that large-scale group formation and its patterns of solidarity originate and operate according to the same principles as those of small groups. In other words, no significant distinction is made between the micro-level interactional social mechanisms at work in small, mostly kinship based, groups and the macro-level organisationally produced social cohesion that characterises vast collective entities such as nation-states. However, as Collins (2004, 2008) rightly argues, long-term intense solidarity is only possible on the micro level, between individuals who can directly interact with each other. The empirical research on the performance of soldiers in combat has persuasively demonstrated that very few of them are motivated by their loyalty to their nation, state, ethnic group or to abstract ideological principles such as socialism, liberalism or religious commitment (see Chapter 7). Instead, the primary motive was a feeling of solidarity with other soldiers in their platoon (Marshall 1947; Holmes 1985; Bourke 2000). The neo-Durkheimian interpretation of social cohesion presumes that in times of war collective effervescence reinforces nationalism to the level that it functions as a single, uniform and highly synchronised group feeling that spreads evenly throughout the entire society. Nevertheless as Kalyvas (2006) documents well, drawing on the example of numerous civil wars, a large-scale normative nationalist narrative is often used by local actors and small-scale groups to map their own private grievances and discords by re-articulating them in official nationalist terms. Rather than operating as a giant all-embracing Durkheimian collective conscience, genuine social solidarity is generated on the micro level – in the patches, tads and fragments of small local social networks. In contrast, the successful production of social cohesion and cultural homogenisation of large collective entities such as nations and ethnic groups requires long-term institutional, organisational and ideological support.

Secondly, the fact that in-group homogenisation and national solidarity is interpreted as functional in times of violent conflicts does not make it inevitable, nor does it explain the link between the two. Most formative approaches adopt some version of the functionalist argument that warfare is beneficial, that is, functional, to in-group solidarity. However, needs are not causes. Not only are there many historical instances where there was a need for intensive solidarity in times of external threat (or war) and it went unfulfilled, but having a particular need cannot possibly explain a specific historical outcome. Germany's WWI experience illustrates this point well. Russia's capitulation in 1917 and the Ludendorff Offensive of March 1918 brought Germany to the brink of victory in WWI, but its domestic political turmoil and intensive social polarisation proved stronger than any calls to national unity. As a consequence of not having substantial domestic support, the morale of German soldiers plummeted and the army was crushed at the Battle of Amiens in August 1918, which 'was the first outright and irreversible defeat that the Germans had suffered in four years of fighting' (Howard 2002: 106). Hence Germany lost the war. While there is no doubt that intensive national solidarity is instrumental for a war effort, it is neither automatic nor universal. Most of all, when it materialises it is an effect – not a cause – that requires proper explanation. In this sense, functionalist arguments are teleological, as they interpret social events and institutions by focusing on effects and needs rather than explaining the origins and causes of these effects. Furthermore, the very fact that, in the context of an external threat, politicians and nationalist leaders have to make repeated calls for national unity is in itself a potent indicator that social solidarity on a large scale is not habitual and natural, but needs to be institutionally created and constantly reinforced through organisational mechanisms.

Thirdly, rather than automatically enhancing cultural homogenisation and national solidarity, wars can in fact destroy the internal national cohesion of the societies involved. Since Simmel and Sumner see inter-group violent conflict as the most important generator of national homogenisation (or in Simmel's case the only such generator) they make no allowance for this possibility. For realists and neo-Weberians such an outcome is simply a sign of the infrastructural weaknesses of small or ethnically heterogeneous states, while well established modern nation-states are perceived as institutionally resistant, capable of withstanding the tendency towards national disintegration even when thoroughly defeated, as for example France in 1940 or Japan in 1945. Since neo-Durkheimians tie national homogenisation and cultural unity to institutionalised memories of warfare, they attribute a great deal of social importance to war victories, as they do to military defeats. However, in both cases the emphasis is on the heroic or cathartic worship of a soldier's sacrifice for the nation and thus exclusively on the integrative factors. Although A. D. Smith (1981: 383) is well aware of cases of war shattering ethnic and national solidarity, citing examples of the adverse effects of war on internal cohesion including the Jewish War of 66–73 CE, the ancient Greek wars between city states and to Austro-Hungary in WWI, he still maintains the view that although protracted wars can strain national cohesion in the medium term, they are most likely to 'reinforce the community's framework, its sense of ethnic individuality and history' in the long term. The only exception to this neo-Durkheimian rule is the case of multi-ethnic states, which are seen as the most likely to collapse under the conditions of protracted warfare. This view overlooks the fact that post-war glorification and the institutional worship of the 'glorious dead' is not a straightforward or natural response to war sacrifices made in the name of the nation, but instead is something created by specific social organisations, requiring continual ideological and institutional support. To put it simply, it is not the experience of war itself that determines long-term post-war solidarity and homogeneity, as this clearly varies from case to case, but it is the organisational and ideological mechanisms of existing state apparatuses as well as civil society groups, that shapes the intensity and character of what and how war memories will be preserved and interpreted. This is quite evident in the contrast between how the WWI and WWII have been commemorated and understood in the Weimar Republic and the federal Germany of today (Mosse 1991; Giesen 2004). Furthermore, the view that only multi-ethnic states are destined to shatter under the strains of war presumes that there is a qualitative difference between ethnic and national wars on the one hand, and civil and ideological wars on the other. Nevertheless, as Kalyvas (2006, 2008) empirically demonstrates using the example of the Greek Civil War (1943–1949), the Algerian War of Independence (1954–1962), the Kenyan Mau Mau insurgency (1952–1960) and the Spanish Civil War (1936–1939), ideological markers can have even stronger salience than ethnic and national markers. As he sums up: 'I point to overlooked evidence suggesting considerable heterogeneity and fluidity in the behavioural expressions of ethnic identities within civil war … these identities do not always remain stable and fixed during conflict; if they do change, they may soften rather than only harden' (Kalyvas 2008: 1045). As ethnicity and nationhood are not given, primordial group properties but dynamic social relations, they often act in a similar way to ideological commitments (Malešević 2006).

Finally, formative approaches overemphasise the sacrificial character of warfare – the propensity to die for others in the name of one's nation. This is especially visible in the neo-Durkheimian accounts, which interpret strong national bonds in terms of an individual's attempt to overcome the problem of personal oblivion. As A. D. Smith (1991: 160) puts it: 'identification with the "nation" in a secular era is the surest way to surmount the finality of death and ensure a measure of personal immortality'. Hence a war sacrifice is an endeavour to symbolically link past, present and future generations through the image of a nation as an everlasting entity. Although coming from a completely different, that is utilitarian, logic, the rational-actor models subscribe to a similar argument while giving it a more rationalist spin: the war sacrifice of a soldier's life in the name of a nation is 'a solidarity multiplier', a trade-off whereby 'an individual gives up autonomy for solidarity' so that beliefs are traded 'for a feeling of belonging-ness to a group' (Wintrobe 2006: 41). Although the willingness of soldiers to sacrifice their lives is an important indicator of the intensity of social solidarity, its near universal exaltation across societies and throughout history just reinforces the fact that its occurrence is quite rare. However, despite its nominal veneration no state is interested in turning the majority of its population into national martyrs. What is much more important in linking warfare with social cohesion is not readiness to die but willingness to kill for the nation. While individual sacrifice largely serves as 'an inner standard for the community, an *examplum virtutis* for subsequent emulation' (A. D. Smith 1995: 63), and, as such, has to remain exceptional and rare, warfare turns killing into a mass practice stimulated and legitimised by the wider society. Although the common perception is that killing is relatively easy, as Collins (2008: 20–7) argues and documents: 'violent interactions are difficult because they go against the grain of normal interaction rituals … we have evolved, on the physiological level, in such a way that fighting encounters a deep interactional obstacle, because of the way our neurological hard-wiring makes us act in the immediate presence of other human beings'. Consequently, and in contrast to commonsense views, 'it is easier to put up with injury and death than to inflict it' (Collins 2008: 74). Therefore as murder is a social taboo in most societies and as the killing of fellow human beings attempts to rescind the bequest of primary and secondary socialisation, it necessitates much more institutional and organisational work than does sacrifice. To transform ordinary placid and moral citizens into bloodthirsty mass killers takes a lot of social pressure, coercion and fear; that is, powerful organisational and ideological support has to be in place and operational for a long period of time. In brief, social solidarity and group homogeneity are not automatic and natural responses to inter-group violence: they are neither the cause nor the direct product of warfare.

The structural origins of national 'solidarity'

If nationalism and war are almost universally perceived as being automatically linked, and if the two dominant analytical interpretations of their relationship are essentially unsound, how can one explain the origins and character of this phenomenon? I argue that rather than being a natural and mechanical reaction to an external threat, or a habitual artefact forged through the process of violent confrontation, national 'solidarity' and group homogeneity stem from events and processes that are for the most part external to the war zone. In other words, strong national bonds are neither the cause nor the result of the battlefield; they originate outside of the conflict and are formed long before any sign of war. Unprecedented nationalist fervour is witnessed in times of intensive warfare, but is not causally linked to war itself, but is, rather, a product of the two historical and structural processes that have been in motion for several centuries: centrifugal ideologisation and the cumulative bureaucratisation of coercion. Instead of simply bringing national 'solidarity' and group homogeneity into the open or creating it on the spot, war acts as a catalyst that institutionally connects these two processes and generates a space for their synergetic manifestation.

Centrifugal ideologisation and nationalism

George Mosse (1991) coined the term 'nationalisation of the masses' to explain the structural phenomenon that occurred throughout the second half of the nineteenth century and the early twentieth century in Europe. By this he meant the gradual expansion of nationalist ideals and practices from the relatively narrow confines of the political and cultural elites and some middle classes to the entire population of respective nation-states. However, this was not only an uncontested, top-down phenomenon developed through state apparatuses but also one that involved civil society groupings. Furthermore, it operated in the context of an ideologically diverse environment (i.e. liberal, socialist, communist and fascist social orders) and so it is better to speak of the ideologisation of 'the masses' or centrifugal ideologisation. What really stands out in this process is not only the spread of a nationalist narrative to the wider population but the fact that through this process large swathes of people become both objects and subjects of fully fledged ideological action. By focusing on the point that nation, rather than class, gender, or religion has become the central ideological master-signifier of the modern age, one is likely to overlook the centrality of the process itself through which this has been achieved – the ideologisation of 'the masses'.

Since the early diagnoses of the sociological classics such as Toennies, Weber, Durkheim, Marx and Spencer, it has become apparent that modern social orders differ from their traditional counterparts in having a more extensive division of labour, greater rationalisation of social action, and impersonality of human interaction, and a general lack of tight mutual bonds. The large-scale character of the modern nation-state, which often includes millions of inhabitants, most of whom will never meet or see each other, stands in stark contrast to small-scale groups, the members of which are able to directly interact with one another. However, as the very existence of a nation-state is premised on a degree of communality, it requires an alternative social glue to keep it together. Furthermore, the nation-state, unlike its predecessors – empires, city- states, or city leagues – legitimises its existence through the idea of popular sovereignty and so it needs this glue more than any of its predecessors. Hence, centrifugal ideologisation emerges as an institutional and extra-institutional attempt to forge something that resembles social solidarity at this macro level of the nation-state. However, given that large-scale entities of this size cannot possibly generate genuine solidarity of the sort that entails face-to-face interaction (Collins 2004; 2008), they are forced to rely on ideologisation as a structural replacement for solidarity. In this respect ideologisation is a continuous process which attempts to make large-scale organisations such as nation-states into entities that possess kinship-based face-to-face communal solidarity.

Nevertheless, it is important to emphasise that this is not a one-way (top-down) process but works in both directions: the state apparatus utilises its key institutions for ideological dissemination (from the educational system, mass media, military conscription to welfare and citizenship obligations), whiles family networks and various civil society groups play an active role in articulating and reinforcing the moral parameters around which the dominant ideological (nationalist) narrative is framed. As Gellner (1983), Breuilly (1993) and Hobsbawm (1990) persuasively argue (and the last two also document well) nationalist ideology is not a simple extension of pre-modern ethnic group loyalties. It is a qualitatively different phenomenon whereby, as Gellner (1997: 74) puts it, nationalist ideology speaks in the language of *Gemeinschaft* but operates along the tracks of a *Gesellschaft*: 'a mobile anonymous society simulating a closed cosy community'. In other words, unlike the traditional agrarian world where a person's loyalty rarely extended beyond the confines of the next village, and sense of solidarity was rigidly linked to his or her social status, the modern social order rests on social and territorial mobility which encompasses large numbers of diverse, but morally equal, individuals. To forge a sense of common purpose but also to function more efficiently in the modern world of interdependency, nationalism emerged as the pivotal ideological glue capable of providing an institutional macro-level substitute for social solidarity. In less than two hundred years, from its first conceptual enunciation in the principles of the Enlightenment and Romanticism and its material expression in the French and American revolutionary upheavals, nationalism has become the dominant operative ideology of nearly all nation-states (Malešević 2002; 2006). Its origins have a firm structural basis: the birth of the modern bureaucratic rationalistic state, the introduction and expansion of mass public education conducted through a single standardised vernacular, the corresponding growth of literacy rates, the proliferation of mass media, the inauguration of universal military conscription and the democratisation and secularisation of public space (Gellner 1964, 1983; Weber 1976; Anderson 1983; Mann 1986). However, none of these structural transformations would come alive and give birth to a society-wide nationalist ideology if it were not for popular mobilisation grounded in local, often family-based networks and civil society associations. Centrifugal ideologisation developed gradually as a long-term process through which, on the one hand, the state relied on its key institutional mechanisms to turn 'peasants into Frenchmen' (Weber 1976), while on the other hand, local actors and organisations were engaged in transforming micro-level solidarity into a national loyalty. However, social solidarity beyond the micro level is difficult to create and even more difficult to sustain: Anderson (1983: 6) rightly says 'all communities larger than primordial villages of face-to-face contact … are imagined'; to have any chance of success the ideologisation of 'the masses' has to be a continuous, almost never-ending process.

Once peasants are made into loyal citizens of their respective nation-states, their sense of obligation and devotion to a nation is never instinctive or automatic but is dependent on permanent institutional and extra-institutional support. Although all nation-states utilise propagandistic techniques (especially at times of war) as Pareto (1966: 44) was already well aware, to be efficient, war propaganda and national stereotyping has to rely on already existing 'sentiments' and perceptions (see Chapter 7). Centrifugal ideologisation is not a simple creation of the voluntaristic and deliberate action of rulers, but a structural phenomenon, thus requiring much more than Socrates's 'sophisticated lies'. The continuous ideologisation of the population typically results in what Billig (1995) calls banal nationalism. In other words the strength of nationalist ideology is not rooted in the sturdy battle cries and heroic images of victory and sacrifice. These highly intense images and actions are rare, exceptional and usually short lived. Moreover, their very existence is dependent on the workings of low-intensity everyday nationalism. Hence, the long-term potency of nationalist ideology comes from its institutional embeddedness – its almost unconscious, habitual reproduction in the daily rhetoric and practice of politicians, administrators, newspapers, marketing brands, coinage and bank notes, weather reports and many other ordinary activities.

As Edensor (2002) demonstrates convincingly, using the example of Britain, banal nationalism is responsible for the spatialisation of the nation, as this is clearly visible in both nationalised rural and urban landscapes (as depicted in popular magazines reinforcing a particular nostalgic image of the past) and everyday, quotidian landscapes characterised by ordinary functional objects such as telephone boxes, fire hydrants, street lighting, post boxes and many other items which, with their distinctive 'national' shapes and colours, underpin the sense of nationhood. Thus, nationalism is strongest not when it is loud and barking but when it is trivial, ordinary and taken for granted. It is this silent and routine process of 'enhabitation' that generates its power: 'thoughts, reactions and symbols become turned into routine habits and, thus become enhabited. The result is that the past is enhabited in the present in a dialectic of forgotten remembrance … These reminders of nationhood serve to turn background space into homeland space' (Billig 1995: 42–3). It is the process of ideologisation that normalises and enhabits national symbols, actions and events into mundane everyday life that act as forceful, daily reminders, 'flagging' one's membership of a particular nation. It is the dull routine and the institutionalised daily repetition that makes banal nationalism such a powerful ideological mechanism that can quickly transform into virulent nationalism in times of war.

In addition to the institutionalisation of banal nationalism, which is largely an external process, the ideologisation of 'the masses' also encompasses its internal counterpart – the subjective disciplining and internalisation of the peculiar nationalist ontology. Since Weber's early works (1946, 1968) on rationalisation, sociologists have identified two central and mutually dependent processes that have characterised modernity: the objective rationalisation of bureaucratic organisations and the subjective rationalisation of individuals inhabiting the modern world. In particular, Weber emphasised the importance of the Christian, more specifically the Calvinist, doctrinal view that rejects emotional action in favour of ascetic determination and 'the alert, methodical control of one's own pattern of life and behaviour' (Weber 1968: 544).

Although Billig (1995) clearly neglects this, banal nationalism operates in a similar way: institutional reinforcement of nationalism regularly goes hand in hand with the personal self-disciplining of 'the soul'. Since nationalism, as a sense of group loyalty and as an ideology of popular sovereignty, is a modern belief system *par excellence*, its society-wide expansion and proliferation requires not only structural transformations but also a dramatic alteration in each person's *Weltanschauung*. As Gellner (1983) argues, illiterate peasants do not make good nationalists. Rather a fully fledged nationalist ideology entails a substantial degree of literacy, subjective reflection and awareness that one lives in the world of nation-states, and that one's interests, goals and social status often overlap with, and can be realised best through, the institutional framework of the nation-state. It is only when the majority of the population starts to conceptualise, understand and identify with the world primarily in national terms (as opposed to the pre-modern focus on the village, manor or a free town), that nationalism becomes the dominant cognitive and normative universe of the world. For this to happen it is paramount that the population at large starts to distinguish sharply between those who are members of the same nation and those who are not. In this sense nationalism is not a simple extension of ethnic stereotyping and primordial xenophobia. Instead, it is a novel social condition. Rather than being a mere emotional response and supposed psychoanalytic 'universal disdain of the other', nationalism involves a new historical context that generates a new sense of individual and collective rationality.

Contrary to the commonsense view, the strength of nationalist ideology is not defined by affective outbursts of hatred, but by instrumental and value rationality, both of which imply a considerable degree of self-direction and self-restraint. As Bauman (1989) points out, there is a substantial qualitative difference between the emotionally driven periodic eruptions of anti-Semitic hatred that characterised pre-modern pogroms and the modernist ideological principles that underpinned the Holocaust. Unlike the sporadic, chaotic and random violence expressed in episodic pogroms, the 'Final Solution' was a thoroughly modern ideological project: it required an efficient modern bureaucratic machine, science and technology for its implementation, and the utopian ideological goal of creating a biologically pure social order. Similarly, nationalism works best not when it is hot, unconstrained and red in tooth and claw but when it is cold, rational, disciplined and almost invisible. There is no need to revert to individual insults and demeaning behaviour when the exclusion and elimination of the national Other can be achieved through the legalistic discourse of law and order and majority rights. While ethnic and national slurs and racist jokes are the subject of near universal condemnation and outrage, institutional discrimination, ethnic profiling by the police and deportation of 'illegal aliens' are either praised or condoned by the majority of those who see themselves as constituting the nation. Centrifugal ideologisation would never succeed if it was not grounded in the instrumental and value rationality of the majority of the population. This process relies on institutions as much as the subjective conditioning that routinises and normalises nationalism into an ordinary, everyday practice. Hence the outbreak of war does not create nationalism. It simply opens the door of an oven that has been cooking for several centuries: it only makes explicit and visible something that has been taken for granted and implicit.

The cumulative bureaucratisation of coercion and nationalism

Although centrifugal ideologisation is a powerful social mechanism that often successfully transforms genuine micro-level solidarity into a broadly shared nationalist narrative, the switch from banal to virulent forms of nationalism also requires direct institutional intervention. While the existence and habitual reproduction of banal nationalism accounts for the cognitive and moral assent exhibited at the battlefields and 'home fronts', in itself it is not enough to turn ordinary men and women into brutal and effective mass killers. In other words, as individual human beings are fearful creatures and not particularly good at fighting, without social organisation to keep large groups of people together and compel them to act in a particular (national and violent) way, it is most likely that the commonly shared grand nationalist narrative of macro-level loyalty would disperse back into patches of mutually incompatible micro-level solidarities.

As Collins (2008: 11) argues, it is social organisation that 'enables individuals to overcome the pervasive fear that keeps most of them from fighting; if it were not socially well organised, wide-participation fighting would not be possible'. Hence, in addition to the ideologisation of the 'masses' another key structural feature of modernity has to be in place for nationalism and war to gel – the cumulative bureaucratisation of coercion. Here too Weber's (1968) legacy is vital. Following his diagnosis, it can be said that modern social orders differ from their traditional counterparts in favouring bureaucratic models of organisation over patrimonial, gerontocratic and other types of traditional authority. Whereas traditional patterns of organisation were grounded in the ruler's personal right of possession and a willingness to act according to his or her wishes, bureaucratic administration derives its authority from a consistent system of abstract rules and regulations. Consequently, unlike traditional authority which tends to be nepotistic, clientelist and status-based, bureaucratic organisation is, in principle, impersonal, meritocratic, rule-bound and strictly and transparently hierarchical. It is these very characteristics that make modern social organisations highly efficient in pursuing their goals. By fostering compartmentalisation of tasks through the delegation of responsibility and the strict division of labour, bureaucratic organisations – the epitome of which is the modern military machine – succeed in prioritising discipline and order over individual initiative and emotional commitment. Although the ultimate goals of bureaucratic systems can be, and very often are, expressed in value-rational terms (e.g. relying on the military organisation to liberate one's nation or to institute a communist, liberal or Islamic social order) their inner logic is almost exclusively shaped by instrumental rationality. Weber's metaphor of the iron cage clearly and tellingly alludes to the uniform, instrumental and machine-like quality of the bureaucratic routine. Nevertheless, what is also important to stress is that bureaucratic efficiency is embedded in its hierarchical and specialised structure. To put it bluntly, because bureaucratic organisation is successfully legitimised through its efficiency – this is after all, as Weber calls it, 'domination through knowledge' – it is the most pervasive mechanism of social control. The fact that the bureaucratic hierarchy is meritocratic, transparent and socially mobile does not make it less domineering. On the contrary, these features make it particularly overbearing, rigid and hierarchical, and individual submission to (legitimate) authority is not only valued, but any sign of incompliance is castigated and formally penalised. The stress on discipline implies obedience and a coercive chain of command. In other words, the functional rationality of bureaucratic organisation has a clear dark side – it is the most powerful structural device of domination. If there was no social organisation in place, warfare would be impossible.

Hence, as war is not an inter-group feud on a large scale but a violent contest between social organisations, the growing potency of modern bureaucracy translates directly into the increased scale of destruction. To put it differently, the ever-increasing rationalisation of organised action paradoxically leads to irrational outcomes as modernity brings much more devastation and greater levels of human casualties than any previous epoch. Unlike their traditional counterparts which had no infrastructural means and resources, and could not rely on a broader sense of national loyalty, modern bureaucratic organisations such as nation-states and militaries are able to legitimately mobilise and keep under control hundreds of thousands and even millions of people in the pursuit of a specific political and military goal. It is the battles between large-scale, well armed, advanced bureaucracies – that is the modern nation-states – that have transformed violent conflicts into total wars.

Although realists and neo-Weberians clearly recognise the unprecedented rise of the infrastructural powers of the modern nation-state, their focus on the changing geopolitical contexts is in some respects too externalist, omitting the internal interplay between ideologisation and the bureaucratisation of coercion. Instead of focusing on the internal stick and external carrot they overstate the role of the external stick and internal carrot. While it is obviously true that the dramatic increase in structural violence that characterises modernity owes a great deal to inter-state rivalries and rulers' ability to mobilise popular support in exchange for extended citizenship rights and gradual democratisation (Tilly 1985, 2007; Mann 1988, 1993), even more important are the internal disciplinary effects of modern social organisations, and in particular the rise of the military iron cage which makes sure that there is no escape from the battlefield. Modern warfare combines the development of sophisticated organisational devices which confine soldiers to the fronts and gradually make mass killing morally and technologically undemanding (long-distance artillery, high-altitude bombing, gas chambers, etc.) with the externally driven struggle for national prestige. On the one hand, the coercive structure of bureaucratic organisation creates conditions that institutionally discourage disobedience, while on the other hand the competitive and eventually conflictual context in which organisations operate fosters a constant striving for the enhancement of the prestige of one's nation. The fact that this process is underpinned by the ongoing ideologisation of 'the masses' in all nation-states involved, contributes further to the eventual transition from banal to virulent nationalism.

The cold, habitual and occasionally calculating nature of banal nationalism goes hand in hand with the detached, rationalist and instrumentally driven ethics of bureaucratic organisation. Whereas in pre-modern social orders there was a ferociousness that provoked and demanded a strong emotional response and involved mutilations, torture, peremptory executions, human sacrifices and ritual war hunts, modernity dispenses with passion by turning violence into a depersonalised means to an end (Collins 1974: 419–20). Overt brutality is replaced with detached and instrumentally driven callousness. It is no accident that murderous ethnic cleansing and genocide are distinctly modern phenomena (Bauman 1989; Mann 2005), since they depend on the availability of large-scale organisation able to implement such mammoth tasks, but also the existence of a specific, depersonalised, callous logic and ethics that perceives mass extermination as the most efficient means of fulfilling a clearly defined goal. Instead of blind hatred and passionate repugnance, modern organisations are simply focused on removing an obstacle to achieve a desired objective.

However, detachment does not imply total lack of commitment. On the contrary, as Merton (1952: 365) notes 'discipline can be effective only if the ideal patterns are buttressed by strong sentiments which entail devotion to one's duties, a keen sense of the limitation of one's authority and competence, and methodical performance of routine activities. The efficacy of social structure depends ultimately upon infusing group participants with appropriate attitudes and sentiments'. Hence, the routinised detachment that one encounters in both banal nationalism and bureaucratic organisation are deeply linked and complementary. While the bureaucratic machine provides a coercive institutional setting that reproduces disjoined and habitual patterns of action, banal nationalism supplies an ideological cement where loyalty to a nation-state and an organisation meet. In fact, banal nationalism is nothing more than a habitual and taken-for-granted sense of loyalty and attachment to a specific bureaucratic organisation – the nation-state. Its apparent invisibility is often mistakenly taken as a sign that nationalism is a weak force in everyday life and that it is only war conditions and other 'aberrant' crises that provoke these 'atavistic' features in human beings. However the reality, as noted by Billig (1995), is that banality does not imply harmlessness. The fact that nationalism is not blatant and loud does not mean that is not pervasive. Actually, as Roland Barthes (1993) was acutely aware, the strength of a particular ideology is best measured by the degree of its everyday naturalisation: how and when particular meanings, discourses, symbols and practices are nearly universally taken for granted and perceived as innocent, normal and natural. When the hegemonic power that bureaucratic organisations enjoy in the modern era is wedded to the ever-present centrifugal ideologisation in the form of banal nationalism, this produces a potentially lethal cocktail. The delegation of tasks decontextualises violence. Orderly obedience to authority and the hierarchal chains of command remove a sense of responsibility. The detached ethic of professionalism and task-driven action fosters a callous attitude towards those who are not members of the organisation (i.e. nation-state). The coercive nature of the bureaucratic machine secures mass recruitment, wide participation and proficient (military) training. The social organisation also supplies the adequate means and technology for mass extermination. Finally, the perpetual ideologisation of 'the masses', infused with the habitual and repetitive practices and values of banal nationalism, provides a compelling ideological glue that projects genuine micro-level solidarity onto the level of the nation-state. Once all of these ongoing processes and actions are synergetically linked in one event – war – nationalism is ready to metamorphose from the banal and ordinary Dr Jekyll into a virulent and venomous Mr Hyde.

Conclusion

There is an almost universally shared perception that modern inter-state warfare and nationalism are profoundly interlinked. The typical images associated with the wars of the last two centuries are those of dying and killing for one's country: the heroic martyrdom of the 'glorious dead' and the nationalist frenzy of overzealous soldiers defending their fatherland cheered on by their equally fervent brethren. However, these and similar images project a strong causality between warfare and nationalism that in fact does not exist. Rather than being a direct product or an inevitable outcome of war, nationalism is a much more complex and contingent modern phenomenon that entails long-term organisational and ideological supports. There is nothing automatic, natural or inevitable in either war or nationalism and there is nothing self-evident and inherent in the relationship between the two. Nationalism is not a simple extension of social solidarity to a wider group but an ideological mechanism institutionally created to be an organisational surrogate for genuine face-to-face interactive bonds. In a similar vein, war is not an extension of group aggression on a macro-level scale but a violent political conflict waged between two opposed social organisations. Most of all, war does not create nationalism, neither does nationalism generate wars. Instead, the development of nationalism owes much to institutional processes that have little to do with actual battlefields: centrifugal ideologisation and the cumulative bureaucratisation of coercion. It is the historical contingencies and the synergetic contexts, rather than warfare itself that bring these two processes together and open the door for the transformation of habitual banality into organised virulence.

7 War propaganda and solidarity

Introduction

Propaganda is often identified as an essential ingredient of warfare. The general view is that propagandistic imagery and messages are effective devices in transforming popular perceptions and attitudes towards a particular war. The assumption is that no matter how unpopular conflict might initially be, effective and well orchestrated propaganda is capable of altering such views and making the war effort plausible and even popular. When one thinks of war propaganda it is Goebbels's fiery speeches, the Nazi Party's use of torchlight parades, brass bands, massed choirs and other propagandistic techniques that quickly spring to mind. War propaganda is often seen as a powerful motivating force able to persuade young men (and more recently young women too) into volunteering to fight and die for their country, ethnonational group, religious creed or ideological doctrine.

However, as with all social phenomena, the workings of war propaganda are much more complex than that. The central argument of this chapter is that rather than being an omnipotent force able, with relative ease, to sway millions of people to change their perceptions of reality, war propaganda is predominantly a mechanism for society-wide self-justification. In other words, instead of having the capacity to dramatically convert public opinion and actions, most propaganda serves as a cognitive, moral and legitimising map utilised by those who already subscribe to the values espoused by the propaganda. The chapter also contests the alleged inherent connections between propaganda and soldiers' motivation on the front line. Using the results of the available research on soldiers' behaviour, it is argued that propaganda has little or no impact on behaviour on the battlefield. Soldiers rarely kill or die for grand abstractions such as the nation's liberty, Islam, democracy or socialism. Instead the principal motivating force for most is micro-level group solidarity. The first part of the chapter dissects the commonsense understanding of war propaganda, while the second part focuses on the real motivation for killing and sacrificing oneself. However, before we embark on this analysis it is important to specify what kinds of actions constitute propaganda. The simplest definition is that propaganda is a strenuous form of organised communication involving production, reproduction and dissemination of ideas, images and messages that are aimed at persuading and influencing the opinions and actions of large groups of individuals. Although the term itself is derived from the seventeenth-century name of the Vatican congregation of cardinals for the promotion of faith (*Congregatio de Propaganda Fide*), the contemporary use of the term has distinctly military origins – WWI (Marlin 2002; Taylor 2003). In this sense all propaganda originated from war propaganda. However, what is distinct about war is its violent character, which means that war propaganda, unlike other forms of propaganda, involves the organised production, reproduction and dissemination of messages that focus on killing, dying, destruction and suffering. As Taylor (2003: 6) puts it: 'propaganda … is about persuading people to do things which benefit those doing the persuading' and 'in wartime that usually means getting them to fight or to support the fight'.

War propaganda

The commonsense view of war propaganda perpetuates the following widely shared myths:

1. Propaganda is a powerful and highly efficient mechanism of social control;
2. Propaganda is essentially a deliberate act of deception;
3. Propagandistic practices are prevalent in authoritarian and rare in democratic political orders;
4. Propaganda is a primeval practice integral to all warfare from time immemorial to the present day.

However, none of these four claims stand up well to scrutiny. Let us examine them in greater detail.

Social control

Wartime propaganda is often understood as a potent device able to quickly transform ordinary, peaceful individuals into bloodthirsty killers and enthusiastic martyrs. A typical example is Chomsky's characterisation of the Creel Commission, which was set up by Woodrow Wilson's administration as the US government's main WWI propaganda tool. According to Chomsky (2002: 11), this commission 'succeeded within six months, in turning a pacifist population into a hysterical, war-mongering population which wanted to destroy everything German, tear the Germans limb from limb, go to war and save the world' (Chomsky 2002: 11). In other words, Chomsky attributes to propaganda a decisive role not only in mobilising until then highly passive and uninterested American citizens for war, but also claims that war propaganda is able to utterly transform human beings. However, this form of reasoning is usually focused on authoritarian rulers such as Goebbels, Hitler, Stalin and Mussolini. It is these political leaders that are regularly invoked as master manipulators able to sway millions of ordinary people to embrace radical doctrines, make them tacitly assent to the most extremist policies and act against their self-interest. Such a view emphasises the emotional character of propagandist appeal and links it to a person's education (Galanter 1989; Moore 1994; O'Shaughnessy 2004). For example, O'Shaughnessy (2004: 39–40) argues that 'emotion is the core of propaganda … The power of emotional prejudice overweighs illuminated factual truth … it proceeds through dogmatic assertion … this is particularly true of the less well educated who tend to use 'liability heuristic', choosing primarily on the basis of feeling'.

However this highly popular understanding of propaganda is based on a simplified view of social action whereby human beings are essentially seen as overly passive, dependent, unreflective and irrational beings that lack wills of their own. In some respects, this position leans on the Marxist notion of 'false consciousness', which presumes that individuals are institutionally constrained, and unaware of the presence of this constraint, and do not realise that they are manipulated to act in ways that are contrary to their individual or collective interests. In other words, propaganda is conceived as an externally imposed form of social pathology which is able in a very short period of time to radically transform human beings. Nevertheless, these and similar arguments operate with an overly plastic understanding of human agency. As Gouldner (1970), Giddens (1991) and Jenkins (2008) convincingly demonstrate, social action nearly always involves a substantial degree of self-reflection. Although human beings are dynamic and changeable creatures, they are rarely, if ever, so malleable that they simply and quickly embrace propagandistic messages that entirely alter their patterns of behaviour. Since Weber's (1968) early works it has become apparent that social action is a complex process that involves not only emotions but also instrumental rationality, value rationality and the everyday inertia of habitual activities. Hence, despite the fact that war propaganda relies on conscious behaviour with a predetermined logic of action, in itself it is not immune to the unintended consequences of purposive action. Not only can propaganda easily miss its target audience, be disseminated at the wrong time and place, and fail to articulate its message properly, but it can also have counter-productive effects. For example, in the dying days of socialism in Romania much of the propaganda put out by the state became the object of ridicule and popular jokes, while Ceauşescu's attempt to organise a large-scale 'spontaneous' meeting in his support on 21 December 1989, which was aired on the main TV channel, quickly turned into a public demonstration against the dictator. The sudden termination of the broadcast of this meeting only provoked anti-Ceauşescu sentiments throughout the country thus fueling the 1989 Romanian Revolution (Holmes 1997).

Similarly, the German attempt to commemorate the sinking of the British commercial vessel, Lusitania, in August 1915 by producing a satirical medal intent on delegitimising British claims that the ship was carrying illegal armaments spectacularly backfired. The artist, K. Goetz, mistakenly engraved 5 May on the reverse instead of 7 May as the date when the ship was sunk, and this was later used by the British propagandists to claim that the sinking of the ship was premeditated murder. In a counter-propagandist coup d'état, a photograph of the medal was published in the New York Times and a replica medal was reproduced and sold 250,000 copies. All this contributed to the depiction of Germany as an aggressor in WWI and had some impact on the decision of the US government to enter the war (Ponsonby 2005). What these examples show is that war propaganda is not a simple device of social control that can easily direct human behaviour. Despite the fact that modern states invest a great deal of time, resources and expertise in war propaganda, much of the propagandistic information has little or no effect in changing the behaviour of those already involved in the conflict. For example, during WWII the US Air Force created a special squadron (of 'Flying Fortresses') and gave it responsibility for the distribution of war propaganda leaflets over enemy lines. By the end of the war, using the so-called Monroe bombs, this squadron was involved in dropping over 7 million leaflets a week.[1] Similarly, in the Gulf War of 1991 the US Air Force dropped over 29 million leaflets over Iraqi lines, that is, more than fifty leaflets per Iraqi soldier (Taylor 2003: 226, 296). However, there is no proof that any of the messages contained in the leaflets had any success in transforming the opinions or behaviour of the

---

[1] The Monroe bomb was a device that carried up to 80,000 leaflets that were be released after the bomb descended to 1,000 feet (Taylor 2003: 227)

opponents of the US. In fact, in the case of the Wehrmacht, there is clear and reliable sociological evidence that the opposite was the case. As the extensive wartime research of Shils and Janowitz (1948) demonstrates, the social organisation of the German military and the intense micro-level solidarity of its platoons were much more powerful in moulding soldiers' behaviour than any (domestic or enemy) propaganda. As a result, despite becoming aware that Germany had lost the war, Wehrmacht soldiers fought stubbornly to the very end. In both of these cases it was only the resounding military defeat of Nazi Germany and the Iraqi armies that brought about the large-scale surrender of soldiers and changed the attitudes of the population at large. Hence, rather than an omnipotent device of brainwashing able to quickly persuade large masses of people on both sides of the conflict, much of war propaganda functions as a mechanism of self-justification. Rather than suddenly and dramatically transforming popular opinions and perceptions, propaganda in fact helps legitimise already existing and developed views which are often grounded in what the majority of individuals perceive to be their individual and collective interest. Instead of changing people's views, war propaganda provides an external outlet, a social mirror that only facilitates the articulation and reinforcement of the attitudes and practices that already permeate public opinion. In times of violent conflict, one reads and listens to the mass media not only to acquire reliable information but primarily to confirm a firm belief (in the righteousness of one's cause) and to find a social proof for the validity of this belief. As psychological research demonstrates, most individuals tend to embrace evidence that conforms to their beliefs while discounting or ignoring evidence against them. Even in peace time a person rarely tests his or her political beliefs by reading newspapers and books that articulate an opposing viewpoint (Weintraub 1988; Heuer 1999).

A great deal of war propaganda is not aimed at the 'enemy' population and when it directly targets this population it generally tends to be highly ineffective. The principal target of war propaganda is the domestic audience and occasionally an audience of already sympathetic external organisations and states. Nevertheless, even here the propagandistic messages are unlikely to lead to rapid and dramatic changes in popular opinion. Instead, when successful, war propaganda draws and feeds off something that is already there. As a human being is not a simple *tabula rasa*, propaganda has to utilise the existing values and perceptions of social reality. In other words, the success of war propaganda is heavily dependent on historically long-term processes such as centrifugal ideologisation and the cumulative bureaucratisation of coercion. As elaborated in the previous chapter, both of these processes have gradually developed over time and in this process have helped bond citizens with their respective nation-states. While the 'ideologisation of the masses' constituted an institutional and societal surrogate for the micro-level solidarity of face-to-face interaction, the bureaucratisation of violence provided an organisational device for the subjective and objective routinisation of compliance. Any attempt to change popular opinions and behaviour which goes against these two processes is highly unlikely to succeed. For example, the Kosovo War of 1999 saw Serbian government propaganda depicting the NATO alliance as Nazis and fascists who were determined to annihilate Serbs through a relentless policy of intensive carpet-bombing of its main cities. While these propagandistic images had little or no resonance outside the borders of Serbia and made no sense to audiences of either the NATO states or the international community at large, since NATO itself was constituted by the states that fought Nazi Germany and fascist Italy, the Serbian population was fairly receptive to these images. By playing on the similarities between the Luftwaffe's destruction of Belgrade in 1941 and the ongoing air attacks, the government propaganda proved highly successful in conveying the message of universal Serbian victimhood (Čolović 1999). In other words, the function of war propaganda was not to change the opinions of either side but to reinforce and legitimise the view that was already shared by the majority of the Serbian population, a view rooted in long-term processes of ideologisation and bureaucratisation.

Truth and deception

War propaganda is also regularly associated with calculated deception whereby the monopolisation of the mass media and continuous repetition of the false messages allegedly easily deceive individuals into believing something that is not true. This is frequently illustrated with Goebbels's (1941: 364) expression that 'when one lies, one should lie big, and stick to it' and Hitler's (2001 [1925]: 168) statement that the essential function of propaganda is to 'serve our own right, always and unflinchingly' and that in this respect propaganda 'must confine itself to a few points and repeat them over and over'. In other words, war propaganda becomes a mere synonym for the well orchestrated dissemination of lies. However, although black propaganda, that is, the deliberate use of false information to misrepresent or belittle the enemy, and usually created by one side in such a way as to make it appear as though it actually comes from the enemy, has occasionally proved useful in the short term, an overwhelming major-ity of successful war propaganda is, in fact, based on truthful statements and genuine sources.

Unlike black propaganda, white propaganda is grounded in the skilful and dexterous, but largely one-sided, interpretation of factual information that truthfully declares its origin. While there is no doubt that WWII radio broadcasters such as the British Gustav Siegfried Eins, Soldatensender Calais, Atlantiksender or German Radio Concordia and Radio Debunk proved effective in disseminating black propaganda by tricking their listeners into believing that they were enemy broadcasters, these radio stations had little impact in changing the attitudes of the 'enemy population' (Lerner 1972). When black propaganda is successful, this just confirms that, rather than transforming popular perceptions, war propaganda works best as a device for bolstering existing values, that is, as a means of self-justification. The broadcasts of Gustav Siegfried Eins and Radio Concordia were instrumen-tal in reaffirming the already shared images and stereotypes of the enemy side and had little impact on changing attitudes. The Gustav Siegfried's main speaker, 'Der Chef' was created as 'a typical diehard loyal old Prussian Army Officer whose colourful and outspoken views showed him as deeply loyal to the Fatherland, and indeed the Fuehrer, but severely critical of many of the Nazi policies and conduct of the war' (Black 1972). Such an image was likely to conform to the British stereotypes of a typical German as much as to German auto-stereotyping. However, Der Chef's messages did not change either German or British attitudes about each other or about the rightness of the two sides' war causes; they just helped cement the stereotypical images that were already prevalent.

Although it is true that in their search for reliable and trustworthy infor-mation German soldiers and officers became much more interested in listen-ing to the Allied-run radio stations at the end of war, this only reiterates the argument that it was the changing war conditions rather than propaganda itself that influenced change in attitudes and behaviour. It was only once the German armies were on the defensive and in retreat that soldiers started questioning the widely shared dominant narrative of the war. Since the win-ning side is more likely to disseminate more realistic information about war conditions – as the situation on the ground benefits the winners – the soldiers and the population of the losing side are often inclined to pay more attention to the enemy propaganda. Hence, even the black propaganda outlets such as the Allied broadcasters proved to gain more from the dissemination of truth than lies. As Daniel Lerner (1972: 28), himself a veteran of information warfare, acknowledges: 'Credibility is a condition of persuasion. Before you can make a man do as you say, you must make him believe what you say'.

The fact that a great deal of effective war propaganda is rooted in factual accuracy does not imply that facts have to be presented in an objective, unbiased manner. On the contrary, white propaganda relies heavily on spin. It is the creative interpretation of events such as the selective presentation of facts that support one's position, phrasing statements in a way that assumes unproven truth, the extensive use of euphemisms and similar strategies that help articulate and direct a propagandistic message so as to benefit a side's cause. Galtung and Ruge (1965) have identified a number of strategic means used to disseminate white propaganda including the Manichean dualist portrayal of actors and events (i.e. reducing the complexities of the conflict to only two mutually antagonistic parties), decontextualisation of violence (the emphasis on the spectacular, dramatic and irrational actions with no attempt to explain the sources of the conflict), a focus on individual acts of brutality or heroism while avoiding the structural causes, and presenting the cycles of violence as inevitable and unstoppable. Since the principal purpose of all propaganda is to legitimise the ideas and actions of one's side, and delegitimise those of the opponents', and since, in wartime, these actions include deeply contested practices such as killing, dying, destruction and suffering, much of war propaganda is centred on justifying, rationalising or vilifying particular courses of action and those responsible for such action.

As large-scale violent conflicts often require mobilisation of the entire population there is a tendency to try to delegitimise entire collectives – nations, ethnic groups or states. According to Daniel Bar-Tal (1989), there are five typical ways of delegitimisation employed in protracted violent conflicts: dehumanisation, outcasting, trait characterisation, the use of political labels and group comparisons. While dehumanisation involves the categorisation of the opponent as subhuman (e.g. animalistic Negros, Jewish parasites, Slavic *Untermenchen*) or non-human (monsters, demons) outcasting emphasises the enemy's continuous disregard for universally shared social norms (e.g. they attack children, the sick and the elderly). The propagandistic messages regularly rely on trait characterisation, which entails attributing (mostly negative) personality traits to entire groups of people (e.g. the perverted and treacherous character of 'Japs'), as well as the use of comparison with groups that are traditionally viewed in an extremely negative light (e.g. the regular reference in the British media to Germans during WWI as 'Huns'). Finally, the actions of the opponents are also delegitimised by invoking ideological labels that are associated with political groups considered to be highly undesirable or dangerous in one's own society. For example, the enemies are typically labelled as 'fascists', 'communists', 'racists', 'capitalists' or 'imperialists'. The use of delegitimising strategies helps justify one's own course of action, re-affirms the moral superiority of one's cause, sharpens the social boundaries between the groups involved and facilitates the ongoing processes of in-group homogenisation. By demonstrating that the enemy, on the evidence of their characteristics and actions, do not belong to the human race, it is much easier to justify the actions of one's own side: monsters and beasts need no human compassion.

However, what is missing in this largely psychological account is the fact that the character, degree and intensity of delegitimisation are deeply linked to the nature of the violent conflict. In other words, rather than there being a universal symmetrical propensity towards delegitimisation on the part of all sides involved, warfare itself dictates the scope and the structure of delegitimising strategies employed. For example the 1991–1995 Wars of Yugoslav Succession were characterised by intensive propaganda warfare between the sides involved. A cursory view of the propagandistic messages would indicate that the two sides used similar techniques in depicting their enemies as unscrupulous and aggressive. However, the asymmetrical nature of the conflict generated rather diverse models of propaganda. In the early stages of war the militarily weaker Croatian and Bosnian sides, which had also lost substantial territories, were heavily dependent on external support, while the Serbian side, inheriting large stocks of armaments from the well-equipped Yugoslav army and making significant military advancements, had little need for the internationalisation of the conflict. In consequence, whereas the Croatian and Bosnian war propaganda was firmly focused on delegitimising the aims, character and nature of Serbian belligerence (and the Serbs as a nation) in order to win the support of an already sympathetic international community and their own population, the Serbian war propaganda was almost entirely focused on self-justification of its actions. In other words, while Bosnian and Croatian propagandists emphasised the moral inferiority of the Serbs and the sheer illegitimacy of their territorial conquests by depicting them as murderous thieves, devils, rats and vultures, the Serbian propagandists were essentially centred on self-stereotyping rather than on the delegitimisation of the other two sides involved in the conflict and portrayed Serbs as peaceful and proud victims of the international conspiracy that was 'the new world order' (Malešević and Uzelac 1997; Malešević 1998).

The use of stereotyping and delegitimisation helps to simplify the propagandistic narrative and to crystallise the coherent message disseminated among the targeted audience. However, while simplification is useful, lying is not. To acquire lasting success war propaganda has to be composed of truthful statements as only truth can be an object of effective spin.

The democratic origins of war propaganda

The invention and excessive use of propaganda is colloquially associated with authoritarian and totalitarian states, while liberal democratic orders are seen as having less need for, and hence being less prone to, propagandistic practices. When democratic orders rely on propaganda, as in times of war, this is ordinarily perceived as a defensive strategy to counter the intensive propaganda messages of authoritarian enemy states. A typical example in literature is Hannah Arendt's (1951: 344) distinction between totalitarian and non-totalitarian propaganda: 'The lies of totalitarian propaganda are distinguished from the normal lying of non-totalitarian regimes in times of emergency by their consistent denial of the importance of facts in general: all facts can be changed and all lies can be made true. The Nazi impress on the German mind consists primarily in a conditioning whereby reality has become a conglomeration of ever-changing events and slogans in which a thing can be true today and false tomorrow.' Nevertheless, this assumption is both sociologically simplistic and historically incorrect. The rigid distinction between the democratic and non-democratic political orders presumes that propaganda is nearly always an externally imposed medium, that its efficient implementation entails either deception or fear and that the existence of political liberty inhibits its proliferation. Hence the commonly expressed view is that, unlike authoritarian states that impose distorted truths and keeps a lid on access to reliable information through fear and repression, democracies, being inherently open, have no need or use for propaganda.

However, not only does this understanding start from the mistaken perception that propaganda is identical to lying but also and more importantly, it operates with a sociologically undeveloped concept of social action. In some respects this view combines elements of the Platonic model of human beings that equates lack of proper information and knowledge with malevolent behaviour and the Marxist teleology that emphasises the structural determination of popular beliefs. In both of these accounts knowledge is wedded to truth whereby the removal of external constraint and repression inevitably leads to enlightenment and hence to virtuous social action. However, following Mannheim, 1966 [1936], Kuhn (1962), Adorno and Horkheimer (1972) and Foucault (1980), it has become apparent that one cannot easily decouple knowledge from power and that the possession of truth and freedom to make up one's own mind do not automatically imply virtuous conduct. On the contrary, since scientifically validated knowledge has acquired a near monopolistic position in the post-Enlightenment age and since the (free) public is highly receptive to scientific-sounding (i.e. factual) interpretations of reality, this opens the door for the proliferation of propagandistic messages. Since in the modern context the possession of knowledge and information is often equated with moral and material progress, the purveyors of knowledge have become enormously powerful arbiters of everyday life and much of this power has been used for anything but benign purposes. To put it simply, a democratic environment is not adverse to propaganda. In fact the opposite is the case, as liberty creates conditions whereby the propagandistic initiative is often taken by groups in civil society and the free media rather than the state apparatuses. It is no accident that the concept of jingoism was born not in authoritarian omnipotent states such as Nazi Germany or Soviet Union but in a distinctly liberal climate of late nineteenth-century Britain. The Russo-Ottoman war of 1877–1878 and the Anglo-Boer war of 1899–1902 saw civil groups, and public and privately owned mass media advocating an extremely belligerent foreign policy, Britain's stringent military intervention against Russia and the war of annihilation against the Boer Republics. Witnessing the emergence of large-scale public opinion, J. A. Hobson was the first to spot the link between the music hall ballads, pulpit, 'yellow' journalism and the wider popular audience all bent on creating and disseminating radical war propaganda. For Hobson (1901: 18–19), jingoism was a product of this new, wider, public opinion that sprung up as a new phenomenon, developed into 'a community of thought, language, and action which was hitherto unknown' and transformed ordinary individuals into a militaristic mob: 'the British nation became a great crowd, and exposed its crowd-mind to the suggestions of the press'. In other words, precisely because citizens, media and civil society are more free in liberal and democratic environments they themselves are more likely to become the key agents of war propaganda. Unlike state-sponsored propaganda, which is always limited by geopolitical, ideological and institutional constrains, and in authoritarian contexts is also firmly controlled by the political authorities, the democratic setting opens the door for the unconstrained proliferation of popular jingoistic propaganda. In times of war this can lead to fierce competition among the various civil groups and mass media to outbid others in demonstrating the degree of their determination and support for the war cause. Hence, democracies are not immune to war propaganda.

In fact, one could argue that the birth of propaganda, and in particular war propaganda, can be traced to democratic, not authoritarian contexts. In other words, rather than being a top–down creation of despotic states, war propaganda is a by-product of democratisation and liberalisation. The English Civil War (1642–1646) caused the collapse of royal censorship and the appearance of the first forms of proto-propaganda, since both sides in the conflict, Royalists ('Cavaliers') and Parliamentarians ('Roundheads'), had also to fight for 'the souls' of those who were wavering between the two camps. The war conditions liberalised the public space and fostered a proliferation of books, pamphlets and the first news-sheets, the predecessors of contemporary newspapers. Both warring sides established their principal mouthpieces (the royalist *Mercurius Aulicus* and the parliamentarian *Mercurius Britannicus*) and relied heavily on the printed word to propagate their causes (Frank 1961). A direct side effect of this protracted conflict was a dramatic expansion of proto-propagandistic publications. For example, between 1640 and 1663 more than 15,000 types of pamphlets were produced and the number of news-sheets rose spectacularly from only 4 in 1641 to 167 in 1642 and a staggering 722 in 1645 (Taylor 2003: 118). What is particularly interesting here is that the civil war not only opened the space for an (albeit intense and aggressive) exchange of ideas but it also helped mobilise broader sectors of the population who combined their puritan zeal with political ambition to create and disseminate ideas that supported their cause.

The English Civil War was a prelude to the development of propagandistic discourse. However, as this discourse was still confined to small sections of the population (the literate and relatively privileged) and had to rely on modest technological and infrastructural means for its dissemination, it was more of proto-propaganda than fully fledged war propaganda. Real, society-wide, technologically and organisationally sophisticated war propaganda did not appear for another two centuries. While this large-scale historical development requires some explaining and elaboration (to be done shortly), the focus here is on the democratic origins of war propaganda. Despite the prevalent perception among the British public that propaganda is the property of (largely non-democratic) others, Britain is, in fact, its institutional cradle. As Taylor (2003: 160) points out, in the late nineteenth century 'Britain was the country that emerged as the unrivalled leader in the field of political propaganda and, in the twentieth century, the undisputed master of war propaganda.' This obviously had nothing to do with the psychological, biological or other characteristics of Britons, but was a product of the type of state Britain had developed into: a state that combined a highly industrialised, liberalised and democratised domestic social order with vast worldwide imperial power. In this context, the expansion of electoral politics, the rapid urbanisation of the population, ever-increasing literacy rates, technological developments and the commercial character of the mass media together with the ongoing imperial wars of conquest all contributed to the general politisation of public opinion. The ever-increasing liberalisation and democratisation of Britain fostered the development of war propaganda. The popular, privately owned, liberal, conservative, Christian and secular media were struggling to feed the enormous popular demand for the reports of exotic exploits from the British imperial campaigns in Africa and Asia. Underpinned by the new quasi-Darwinian paradigms of racial hierarchies and the 'struggle for survival' the nearly universal depictions of British superiority were equally shared by the wider public, most civil groups and mass media (Mackenzie 1984). As Taylor (2003: 165) puts it: 'Military success appeared to prove British racial superiority over inferior peoples, and this myth was perpetuated in a variety of media, from newspapers to novels, from parades to postcards, from school textbooks to societies, from board-games to biscuit tins.' By the beginning of WWI Britain had the most experience with putting out propaganda messages, and this involved general public, civil society groupings, mass media as much as the state apparatuses. Hence, the origins of war propaganda can be traced not to authoritarian, but chiefly to democratic and liberal, historical contexts.

The fact that authoritarian states do indeed produce quantitatively more propaganda does not tell us much about the supposedly inherent link between propaganda and authoritarianism. Instead, this only confirms the argument that much of propaganda is essentially a means of internal legitimation. The Nurnberg rallies and the giant portraits of Stalin, Lenin and Marx made no impact on the Allied population apart from reinforcing the already existing ideological divide between the opposing camps. Similarly, the self-depictions of the British and US mass media as beacons of liberty and free thought made little headway among the general population in Nazi Germany and the Soviet Union. The cruder and almost caricatural nature of the Soviet or Nazi propaganda only illustrates the universal purpose of all propaganda: rather than being an attempt to change the opinions and actions of non-subscribers, propaganda is a device of self-justification. One needs propaganda to feel comfortable in one's own (ideological) skin; to hold the same world-view as those who are the closest and dearest to oneself and as those who are greatly admired; to feel reassured when in the slightest doubt, and for many other reasons too. Most of all one needs propaganda when the dominant interpretation of social reality is vigorously and persistently contested by (external) others. Since wars are nearly universally seen as illegitimate social situations, they require more propaganda than most other social situations. In this sense there is not much difference between the democratic and other social orders: to justify the extraordinary situation that is war their citizens all require ideological comfort, mass-scale reassurance and a sense of fraternity.

Modernity of war propaganda

The use of propaganda in general and war propaganda in particular is often conceptualised as a trans-historical phenomena occurring in all historical epochs with a similar level of intensity and prevalence. In this way, propaganda is identified with 'psychological warfare' and as such is understood to be an integral element of all wars. For example, the leading textbook on propaganda states that: 'The use of propaganda as a means of controlling information flow, managing public opinion, or manipulating behaviour is as old as recorded history. The concept of persuasion is an integral part of human nature, and the use of specific techniques to bring about large-scale shifts in ideas can be traced back to the ancient world' (Jowett and O'Donnell 2006: 50). Leaving aside the highly dubious notion of 'human nature', this view makes no distinction between persuasion and propaganda. Unlike persuasion, which is a nearly universal form of social influence, the rudimentary form of which is old as the language itself (both dating back to the upper Paleolithic), propaganda is organised communication that involves relatively systematic production and dissemination of ideas and images in order to influence the thought and behaviour of large groups of people. In other words, rather than being a mere synonym for propaganda, persuasion is a rhetorical technique that is an integral element of propaganda. While there is no propaganda without persuasion there is persuasion without propaganda.

Furthermore, while there is no doubt that throughout history many rulers, high priests, military leaders and wealthy individuals have relied heavily on various models of persuasion and even occasionally were successful in developing proto-propagandistic forms of social influence, they clearly lacked the organisational capacity, infrastructural means for its creation and dissemination and a sufficiently literate and politicised public sphere receptive to propagandistic messages on a regular basis. Whereas the stone tablets and obelisks of Assyrian kings and the public architecture of Egyptian pharaohs were built in part to convey the message of rulers' absolute superiority and military invincibility, their attempts at persuasion were 'erratic and spor-adic' with 'no coherent pattern or organisation' (Taylor 2003: 24). Although ancient Greece and Rome provide examples of more elaborate attempts to boost popular, and in particular soldiers', morale in times of war by manipu-lating and utilising local mythologies for military purposes, the small-scale and ad hoc character of these practices indicate that this was a far cry from fully fledged propaganda. Alexander the Great was a master manipula-tor who exploited Greek beliefs in omens, portents and oracles to mobilise his troops for combat. For example, before a major battle he would use 'a tame snake with a linen human head to demonstrate to his soldiers that the god Asclepius – often portrayed in serpent form – was with them' or the word 'victory' would be dyed on the liver of a sacrificial animal and shown to troops before the battle to indicate that there is a reliable sign that gods favour Alexander's army (Taylor 2003: 29). Similarly, Julius Caesar employed Roman imperial doctrine and his own military successes to create an elab-orate cult of personality which was then used to galvanise public support for further military adventures. His portrait was stamped on Roman coins and statues of him were erected throughout the empire during his lifetime, he had 'a golden seat in the Senate house and on the tribunal, a ceremonial car-riage and litter in the Circus procession, temples, altars, images next to those of gods, a ceremonial couch' and even a month named after him (Gardner 1974: 90). Nevertheless, regardless of how influential these practices were, simple tricks that boost military morale and even extravagant cults of per-sonality do not represent propaganda in any sociologically meaningful sense, since propaganda, as will be demonstrated shortly, has little to do with the soldiers' fighting morale.

Even the arrival and proliferation of monotheistic religions such as Christianity and Islam did not lead to the birth of proper propaganda. Despite the fact that the Catholic Church made extensive use of visual imagery such as statues, icons, crucifixes, religious paintings, copperplate engravings and etchings, and that the rulers in the Islamic world have heavily utilised the Koranic notion of jihad to mobilise mass support, the deeply stratified char-acter of these societies before modern times, their infrastructural and organ-isational backwardness and their inability to provide instant and continuous message dissemination throughout the entire social realm points to the lim-ited character of their persuasive powers. As Hall demonstrates in his histor-ically nuanced analysis, the socially hierarchical pre-modern world was no place for ideological unity. On the contrary 'the sharing of norms is an excep-tion in history … In the medieval Pyrenean village of Montaillou everybody did think of themselves as Christian; but the peasants regarded the Bishop of Pamiers as a feudal exploiter' (Hall 1985: 29–30).

Gutenberg's invention of the printing press, the standardisation of vernacular languages, the Protestant Reformation and the Catholic Counter-Reformation followed by two centuries of religious wars have all had a direct impact on the politisation of a wider strata of population thus creating the structural conditions for the eventual birth of propaganda. The religious schism fostered an extensive reliance on the pulpit and printing presses to disseminate pamphlets, religious handbooks, bibles, paintings, posters, leaflets and single-page news-sheets in vernacular idioms, hence making them accessible to broader audiences. For example by 1520 Luther's key publications were sold in over 300,000 copies while the Catholic handbook on heretic practices and witchcraft, *Malleus Maleficarum*, had been reprinted thirty six times by 1669 (Dickens 1968: 51; Russell 1984: 79). In all of these cases it was war that encouraged the proliferation of the published word.

By the end of the Napoleonic wars in 1815, the techniques of persuasion and the mass circulation of printed material had dramatically increased while the warring sides had become well aware of the significance of propagandistic discourse in articulating their war causes. Napoleon was especially attentive to the significance of building a potent war propaganda machine arguing that 'three hostile newspapers are more to be feared than a thousand bayonets' (McLuhan 2001: 14). Not only did he introduce severe censorship and close down all independent media outlets, thus reducing the number of newspapers in the Paris region from 70 to only 4 in 1811 (Dunn 2004: 126), but his propagandists penetrated all important spheres of social life and focused on even the most minute details in planning and executing state propaganda. This included the introduction of a highly centralised propaganda state apparatus, 'Direction generale de l'Imprimerie et de la Librairie', which directed and monitored all cultural production and dissemination of art, literature and publishing. The newspaper *Moniteur*, instituted as an official government propaganda organ, also contained articles written by Napoleon himself and was freely distributed to the military. Following in Julius Caesar's footsteps, but on a much grander scale, Napoleon created and was able to propagate his own cult of personality: Napoleon's image was stamped on coins, medals, medallions and trinkets. By becoming a patron of artists and writers, Napoleon was able to extensively utilise art and the humanities for propagandistic purposes with numerous statues, paintings, engravings, architecture and literature reflecting his image. In addition, the letter 'N' was imprinted on most public buildings while popular biographies of Napoleon became huge bestsellers (Hanley 2005). In many respects, the Napoleonic era was the beginning of propaganda as a mass, sociological, phenomenon. Since war propaganda is first and foremost a society-wide means of self-legitimisation it requires the existence of politicised masses receptive of such messages. The rapid industrialisation, increasing levels of urban living and the dramatic rise in literacy rates coupled with the expansion of electorates in most Western states and new technological discoveries have helped create a much wider audience amenable to, and often in need of, propagandistic imagery. The upsurge in the infrastructural powers of modern states throughout the nineteenth century, including the development of robust and extensive transport systems (railways, steam-powered ships, wider roads), the invention and expansion of cheap and mass circulated newspapers,[2] the wide availability of maps, the growth of postal services, the invention of photography, wireless telegraph and cinematography, all contributed towards making propaganda an integral and indispensable element of warfare.

Furthermore, with the emergence of the new role of war correspondent in the early nineteenth century a direct link between the front and the civilian audience at home was established for the first time. Thus William Howard Russell's dispatches and reports from the battlefields of the Crimean War (1853–1856) were decisive in engaging popular opinion in discussing the efficiency and competence of military authorities. According to Knightley (2002: 4) this was the first organised attempt 'to report a war to the civilian population at home using the services of a civilian reporter'. Nevertheless, what is of particular importance here is not so much the fact that from now on the civilian population was able to 'directly participate' in the war effort by following the regular information coming from the front and, hence, reflecting on and politically engaging with these news, but the fact that the events on the battlefields, now witnessed at source, could be articulated and propagandised in a variety of different ways. For example, what was to become the most quoted speech in American history, Lincoln's Gettysburg Address of 1863 during the American Civil War, had little or no effect when it was given, in part because one of the newspapers that was reporting the event dedicated only one line to Lincoln's speech stating that 'the President also spoke' (Taylor 2003: 167) and in part because it still lacked popular resonance. The propagandistic potential of this speech became apparent much later and it was only during the two world wars that this speech, which invokes the soldier's sacrifice for national freedom,

---

[2] For example 'whereas there had been 76 newspapers and periodicals published in England and Wales in 1781, the figure had risen to 563 in 1851. Between 1840 and 1852 the circulation of *The Times* quadrupled from 10,000 to 40,000 copies per issue. (Taylor 2003: 159).

self-determination and a democratic form of government, was used on a massive scale to galvanise support among the American public for the causes of the two world wars. Hence, the capacity of the event to be presented in a particular, propagandistic, light became relevant only when there was a popular hunger for such a presentation. As pioneer of propaganda studies Jacques Ellul (1965) noticed a long time ago, propaganda is most effective when it conforms to needs that already exist.

Since propaganda is essentially a device of self-legitimation and since in the war context this principally involves the justification of murder and death, the establishment of a continuous information link between the front and the civilian rear meant that war propaganda had become, from now on, a powerful tool for the popular mobilisation of the domestic audience. In other words, rather than having much impact on the troops on the front (of either side), war propaganda established itself as a potent mechanism of civilian self-legitimation. It was the civilians, not the soldiers, who found propagandistic imagery and messages believable and comforting. It was the popular masses who needed and wanted to hear that WWI Germans are bloodthirsty Huns who boil down human corpses to make soap,[3] that Russians were savage Bolshevik hordes of *Untermenchen* as depicted by the Nazi mass media or that 'our boys' were heroic martyrs who unhesitatingly sacrificed their lives for their freedom. Once this link was firmly established and once civilian audiences became fully receptive and involved with war, propaganda became an obligatory feature of warfare. The total wars of the twentieth century made this link irreversible, as war propaganda developed into a total, mass phenomenon penetrating entire societies. Therefore, propaganda is essentially a modern phenomenon that entails mass mobilisation and public involvement in politics, a substantial degree of infrastructural and technological sophistication, society-wide egalitarian ethics, effective and durable social organisation and an ideologised social order.

Killing, dying and micro-level solidarity

If much of war propaganda is nothing else but an exercise in society-wide self-legitimisation, then the central questions become: Why do individuals

---

[3] Among many atrocity stories of WWI one of the most popular was the alleged existence of a German 'corpse-conversion factory'. This story was based on a German newspaper article that wrote about the factory being used to convert dead horse flesh into soap, candles and lubricants, but the British press mistranslated the term '*kadaver*' to mean human corpse, and wrote that, because fats were scarce in Germany (due to the British naval blockade) battlefield corpses were being rendered down for fat (Knightley 2002).

take part and/or support wars? More specifically what motivates soldiers and civilian participation and corroboration in killing and dying?

Here, too, several popular myths prevail. Firstly, it is assumed that once an individual undergoes extensive and strict military training (including intensive 'brainwashing') he has no difficulty in killing the hated enemy. However, nothing can be further from the truth. Since Ardant du Picq's (2006 [1921]) early studies on battlefield behaviour it has become apparent that in the combat zone human actions are much more complex and contradictory than ordinarily expected. Not only is it true that a great majority of soldiers will not respond in the same way as when in combat or the boot camp, but also, unless there is external coercive or other pressure, most are unlikely to fight at all. There is overwhelming historical and contemporary evidence that, despite intensive military training, the availability of high-quality weaponry and clear military strategies and goals, most soldiers are reluctant to actively engage in face-to-face fighting. Colonel Marshall's (1947) empirical studies on the behaviour of American soldiers in WWII demonstrated that only between 15 and 25 per cent of front-line combatants were able and willing to aim and fire their weapons at the enemy, whereas the remaining 75 to 85 per cent either declined to shoot, misfired or deliberately fired in the air. Marshall interviewed soldiers immediately after combat in 400 infantry companies throughout the theatres of war in Europe in 1944 and the Central Pacific Area in 1943, and these interviews all yielded almost identical results. Dyer's (1985) research on German and Japanese militaries indicates that these soldiers too had a similar level of non-firing during WWII.

As Holmes (1985), Griffith (1989), Grossman (1996), Bourke (2000) and Miller (2000) document, a similar pattern was observed in previous wars. For example, in the American Civil War, rather than directly shooting at the enemy a large majority of combatants engaged in mock firing, which is evident from the multiply loaded weapons left on the battlefields. With loading taking 95 per cent of soldier's time and shooting only 5 per cent, soldiers could, and mostly did, reload without actually firing without being noticed by their commanders. Grossman (1996: 22) illustrates this point well with the data from the famous Battle of Gettysburg where nearly 90 per cent of the around 30,000 muskets recovered from the battlefield were multiply loaded, with one weapon having been loaded as many as twenty-three times, thus rendering most of them useless for firing. Despite enormous casualties, WWI became renowned for the 'live and let live' principle in which the trench soldiers of both sides had a tacit agreement not to fire if the other side did the same (Ashworth 1980). According to Bourke (2000: 73) only 10 per cent of soldiers in this war were regarded as willing to fight, while the great majority of servicemen were deemed by their superiors as lacking 'an offensive spirit'. The 1986 British Defence Operational Analysis Establishment conducted a large-scale study on more than one hundred battles of the nineteenth and twentieth centuries using test trials with pulsed laser weapons to determine the killing efficiency on the real and simulated battlefields. The study concluded that the real casualties were significantly lower than those in the test trials, indicating that the soldiers' unwillingness to fight was a determining reason for the lower killing rates in the actual battles (Grossman 1996: 16). What stands out in all of these studies are the findings that once on the battlefield most soldiers become paralysed by fear or a conscious inability to kill other human beings and that only a small minority do all the fighting.

The rise in the firing ratios and more active participation in battles, witnessed since the end of WWII, are clearly linked to the two sociological interventions: the increase in coercive regulation, command and control, and the institutional reliance on the social mechanisms of micro-level solidarity. The increase in coercive pressure on the front line was an extension of the ever-increasing bureaucratic power of the military organisation and, in this respect, is an integral component of the large-scale phenomenon that is the cumulative bureaucratisation of coercion. To foster greater combat efficiency the military organisations have focused on implementing a stronger command hierarchy with officers giving direct (mostly face-to-face) orders to soldiers on the battlefields and supervising their actions, as well as the use of psychologically realistic training methods that resemble the chaotic and brutal character of actual war conditions (Grossman 1996). In the two world wars, and many other recent violent conflicts, all major militaries had battle police responsible for preventing soldiers from running away and making sure that they fought (Collins 2008: 49). When such external controllers are not present, soldiers are reluctant to fire. This is well illustrated with the comments of Lieutenant-Colonel Robert G. Cole, a commander of 502nd Parachute Infantry, which was deemed to be one of the best units in the US Army during WWII, when describing the behaviour of his soldiers under attack in 1944: 'Not one man in twenty-five voluntarily used his weapon ... they fired only while I watched them or while some other soldier stood over them' (Bourke 2000: 74).

In addition to greater organisational control, modern militaries have also focused on using and, when possible, replicating the cohesive benefits of social solidarity that arise in small-scale group interaction. Marshall (1947: 56) was already aware that 'the really active firers were usually in small groups working together' and Shils and Janowitz (1948) were able to identify small-group cohesion as central for the Wehrmacht's early military successes and stubborn resistance at the end of war. Holmes (1985: 291) provides a historical analysis of this experience confirming that it is 'the comradeship that binds soldiers together' and argues that to find what 'makes men fight' one has to look hard 'at military groups and the bonds that link the men within them'. In other words, the greater military efficiency was the product of small-group integration. Not only do individuals in small-scale, face-to-face, interactional networks more readily develop kinship like feelings of social attachment, but they also build a sense of collective responsibility towards their fellow members. Both Durkheim (1933) and Weber (1968) have sociologically articulated this phenomenon. For Durkheim (1933: 415) social solidarity is linked to one's sense of (in-group) justice and collective ethical responsibility. As he put it, solidarity is 'perhaps the very source of morality'. It unifies individuals around common ideals and establishes strong bonds of mutual obligation. For Durkheim (1933), this has little, if anything, to do with the utilitarian motives of its members (as it would be just as rational to extend this sense of belonging to the entire army organisation and to shoot at those that shoot at you), but solidarity stems from one's normative self-imposed feeling of commitment to the group. A WWII American soldier, who escaped the hospital to rejoin his platoon on the front line, expressed this feeling: 'Those men on the line were my family, my home. They were closer to me than I can say, closer than any friends had been or ever would be. They never let me down, and I couldn't do it to them … Any man in combat who lacks comrades who will die for him, or for whom he is willing to die, is not a man at all' (Holmes 1985: 300). Weber (1968) emphasised that rather than being set around given characteristics of individuals, group formation is a process that requires intensive social action. The fact that soldiers might share common descent, nationality, religion, geographic location or political ideology is unlikely to automatically translate into co-ordinated group mobilisation. On the contrary, what matters is the action itself, as it is through shared social action that groups become groups in a sociologically meaningful sense. Hence, as individuals, human beings are reluctant and inefficient killers. They require social organisation and micro-level solidarity to spur them towards co-ordinated joint action. Combativeness is not an individual but a group phenomenon.

Secondly, the popular view is that efficient and dedicated fighting entails a strong ideological commitment. It is often alleged that the sheer determination of Wehrmacht soldiers was driven by Nazi doctrine, that communist ideals underpinned Soviet sacrifices in WWII or that Al Qaeda suicide bombers are motivated by religious fanaticism. However, despite this perception, a century of combat research compellingly shows that for an overwhelming majority of soldiers this is not the case. Rather than fighting out of religious zeal, nationalism, a strong commitment to defending democratic liberties, establishing an Islamic caliphate or spreading a socialist doctrine, most soldiers go into battle out of a sense of loyalty for their platoon and mutual protection. This is not to say that ideology, and in particular the long-term institutional processes that buttress its impact such as bureaucratisation and ideologisation, are not important. On the contrary, they are fundamental for articulating the character of the violent conflict, are indispensable in mobilising the large-scale support of the non-fighting (mostly civilian) public and are crucial organisational devices for military recruitment. However, the battlefield context changes people's perceptions of social reality: a great majority of soldiers substitute macro-level ideological motivation for the micro-level solidarity of a small-group bond. Although WWI is regularly depicted by official historians as a conflict caused by rising nationalism, there is little evidence that this attitude was widespread in the trenches. Graves (1957: 157) describes the commonly shared view among the British soldiers of nationalist euphoria as 'too remote a sentiment, and at once rejected as fit only for civilians, or prisoners'. Similarly Dollard's (1977: 42) research indicates that most US soldiers were not driven by ideological commitments during the battle. Rather than spurring soldiers to fight, as he puts it, 'ideology functions *before* battle, to get the man in; and *after* battle by blocking thoughts of escape'. WWII was no different in this regard. Not only were talk of patriotic motives and flag-waving resented by experienced soldiers but any reference to democratic or other ideals as the primary fighting aim was mostly taboo and discouraged on the front line (Stouffer *et al.* 1949; Holmes 1985). More recently, suicide campaigns are not markedly different in the sense that, rather than being a product of religious zealotry, they are, as Pape's (2006: 21) extensive research clearly shows, 'not isolated or random acts by individual fanatics but rather occur in clusters as a part of larger campaign by an organised group to achieve a specific political goal'.

Although front-line soldiers are in principle largely immune to propagandistic messages, it is the process of centrifugal ideologisation (and bureaucratisation) of violence that is decisive in bringing them to the battlefield in the first place. As elaborated in the previous chapter, ideologisation combines subjective and institutional conditioning that draws upon instrumental and value rationality and in this process normalises and naturalises nationalist and other doctrines. Fighting (killing) and sacrificing (dying) for one's nation becomes an established and organisationally perpetuated ideal shared throughout the society. What war propaganda does is to link, position and crystallise the immanent or already ongoing violent conflict within the society-wide internalised ideological narrative. In this way, the new war is situated within the familiar moral discourse of collective justice, responsibility and honour, which often appeals to the population at large, including the future war-bound recruits. Since the volunteers, as much as the conscripts, are exposed to the same process of ideologisation and bureaucratisation, war propaganda builds on these recognisable, habitual images to help internally justify the aims and character of a particular war. To put it simply, successful war propaganda draws from the ideological repertoire of already existing and familiar social and cultural resources to legitimise the beliefs and actions of the people. In this way, war propaganda is most likely to find resonance among those who are the least likely to kill and die. In other words, while front-line solders are by and large ignorant of propaganda,[4] the new, inexperienced recruits, rear-side military personnel and civilians are most susceptible to propagandistic imagery. The research confirms that the further away from the battlefield a person is, the more likely he or she is to hate and dehumanise the enemy, and generally to engage in a more ferocious rhetoric against the enemy (Stouffer *et al.* 1949: 158–65; Bourke 2000: 137–70). For example, Stouffer's study of attitudes during WWII shows that while recruits who had not left US soil expressed extreme prejudice against the Japanese, with 67 per cent agreeing with the statement that they should be 'wiped out altogether', a much smaller percentage of soldiers stationed in the Pacific shared that view (42 per cent) and it is reasonable to conclude that that percentage would have been even smaller (or much smaller) if the survey included only those who actually took part in the protracted face–to–face fighting against the Japanese military. Research on the attitudes of the civilian population shows a similar trend, as those who had direct experience with war (e.g. civilians subjected to aerial bombardment) were less likely to call for revenge. As a 1941 British Institute of Public Opinion study demonstrates, the demand for reprisal bombing against German cities came not from the inhabitants of cities that had experienced intensive bombardment but from the unaffected rural areas of England (Garrett 1993: 95).

---

[4] For example, in a survey conducted in 1943–4 on nearly 5,000 US soldiers only 13 per cent concurred with propagandistic images of German and Japanese soldiers as employing 'dirty or inhuman' tactics of fighting (Stouffer *et al.* 1949: 162).

More recent studies just confirm this tendency. In the 1991–1995 Wars of Yugoslav Succession the attitudes and behaviour of soldiers and civilians stand often in stark contrast. While the front-line soldiers would often fraternise with the enemy side (e.g. share music tapes, play football during the ceasefires, trade with their adversaries and even address each other across the front line with the affable nicknames, 'Čedo' and 'Ujo', civilians, who had no direct war experience, such as university students, would express utter disdain towards the enemy (Čolović 1999). For example, 15.3 per cent (in 1992) and 14.1 per cent (in 1993) of Croatian students demonstrated extreme hostility towards Serbs, as they agreed with statements such as 'I would like someone to kill them all' or 'I would personally exterminate them all'. In addition, a further 24.4 per cent (in 1992) and 26.5 (in 1993) wanted to avoid any contact with Serbs or expel them all from Croatia (Malešević and Uzelac 1997: 294–5). Once they are on the battlefield, soldiers quickly realise that instead of encountering bloodthirsty cannibals and three-headed monsters they face two-legged creatures not so different from themselves. As recruits are transformed from civilians into fully fledged front-line soldiers the propagandistic imagery inevitably fades away. As Bourke (2000: 236–7) concludes: 'Dehumanisation worked quite well in basic training; not so well in battle. In combat situations, where human slaughter was ubiquitous, atrocities were difficult to define and were often ignored. It was impossible to maintain the fiction that the enemy was any different from oneself for very long.'

In fact, rather than indulging in perpetual hatred of the enemy many experienced soldiers develop feelings of respect, admiration and even reverence for the adversary. While there is a long history of mutual esteem for the bravery, skill and discipline of the enemy military, the sheer distance of modern fronts, the bureaucratic organisation of violence and the ideological character of modern warfare have all transformed the perception of combat as something involving chivalry and duelling. However, while the noble image of the adversary has largely disappeared with the emergence of total warfare and the development of extensive propagandistic machines that deny the universal humanity of the enemy, the encountering and interacting with enemy soldiers face-to-face often changes this perception. T.E. Lawrence (1935: 634) described his veneration of his German adversary in WWI in the following words: 'I grew proud of the enemy who killed my brothers. They were two thousand miles from home, without hope and without guidelines, in conditions bad enough to break the bravest nerves. Yet their sections held together ... when attacked they halted, took position, fired to order. There was no haste, no crying, no hesitation. They were glorious.' The adversary is often valued for his determination, the strength of resistance and ability to survive in severe conditions, but most of all for the universal human characteristics that indicate the degree of similarity between the soldiers on the opposing sides. Caputo's (1977: 117) memoir of the Vietnam War illustrates this well: finding letters and photographs of dead enemy soldiers 'gave the enemy the humanity I wished to deny him'. Realising that the Vietcong 'were flesh and blood instead of the mysterious wraiths' provoked 'an abiding sense of remorse' with a soldier commenting that 'they're young men … just like us, lieutenant'. The dead foe was often accorded a dignified funeral. The prisoners were treated with respect and even the ruthless policy of not taking prisoners was an organisational development introduced to prevent the almost inevitable fraternisation with the enemy. Therefore, rather than depending on fierce ideological devotion, direct involvement in combat entails a substantial degree of de-propagandisation. To put it simply, the war experience and the power of propaganda are, in most cases, inversely proportional: susceptibility to, and need for, propagandistic imagery progressively increases with distance from the battlefield.

Finally, the commonsense view, and much of military history, starts from the assumption that in war it is much easer to kill another human being than to die for others. Such a perception is clearly grounded in the Hobbesian ontology that posits human beings as utilitarian and rational self-preservers. From this point of view it perfectly and obviously makes sense that killing others is more rational and easier than volunteering to die for others. After all, the examples of numerous wars throughout history and especially the modern-day total wars clearly show that killings occur on a massive scale while individual gestures of self-sacrifice seem rare and exceptional events. However, this conclusion is built on faulty premises. While there is no doubt that modern warfare has produced large-scale devastation, including millions of war dead, an overwhelming percentage of these deaths were not inflicted through face-to-face contact. Since the musket era, cannon fodder has consistently accounted for more than 50 per cent of casualties (Collins 2008: 58). Despite the standard and widely reproduced imagery of the WWI battles where soldiers attack each other with bayonets, more than two thirds of all soldiers who died in this war were killed by long-distance artillery 'while less than half a per cent of wounds were inflicted by the bayonet' (Bourke 2000: 51).[5] Interestingly enough,

---

[5] For example, the breakdown of the British military casualties in WWI was as follows: 'shells and mortar bombs caused 58.51 per cent of British casulties, bullets 38.98 per cent, bombs and grenades 2.19 per cent and bayonets 0.32 per cent' (Holmes 1985: 210).

even in the earlier periods when it was regarded as an essential battlefield weapon, such as at Waterloo in 1815, less than 1 per cent of all killings were inflicted by the bayonet (Keegan 1976: 268–9). Long-distance killings have only increased since that period and artillery has been responsible for the large majority of combat deaths 'from the time of Napoleon on down to today' (Grossman 1996: 27). For example, in WWII, 75 per cent of British military casualties were caused by mortars, grenades, aerial bombs and artillery shells, with bullets and anti-tank shells accounting for only 10 per cent, while the remaining 15 per cent were caused by blasts, crushes, phosphorus and other agents. The Korean War continued this tendency with small arms accounting for only 3 per cent of American casualties (Holmes 1985: 210). Furthermore, the development of new, more sophisticated, more deadly and more precise weaponry has not significantly increased killing ratios, as one would have expected. For example, muzzle-loading muskets were already capable of reaching a 50 per cent hit rate, which would amount to a killing rate of hundreds per minute, but the soldiers using them rarely managed to kill more than one or two enemy combatants; in the 1870 Battle of Wissembourg the French soldiers fired 48,000 rounds to kill only 404 German foes with a hit ratio of 1 per 119 rounds fired; in Vietnam more than 50,000 bullets were fired for every enemy soldier killed (Grossman 1996: 12). In all of these cases it was not technology but the human reluctance to kill that was responsible for such low kill ratios. In WWII most front-line infantrymen were certain that they actually had not killed anyone during the entire war (Holmes 1985: 376). The distinct feature of all modern wars is that an overwhelming percentage of killings are not done directly, in face-to-face interaction with the enemy, but in ways that are detached both territorially and organisationally: long-distance artillery, high-altitude bombing, the firing of missiles and so on. The almost universal aversion to close-encounter killings is best illustrated by the fact that those who are not directly involved in such activities experience significantly fewer psychiatric disorders. For example, the data shows that sailors and high-altitude pilots who kill at distance have little or no psychiatric problems. The situation is similar with civilian victims of bombing and prisoners of war under fire, who, despite their ordeals, express fewer symptoms of psychological illness than the military prison guards who remain in combat mode or the front-line soldiers involved in close encounter killings (Gabriel 1987; Grossman 1996: 57).

It was the ever-increasing coercive power of social organisations that created the conditions for mass slaughter. The quasi-duelling character of close-encounter pre-modern warfare with very low casualty rates has been replaced by efficient, anonymous, bureaucratic and banal extermination with high killing ratios. A WWII veteran summarised the impersonal nature of modern warfare: 'A thing few people realise is that you hardly ever see a German. Very few men – even in the infantry – actually have the experience of aiming a weapon at a German and seeing the man fall' (Grossman 1996: 92). For example, in the Vietnam War only 14 per cent of soldiers were involved in combat (Holmes 1985: 76); more specifically, of 2.8 million soldiers who were deployed to serve in Vietnam less than 0.3 million faced battle (Gabriel 1987: 26–30). In other words, the dramatic increase in killing ratios had nothing to do with people's supposedly intrinsic propensity to kill other humans with ease. On the contrary, as Collins (2008: 469) rightly points out: 'we have become deadly in battle, not because of greater individual ferociousness but because we have found social and technological ways around confrontational tension/fear'. It is precisely because killing others is difficult that it took centuries for the state and military organisations to perfect mass-scale killing strategies, and in even in contemporary wars the best military machines in the world still require a great deal of continuous organisational and ideological effort to maintain high killing ratios. The available data on WWI and WWII pilots shows that the great majority never shot down an enemy plane or dropped a bomb at close distance. While in WWI only 8 per cent of all pilots accounted for 68 per cent of the enemy planes destroyed, in WWII just 1 per cent of US and 5 per cent of British pilots gunned down 40 per cent and 60 per cent of German planes respectively; two top German pilots were responsible for shooting down 300 allied planes (Gurney 1958: 83; Grossman 1996: 30; Collins 2008: 388). When forced to make kills at low altitude, most pilots were in distress and 'profoundly shaken', as they found it very difficult to run down 'human beings, opening up all the guns, and bullets spraying, killing and maiming many of those unknown individuals' (Bourke 2000: 65). As Browning's (1992) detailed behavioural study of some middle-aged German reserve policemen's liquidation of a Jewish village in Poland shows, most 'ordinary men' are reluctant killers. Despite strong group cohesion, prevalent ideological indoctrination and an efficient bureaucratic system in place,[6] the majority of men involved in these killings found the entire process revolting, depressing and often physically sickening. In addition, despite the close proximity many 'individual

[6] As Browning (1992: 48) makes clear, 25 per cent of these policemen were members of the Nazi Party.

policemen "shot past" their victims' (Browning 1992: 62). As killing other human beings stands in stark opposition to most processes and values inculcated through primary socialisation, the act of taking a life is almost never easily committed. Close-range killing often demands nothing short of the tearing apart of a person's moral universe. This sentiment is well echoed in the remorseful reflection of an American WWII veteran who personally killed a Japanese soldier: 'I can remember whispering foolishly, "I'm sorry" and then just throwing up … I threw up all over myself … I had urinated in my skivvies … It was a betrayal of what I'd been taught since a child' (Grossman 1996: 88; Bourke 2000: 247). Similarly, for a Vietnam War veteran who was an experienced killer, close-range shootings were highly disturbing: 'But we started having a very personal contact with the people we were killing … [and] I started to get really bad feelings. Not feeling of morality either. Just fucking bad feelings' (Baker 1982: 123).

In a nutshell, despite the popular view that wars release the hidden beast within all of us, thus showing our supposedly 'true predatory nature', killing is, in fact, tremendously difficult, messy, guilt-ridden and, for most people, an abhorrent activity. The dramatic rise in the mass slaughter witnessed in the last two centuries has nothing to do with 'human nature' and all to do with the increase in the coercive power of modern social organisations. By employing various psychological and sociological strategies, the modern military machine is now able to combine all-embracing bureaucratic control, sophisticated weaponry and impersonal, detached battlefields with the integrative, conformist and uniting energy of small-group cohesion to expand the scope and quantity of mass killings. Drawing on this experience, the US military has been able to utterly transform soldiers' behaviour on the front line: the willingness to fire increased substantially from 12–25 per cent in WWII to 55 per cent in the Korean War to as much as 90 per cent in Vietnam (Grossman 1996).

While it is obvious that human beings, just as all other living creatures, are ingrained with a strong determination to survive and live, the human experience of and attitude to dying is just as complex as that to killing. There is no doubt that most people in most circumstances will try to avoid death: the war environment is no different in this respect. Nevertheless, because in war death is a more present, more frequent and more visible phenomenon, the ordinary fear of death often acquires different forms. In situations where death is experienced on an everyday basis, as on the battlefield, soldiers generally tend to fear loss of face more than loss of life. As Dollard's (1977) research on 300 American veterans of the Spanish Civil war shows, most soldiers were afraid not of getting killed, but of being deemed cowards. Furthermore, while most were afraid before the first battle (71 per cent) only around 15 per cent had that feeling during or after the battle. Other studies (Berkun 1958; Shalit 1988; Grossman 1996) also confirm that the central concern for most soldiers as they approach battle is the fear of 'letting others down' or disgracing themselves in front of their peers. As one WWII soldier put it, what really matters to most soldiers is 'how you are going to behave in front of other people' (Holmes 1985: 142). Shalit's (1988) study on Israeli soldiers and Swedish peacekeepers clearly demonstrates that fear of death and the combat experience are inversely correlated: while for peacekeepers without combat experience, the possibility of losing one's life was the number one concern, the more experienced combatants feared most how their comrades would view their actions. The research also confirms that those in positions of greater responsibility on the battlefield such as officers, medics and priests are in principle even less fearful for their lives (Holmes 1985: 142–6; Grossman 1996). Since they focus their attention on maintaining the platoon's operational capability (through command or pastoral or medical care), and rarely or never participate in killing, they are able to avoid the tension and the emotionally draining process that participation in killing involves. Simultaneously, their exceptional position grants them a sense of group importance which enhances their feeling of attachment and thus obligation to a group. This all makes officers, medics and priests often more willing to sacrifice their lives for the group.

However, willing sacrifice is not only a prerogative of these non-combatants. Although it is not a mass practice by any standard, dying for others is not as uncommon as ordinarily thought. While popular films and novels paint a picture of self-sacrifice as an individual heroic feat of an unusually altruistic person, the sociological truth is that most voluntary acts of dying for others are in fact collective phenomena. In Durkheimian (2001: 221–35) terms such an altruistic deed stems from an exceptionally integrated and cohesive sense of belonging to an exclusive group whereby the group becomes a realm of the sacred: ascetic practices and jointly shared suffering transforms its members into a special, selected fraternity. The more integrated the group is, the more likely it is that its members will be willing to die for each other. An experienced Vietnam War veteran who was a member of such a tight platoon expressed his admiration for the behaviour of an even tighter and more exclusive group: 'I was fascinated with this group of men. They were all on their second or third tour of Nam … Their kinship was even stronger than ours … They didn't even think of anyone else around' (Baker 1982: 121). It is no accident that the term 'kinship' is used to describe this sense of group attachment. The extremely adverse, unpredictable and hostile environment of warfare helps reinforce an intensive feeling of micro-level solidarity that, in many respects, resembles kinship ties. Although there is a utilitarian element present in this relationship (whereby one is willing to sacrifice oneself for others on the presumption that others would do the same for one) a great deal of this relationship is grounded in one's sense of normative obligation. Just as in close family relationships a mother or father would do anything to save their sick or dying child, so the members of a close-knit platoon embrace a similar feeling of kinship-like solidarity. As Simmel (1917) argued, war is an 'absolute situation' where soldiers' experience is heightened to the extremes and one's sense of sociability is dramatically intensified. When one can easily and instantly die at any moment in time and when this thin line between life and death hinges on the strength of group ties, than these ties become sacred and the group itself becomes greater than oneself. In other words, despite official, and even personal, pronouncements that a particular soldier has given his life for his country, an ethnic collective or an ideological doctrine, most willing battlefield sacrifices are in fact made for a much smaller group – one's platoon, troop, squad or crew. The importance of small-group unity is well recognised by the military establishment. The American defeat in the Vietnam War was in large part linked to the progressive disintegration of small-unit solidarity, whereas the Vietcong's policy was focused on 'primary group cohesion' (Gabriel and Savage, 1979; Henderson 1979). Similarly, the early success of the Chinese military in the Korean War stemmed from a strategy which ensured 'that the aims of the small group did not diverge from those of the larger organisation' (Holmes 1985: 296). In the 1982 Lebanese War the Israeli Army made extensive use of platoon micro-level solidarity to deal with psychiatric casualties. They set up front-line psychiatric centres where the patients would be visited regularly by their platoon comrades 'who assured them that they were in no way disgraced and would be welcome back'. As a result of this practice 'almost 60 per cent of patients were returned to duty' (Holmes 1985: 259). The fact that most militaries have moved from the use of large weapons used by a single soldier towards group-operated weaponry systems is also a potent indicator of how small-unit cohesion is valued. Despite the fact that many of these weapons do not necessarily require more than one soldier to operate them, introducing teams to man rocket launchers, mortars, machine guns or bazookas enhances micro-level solidarity, as soldiers who interact on a daily basis, are mutually dependent and fight together.

To sum up, rather than killing being easy and the willingness to die for others difficult and rare, both of these activities are difficult and require concentrated organisational support and intensive micro-level solidarity. The war environment radically transforms human relationships and creates conditions whereby, on many occasions, self-sacrifice becomes the preferred option to face-to-face killing.

Conclusion

Although it is difficult, if not impossible, to imagine modern warfare without propagandistic imagery and messages, propaganda does not possess as much omnipotence as is often attributed to it. Rather than being a giant, all-embracing brainwashing device capable of transforming peace-loving individuals into bloodthirsty thugs, its role is significantly more modest. In many respects war propaganda is not an autonomous force but a parasitic entity that feeds off already existing practices including long-term processes such as centrifugal ideologisation and the cumulative bureaucratisation of coercion. Propaganda does not and cannot create solidarity where it does not exist. Instead, its messages and imagery are severely constrained and shaped by the social order it is part of and it aims to address. In this sense, war propaganda is first and foremost a means of society-wide self-legitimisation. Rather than converting opinions and changing behaviour, much of propaganda acts as set of traffic lights: it gives a clear signal about who and where is the enemy; how to treat that enemy and why it is justified to treat him this way. In the context of war this essentially involves the justification of killing and dying. However, much of this justification is aimed not at those who are directly involved in killing and dying but at the broader audience of the battlefield spectators. In real front-line experience of face-to-face interaction, propagandistic visions quickly deflate and evaporate. The realisation that a soldier is not facing a monstrous ogre but a human being just like himself makes close-encounter killing a very difficult thing which only a few can efficiently perform. To circumvent this almost intrinsic human incapacity to kill other humans, modern social organisations have devised potent coercive apparatuses to make killing more anonymous, banal, distant, bureaucratic and efficient. Most of all, once military organisations understood the strength, intensity and importance of small-group bonds and that most combatants fight not for great ideological abstractions, but out of necessity and micro-level solidarity, willingness to die for one's platoon became a cornerstone of a broader military strategy. From that moment on the central task of the bureaucratic machine was to ensure that the principles, practices and benefits of micro-level solidarity were effectively translated onto the ideological and organisational macro level and vice versa.

Part IV

War, violence and social divisions

8 Social stratification, warfare and violence

Introduction

Just a brief glance through the contemporary textbooks that narrate events over the last 2,000 years of human history would show that if there are any near universal processes that have shaped our global past, these must have been collective violence and social exclusion. While it is certainly true that much of early historiography is full of overblown descriptions of imperial power, embellished portrayals of social hierarchies and inflated narratives of battlefield deaths, there is no doubt that violence and inequalities were prevalent for most of recorded human history. Notwithstanding this fact, contemporary sociology has ignored and, for the most part, continues to ignore, the relationships between organised violence and social hierarchies. Although social stratification is one of the most extensively studied topics in sociology, an overwhelming body of empirical research and theorising in this field has focused exclusively on social inequalities between people in times of peace. Rather than looking at warfare and organised coercion sociologists were preoccupied with the role economic and cultural forces such as capitalism, globalisation, individual self-interests, social norms and discourses play in generating social inequalities. However, this chapter starts from the proposition that since, as demonstrated later in the chapter, social stratification originated in warfare and violence, it cannot be properly explained without tackling this inherent link between the two. Moreover, I argue that despite its apparent invisibility in the modern age, organised violence remains one of the most important factors in the maintenance and proliferation of social inequalities. Here, too, the cumulative bureaucratisation of coercion and centrifugal ideologisation are identified as crucial processes that have shaped the relationship between violence and social stratification.

The chapter is divided into four parts. The first part focuses on the dominant sociological perspectives in the study of social hierarchies and emphasises the general lack of interest in studying violence and warfare. The second part critically assesses the two most important exceptions: the writings of Stanislav Andreski and Michael Mann. The third part explores the violent origins of social stratification and its gradual transformation through the cumulative bureaucratisation of coercion. The final part analyses the role of ideology and especially the process of the mass ideologisation of coercive action.

Stratification without collective violence?

Since its inception as an academic discipline sociology has been preoccupied with the study of social stratification. In fact, for much of the second half of the twentieth century stratification was regarded as the most important theme in sociology. The study of the origins and causes of social inequalities and the asymmetrical access to wealth, power and prestige have dominated theoretical and empirical research (Collins 1988; Crompton 1993; Grusky 1994). Despite the variety of models developed, two approaches have become central: the Marxist and Weberian concepts of social stratification. Whereas the Marxist models focus on the economic foundations of inequality and in particular on the ownership of productive wealth, the Weberian models emphasise the multiplicity of group cleavages by identifying political, cultural and economic sources of social divisions. In Marxist analyses social stratification is essentially seen as class conflict generated by the irrationalities of capitalist economic organisation and driven by profit maximisation which, it is alleged, inevitably pits those who own the means of production against those who only possess their labour. In this view, economic classes are the essential agents of social change, with history being interpreted as an arena of class struggle: from the slaves and slave owners of the ancient world, the lords and serfs of feudalism to the capitalists and proletarians of the industrial era (Marx 1972 [1894]).

In contrast, for Weberians stratification is a multi-dimensional phenomenon: in addition to economic classes it also involves political power and social status with all three of these categories exhibiting significant autonomy. While social status stands for a hierarchically ranked position in society that a person has and shares with a community of individuals who have a similar lifestyle, power is linked to individual or collective ability to acquire and use political domination in order to influence or control the behaviour of others. Even the concept of social class differs from the Marxist version since in the Weberian model it refers to the occupational market position rather than to property relationships (Weber 1968). In the Weberian view the patterns of stratification vary and oscillate through time and space: while in some social contexts status, class and power can overlap, there are many instances where one's social status is not determined by one's market position, personal wealth or ownership of the means of production. As Weber (1946: 187) puts it: 'status honour need not necessarily be linked with class situation. On the contrary, it normally stands in sharp opposition to the pretensions of sheer property'.

Although the central propositions of these two approaches have not been significantly altered, both models have evolved over time into what is now known as neo-Marxist and neo-Weberian perspectives. Much of contemporary neo-Marxist views focus on the political economy of labour migration, 'the racialised fraction of working class', the role of the managerial, technocratic and middle classes in capitalism and on the proletarisation and embourgeoisement of the labour force (Braverman 1974; Poulanzas 1974; Wright 1979; 1989; Miles 1984; 1988). More recently attention has shifted to the study of the exploitative character of neo-liberal economic policies, the link between globalisation and widening income inequality and the emergence of the so called 'transnational capitalist class' (Wallerstein 2000; Sklair 2001; Sassen 2006).

The focal point of neo-Weberian research includes the role of structurally produced status disparity and relative deprivation (Lenski 1966; Wegener 1991; Baron 1994), the relationship between social status and citizenship rights (Turner 1986; 1988; Brubaker 1992), the growing importance of educational success and academic credentials (Collins 1979; 1988) and the study of consumption practices and lifestyles (DiMaggio 1987; 1991; Lamont 1992; 2002). However, most attention has been given to the organisational devices of social exclusion and, in particular, to Weber's concept of monopolistic social closure (Parkin 1979; Rex 1986; Goldthorpe 1987; Wimmer 2008). These neo-Weberian studies explore the processes through which groups and social organisations create and enforce rules of membership: using monopolistic tactics they close access to non-group members thus preventing them from acquiring material and symbolic benefits. In other words, social stratification is often the product of structurally and monopolistically imposed exclusionary processes.

Some researchers have attempted to synthesise Marxist and Weberian models by situating class transformations in the changing character of industrial society. These studies explore the links between political power and social class (Dahrendorf 1959), the specific position of lower non-manual and white-collar workers in advanced capitalism (Lockwood 1989), the transformation from industrial labour towards service- and information-oriented post-industrial society (Bell 1973) and the structural symbiosis between class and cultural lifestyles (Bourdieu and Passeron 1977). Pierre Bourdieu's work (1984, 1990, 1996) has been particularly influential in attempting to bring together the Weberian understanding of status as domination and the Marxist stress on the centrality of economic classes in social relations. By focusing on the structural reproduction of knowledge, taste, linguistic competence and artistic expertise, Bourdieu identifies cultural capital and habitus as key social mechanisms of inequality. Hence, it is not only economic assets or position in the political organisation that determines one's place in the social structure; it is also one's own, socially produced, cultural resources. In a nutshell: for Bourdieu social stratification is rooted in economic and political domination as much as is the aesthetic dispositions of dominant classes.

Although there is no doubt that both neo-Marxist and neo-Weberian approaches have provided valuable and rich analyses of stratification processes, an overwhelming majority of these studies have neglected to tackle what is probably the most important feature of stratification: the role violence and war play in the creation and maintenance of social hierarchies. Considering, as I will demonstrate later, that the institution of social stratification for the most part originated in warfare and violence and that its persistence through history has been and remains heavily dependent on the ability of social organisations to control violence, it is quite astonishing that war and violence have been almost completely ignored by the contemporary sociologists of stratification.

What is apparent here is that most studies written from the neo-Marxist or neo-Weberian perspectives have adopted either the position of 'methodological nationalism' (Martins 1974; Wimmer and Glick-Schiller 2002) or 'methodological cosmopolitanism' (Beck 2002) thus remaining oblivious to the role state borders, and in particular, the state's monopoly on violence, play in cementing the patterns of stratification. In other words, the 'conventional' approaches tend to study social inequalities and the process of inclusion and exclusion in two ways: either by looking solely inside a particular society where 'society' and nation-state are, wrongly, understood as coterminous; or alternatively by overextending the notion of 'society' to the entire globe whereby stratification is analysed through the prism of transnational phenomena such as capitalism or globalisation. However, both of these research strategies are deeply problematic, as they fail to see states as 'the pre-eminent power containers' (Giddens 1985) and especially the interdependence of the internal social hierarchies with the external geopolitical contexts. To put it differently: rather than exploring the inter-relationships between domestic class or status politics and the use of violence in the 'international' political arena, the conventional approaches start from the wrong assumption that stratification is either a product of global economic forces (such as capitalism) or that social inequalities stem from internal, society-specific, causes such as historical traditions or socio-economic development. Both of these approaches, the inward looking and the globalist position, operate with an overly 'pacifist' view of social stratification: there is no engagement either with the gory, physically brutal, origins of human inequality nor with the contemporary coercive apparatuses that remain paramount in maintaining such inequalities. Although social stratification is a nearly universal feature of all societies, no human being would easily assent to occupying the bottom place in any social hierarchy. Whereas neo-Marxists and neo-Weberians clearly recognise the exploitative, functional and instrumental character of stratification there is still little or no recognition of the role force plays in establishing and preserving social hierarchies and inequalities. There is no doubt that the dominance of such 'pacifist' interpretations of stratification are in a significant way linked to the legacy of European and North-American economic prosperity and the political stability of the post-WWII era whereby the imagery of the emerging welfare state has fostered the decoupling of social inequality from violence.

This clearly was not the case with the 'founding fathers' of these approaches since both of them, Weber and Marx (see Chapter 1) did make explanatory links between stratification and collective violence. While for Marx, historically the class struggle was defined by organised violence and capitalism was seen as a coercive system, the transformation of which would necessitate the use of revolutionary bloodshed, Weber identified political power with coercive action and tied the cultural and political status of the ruling strata to their victories in wars.

It might seem that Bourdieu is an exception here as he developed the concept of symbolic violence to explain the coercive character of class domination and in particular the imposition of culturally arbitrary 'pedagogic action' on unresisting human subjects (Bourdieu 1990; 1996). However, since this idiom refers to the tacit, habitual, unconscious forms of cultural domination which are enforced through cultural reproduction rather than actual physical harm, this concept is little more than a subtle metaphor. To put it bluntly: since 'symbolic violence' does not involve killing, injuring, destruction or any other form of physical devastation, it is not violence at all but a form of hegemonic socialisation. If we were to treat any form of cultural and symbolic pressure as violence then the concept of violence would be relativised in the extreme and lose its meaning. Surely there is a qualitative difference between penalising a working-class child for mispronouncing a Latin phrase and guillotining thousands of revolutionaries for attempting to overthrow the government?

Stratification through war and violence

There are only a few exceptions among contemporary sociological analysts of social stratification who have taken the study of war and violence seriously, among which two stand out: Stanislav Andreski and Michael Mann.

For Andreski (1968) military power is the backbone of all power while warfare is intrinsically linked to patterns of social inequality. In his empirically rich analysis, Andreski (1968: 25–6) argues that economic inequalities are a reflection of political, and more specifically coercive, power, whereby economic rights of property possession and asset ownership are 'not self-sufficient but derivative' as they 'designate the right to control, to use and dispose of objects, the access to which is prohibited to all except the owner'. Hence economic dominance implies 'the ability to compel through the use or the threat of violence'. Consequently, those who control the means of military power regularly, if not always, occupy the highest positions in society's stratification chain. However, this does not imply that the top generals wield disproportionate political power or that they rank high in terms of social status but that those who rank high in the social hierarchy will, for the most part, be able to directly use or indirectly rely on the structures of military power.[1]

Furthermore, Andreski argues that the link between stratification and military organisation is rooted in group size. Unlike small and dispersed hunter-gatherer groups, which do not require much co-ordination, large-scale societies cannot operate without some form of social organisation. To facilitate group co-ordination it becomes necessary to introduce social

---

[1] Andreski (1968: 26) argues that even big business has to rely on military might (via the state) in order to secure its wealth, and plutocrats can rarely rule on their own: 'The pure plutocracy, that is to say, the rule of the rich who do not control the military power, can only be a temporary phenomenon. Purely economic factors produce, no doubt, fluctuations in the height of stratification, but as the following evidence will show, the long-term trends are determined by the shifts of the locus of military power.'

hierarchies with a clear division of labour and mutually exclusive delegation of responsibility. With the huge numbers of people involved and the need to act promptly in the context of external threats, control by a few proves to be more effective than any other, more inclusive, form of rule. Consequently, the first organisations tended to be military organisations. The fact that your neighbours have developed a (military) organisation means that there is little choice left: 'Peoples who could not evolve or adopt such organisation were inevitably destroyed' (Andreski 1968: 23). Nevertheless, once chains of command and control are established, they tend to lead to the acquisition and accumulation of privileges and are also difficult to undo. For Andreski, group size is a good predictor of the level of inequality: the larger the society, the greater the need for efficient co-ordination, and hence greater social stratification. However it is the war experience that most influences the patterns of social inequality: 'Success in war, more than in any other human activity, depends on co-ordination of individual actions, and the larger a group the more necessary is the co-ordination, the larger the hierarchy required … therefore the larger the group the more pronounced should be the stratifying effect of militancy' (Andreski 1968: 29).

What also matters is the scale of participation in warfare. By comparing the available data on the involvement of the wider population in military units throughout history, Andreski identifies what he terms the 'military participation ratio' (MPR) as the most important indicator of social inequality. In his view, the military participation ratio, which stands for 'the proportion of militarily utilised individuals in the total population', is 'one of the strongest determinants of stratification' (Andreski 1968: 33, 73). Whereas simple, pre-modern, forms of collectivities, such as tribes and chiefdoms, are characterised by exceptionally high levels of participation in combat whereby all men are warriors, the more complex societies have much lower levels of MPR. Furthermore, as the monopolisation of weaponry eventually leads to the monopolisation of various privileges and positions of power, in complex social orders the MPR tends to decrease gradually. This is particularly the case when new technological developments in weaponry production provide means to close access to military participation. As Andreski (1968: 35) emphasises 'the predominance of the armed forces over the populace grows as the armament becomes more elaborate'. The use of bronze swords, war chariots, composite bows and heavy-armed cavalry helped institute a small and select warrior caste where being a soldier entailed enormous expense that required the protracted labour of a large non-soldiering, subordinate, population. Although in early history conquest was the main source of the labour supply, as Andreski (1968: 38) argues, extensive predation could be counter productive in the long term as it dramatically lowers MPR, thus weakening a state's defensive potential: 'states try to subjugate as much territory as they can, there is the constant tendency for the actual MPR to be reduced below the optimum'. Territorial over-extension that is not followed by an increase in the military participation ratio has often led to the situation where 'tremendous empires fall prey to small tribes where all men bear arms'. Hence, for Andreski, social stratification and military participation are inversely proportional: social orders where there is wider involvement in warfare and where there is more open access to weaponry tend to be more egalitarian, while a monopoly on the use of violence and the professionalisation of military roles is linked to high levels of stratification.

Michael Mann (1986, 1988, 1993) also focuses on the role of warfare in transforming patterns of inclusion and exclusion. He conceptualises social stratification as 'the overall creation and distribution of power in society' and as such sees it as '*the* central structure of societies' since 'in its dual collective and distributive aspects it is the means whereby human beings achieve their goals in society' (Mann 1986: 10). As discussed in Chapter 2, Mann extends the Weberian tripartite division of stratification by identifying military power as an autonomous source of social control. He justifies the separation between political and military power on the grounds that for much of history there was little or no overlap between administrative control and the use of large-scale violence. Before the era of absolutism, to fight wars most European rulers required both consent and military support from the fairly independent aristocrats who possessed their own armies. Similarly, most powerful world despots and emperors in the pre-modern age were unable to prevent periodic invasions of nomadic warrior tribes, the pillage of pirates, organised banditry or to curtail tribal feuding. It is only in modernity that states are able to legitimately claim and politically enforce a monopoly on the use of organised violence (through state-controlled military and police). Hence, what distinguishes the two forms of power is that 'political powers are those of centralised, institutionalised, territorial regulation' while 'military powers are of organised physical force wherever they are organised' (Mann 1986: 11).

What is particularly relevant here is that the nearly perfect overlap between the political and military power that characterises contemporary nation-states is firmly tied to historical transformations in social stratification. Mann argues that the gradual extension of state power, both internally and externally, is structurally linked with the rise of classes and nations as the two dominant agents of the modern era. Whereas agrarian civilisations were too wide, too hierarchical and too decentralised to accommodate the existence of clearly formed classes or society-encompassing nations, these two actors became 'central to social development' in modernity. However, Mann's account differs significantly from the conventional sociological common sense that posits industrialisation or capitalism (or both) as key generators of this transformation. Instead, for Mann, the spread of capitalism and industrialism remained dependent on military and political powers. In his words: 'Capitalism and industrialism have been overrated. Their diffused powers exceeded their authoritative powers, for which they relied more on, and were shaped by, military and political power organisations. Though both capitalism and industrialism vastly increased collective powers, distributive powers – social stratification – were less altered' (Mann 1993: 726). Hence, neither industrialism nor capitalism dramatically transformed patterns of stratification for much of the eighteenth and nineteenth centuries. It was geopolitics, warfare and the general increase in military power that proved decisive in the alteration of social structure. The transformation of coercive power was a slow and gradual process whereby it gradually lost its role as agent of internal social repression and retained only its external, war-fighting, role. As Mann notes, this separation was achieved in Europe and North America only in the twentieth century as a result of prolonged struggles over the extension of citizenship rights. In other words, before WWI, strikes and political protests were suppressed by military force as much as by the police. For example, both France and the USA relied on soldiers to quash labour movements and urban riots throughout the nineteenth and early twentieth centuries (Goldstein 1978; Tilly 1986).

Geopolitics had a profound impact on the emergence and spread of classes while, once classes gained a strong footing in the domestic political arena, they themselves influenced the geopolitical actions of their states. Mann charts the cumulative development of various social classes and their impact on military and state power from the early emergence of the bourgeoisie and petite bourgeoisie, to the gradual expansion of the middle class and finally to the organisation and fully fledged incorporation of the working classes and peasantry into the national social structure. In all these cases citizenship is identified as a key terrain of social struggle whereby the slow, class-wide, extension of civil and political rights was paralleled by the military, fiscal and political requirements of rising nation-states. By drawing indirectly on Hintze (1975), Mann contends that citizenship was utilised as a mechanism of social control for political and military elites. That is, by incrementally and selectively granting civil, political and social rights to various classes state rulers were able to pacify domestic politics while simultaneously pursuing their own geopolitical ambitions. In other words, the expansion of citizenship is on the one hand linked with the steady rise of classes in Europe and North America, while on the other hand it was a principal instrument of political and military rulers in controlling the potentially disruptive influence at first of the rising bourgeoisie and middle classes and later of the workers and peasants. For Mann, diverse historical and social contexts determined the development of different citizenship regimes. While the early emergence of economic liberalism (coupled with popular participation in the American Revolution) were decisive for the development of a constitutional model of citizenship in the UK and USA, absolutist regimes with extensive agrarian bases, such as those of Germany, Austria, Japan and Russia, have experienced prolonged and often extremely violent struggles over citizenship. However, in all of these cases rulers were prone to use citizenship as both a divide-and-rule strategy and as a bargaining chip to solve fiscal crises and mobilise participation and support for wars (Mann 1988; 1993).

These different trajectories of citizenship development had a profound impact on the geopolitical actions of individual states, as the extension of citizenship rights to various classes usually implied greater cross-class commitment to the geopolitical goals of these states. Thus, before WWI, workers and peasants were largely excluded from citizenship in much of Europe, which meant that they did not perceive the states as their states and were mostly opposed to war efforts. In contrast, once the bourgeoisie and middle classes were granted significant civil, social and political rights they tended to organise nationally and embrace nationalist causes. However, Mann argues that not all middle-class groups succumbed to rampant nationalism. Rather it was the state careerists and highly educated upper middle classes that became the key proponents of imperial claims and the principal warmongers in Europe at the end of the nineteenth century and beginning of the twentieth (Mann 1993: 786). An outcome of the two world wars was the emergence of 'cross-class nations', whereby in much of Europe and North America citizenship rights became more inclusive. As a result, there was and is more stability in both domestic and geopolitical politics. In contrast, in the regions where labour relations were not institutionally conciliated and where citizenship rights have not been fully extended, such as many parts of Africa, military power remains unconstrained and is often used to quell domestic disturbances. Similarly, since authoritarian regimes rely on military might to regulate class politics, they are more vulnerable to war-induced demise

(Mann 1993: 730). Hence to sum up, for Mann, 'nations are not the opposite of classes, for they rose up together, both (to varying degrees) the product of modernising churches, commercial capitalism, militarism, and the rise of modern state' (Mann 1993: 249). The institutional pacification of labour relations was often achieved because and through warfare, since universal conscription and full participation in wars was rewarded through greater social inclusion and the extension of citizenship rights after wars.

Both Andreski and Mann tie social stratification to military power and argue that historically, warfare was a significant device in transforming patterns of social inclusion and exclusion. Furthermore, they both emphasise the role of war and violence in generating complex and socially hierarchical social organisations that eventually developed into modern nation-states. However, their accounts differ in scope: while Andreski focuses on group size and the scale of popular participation in military force, Mann is more interested in the interdependent rise of classes and nations in the context of changing geopolitics and warfare. Although the two accounts are highly compatible and as such contribute a great deal to the understanding of the relationships between war, violence and social stratification, they also require a degree of modification to accommodate issues they do not adequately address.

Despite rightly identifying the links between group size and organisational inequality, as well as the inversely proportional relationship between stratification and military participation, Andreski's model is based on a very static and overly mechanical measurement. Such a measurement cannot explain the complexity, variety and changing character of social stratification. While there is no doubt that larger social entities require complex and hierarchical social organisations, size alone does not predetermine the scale of social inequalities. For example, by comparing contemporary Russia with its Soviet era counterpart it is possible to see that size and stratification are not necessarily equivalent. In fact, this case clearly demonstrates that size of territory and population can be inversely proportional with levels of social hierarchy and inequality. The fact that modern-day Russia has significantly fewer people and less territory than the Soviet Union had does not imply that it is automatically a less hierarchical and less stratified society. On the contrary, as all available research shows, levels of social inequality among Russian citizens have dramatically increased with a small wealthy elite and large numbers of impoverished middle classes (Holmes 1997; Pickles and Smith 1998; Sakwa 1999). Whereas in the late Soviet era only 1.5 per cent of the population were living below the poverty line, by 1993 this figure had risen sharply to between 39 per cent and 49 per cent (Milanović 1998). Furthermore, the decrease in population and territory size has not resulted in a smaller state apparatus. On the contrary, the bureaucratic machine has substantially increased: by 1993 the Russian administrative apparatus was 'larger than the combined central state and party apparatus of the former USSR and RSFSR' while the government was up to three times larger than its Soviet equivalent (Holmes 1997: 184).

Similarly, the military participation ratio is too crude an instrument to gauge the intricacy of the relationship between stratification and war. Although it is highly valuable to know that greater popular participation in war is often related to more egalitarian social formations, it is also just as important to look at the structure and composition of military apparatuses and wider societies in order to explain the variety of historical experience. Although Andreski is right that in small-scale tribal and clan-based egalitarian social orders virtually all men are warriors, this fact in itself does not tell us much about the relationship between stratification and popular participation in warfare simply because there is very little if any warfare fought by and among such egalitarian groups. As Textor (1967), Eckhardt (1992) and Fry (2007) document, there is no archaeological evidence for warfare among nomadic foragers and only scant evidence for warfare among simple sedentary tribes. Eckhardt (1990, 1992) emphasises that, in all the abundance of cave paintings depicting aspects of the social life of the Homo sapiens, including hunting, there are no paintings of warfare. Fry (2007: 56) concludes that 'the archaeological record shows no evidence of war at 12,000 BCE and then evidence for sparse war about 9,500 BCE' with large-scale warfare 'evident only in the last 1,800–1,500 years before the present'.

In a similar vein, low levels of popular participation in military organisations do not necessarily indicate sharp stratification patterns. For example, the abolition of conscription in the Netherlands in 1996 and the establishment of a professional military had no direct impact on social stratification (Ajangiz 2002). The fact that Sweden has compulsory military service and is generally regarded as one of the least stratified modern societies might, at first, signal that Andreski's model is fully applicable here. However, if we take into account the facts that Swedish soldiers have not participated in any war for the past two centuries and the current Swedish Armed Forces consist of less than 20,000 troops, it becomes apparent that the patterns of stratification are not linked in any recognisable way to the military participation ratio (Perry 2004). The point is that mere participation in the military cannot tell us much about the social structure of a particular society. What is more important is the presence or absence of prolonged warfare. Most simple hunter-gatherer societies do not experience warfare, and neither do most contemporary European states (since 1945), so the military participation ratio is not a reliable indicator of social stratification in such cases. This measure might not even be trustworthy in the context of warfare, since there are significant differences between the societies and militaries involved. For example, despite the fact that the Carthaginian Empire (575 BCE-146 CE) was an oligarchic republic the wars of which, (in particular the Punic Wars) were fought by mercenaries, the empire was less stratified and more democratic than many of the Greek city-states that practised almost universal conscription. Not only did Carthage have elected legislators, trade unions and town meetings, but also the Carthaginian popular assembly often had the decisive vote in matters of public concern such as waging a war (Stepper 2001). On the opposite side, the protracted 1980s Iraq–Iran war involved high levels of military participation on both sides, but this did not result in a lessening of social inequalities in the two societies. In fact, the war was responsible for sharpening social stratification and the increasing the influence of the military establishment in Iran (Cordesman and Kleiber 2007). All of this suggests that the relationship between popular participation in warfare and social inclusion and exclusion needs more nuanced analysis.

Mann provides a much more subtle model that ties transformations in social stratification to geopolitical changes and citizenship rights. While this theoretically comprehensive and empirically rich model sheds much light on the relationship between collective violence and social inequalities, it unduly emphasises the separation between military and political power, as well as the roles of class and citizenship, while downplaying the process of ideologisation, which is crucial in accounting for the patterns of stratification. Mann is right that for much of history collective violence remained outside centralised administrative control and it is only in modernity that states have managed to monopolise the use of violence. However, this does not imply the separate and independent existence of political and military power. On the contrary, political power stems directly from a state's ability to use force or coercive pressure in the process of pursuing its goals. Unless political action is tied to force it lacks proper 'anthropological grounding' (Poggi 2006: 138). Administrative control can have institutional resonance only when rooted in the use, or the threat of the use, of violence. The fact that in the pre-modern world there was little territorial centralisation of power does not really tell us much about the relationship between political control and violence; it only points out that power and violence were territorially dispersed. The existence of independent aristocracies who possessed their own military apparatuses only suggests that there was no monopoly on the use of violence, not that political control and violence are separate social spheres.

The point here, as Weber (1968) argued, is that political organisations derive their ability to enforce rules from violence. As such, political organisations have no ultimate ends (as their ends are subject to change) but can only be defined in terms of the means they have at their disposal, that is, violence. As Poggi (2004: 39) argues, 'exactly because violence constitutes a means to so many ends, the possibility of exercising it becomes the target of multiple, competing ambitions on the part of individuals and groups. These contend with one another not just by *means* of violence means, but also over violence itself, and particularly over the control of the dominant material and social technology of organised violence'. In other words, political power presupposes coercive domination. This is not to say that any use of brute force would guarantee long-term obedience. Although successful utilisation of political power rests on sound ideological justification, administrative control has to be grounded in the organised ability to invoke the threat of coercive action. This is particularly relevant in the context of social stratification since, as I argue later, the continual maintenance of a stratified social structure is always underpinned and heavily dependent on this institutionalised coercive threat regardless of how invisible such a threat is in modern democratic political orders. Since both social stratification and large-scale political power originate in warfare and have dramatically expanded with the proliferation of organised violence, little, if anything, is gained analytically by treating political power separately from military power.

Secondly, Mann's theory devotes much attention to class and citizenship while largely neglecting other forms of social divisions. There is no denying the importance of the role that social class and citizenship rights have played in the construction of modern social orders and in particular how they have shaped and have been shaped by geopolitical transformations and modern warfare. Nevertheless, for much of history it was not class but social status, caste, estate, gender, age and other types of social divisions that dominated patterns of stratification. While Mann rightly recognises that in modernity classes become central agents of inclusion and exclusion, he also operates with an exceptionally wide and unusually trans-historical understanding of class relations. Hence, he regularly subsumes status, estates and caste-based institutions in the concept of class. For example, he writes about classical Greece as 'the first historical society in which we can clearly perceive class struggle as an enduring feature of social life' (Mann 1986: 216), about 'class-conscious rules of medieval warfare' or about class divisions in medieval Europe where 'religion widened the cultural gulf between classes' (Mann 2005: 42–4). At the same time he finds little or no place for social status in modernity. However, to understand the workings of social stratification it is paramount to make a clear distinction between the largely unchanging and unchangeable forms such as status, caste and membership of estates characterizing the pre-modern world, and the more economic, and thus more open and market-dependent class associations that one encounters in modernity. Not only are classes in many respect modern forms of association (including their specific market condition, the greater importance of consumption and the sense of class identification) but they are also much more fluid forms of group attachment by comparison to caste or estate-type systems. Furthermore, even though Mann (1993: 24–30) operates with a more dynamic concept of class than classical and contemporary Marxist thinkers, he still conceives of classes as tangible groups who 'share a cohesive community and a keen defence of their own interests' which means that 'class consciousness is also a perennial feature of modern societies'. However, class is not such a coherent, stable and self-conscious group.[2] As Weber (1968) rightly points out, classes are quasi-groups that consist of individuals sharing a similar market situation. In addition, in the modern era, a person's class position does not necessarily overlap with his or her social status. While modern status associations are more mobile and fluctuating than their pre-modern counterparts, status – defined as accepted distribution of social honour – remains a potent mechanism of social inclusion and exclusion in modernity. Weber (1968: 405) was well aware that status and class can underpin each other but also that status cannot be subsumed in class: 'Social honour can stick directly to a class-situation, and it is also, indeed most of the time, determined by the average class-situation of the status-group members. This, however, is not necessarily the case. Status membership, in turn, influences the class-situation in that the style of life required by status groups makes them prefer special kinds of property or gainful pursuits and reject others.' This conceptual separation is especially important when exploring the relationships between warfare, violence and stratification. As I demonstrate later, it is social-status hierarchies that play a central role in linking organised violence with patterns of social stratification rather than class divisions.

Finally, since Mann's focus is primarily on the historical development and transformations of states rather than on warfare as such, he does not devote

---

[2] When directly confronted with this criticism Mann states that he simply does not like the category of 'status'. See our exchange in J. Breuilly et al. (2006).

much attention to the processes of the justification of violence. While, as already discussed in Chapter 2, Mann articulates a potent theory of ideological power, he underestimates the strength of ideology in the modern age. The entire period 1760–1914, which is often understood to be the age when modern ideological doctrines were born and expanded dramatically, Mann describes as a period of ideological decline. In his own words: 'Ideological power relations were of declining and lesser power significance during this period'; that is, ideological power 'was more "immanent" than "transcendent" … aiding the emergence of collective actors created by capitalism, militarism and states' (Mann 1993: 2). The problem here is that by equating ideology with culture and religion, Mann is unable to assess correctly the significance of modern ideological doctrines in legitimising transformations in social stratification influenced by wars and other forms of collective violence. Rather than looking at both ideology and warfare as second-order realities and mere means of state power, it is imperative to explore their structural autonomy and the processes through which they have shaped each other. While Clausewitz was right that war is a form of state policy, what is sociologically more interesting is to study wars through their own unpredictable dialectics. If wars were only just another type of policy (though 'by other means'), an activity controllable and regulated by omnipotent states, then warfare would be utilised much more frequently and would be an easily justifiable practice. The fact that the initiation and the conduct of wars remains a highly contentious, thorny, polarising and volatile activity, an activity that generates its own dynamics, indicates that warfare is much more than just a tool of state power. War is an autonomous sociological phenomenon often capable of creating new social realities. Similarly, ideological power is rarely just an instrument of political manipulation: it too possesses independence and produces unintended consequences of social action. Hence, to fully understand the origins and development of social stratification it is crucial to analyse collective violence and its ideological underpinnings.

Warfare and the origins of social stratification

Most archaeologists and anthropologists agree that there was little inequality between human beings before the emergence of agriculture and the sedentary lifestyle (Cashdan 1980; Angle 1986; Fry 2007). The extensive studies of remaining hunter-gatherer bands clearly indicate that they operate on strictly egalitarian principles with little or no leadership involved (Boehm 1999;

Winterhalder 2001; De Waal 2005). Moreover, such groups are not prone to violent actions and are generally incapable of and unwilling to engage in protracted feuds, let alone wars. Hence, there is an overwhelming body of evidence that agriculture and permanent human settlements develop in parallel with social stratification and warfare (Wright 1965; Textor 1967; Kohn 1987). In other words, there are clear links between the birth of civilisation, warfare and institutionalised social inequalities (Toynbee 1950; Eckhardt 1990; 1992). Nevertheless, there is no agreement on whether the development of agriculture and sedentary lifestyles generated stratification and wars or it is the other way around. Marxist-inspired theorists argue that agriculture was decisive in this process, as the production of surplus food allowed the emergence of a non-food-producing upper class able to live off the labour of peasant food producers (Childe 1950; Mandel 1968). The other economistic, but more organisationally centred, approaches have focused on the indispensable role of social organisation in providing and preserving surplus production. For example, Sahlins (1972) and Hayden (1995) argue that the ability to store food is more important than its production since without organised systems in place, unstored surpluses are wasted instead of generating the wealth that is a prerequisite of a stratified social order. Hence, it was not the availability of surpluses by itself that led to the development of civilisation, but the social organisation that enabled the storage of surpluses. However, both of these positions overemphasise production at the expense of coercion and see warfare as a mere by-product of economic or material growth. The view is that once sedentary, agriculture-based life developed, it resulted in violent conflict over the available farming land and the food storages in possession of other groups. In a nutshell, the emergence of warfare is interpreted as a consequence, rather than a cause, of social stratification.

Nevertheless, drawing in part on classical 'bellicose' sociology, one can argue that social stratification was in fact born of warfare. It was co-ordinated collective violence that initially generated and also helped later establish relatively stable patterns of social inclusion and exclusion. Gumplowicz (2007 [1883], 1899) was right when he argued that organised collective violent action was crucial in creating stratified social orders. It is through the conquest of disorganised neighbours that organised minorities were able to impose themselves on the rest and eventually establish the dominant warrior strata. Gumplowicz (1899: 119, 123) argues that since 'the human labour could not be exploited without violence' the clans and tribes had to be 'united by the forcible subjection of one to the other'. In a similar vein, Oppenheimer (2007) argues that war raids lead to the centralisation of the warring group which is then able to utilise its organisational capacity to enforce its domination over other groups. Although classical theories of conquest focus more on the genesis of the state, rather than on the origins of social divisions, they point in the right direction as they tie the development of organisational power to the emergence of stratification. Since social hierarchies require organisational underpinning, there is no enduring social exclusion without organisation. Hence to wage war means to create a stable and durable social organisation. By overemphasising the production of surpluses, the Marxist and other economistic theories simply and wrongly presume that those who create surpluses are destined to be exploited. It seems more realistic that those who were initially able to use their strength, skill, intelligence and most of all organisational capabilities to produce more food than others were just as capable of using these same qualities to protect their surpluses.[3] As the example of Greek hoplites illustrates well, it is quite possible to be a warrior and farmer at the same time (Goldsworthy 1997).

While there is no doubt, as most classical and contemporary 'bellicose' historical sociologists demonstrate, that this organisational power eventually gave birth to the pristine states, this still does not explain the origins of military organisations. Since conquest and warfare are not practised by nomadic bands and tribes, it is not clear how this organisational power eventually emerged. That is, whereas it is evident that, once established, military organisations were instrumental in reinforcing stratified social orders and ultimately creating states and civilisations it is far from evident how this outcome was achieved.[4] Mann (1986: 105–27) argues that this was a two-stage process which at first relied on 'circuits of economic praxis', that is, the availability of economic surpluses generated by alluvial agriculture helped establish 'territorial centredness' and political authority through small city-states that 'provided a merged form of economic and political authoritative power organisation'. Secondly, the fact that these city-states generally appeared within a broader, diffused religious and geopolitical environment, linked to regional cult centres, meant that in the second stage the economic and political powers (of city-states) tended to merge gradually with those of more extensive ideological and military powers. In other words, Mann (1986: 127) endorses 'a broadly economic view of first origins' while 'for later stages of the process the militaristic mechanisms have greater relevance'.

---

[3] Furthermore it also seems that such individuals and groups were more likely to initially distribute this surplus in order to acquire support and favours from others within their collectivity (cf. Mann 1986).

[4] Although, as Gellner (1988b) and Mann (1986: 124) rightly point out, the emergence of statehood and civilisations was an exception rather than a rule, a structural aberration, a historical contingency and 'an abnormal phenomenon'.

However, this interpretation still provides too economistic an answer that focuses on surplus production and does not really explain the transition from egalitarian nomadism to sedentary stratified orders. Since Mann, just like some of the classical 'bellicose' theorists, is essentially interested in tracking down the origins of pristine states, he pays less attention to the crucial issue of the transition from nomadic hunter-gatherers to complex sedentary hunter-gatherers. This transition is very important as it indicates that real stratification originated before the birth of statehood. While there is no question that the pristine states and the further development of civilisation have reinforced and institutionalised social hierarchies, it was the pre-state formations such as chiefdoms where social stratification emerged. Although there is great variety between these complex sedentary hunter-gatherer groupings, whereby in some instances chiefs have substantial powers and in others their influence is weak in most cases 'chiefs are entitled to special privileges' including paying of tribute, 'some of which the chiefs then redistribute back to their subjects' (Fry 2007: 71). In terms of the development of organisational power, as Service (1978: 6) argues, chiefdoms are a 'watershed in human political evolution' since here, for the first time in history, one can encounter 'centralised leadership' that acts as a 'central nervous system of society'. Chiefdoms have often emerged in areas with rich natural resources, and as result tend to have higher population densities than bands and tribes. However, as they are ethnographically very rare they have not been as extensively studied as other forms of human association. According to the archaeological evidence, chiefdoms developed very late in human evolution, mostly within the last 13,000 years (Kelly 1995: 302; Fry 2007: 71).

What is most important here is that they provide evidence of the link between the development of military organisation and social stratification. Although the chief's superior position is dependent on periodic and regular distributions of wealth, what makes somebody into a chief is military experience, leadership in battle. Unlike nomadic hunter-gatherers, these complex sedentary hunter-gatherer groups are prone to regular and intensive warfare. For example the Nootka of British Columbia often engage in ambushes and surprise attacks with violent raids involving 'complete destruction of the enemy. Whole heads are taken as trophies – even of women and children – and carried aloft on the points of the spears, and after the return home, a great dancing celebration is held around them. The booty is later distributed at a potlatch' (Service 1978: 238). The chiefdoms are structured around kinship with single lineage or family providing hereditary leadership. The stratification patterns involve distinctions on the basis of age, gender, marriage and military position. However, the most important dividing line is often between the slaves or serfs and the rest. What can be witnessed here is that organised violence is not linked either to agricultural production or to state formation, as agriculturalists do not develop chiefdoms (Kardin 2002; 2004). Since chiefdoms lack stable institutions they are prone to periodic cycles of collapse and renewal. As Service (1978: 8) summarises: 'chiefdoms are familial, but not egalitarian; they have central direction and authority, but no true government; they have unequal control over goods and production, but no true private property, entrepreneurs, or markets; they have marked social stratification and ranks, but no true socioeconomic classes'. In other words, these complex sedentary hunter-gatherer groups provide an ideal laboratory to analyse the emergence of both military organisation and social stratification. The historical importance and military might of chiefdoms are often overlooked, despite the fact that this form of social organisation has on many occasions proved to be equal to and even more powerful than pristine states. For example, the Germanic and other 'barbarian' invaders who overran and eventually conquered the western half of the Roman Empire in the fifth century were 'confederations' of various chiefdoms. Similarly, most nomadic populations of Eurasia developed complex and vast chiefdoms that were able to rival many states and some of them, such as Khitan, Jin and most of all the networks of Mongol chiefdoms that were eventually united by Temüjin (later Genghis Khan) in the thirteenth century, developed a supreme military capability. The origins of the largest contiguous empire the world has ever known, the Mongol Empire covering some 33 million km^2, can be directly traced to the military organisation of early Mongol chiefdoms (Taagepera 1997). Therefore, as organised violence emerges before agriculture and state formation, neither agriculture nor state formation can be a cause of social stratification.

To understand the origins of stratification it is necessary to look at the role violence played in the transformation of chiefdoms. As Gumplowicz (2007 [1883]), Ratzenhofer (1904), Rustow (1980) and other early representatives of the 'bellicose' tradition have argued, the first real form of stratification was the one involving warriors and non-warriors. Following in part this line of thought, Andreski (1968: 39–62) provides empirical evidence for the theory that a clearly defined hierarchical social structure principally emerges through conquest: examples include the subjugation of 'Negroid agriculturists' by 'Hamitic pastoralists' in East Africa, the conquests of the formerly theocratic cities of Mesopotamia by other, more expansive, cities, and the Dorian invasion of Greek *poleis* among many other historically documented cases. Although he acknowledges that a warrior class could have emerged gradually through differentiation from the rest of the population (by the restriction of military service to some individuals or through the monopolisation of arms-bearing), Andreski (1968: 32), just like Mann (1986), agrees that this is more likely to happen in more complex social orders 'where costly armament beyond the means of many may render the services of the majority useless, or where internal and external security are such that disarming the population is feasible'.

What is particularly relevant here is the origin of city-states, as they represent the first form of settled life and eventually gave birth to civilisation and pristine states. While there is little doubt that their origin owes a great deal to the appearance of broader regional cult centres emerging around temples, as suggested by Mann (1986), Stein (1994) and others, the transition from tribes and chiefdoms to networks of city-states is largely grounded, not in economic, but in military factors. Not only does the archaeological evidence point in the direction of the first high priests often gradually taking on the role of military leaders – as was the case for example with the early Sumerian state and the Mayas of Yucatan (Webster 1976; Postgate 1994) – but more importantly, the city-states themselves emerged mostly through and for military reasons: defence and attack. The Sumerian case is highly illustrative here as this was the earliest literate world, whereas the later Sumerian Empire (pristine state) evolved from networks of very small settled congregations. What is distinctive about these first settlements is that they seem to have been fortified by defensive ditches and walls (e.g. the excavations of Tell-Sawwan village, present day Samarra, indicate the presence of such a wall dating to 5500–4800 BCE), which is often a reliable indicator of violent intrusions and military activity. Furthermore, most Sumerian city-states emerged in clusters, which suggests the existence of micro-level geopolitics with trading, exchange and periodic feuding between these entities. The fact that up to 90 per cent of the Sumerian population lived in these city-states, while the principal source of economic life was non-urban in character (i.e. food production and farming), would imply that the walls of the city-states provided defensive security (Nissen 1988). In other words, early urban settlements were mostly composed of rural populations who required protection from external attacks and the periodic pillages undertaken by neighbouring city-states. Hence, the principal purpose of the early walled city-states was military in nature. As Gat (2006: 277) rightly argues: 'City-states emerged where large-scale territorial unification did not take place early in political evolution … Space was divided between small antagonistic political units, which meant *both* high threat levels from close-by neighbours and the ability of peasants to find refuge by living in the city while working outside it.' Hence 'city-states were the product of war'.

The counter-example of early Egypt, where an unusual geographical location and an agricultural abundance (linked to the River Nile) fostered a quicker transition towards relatively unified central authority, clearly shows that where there is no external threat there are fewer cities and walls, and more peasants in the countryside (O'Connor 1993). Hence, in spite of what Mann (1986) says, it seems that violence was just as important in the first stage of development as it was in the second stage. The imperfect transformation from tribes and chiefdoms to city-states, and eventually to pristine states, was for the most part a violent process involving conquests, raids and pillage of weaker neighbours. In other words, social stratification was in many cases imposed directly from the outside (by conquest) or through the invocation of such a threat by organised insiders (i.e. political racketeering). Thus the violent origins of settled life confirm Gumplowicz's (1899: 120) point that 'civilised men cannot live without the service of others'. Once the monopolisation of weaponry and military roles were complete, the seeds for later rigid patterns of stratification were in place.

As Lenski (1966) demonstrates, further historical development from 'horticultural societies' characterised by differentiation of strong and weak kinship groupings, towards agrarian societies, usually dominated by the warrior aristocracy, all indicate a gradual, steady and sharpening increase in social inequalities between different strata. In all of these cases it is possible to observe the parallel development of coercive social organisation, monopolisation of violence in the hands of a military caste and a dramatic rise in social inequalities. Agrarian societies such as the Roman Empire, medieval China and twelfth century European Christendom – all of which were rooted in elaborate and rigid social hierarchies – are indicative examples of how monopoly of arms control was instrumental in preventing social mobility and eventually establishing hereditary warrior strata. It is no accident that the most commonly used term for stratification, class, is itself the product of the military context. The Roman term *classis* meant a military division of Roman citizens (Turner 1988: 31).

As elaborated in Chapters 3 and 6, much of the pre-modern era was a world were the sword ruled the plough; that is, where a military aristocracy used its monopoly of organised coercion to enforce a profoundly hierarchical social order and dominate the large swathes of the peasantry. Although only a few sociologists contest the view that war and violence were important in establishing and maintaining patterns of social stratification before modernity, most of them would deny such a role to coercion in modern industrial social orders. For example, even Lenski (1966) interprets industrial social orders as essentially built on pacifist principles where technological development and a substantial increase in economic surpluses have reduced inequalities in wealth and power. Similarly, Gellner (1988b, 1997) contrasts two types of society: the agrarian, which is rigidly hierarchical, torpid and poverty stricken, and the industrial, which is a vibrant, socially mobile universe sustained by economic growth and continual scientific development. Nevertheless, such interpretations omit a simple truth, that human beings do not easily tolerate unequal distribution of wealth, power and prestige. In fact, acute social inequalities and rigid forms of group exclusion need to be maintained either by coercive control or through elaborate ideological justification and most of the time they require both of these processes. While the role of ideology will be discussed later, let us focus a bit more on the coercive underpinning of social stratification in modernity. What is apparent here, as I will demonstrate shortly, is that stratification, just as other sociological phenomena already analysed, has been and remains shaped by the cumulative bureaucratisation of coercion.

The first thing that needs pointing out is that the system of stratification that currently prevails in much of Europe and North America, and which underpins nearly all neo-Weberian and neo-Marxist theories of stratification, is itself a product of the two total wars. Despite the enormous economic growth, the unprecedented industrial development, the gigantic structural transformations and the scientific and technological innovations witnessed throughout the eighteenth and nineteenth centuries, there was little actual change in social stratification before WWI. Although the rulers were forced to concede some citizenship rights to various social strata, the medieval warrior legacy remained firmly entrenched such that by the beginning of the twentieth century most European states were still ruled by the landed aristocracy. For example, even in 1910 nine out of eleven ministers of the German government were nobility; the aristocracy completely dominated the German parliament (all of the upper house and a quarter of the lower house); administration (over 90 per cent of top civil service posts); diplomacy (80 per cent of ambassadorships); and military (55 per cent of top army ranks) (Goldstein 1983: 252). In the UK, landed aristocracy dominated every government until 1905, while in France at the end of the nineteenth century over two thirds of the parliamentarians in the Chamber of Deputies came from aristocratic families (Thomas 1939; Cole and Campbell 1989). Furthermore, much of eastern and central Euro[pe] [aristoc]rats, who successfully monopolised ne[...] and military positions.

In addition, although Europe[an] [dem]ocratisation, by 1910 most devel[oped] their populations enfranchised, rangi[ng] [...]ls, 18 per cent in UK to 21 per cent in Austria, 22 per cent in Germany and 29 per cent in France. By 1914 Norway was the only European country with universal and equal suffrage (Goldstein 1983: 241). Even in the USA, 'indentured servitude' lasted until the early nineteenth century, property ownership qualifications for voting were present in many states; slavery formally barred 15 per cent of the population from suffrage until 1870 and in reality until the 1960s. Women were excluded from voting until 1920 and Native Americans were granted the right to vote only in 1924 (Collins 1999: 118).

WWI was a turning point in history as it brought a dramatic decline in the strength and prominence of the aristocracy, thus causing an upheaval in the traditional social hierarchies. As Halperin (2004) demonstrates, the end of WWI was in many respects the real 'passing of feudalism', since the medieval legacy of the landed (warrior) aristocracy was blown apart by mass participation in warfare of the workers, peasants and other social strata.[5] As a result, the end of the war saw an unprecedented transfer of land throughout Europe. While peasants and other impoverished groups who fought in the war benefited from the redistribution of land throughout Europe, and in particular in central and eastern Europe, the main beneficiaries were the financiers and merchants, who profited from war contracts, the tenant farmers and the county and rural district councils. For example, in England one-quarter of all land changed owners, making this the biggest land transfer since the Norman Conquest (Montagu 1970). Even though WWI signalled the decline of aristocracy it did not dramatically alter the patterns of social stratification for other strata. As Halperin (2004: 153) argues and documents, 'wartime and postwar conditions generally decreased wealth throughout the social structure', meaning that 'Europe's prewar social structure survived'; this was reflected in the small changes to the dynamics of industrial expansion after the war. A much more substantial transformation of the social stratification had to await the WWII. 'It was only after WWII that there was a shift to a system of production oriented to the improvement of the standard of living

---

[5] For example as many as 5 million industrial workers joined the British armed forces during WWI (Halperin 2004: 154).

of workers. It came, as it had previously come in the USA (in the 1860s) and Russia (1917–22), as a result of protracted and bloody civil war among elites' (Halperin 2004: 118).

Although WWII did not prove to be, as it is sometimes described, 'the complete leveller of classes', the state's dependence on the full participation of all social strata meant that some sectors of the population greatly benefited from their involvement in war. However, different social and geopolitical conditions of states impacted social stratification in different ways. In the USA, the strong industrial base and the distance from the battlefields were instrumental in the rise of the middle classes, generated in part through the emergence of so-called 'war-boom communities'. One of the sociologically most interesting of these was the Willow Run community in Detroit run by the Ford Motor Company as the biggest airplane bomber factory in the world. While the factory employed over 40,000 workers, up to 250,000 people from all over the USA moved into what had been a tiny farming community. As Lowell Carr's study shows, the Willow Run community was perceived and used as an important vehicle of social mobility for the thousands of lower-class families who successfully and relatively swiftly climbed the social ladder to become members of the middle classes (Carr and Stermer 1952). The European experience was quite different: in some instances peasants and industrial workers were the main winners. In Britain, the government used food subsidies to keep the cost of living under control while raising wages in war production industries by 80 per cent. In addition, to motivate the full participation of workers in the war effort, it introduced a 'fair shares' model of distribution, the class-sensitive policy of rationing, higher nutritional standards for all and major social policy programmes. Service in the army also offered educational opportunities not available to workers elsewhere (Marwick 1981: 216–22). As France was occupied early there was less demand for industrial workers and since food was scarce the real beneficiaries of war were the peasantry. Nevertheless in all of these cases total wars proved to be key catalysts of social stratification.

The second point is that stratification remains wedded to the coercive apparatus of social organisations. Although it is clearly apparent that in the 1970s Sweden was much less socially hierarchical and less violent than its fifteenth century counterpart, the sources that shaped social structure in both of these periods were, in fact, the same: the organisational control of violence moulds the character of social stratification. The fact that in one of these social orders the control of violence was territorially dispersed and dominated by a small minority of aristocratic warriors, while in the other the coercive apparatus was legitimately monopolised by the nation-state, does not indicate that in the 1970s Swedish patterns of social inclusion and exclusion had nothing to do with violence. On the contrary, the very existence and stability of the modern stratification system is deeply rooted in the state's organisational monopoly of the use of violence. Not only does this monopoly prevent arbitrary beatings and killings of members of one social stratum by members of another, but it also thwarts the unsanctioned collective and individual usurpation of class or status roles. Modern, industrial, social orders are not inherently pacifist and industrious, thus allowing greater upward mobility. Instead they are internally peaceful and economically productive precisely because there is a nearly absolute monopoly of coercion and ideology by a single social organisation – the modern nation-state. Not only is the externalisation of violent conflicts at the borders of nation-states the cause of this internal pacification (Giddens 1985; Hirst 2001), but it also helps states to centralise and concentrate violence in its institutions.

Consequently, unlike earlier polities, modern states are able to rely on courts, police and military to firmly uphold the existing systems of stratification. Whereas in medieval Europe those who owned the means of destruction were capable of swiftly redrawing existing social hierarchies, the modern state's coercive monopoly guarantees the persistence of existing social hierarchies. Nevertheless, none of these processes have stifled internal social conflicts nor have they removed violence from social life. Rather, violence has become indiscernible. Since this monopoly is so ingrained and routinised it becomes normalised and, hence, popularly invisible. However, any attempt to forcibly defy the existing social order reveals the coercive nature of social stratification in modernity. We, as moderns, can enjoy unprecedented freedoms as long as we do not decide to address economic, political and social grievances ourselves: a homeless person who squats in an uninhabited house owned by a private corporation will be quickly and vehemently evicted; a brawl between two drunken friends can land them both in prison; parents who opt not to send their children to primary school (and do not educate them themselves) will be rigorously punished; a private house built without permission will be demolished; an unemployed single mother who cannot pay her bank loans and her household bills can expect to lose her children to the social services; and a teenager who carries a pocket knife is likely to end up behind bars. In other words, since stratification originated in violence it can never be truly decoupled from violence. In this respect, modern social orders are no different from their pre-modern counterparts, since the control of coercion was and remains a central element of any stratification system.

For example, no modern nation-state tolerates violent attempts to radically challenge the existing social structure. Nowhere is revolution or large-scale violent social action officially condoned. Instead, such attempts are quickly delegitimised and often ruthlessly crushed with the use of the police or military. Not only is no one allowed to practise law, open up a surgery or teach without state-sanctioned qualifications and permission, but any attempt to fraudulently use professional titles such as doctor, lawyer or professor is coercively penalised by the state. In a normatively meritocratic social order, such as most of us now live under, it is the state-sponsored and controlled educational systems that determine patterns of social inequality. As researchers have demonstrated on numerous occasions (Collins 1979; 1988), education has become a much better predictor of a person's occupational achievement than his or her parents' socio-economic and class background.

Nevertheless, ever-increasing levels of formal education of the world's population have not translated into greater social mobility. Instead, while the degree of social mobility has largely remained constant throughout the twentieth century in the developed world (Boudon 1973; Hauser and Featherman 1976; Collins 1988), structural disparities and social inequalities between the North and South have continued to increase (Milanović 1998; Gafar 2003). However, the key point here is that the education system is both coercively imposed and popularly accepted as a justifiable form of social hierarchy. On the one hand education is coercively enforced (no one can opt out from primary education), coercively preserved (no one can set up an alternative educational system without the state's approval) and, for the most part, coercively structured (no one can gain appropriate employment without adequate education). On the other hand, a person's level of education is popularly accepted as the most legitimate criterion for the existence of social inequalities. This is not to say that the educational system as such is a form of 'symbolic violence', since it obviously does not involve physical harm. To partially rescue Bourdieu's argument it is necessary to turn it around: it is not that 'symbolic violence' is used to preserve the existing system of stratification; it is the stratification system itself that is used to maintain the state's coercive monopoly. The point is that any attempt to set up an alternative form of education would not really affect the dominant patterns of social inequalities but would challenge directly the state's monopoly on the legitimate use of violence. That is why education as such is not violent but any attempt to directly interfere with existing educational systems can provoke a coercive action on the part of the state, using the principal tools of its monopoly – the judiciary and the police.

Similarly, the modern welfare state could not have arisen without the cumulative concentration of force, since coercive power is the cornerstone of any distributive system. While modernity is much more open to social mobility in principle, it allows no room for the dramatic, collective appropriation of social organisations with a view to quickly transforming patterns of inequality. Hence, what is crucial for the persistence of stratification is the coercive role of social organisation: the modern nation-state. As Collins (1988: 450–9) rightly points out: 'Organisations are the original site of stratification. Social classes are based on different control positions within organisations (including the ownership of organisations). The state, as a centre for political control, a prop for the property system, and locus of struggle, is a particular kind of organisation … any property system is ultimately backed up by the state, and hence rests ultimately upon some coercive control.' None of this is to deny the obvious reality that modern social orders are internally less violent and less stratified than those of the pre-modern world. The point is that despite its invisibility in the contemporary world, it is control of the coercive apparatus that upholds social stratification in all social orders. What we see in modernity is not the disappearance of violence but its transformation and that is how the cumulative bureaucratisation of coercion operates. However, what makes coercion durable, bearable and less visible is ideology. Hence let us now focus on the relationships between social stratification, violence and ideology.

Justifying social hierarchies

Neither war nor social inequalities come naturally to human beings. Most individuals avoid violent confrontation and are not particularly good at it, while very few people, if any, would lightly accept being categorised as socially inferior. Nevertheless, most of recorded history clearly demonstrates the prevalence of warfare and rigidly hierarchical social structures. Moreover, not only have the evolution of social institutions, the rise of complex and sophisticated social organisations and unprecedented technological improvements not ended wars or social exclusion, modernity has been, in fact, a witness to a dramatic increase in both large-scale violence and social inequality. While the process of the cumulative bureaucratisation of coercion can account for this rise of violence and inequality it cannot explain the popular acceptance of this situation. Hence to answer this question it is important to historically situate and tackle the role that ideology – and particularly the mass (centrifugal) ideologisation of coercive actions – plays in this process.

As argued in the previous chapters, the pre-modern world lacked the organisational, technological and structural means for the development, articulation and dissemination of clearly defined ideological doctrines. In addition, such relatively coherent, this-worldly doctrines, were of no use to the sedentary hunter-gatherers and peasants. Ideas such as the moral equality of human beings, racial superiority rooted in biology, the unity of the world's proletariat or national sovereignty would have been utterly incomprehensible and senseless to most individuals before the age of modernity. As Weber (1968) was aware, collectively shared beliefs and practices require and underpin large-scale structural transformations: one's *Weltanschauung* is grounded in one's social and historical position. Hence there were many religious, magic-based and other non-secular belief systems and very little, if any, ideology before modernity. Ideologies appear and proliferate in the modern, politically secular, era when there is popular demand for relatively coherent frameworks of meaning, when there are institutional and other devices available to organise those meanings and when there is a public sphere where such meanings and corresponding practices can compete and cooperate. It is worth emphasising that the idea that ideology is quintessentially modern and qualitatively different to magic and religion does not imply that ideologies are necessarily secular. Not at all: many contemporary ideological movements such as political Islam and Christian Identity heavily utilise religious rhetoric. Nevertheless, the point is that they too operate in a secularised (i.e. post Machiavellian and post Nietzschean) political environment, which forces them to work within and through secularised social categories. In this sense, political Islam is not a religion but an ideological and political movement with a clearly defined political blueprint and with a focus on popular mobilisation and the broad-based political legitimisation of its actions. Hence despite its official religiously infused discourse that invokes metaphors of afterlife, political Islam is really concerned with the here and now, which does not make it necessarily secular, but it does make it a secularised ideological doctrine (Ayubi 1991; Pape 2006; Gambetta 2006).

However, none of this is to say that traditional, magical and religious world-views have nothing in common with modern ideologies. There is little doubt that throughout history rulers and other dominant groups relied heavily on commonly shared belief systems to justify existing social hierarchies and to wage wars. For example, the common practice among European rulers and higher clergy from the Roman Emperor Julian in 360 to the Visigoth

King Wamba in 672, culminating in the coronation of Charlemagne in 800, was to initially refuse the honour of holding the imperial or royal office and to eventually accept it 'when threatened with death'. Hence Charlemagne's coronation was officially depicted as a 'sudden' and 'inspired' choice by Pope Leo III that aimed to restore the glory of the Roman Empire that had 'fallen into degradation' under the Byzantines. The official narrative states that Charlemagne knew nothing about this event and once informed was fiercely opposed to the coronation (Collins 2005: 52–70). Nevertheless, this ritualistic quasi-rejection had a clear proto-ideological purpose: to justify an illegitimate usurpation of political and religious power. Both Pope Leo III and Charlemagne had an interest in reclaiming the disputed imperial status (*Imperator Romanorum*) from the Byzantine Empress Irene and this act of coronation was undertaken to give credence to Charlemagne's political claim as the one and only 'Emperor of the Romans' while simultaneously reinforcing Leo III's claim to be the only legitimate religious authority in the whole of Christendom. In a similar vein, Charlemagne's attempt to standardise the use of coinage within his realm by replacing all the existing Roman and other coins with ones that bore only his image can also be interpreted as a proto-ideological move to legitimise his rule (Coupland 2005: 211–29).

However, although such practices were common throughout history, their target audience was mostly a small elite of top clergy and aristocracy able and willing to contest the ruler's legitimacy. In this respect, in the pre-modern world, there was less need for the legitimisation of wars and almost none for the justification of social inequalities. It is true that before the era of absolutism, kings usually required financial and political support from the aristocracy to wage wars, but with the possible exception of the Ständestaat (polity of estates), (by which the rulers had to consult with various assemblies of noblemen, clerics and some representatives of the free cities), they rarely had to justify war aims. The kings had the final say on whether wars would be fought and the support of the aristocratic warrior caste hinged mostly on their personal interest (Poggi 1978; Mann 1988).[6] Warfare was understood as a legitimate royal prerogative that involved competition over land, heiresses, honour and dynastic claims.

Rigid patterns of social stratification required even less justification. Strict social, political and economic hierarchies were generally taken as representing the natural, God-given, cosmic order. As Gellner (1997: 20) puts

---

[6] However, even in the polity of estates period there was no need to justify wars to the peasantry as 'the great majority of population appeared purely as the object of rule' (Poggi 1978: 55).

it: 'Agrarian society is generally inegalitarian in its values. It even exaggerates its own inequality and hides such mobility as occurs, just as our society tends to do the exact opposite … Agrarian society depends on the maintenance of a complex systems of ranks, and it is important that these be both visible and felt, that they be both externalised and internalised.' In other words, the entire ethical universe of this social order is defined in rigorously hierarchical terms: 'morality consists of each element in the hierarchical social structure performing its assigned task, and no other'. Although religious ceremonies and rituals were extensively employed by the ruling warrior caste, their essential role was to sanctify one aristocratic group or an individual in the eyes of other aristocrats – not to make their actions popularly legitimate.[7] In principle, before the early modern era there was little need to justify either social inequalities or the waging of wars: the entire system was built on a religiously validated cosmic order that separated those who fought and those who prayed from those who toiled. In other words, the control of the means of destruction (warrior caste) sanctified by the religious monopoly (clergy) provided also the control of the means of production (slaves, serfs and land). In such a social order both war and social inequalities were understood by all as normal, natural and inevitable.

The arrival and spread of modernity utterly undermined both of these assumptions. The philosophy of the Enlightenment posited the moral equality of all human beings, reason and rational conduct and the peaceful resolution of conflicts as the moral imperatives of the post-traditional age, and thus attempted to delegitimise any claims for natural hierarchies and violent confrontations between humans. As the pre-eminent philosopher of the Enlightenment, Immanuel Kant (1991 [1784]), put it 'Enlightenment is man's release from his self-incurred tutelage. Tutelage is the incapacity to use one's own understanding without the guidance of another. Such tutelage is self-imposed if its cause is not lack of intelligence, but rather a lack of determination and courage to use one's intelligence without being guided by another.' Hence, inspired by the principles of the Enlightenment, modernity abhors paternalistic social relationships and divinely ordained hierarchies. Moreover, the firm belief in the autonomy of human reason generates an optimistic assumption that once human beings were left to rely on their reason alone their actions would lead towards 'perpetual peace'. In Kant's (1991 [1794]) formulation 'the progress of civilisation and men's gradual approach

---

[7] For example, even the word 'people' was generally used not to refer to the peasant majority but to the gentry and aristocracy vis-à-vis the crowns as in seventeenth century England (Collins 1999: 112).

to greater harmony in their principles finally leads to peaceful agreement'. This attitude of the early Enlightenment thinkers has become a cornerstone of modern ethics: both violence and social exclusion are detested and popularly understood as remnants of the past, uncivilised, eras. From UN charters to the constitutions of nearly all contemporary states, violence and social inequality are deemed as residual evils that have no place in the modern world. In this sense Elias (2000) is partially right when he says that modern men and women have developed a sense of repugnance and shame towards rituals of hierarchical submission, public torture and other public displays of inhumanity.[8] For most moderns, war and violence are abhorrent and despicable activities not worthy of 'civilised people'.

Nevertheless, these hopes of the early Enlightenment thinkers have for the most part turned into nightmares, with modernity exceeding all previous epochs in the scale of violence and brutality while also seeing a great increase in the scope of social exclusion. As already indicated, no period in recorded history can compare with the killing ratios of the twentieth century (see Chapter 5). Although modernity has largely dispensed with overt and publicly visible expressions of inequality and violence, this era is also the time when both violence and inequalities have proliferated to unprecedented levels. It is not only that modernity bestows total wars, genocides and violent revolutions on us but it is also in this historical period that one can see an unrivalled increase in economic and social disparities between individuals and groups worldwide. For example, the current global distribution of wealth shows stark polarities whereby 1 per cent of the world's wealthiest population owns 40 per cent of all global assets with a further 9 per cent owning the remaining 45 per cent. At the same time more than 50 per cent of the world's population owns less than 1 per cent of global wealth (Davies *et al.* 2006: 26). To better understand this discrepancy in economic inequalities, consider that the world's three richest individuals possess assets which are worth more than the combined gross domestic product of the 48 poorest countries (Gafar 2003: 85).

---

[8] However, Elias is wrong to attribute such feelings entirely to cultural and psychological 'conditioning'. His largely Freudian argument states that the contemporary repugnance towards the popular sixteenth century practice of cat burning is a product of historical conditioning that he terms a 'civilizing process': 'someone who wished to gratify his or her pleasure in the manner of the sixteenth century by burning cats would be seen today as "abnormal", simply because normal conditioning in our stage of civilisation restrains the expression of pleasure in such actions through anxiety instilled as self-control. Here, obviously, the simple psychological mechanism is at work on the basis of which the long-term change of personality structure has taken place: socially undesirable expressions of drives and pleasure are threatened and punished with measures that generate displeasure' (Elias 2000: 171–2). This view wrongly presumes that aggressive behaviour in humans is a natural condition held back only by the thin walls of the 'civilizing process'.

Furthermore, most economist believe that income inequality, as well as disparities in wealth distributions, have been on the increase in the second half of the twentieth and the beginning of this century (Milanović 1998; Atkinson 2002). Obviously, wealth ownership and income are too crude as measure to account for the subtlety of social relations and they do not necessarily provide a clear picture of social stratification. For example, ownership and income had little or no bearing on a person's social status or political influence in most of the communist states, but that in itself was no obstacle to the generation of rigid social hierarchies. However, these measures do indicate that modern social orders are very far from achieving the universally proclaimed values of social inclusion and greater equality. Although pre-modern rulers were just as able to monopolise existing wealth, they lacked the organisational means and the ideological know-how to concentrate such vast quantities of wealth. Most importantly, unlike earlier royalty and aristocracy who needed little or no justification of such staggering social inequalities, modern social orders require an elaborate and popularly acceptable validation of such class and status asymmetries.

Hence the central question is how can anyone reconcile such apparent social inequalities and the cumulative expansion of large-scale violence while simultaneously advocating the non-hierarchical principles of social inclusion and peace? One way to answer this question is to view human beings as cynical individuals who pursue their interests whereby espoused principles are no more than 'a fig leaf' used to camouflage their real (egoistic) interests. For example, both Marxist and rational choice models embrace a version of such a position. While Marxists (e.g. Lukacs 1971; Althusser 1994) focus on the structural determinants of 'commodity fetishism' as a form of (false) class consciousness, a potent symptom of malaise that shapes human relations in capitalism, rational choice advocates (Elster 1985; Boudon 1989; Hechter 1995) interpret such behaviour as instrumentally rational in given circumstances. However, both of these models operate with overly economistic, voluntaristic and ahistorical views of social action. The central points are that this ontological dissonance is not unique to capitalist social orders, it is often not a matter of simple individual decisions and choice, and it is a historically specific phenomenon. Unlike the pre-modern world where there was a clear congruence between the dominant moral universe and the corresponding hierarchical and violent practices, modernity preaches inclusion, equality and peace while practising mass slaughter and extreme forms of social exclusion (Malešević 2007). For the most part this situation is a structurally produced phenomenon whereby the increase in the cumulative power of social organisations, and particularly in the monopolisation of coercion by modern states, leads to a series of unintended consequences of social action. The more coherent answer to this question is to be found in the ideological relationship between warfare and social exclusion. I argue that modernity has generated unintended structural conditions whereby social organisations are able to rely on the processes of centrifugal ideologisation to counterpoise warfare and social inequalities thus simultaneously validating the existence of both. Although in modernity the practice and rhetoric of social inequality or collective violence are largely deemed to be detestable and generally illegitimate forms of action per se, deploying one to contest the other has proved to be a successful policy. When these two appear separately they are quickly invalidated and denounced: no modern government can easily embark on a war of conquest and for most states any attempt to engage in organised violence requires an enormous effort of justification in both the domestic and the global arenas. Similarly, no modern state can enslave its citizens or institute judicially discriminating provisions without invoking loud worldwide condemnation, including expulsion from leading international organisations.

However, when social exclusion and violence rhetorically and empirically blend together through the process of ideologisation, the actions of social organisations often receive popular legitimisation. Since ideological doctrines are complex, sophisticated and often contradictory tapestries of ideas and practices they are able to reconcile what ordinarily would seem irreconcilable. For example the French Revolution of 1789, the Russian Revolution of 1917 and the Romanian Revolution of 1989 were all undertaken in the name of higher ethical principles, grounded in the Enlightenment goals of equality, liberty, fraternity, reason, peace, justice, toleration and democracy. Moreover all three were envisaged as attempts to radically transform patterns of social stratification by removing the dominant economic, political and social classes and status groups from power. Yet all three revolutions were inherently violent and bloody events that directly involved trampling over all of these ideals and killing large numbers of human beings. In addition, instead of removing social inequalities all three revolutions have generated new forms of social exclusion.

Similarly, the bombing of Dresden, the baroque capital of the German state of Saxony, which had no military or strategic relevance, and the killing of up to 40,000 civilians thereby caused was conducted, as the Air Chief Marshal Arthur Harris put it, to 'shorten the war' (Taylor 2004) and remove the Nazi political elite from power in Germany. Nevertheless, such extremely violent episodes are popularly perceived as justified since their outcome was a (supposedly) freer, more just and better social order. Hence when violence is ideologically coded as a mere technical means for accomplishing grand ideological blueprints – that is establishing a socially inclusive society – then it becomes a fully legitimate practice. In this respect, most modern ideological grand vistas are similar, as they all project an ideal social order where a particular social group would achieve a state of absolute social inclusion. In a Nazi utopia all members of the Aryan race would improve their social status and class position by becoming members of a master race; in the Soviet model of the communist paradise the impoverished and wretched proletariat would overpower the despised bourgeoisie and all would eventually live according to the principle 'from each according to his ability, to each according to his needs'; in Hizb ut-Tahrir and al-Qaeda's vision of the future, the social prestige of all Muslims would dramatically rise as they join the universal brotherhood and sisterhood in the restored Islamic caliphate run on the principles of Sharia law; in the blueprint of the ideal liberal majoritarian, meritocratic democracy, it is personal talent, educational achievements, hard work and individual freedom that are seen as determining personal success and any deviation from this model is seen as authoritarian and unjust.

What is common to all of these and many other ideological grand vistas is the popular perception that since these goals are so noble they are also worth fighting for, meaning that the use of violence in building or preserving such social orders becomes justified. Even though most individuals might nominally be opposed to the use of force, when presented with stark scenarios, as in times of wars, revolutions, terrorist threats, large-scale environmental disasters or deadly pandemics, most people tend to accept the use of violence as a necessary evil. Hence modern justifications of bloodshed are often couched in words that depict the 'enemy' not as an honourable or worthy adversary but as a subhuman, monstrous creature hell-bent on destroying the social order: 'the Jap rats', 'the Hun beasts', 'the Jewish parasites', 'the Gooks', etc. As already discussed (see Chapters 5 and 8), when individuals and entire nations are dehumanised and depicted as animals, things and monsters, they are removed from the ethical codes reserved for humans; thus they become dispensable and any violent action towards such non-human creatures becomes justified. Even when there is no direct danger to one's society the ideological justification often resonates widely. For example, the bombing of Baghdad in the 1991 Gulf War, which resulted in the death of numerous civilians, was deemed by many in the mainstream American newspapers as legitimate. This is well illustrated by the rhetoric of the Washington Post: 'When a war is just, it must be faced with a kind of nerve … So long as we scrupulously attack what we reasonable believe to be military targets, the bombing of Baghdad is a cause for sorrow, not guilt' (Sifry and Cerf 1991: 333).

However, the dehumanisation of the enemy which regularly follows the justification of external cruelty is not just a psychological phenomenon. There is a sociological reasoning involved too. What is crucial in these discourses is the link between violence and social hierarchies. The dehumanisation of the enemy helps externalise social conflicts and in this process disguises existing social inequalities. Since the war rhetoric entails the externally exclusive language of hierarchies and the internally inclusive language of egalitarianism and calls for in-group unity, it is bound to transfer the domestic hierarchies to the external sphere. This ideological move, referred to as 'the lowest common denominator' policy, often 'sacrifices those less powerful and privileged' within the group to those who are in a higher social stratum (Gamson 1995: 11). Nevertheless, it is important to emphasise that such processes rarely, if ever, go against the grain of the popular mood. Rather than acting as a form of giant brainwashing machine this ideological process is fully grounded in what Weber would call the material and ideal interests as well as the emotions of most individuals involved. By combining Durkheimian (2001 [1915]) and Weberian (1968) concepts it is possible to see war and other similar extraordinary events as the particular social and historical moments when social stratification is temporarily displaced from the social order: initially through the overwhelming feelings of collective effervescence and later through sudden and dramatic enhancement of collective social prestige brought about by war victories. In other words, officially proclaimed calls for national unity often resonate well with the public, caught up in the quasi-religious mood of the collectively shared extraordinary experience that the early stage of war frenzy brings. Nonetheless, as such collective expressions of emotion cannot last very long, the 'war enthusiasm' is often sustained by, real or fictitious, successes on the battlefield which are simultaneously interpreted as individual and collective or national status advancements. For Weber, state legitimacy is in part an emotional state: 'the emotion that individuals feel when facing the threat of death in the company of others'. Such an exceptional state produces intensive social bonds – 'a community of political destiny' (Weber 1968: 910–26; Collins 1986: 156). More specifically, the legitimacy of the entire social order is linked to the military experience, since once stratification is tied to 'the national prestige', any military losses on the battlefield automatically translate into losses of individual prestige, thus making the existing social ladder visible again. Hence as Collins (1999) rightly argues, the social prestige of individual states has internal and external reflection: while war victories improve a state's geopolitical status and influence they also legitimise the position of its rulers. More importantly in the context of stratification, geopolitical and military successes help reinforce the existing patterns of social hierarchies. For example, not only did authoritarian regimes such as Nazi Germany, fascist Italy, and the communist Soviet Union galvanise public support through military conquests and in this way helped justify established models of stratification, but so did more liberal states such as the Dutch Republic, Britain and France, through the various colonial wars of the nineteenth century or as the US did during the Philippine–American War of 1899–1902. Colonial conquests and victories in wars legitimise the existing social order as they often provide emotional comfort for individuals and groups that ordinarily would find themselves at the bottom of the social pyramid: since war is popularly perceived as a zero-sum status game, winning implies automatic enhancement of one's social prestige at the expense of the defeated and thus humiliated enemy. In addition, as the rhetoric of national solidarity is premised on the displacement of class and status conflicts outside one's borders, it is the enemy who is often considered to be the cause of all social inequalities and injustices. It is the Western imperialists, the despotic Easterners, the cowardly terrorists, the greedy and immoral capitalists, the ruthless secessionists and barbaric nationalists, the godless communists, the religious Islamic fanatics and so many others who are to blame for our current social problems. In other words, despite the popular perception, war is not a 'complete leveller of classes'. Rather, the rhetoric of internal egalitarianism is ideologically grounded in the externalisation of social stratification whereby war aims are tightly linked to the legitimacy of the entire social order and in particularly to one's social status. All of this indicates that since stratification originated in violence, its long-term preservation requires coercive underpinning. However, as modernity is normatively built on principles that loathe bloodshed, this era, more than any other, has a greater need for the justification of violent action. Hence the link between stratification and violence is often made as invisible as possible: it is the cloak of ideology that has provided the most potent device for the justification of violence in the modern era.

Conclusion

Although much of the mainstream sociological research perceives social inequality as a phenomenon caused by internal or global economic factors such as capitalism, property ownership, consumption practices and unequal development, this chapter has argued that, for the most part, social stratification is grounded in the organised control of coercion and ideology. To put it bluntly: any process that involves the long-term subordination of some human beings entails some form of violent action and ideological justification. To borrow Gellner's (1988b) terminology (if not his diagnosis): for our illiterate pre-modern ancestors the sword was more important and more discernible than the book whereas in the modern age the book becomes paramount, as nobody wants to be reminded of the hanging sword above their head. In other words neither violence nor social hierarchies disappear in modernity: they are just transformed and demand much more justification. More importantly, despite popular perceptions to the contrary, modernity does not succeed in cutting the umbilical cord between violence and stratification. In this age, just as in all that came before it, social inequality retains its coercive coating. The difference arises from the structural development whereby in the modern era ideology helps sooth and externalise both violence and stratification and thus make them less visible. However, since modernity is built on principles that proscribe violent action while at the same time it is a witness to an unprecedented increase in large-scale slaughter, our age requires more ideological know-how than any previous historical epoch.

9 Gendering of war

Introduction

If there is one unique feature that sets apart war from all other sociological phenomena this must be its staggering gender asymmetry. As archaeological and historical records clearly demonstrate, there is a great diversity in how human beings organise patterns of social inclusion and exclusion, which spawn hierarchies and divisions based on economic, political, religious, ethnic, educational or many other criteria. However, fighting in wars is the only human activity from which an entire gender is almost completely excluded. While one can find many historical instances where education, ethnicity, religion or wealth had some, much or no bearing at all on the possibility of a person's participation, warfare seems to be the sole group activity that generally excludes women. Despite a handful of exceptions, battlefields have been and remain the exclusive arena of men, with less than 1 per cent of all combatants in recorded history being women (Ehrenreich 1997: 125). Although women have often played an important supportive role in the war effort in many societies, throughout history they have regularly been excluded from the actual fighting. Furthermore, even though modern states have made significant attempts to increase women's participation in the military, this has had little or no impact on the numbers of females involved in fighting wars. As Goldstein (2001: 10) concludes: 'Designed combat forces in the world's state armies today include several million soldiers ... of whom 99.9 per cent are male'. This astonishing fact raises two central and inter-related questions that demand a sociological answer: Why is warfare, unlike almost any other social activity, so gender exclusive? And why are women nearly universally barred from the battlefield?

The first part of this chapter critically assesses the three currently prevalent explanations of this puzzle, which I term the masculinist, culturalist and feminist views, while the second part develops an alternative interpretation that links gender segregation in warfare with the processes of cumulative bureaucratisation of coercion and centrifugal ideologisation.

The innate masculinity of combat?

Although there is near unanimity among scholars on the view that fighting in wars has been and largely still remains the 'privilege' of men, modern scholarship on gender and war is still profoundly divided over the reasons why this is so. Despite the great diversity of answers provided, it is possible to identify three distinct and, in most respects, mutually incompatible perspectives which dominate current debates: the masculinist, the culturalist and the feminist interpretations.

The masculinist view comes in a variety of forms but two versions prevail: biological and social masculinism. While both approaches argue that there is an innate link between warfare and masculinity, they single out different factors as being decisive for explaining this link. For biological masculinism, the gendering of war roles is related to anatomical, physiological, genetic and cognitive differences between men and women, whereas social masculinism emphasises the intrinsic discrepancies in the way male and female group dynamics operate. Since biological masculinism interprets warfare as an extension of individual hostility on a larger scale, their focus is on the biological differences between the two genders which supposedly determine the male proclivity for war. As sociobiologists Shaw and Wang (1989: 179) argue, the evolutionary principle of inclusive fitness operates differently for the two genders: whereas women assume 'defensive/protectorate roles for the group's offspring and means of genetic reproduction' the greater physical might of men indicates that 'where warfare was involved, this strength was readily transferred to the battlefield'. Hence, the focal point of these types of analyses is the gender-specific differences in body size, genetic predispositions and bio-chemical variation. The general argument is that men are genetically predisposed for warfare as they are physically stronger, taller and heavier than women, which allegedly makes them better soldiers. Hence biologists point out that on average men are 8–9 per cent taller, 10 per cent faster, and 50 per cent stronger in their upper-body constitution than women and have a smaller percentage of body fat (15 per cent vs. 27 per cent), all of which are seen as natural advantages on the battlefield (Lentner 1984; Goldstein 2001: 159–66). Sociobiological research draws parallels between human and animal behaviour, arguing that human males exhibit similar patterns of behaviour to the males of other advanced apes such as chimpanzees. According to Goodall (1986), male chimpanzees are violent, domineering, patriarchal, promiscuous and prone to attacking other groups of chimpanzees. In this respect, they are seen as resembling early humans, with both groups engaging in periodic lethal conquests, killing the males and assimilating the females of the conquered group. More specifically, the use of strategic planning and coalition building for attack are interpreted as reliable indicators that both chimpanzees and early humans were involved in 'primitive warfare' (Van Hooff 1990). Hence, biological masculinists argue that 'as throughout human history fighting has been a trial of force, this sex difference has been crucial' (Gat 2006: 77).

In addition, empirical research on brain function and cognitive abilities suggests that, on average, men seem to be better in spatial orientation, quantitative proficiency and visualising objects rotated in space, while women demonstrate better ability in attention to details, verbal skills and speed and accuracy of perception (Linn and Petersen 1986; Hampson and Kimura 1992). These findings have been interpreted as giving further proof that the gendered character of war is rooted in firm biological differences, as fighting requires a good sense of orientation including the ability to read maps, recognise shapes and objects embedded in convoluted patterns, engage in complex mathematical reasoning and use spatial and long-distance navigation.

Furthermore, biological masculinism emphasises the apparent gender differences in the prevalence of distinct sex hormones, with the average adult female having between three and twenty-five times more estrogen than an average man,[1] whereas the body of an average adult male produces around twenty times more testosterone than that of an adult female (Norman and Litwack 1987). Since experimental studies on rats have demonstrated that high testosterone levels are strongly (positively) correlated with aggressive behaviour, the biological masculinists have concluded that testosterone is a cause of human aggressiveness and hence of much violent behaviour including war (Wilson 1975; Eibl-Eibesfeldt 1979; Konner 1988). On the other side, the inherent link between high levels of estrogen and progesterone with the menstrual cycle and pregnancy have been interpreted as biological givens that make women 'natural carers' and 'life givers and preservers', who are more vulnerable to the stringent demands of the battlefield. Consequently, biological masculinists conclude that only one gender is genetically and anatomically wired for warfare: men.

While sharing similar conclusions, social masculinists devote less attention to genetic predispositions for warfare and focus more on the social,

---

[1] This huge variation is linked to the menstrual cycle in which the female body produces wildly fluctuating quantities of estrogen.

anthropological and psychological influences that produce the universal gendering of war. They too interpret aggressiveness as an indispensable feature of war and argue that males are significantly more aggressive than females. Synthesizing the results of numerous psychological studies on aggression, Eagly and Steffen (1986) and Hyde (1986) find men, generally, substantially more physically aggressive and slightly more psychologically aggressive than women. However, unlike biological masculinists, they understand aggression as a socially learned behaviour which is bolstered through rewards and punishments as well as through the imitation and emulation of important role models. Military historians and some anthropologists find small-group bonding as exhibited on the battlefield as a distinctly masculine process premised on demeaning the ability of women. The military effectiveness of small-group solidarity, which is often accompanied by misogynist discourse, is understood as resting firmly on the negation of the civilian male-female bond. Consequently, any attempt to introduce all-female or mixed-gender combat units is viewed as undermining battlefield efficiency, as they allegedly are not able to operate in the masculine world of front-line warfare (Tiger 1969; Tiger and Fox 1971). Some social masculinists (Dart 1953; Morris 1967; Keegan 1994: 102); explain the gendering of war through its primeval origin in hunting. This argument is premised on the similar skills required and almost identical tactics used in hunting and war (e.g. handling of weaponry, use of ambush and attack, ability to act or hide quickly etc.). Most of all, both activities are seen as resting on successful and gender-specific group co-ordination. This view interprets the hunting experience of early men as something that, on the one hand, generated peculiar and long-term male-bonding patterns while on the other hand it gave rise to the nascent military organisation. As a key proponent of this thesis Desmond Morris (1967: 159) put it: 'Organised assault forces cannot operate on a personal basis … They grew originally out of the co-operative male hunting group, where survival depended on allegiance to the "club", and then, as civilisations grew and flourished and technology advanced, they were increasingly exploited in the new military context.' The central issues here are the alleged unique quality and the exclusive dynamics of the male fighting group, forged through generations of hunters and warriors.

Despite the meticulous and reliable research results provided by both biological and social masculinists, much of their interpretation of the gendered characteristics of warfare is flawed. Firstly, the obvious anatomical and physiological differences between men and women such as physical strength, body size, speed and endurance cannot possibly explain the low participation of women in warfare for two reasons: they are relative rather than absolute differences and they are for the most part irrelevant in success in combat. Not only are some women taller, stronger and faster than some men and are still excluded from military action,[2] but the anatomic constitution of human beings varies greatly in time and space and is often determined by position in social stratification, dietary regime and other influences. Today's soldiers are significantly taller than their medieval counterparts and in most armies throughout history officers and middle-class soldiers were on average taller than ordinary soldiers recruited from farming and working-class stock (Floud *et al.* 1990; Komlos 1994). Nevertheless, the fact that working-class soldiers were significantly smaller had no impact on their participation in combat.[3] Similarly the exceptional height of the Dinka and Maasai made little difference in determining the outcome of the Sudanese civil war or British colonial expansion. More to the point, physical strength and soldiers' heights do not win wars, for if this was the case then militaries would spend millions on gyms and eugenic projects to enhance physical characteristics rather than on armaments or skills and logistics training. Perhaps having taller, stronger and faster combatants was an advantage in small-scale face–to-face medieval duels but what defines warfare now is large-scale organised combat for which the body size and physical strength of individual soldiers is irrelevant. As Biddle (2004) rightly argues, in modern wars even the gross numerical strength of armies does not count for much, as what determines whether wars are lost or won is the skill, tactics and strategy of force employment. The ever-increasing recruitment of children in modern conflicts from the Ivory Coast, Sierra Leone, Uganda, Democratic Republic of Congo to Burma and Philippines, with over 300,000 child soldiers currently fighting in various military units throughout the world (Human Rights Watch 2008) indicates that size and strength matter little in war. The fact that many of these child soldiers have proved to be highly efficient combatants demonstrates that physical strength per se is not the reason why women are excluded from combat.[4]

Secondly, despite some gender-specific cognitive differences between men and women, they are too subtle and too small to have any significant impact on participation in warfare (Levy 1978; Kimura 1992). Obviously, not all

[2] A large-scale study of human height among US eighteen-year-olds has shown that around 15 per cent of women are taller than men measured in the same sample (Lentner 1984).

[3] As Floud *et al.* (1990: 184–5) research shows, the average male height in Britain has increased by 10 cm over a period of 260 years (1790–1950) with fifteen-year-old boys from the upper echelons of society being 10 per cent taller than working-class boys.

[4] As Boothby and Knudsen (2000) document, in Sierra Leone's civil war up to 80 per cent of soldiers in the rebel military force were children ranging from 7 to 14 years of age.

soldiers have to be excellent map readers, ship navigators or top mathematicians, while women's better communicative and perceptive skills would be just as useful on the battlefield. The standardised IQ tests show no statistically significant difference between men and women, and while men rely more on the left side of their brains and women on both sides equally, they exhibit 'similar cognitive ability despite sometimes using different cognitive tools to solve problems' (Goldstein 2001: 171). However, even if cognitive differences did matter greatly they would not represent an obstacle to women's participation in warfare. As military organisations require a range of skills and implement a strict division of labour on the battlefield, it would be easy to find roles for combatants with different cognitive abilities. Hence, exclusion from the battlefield has nothing to do with gender-specific cognition.

Thirdly, notwithstanding popular mythology and the flawed reasoning of biological masculinists, hormonal differences between genders have little or no relevance to participation in wars. Although the testosterone levels of laboratory rats are linked with aggressive behaviour this is less the case with apes, and with humans it seems not to be the case at all. Studies on men with high levels of testosterone, such as those with an extra chromosome (XYY syndrome), have shown that they were involved in violent crimes more than other men but this group was also affected by a series of problems unrelated to testosterone, such as having a greater level of mental retardation (Baron and Richardson 1994), and hence it cannot be proved that testosterone, and not some other problem, links this group with crime. Research results find little direct link between violent behaviour and high levels of testosterone. Instead, there is solid evidence that high levels of testosterone are strongly linked with individual competition, sexual stimulus and social success (Mazur and Booth 1998; Goldstein 2001: 153–6). However, rather than causing group competition and conflict, increases in hormone levels are themselves caused by successes in the social arena: wining in competitive encounters is likely to increase one's testosterone levels (Monaghan and Glickman 1992). As biologist Natalie Angier (1995) concludes: 'In humans, if we exclude sexually related actions, it is difficult to see a direct effect of hormones on aggressive behaviour.' Not only do testosterone levels fluctuate from person to person and vary during the day and week, but more importantly, lowering or completely removing the impact of this hormone does not necessarily make men less war-prone. On the contrary, eunuchs have often made excellent and vicious military commanders, as examples such as the Byzantine general Narses, Vietnamese general Ly Thuong Kiet and Chinese admiral Cheng Ho clearly show, while the castration of rapists and violent prisoners has not stopped them acting violently (Scholtz 2001).

Furthermore, high levels of estrogen, the menstrual cycle and pregnancy do not represent an insurmountable obstacle to women's participation in warfare. None of these biological impediments proved to be too problematic or too distracting for the Dahomey women warriors of the nineteenth century or for Soviet female soldiers during WWII. While the Dahomey 'Amazon' army combined strict celibacy with the use of a herbal concoction as a contraceptive, the Soviet women soldiers postponed their motherhood and their menstruation did not prove a handicap on the battlefield (Cottam 1983; Edgerton 2000). In modern militaries this is not even an issue any more: 'In recent years, menstruation has seldom been mentioned as a problem by either women or men in Western armed forces' (Edgerton 2000: 152). In addition, high levels of estrogen do not make women 'natural carers' and 'life preservers'. On the contrary, as both the Dahomey and Soviet cases illustrate so well, women soldiers were often more ferocious and militant in combat then their male counterparts. The Soviet female soldiers were exceptionally efficient bomber pilots and anti-aircraft unit commanders, wreaking havoc on the German military and air force and in the process acquiring the nickname 'night witches'. They were also reliable and effective in infantry and sniper units, with one women soldier killing off 'an entire German company over 25 days' and another being decorated 'for killing over 300 Germans' (Goldstein 2001: 69). The Dahomey women were elite warriors universally considered as 'more disciplined, audacious, and courageous than Dahomey's best full-time male soldiers' and were also ruthless and merciless combatants who would cut up the bodies of their enemies and take 'their genitals, scalps, and intestines as trophies' (Edgerton 2000: 16, 32). European visitors have described them as being 'far superior to the men in everything – in appearance, in dress, in figure, in activity, in their performance as soldiers, and in bravery' (Alpern 1998: 173).

Hence neither testosterone nor estrogen matter much on the battlefield. If there is a hormone that plays an important role in soldiers' performance in combat situation this can only be a stress hormone – adrenaline. As Goldstein (2001: 158) rightly argues: 'A soldier charged up in the heat of battle is charged with adrenaline, not testosterone.' And this stress hormone is not gender specific but universal.

Finally, biological and social masculinists see aggression both as a predominately male characteristic and as an indispensable feature of warfare. However, neither of these two assumptions is correct. The sociobiological arguments that draw on a comparison with male chimpanzees overlook the fact that not all apes behave in the same way. As Goldstein (2001: 184–94) shows, bonobos (so called 'pygmy chimpanzees'), who are as closely related to humans as chimpanzees, live in a much less hierarchical social environment.

The two genders are more integrated, less aggressive and use sexual contact rather than violence to resolve conflicts within the group. Unlike the chimpanzee world of alpha males, at the pinnacle of the bonobo social order stand the oldest females. It is females who direct the group activities, who determine the social standing of the bonobo males and who use sex to prevent violent conflict with neighbouring bonobo groups.

Although cultural masculinists have a point when they argue that aggressive behaviour often results from social conditioning, they are wrong in viewing this process as being solely the preserve of male soldiers. It is true that the intensity of male-group bonding is often articulated through misogynist language and practices, but this is equally the case for exclusively female groups. The Dahomey women warriors exhibited an exceptional degree of group loyalty which was initiated with 'the blood oath' when new recruits would mix and drink the blood of other women warriors and was further developed through joint participation in combat and reinforced through regular performance of common rituals, singing and dancing. Their relentlessness on the battlefield was matched by their unquestioned willingness to self-sacrifice for their corps, which found its expression in a favourite martial song declaring 'May thunder and lightening kill us if we break our oaths' (Edgerton 2000: 25). This strong form of group bonding was also underpinned by a loathing of men, who were deemed to be weak or cowardly as soldiers. Nevertheless, the language used to discredit such men was no less misogynist than that of groups of male warriors, as Dahomey 'Amazons' would sing: 'We marched against the Atahpahms as against men … and found them [to be] women' (Edgerton 2000: 26). The experiences of Soviet female pilots and women in the Yugoslav partisan army during the WWII, the Republican women militias in the Spanish civil war, the Vietcong female soldiers in the Vietnam War, the Sandinista women guerrillas in Nicaragua, and the US women soldiers in the Gulf and Iraq Wars all confirm that the principles of small-group bonding are not gender specific.

Similarly, the link between primeval male hunting and warfare is largely untenable. Not only has much of recent archeological research corroborated the opinion that long-distance male hunting parties appeared much later in evolution than was originally thought,[5] but more importantly, most hunting raids would usually involve entire communities: men, women and children. The killing of large animals required elaborate social coordination

---

[5] It seems that big-game hunting emerged only around 70,000 to 90,000 years ago (Binford 1987; Ehrenreich 1997: 39).

to ensure that herds were encircled or driven off cliffs, requiring the participation of the whole tribe. In addition, there were no means available for the transport of large quantities of meat: the animal carcases had to be cut up, distributed, carried away and consumed by the entire collective (Taylor 1996; Goldstein 2001: 222). As Ehrenreich (1997: 39) sardonically and rightly comments: 'It had always seemed a bit suspicious that the sexual division of labour postulated by the hunting hypothesis – with the males striding out to hunt while the females remain home with the young – bears such an uncanny resemblance to that of American suburbanites in the mid-twentieth century, when the framers of the hunting hypothesis were coming of age.'

Nonetheless, even if all the arguments made by the biological and social masculinists about the inherent link between masculinity and aggression could be corroborated by indisputable evidence, this still would tell us little, if anything, about the relationship between gender and war. As I have argued in Chapter 2, not only is it the case that the psychological process of aggression can never be a synonym for the sociological phenomenon that is warfare but, in most instances successful military conduct is premised on the restraint and institutional control of aggressive impulses. The dramatic, and for the most part, cumulative expansion of mass-scale violence in the modern era is deeply rooted not in the simple extension of our genetic predispositions, but precisely in organisationally induced containment, control and direction of such predispositions. War is nothing like a tussle between two chimpanzees or rats, regardless of how violent this tussle may be. Instead, it is a co-ordinated large-scale process that involves violent confrontation between two social organisations. It is no accident that war and civilisation have emerged on the historical stage simultaneously, for successful military means (if not necessarily the ends) entails the use of reason and rationality. Victorious armies are not built from innately aggressive and overly emotional individuals, be they male or female. Instead, an efficient military machine requires stringent discipline, controlled behaviour and unquestioned obedience to authority. Neither the division of labour and bureaucratic hierarchy nor small-group solidarity could develop and operate if armies were composed of aggressive and inherently violent individual soldiers. Thus, it makes little relevance whether men are inherently more aggressive than women, as psychological or biological aggression has very little to do with the social and historical institution that is warfare. In other words, even if there is an inherent male propensity towards violent behaviour (and obviously there is not) this does not explain either the universal gendering of war nor the exclusion of women from combat roles.

Cultural givens?

The culturalist explanations of the gendered character of warfare downplay the importance of biology and do not see aggression as an innate male characteristic. On the contrary, they argue that the gendering of war, just like the gendering of other social roles, is rooted in the different patterns of male and female socialisation. While early culturalists interpreted this sexual division of labour as functional to social order, contemporary culturalists are more focused on the structural basis of this phenomenon. For example, early functionalists such as Bowlby (1953) and Parsons and Bales (1956) understood the gendering of social roles as conducive to family stability and thus to a successful process of socialisation. For Parsons and Bales, the division of gender roles in the 1950s model of the nuclear family, with men performing 'instrumental roles' (i.e. providing financial and security function) and women undertaking 'expressive roles' (i.e. offering emotional support and care to children), was seen as the backbone of family solidarity. In contrast, contemporary culturalists focus on the impact of primary and secondary socialisation on a person's internalisation of gender roles. For example, Lever (1978) explores gender specialisation in the organisation of children's play activities, which equips boys and girls with different social skills; Bernard (1987) looks at the role family performs in creating and reproducing gender-specific understandings of social reality; Gilligan (1982) identifies different patterns of moral reasoning taught to and adopted by boys and girls in the education system and in peer groups. More recent research in this tradition has established that, although there is little gender-specific difference between children on the individual level, the peer-group dynamics of boys and girls show much greater diversity (Maccoby 1998). Not only is it the case that from three to five years of age to around ten or eleven most children prefer to play with members of the same gender, but also it seems that this form of play-related gender separation and gender coding in early childhood is nearly universal throughout the world (Hartup 1983; Whiting and Edwards 1988). Peer group pressure is often identified as a decisive social device in enforcing gender segregation, as those who attempt to transgress gender boundaries are often stigmatised by their peers (Maccoby 1998). The culturalist views emphasise the role of parents, and especially fathers, teachers, carers and mass media advertising in reproducing the gendered character of social relations among children. Maccoby (1998) identifies several ways in which parents and carers promote gender-specific socialisation, among which the most important are offering inducements to play with gendered toys, participate in gender-specific activities, avoiding direct expressions of affection with boys but not with girls and engaging in rough-and-tumble games with boys but not with girls. Experimental psychological studies have also confirmed that parents and carers are prone to make gendered interpretations of emotional responses given by children, whereby the same emotion is often interpreted as 'anger' if the child was perceived to be a boy and 'fear' if the same child was seen to be a girl (Coie and Dodge 1998). A father's role is particularly singled out as being crucial in maintaining sharp gender boundaries. There is vast empirical evidence that substantiates the claims that fathers tend to be more strict with their sons than with their daughters and that they consciously or unconsciously encourage the avoidance of what is popularly perceived to indicate feminine behaviour: open displays of affection and tenderness, crying, beautifying one's appearance and acting 'soft and submissive' (Campbell 1993; Maccoby 1998). In addition, much of advertising aimed at children, entertainment programmes, video games and toy stores reinforce gender segregation, with clearly demarcated products aimed exclusively either at boys or girls. Of particular importance here is the wide repertoire of militaristic toys available to boys such as replica guns, knifes, swords, walkie-talkies, miniature toy soldiers, military aircraft, ships, tanks, cannons, grenades etc.

Drawing on these findings, the culturalists argue that society-wide gendered socialisation moulds boys into future soldiers. As Goldstein (2001: 249) puts it: 'Childhood gender segregation is a first step in preparing children for war. All-boy groups in middle childhood develop the social interaction scripts used later in armies.' More broadly this approach stands on the position that 'cultures use gender in constructing social roles that enable war', that is, 'various cultural themes and scripts play functional roles, and are passed on to succeeding generations as cultures evolve' (Goldstein 2001: 251). In a similar vein, Holmes (1985: 101–4) argues that strong opposition to women partaking in combat roles is a product of 'cultural conditioning' as most societies 'are structured upon sex stereotyping which has immense force'. This perception is in part linked to the gendered process of socialisation and in part is a crucial source from which military men 'derive their self-identification and feelings of masculinity'.

The central proposition here is that warfare is dependent on the cultural construction of gender roles. Male children are socialised so as to internalise aggressive behaviour as something that constitutes the essence of masculinity, and masculinity is seen as an indispensable ingredient of warfare. Just as boys were urged by their fathers not to cry when hurt and to 'toughen up', so are soldiers expected to endure pain, physical and psychological suffering to demonstrate that they are 'real men'. In other words, not only is masculinity defined in opposition to femininity, but this cultural construction of gender roles is also interpreted as functional to the war effort since it is premised on denying that those who reject participation in combat are real men. The fact that in many societies through time and space ideals of masculinity largely overlap with those that constitute the warrior ethos (i.e. courage, honour, sacrifice for one's group, endurance and determination) is seen as a clear indicator that masculinity is a direct product of cultural norms. In this interpretation, the gendered nature of warfare is a functional necessity that originated in the traditional world where men were mobilised to protect the entire group from attack. In this context, it is no accident that in many traditional social orders boys had to undergo painful and often dangerous initiation rituals in order to be deemed fully fledged men. Training boys to suppress their emotions, to be obedient to paternal authority or to act bravely is a functional prerequisite for having a disciplined, motivated and robust military force in the future. As culturalist Goldstein (2001: 283) argues: 'The omnipresent potential for war causes cultures to transform males, deliberately and systematically, by damaging their emotional capabilities … Thus manhood, an artificial status that must be won individually, is typically constructed around a culture's need for brave and disciplined soldiers.'

The problem with the culturalist interpretation of the gendered nature of warfare is not so much that it is erroneous, but that it simply does not go far enough in accounting for this puzzle. In other words, where culturalist arguments work well, such as for example in detecting the different patterns of gender socialisation, they adequately map the specific sociological processes at stake but they do not provide a fully fledged explanation for these processes. In a nutshell: we know that gendered socialisation is functional for warfare but we still have no proper answer to the question of why women are excluded from combat and why warfare is so gender-exclusive. More specifically, there are two pronounced weaknesses of this interpretation.

Firstly, for the most part, culturalists operate with a functionalist account of gender and war. While for early culturalists the sexual division of labour was seen as functional to social order, contemporary culturalists interpret the gendered character of warfare as a culturally produced social device that impels men to fight. However, the fact that a particular role is functional to a larger social system does not either make it inevitable or explain its origin. To put it simply, knowing that the gendering of war is reinforced through persistent cultural reproduction (e.g. education, mass media, advertising etc.)

does not explain the source of this gender polarisation. The functionalist arguments are epistemologically problematic as they rely on teleological and circular reasoning whereby different situations and different outcomes are all explained with reference to the same social process. For example, Goldstein (2001: 331) argues that: 'Cultures need to coax and trick soldiers into partici-pating in combat … and gender presents a handy means to do so by linking the attainment of manhood to performance in battle. In addition, cultures directly mould boys from an early age to suppress emotions in order to func-tion more effectively in battle.' Similarly, Holmes (1985: 104) sees 'cultural conditioning' as a chief reason why women are excluded from warfare: 'such is the strength of cultural conditioning that killing a woman, even when she is identifiably hostile, non-plusses many soldiers'. Nevertheless, 'cultural needs' and 'cultural conditioning' cannot explain why only one gender is involved in warfare and why this particular gender needs to be coaxed and tricked by 'culture'. It also cannot explain why some soldiers have great difficulty in kill-ing women (and children) and others do not. The experience of the Vietnam War clearly illustrates that despite the fact that many American soldiers were a product of similar socialisation processes, their behaviour on the battle-field and their attitude to Vietnamese women (soldiers and civilians) were highly diverse: some had no problem raping and murdering women while others were firmly opposed to these practices (Baker 1982; Ruane 2000). Similarly, many of those involved in the insurgency in Iraq have undergone strict gendered socialisation processes that emphasise the religiously under-pinned principle that women (and especially Muslim women) should never be involved or killed in warfare. Nevertheless, not only were women targeted by insurgents as much as men, but women were also trained and used as suicide bombers. Clearly 'cultural conditioning' and 'cultural needs' cannot explain the obvious diversity in social action. Functionalist arguments rely on a static view of the social world, and leave little or no room for social change, internal group tensions or for contested interpretations of reality, as different situations and different courses of action are all labelled as products of 'culture'.

Secondly, if the gendered character of warfare is understood as a nearly universal phenomenon, and in the modern era that seems to be the case, then there is no explanatory gain if one focuses on culture to interpret this phenom-enon. For what distinguishes culture is not universality but particularity: cul-tural action is identified by something that is specific, relative, unique, not by something that is regular, absolute, uniform and nearly universal. Female genital mutilation is a culturally unique practice; excluding women from

combat roles is a universal, trans-cultural phenomenon. The sheer prevalence of this phenomenon clearly indicates that this is not a product of a
single or several cultural traditions, but a sociological regularity that requires
supra-cultural explanation. There is no doubt that cultural specificities add
to this process and that cultural means can and do help reinforce and reproduce it, but they are not the ultimate causes of this process.

Furthermore, culturalism overemphasis the strength of social norms and
underemphasises the scale of individual resistance, conflict and micro-level
group re-interpretation of these norms. Human beings are much more than
simple carriers of their normative universes. Not only are cultural influences
rarely, if ever, free from political contestation, but individuals and social
organisations reflect on their actions and are often aware of 'the cultural conditioning' that is taking place. Despite this awareness many still find that
following a 'culturally proscribed' course of action frequently overlaps with
their own political or economic interests. The fact that most girls and boys
are exposed to different cultural contexts does not really explain why some
men volunteer to fight in wars and most do not, nor why men are selected
for battlefield and women are barred from it. There is no doubt that in most
societies the division of labour is gendered, as are the processes of socialisation. However, the scale of gender segregation in warfare is so immense and
so absolute that it has no equivalent in the civilian sphere. Moreover, while
the arrival of modernity has seen a gradual and steady decrease in gender
segregation and gendered division of labour, this has not been the case in
the sphere of warfare. On the contrary, modern wars have seen an even more
rigorous implementation of gender segregation. A view that treats human
beings as mere products of their culture cannot explain a paradox like this.

The patriarchal legacy?

Since the study of war and gender still remains on the margins of many mainstream disciplines, much of contemporary analysis comes from feminist circles. Feminist interpretations of the gendered-war puzzle appear in a variety
of guises among which three diverse approaches predominate: rights-based,
differential and post-essentialist feminism. Although all three perspectives
focus on the study of pervasive gender inequality throughout history, and in
particular on the structural mechanisms and ideologies that establish and
justify male domination, exploitation and oppression of women, they significantly differ in their accounts of these processes.

For rights-based feminists the central issue is gender discrimination, which is identified as prevalent in nearly all spheres of human life. They take the position that despite some innate and acquired gender differences men and women are basically similar. This approach focuses on the social obstacles that prevent women from reaching their potential and capabilities as individuals. The central proposition is that for much of human history women have been the subject of systematic discrimination, and traditional patriarchal social structures have prevented women from high achievement. In this view, the fact that the patriarchal model of domination remains so resilient testifies not that the system is rigid, but that it is able to quickly adapt to changed social and historical conditions. In this context, women's exclusion from military roles is understood as just another form of sexist discrimination whereby non-participation in military and warfare lessens the extent to which women have acquired full citizenship rights (Stiehm 1989). In other words, their non-participation in combat roles is used as an indicator of their 'inherent' weakness and dependency on men: wars are fought by active subjects, men, to defend passive objects, 'womenandchildren' (Enloe 1990). Yuval-Davis (1997: 93) formulates it as follows: 'As sacrificing one's life for one's country is the ultimate citizenship duty, citizenship rights are conditional on being prepared to fulfil this duty.' By identifying cases of successful individual women soldiers in various wars, rights-based feminists emphasise that women can be as capable soldiers as men. Hence, they interpret women's exclusion from the military draft or combat roles as nothing else but discrimination aimed at preserving male domination in the military. However, advocating gender integration in the military does not mean that rights-based feminists espouse militarist values. Rather, as Enloe (2000: 287) argues, the presence of women soldiers 'may provide a platform from which feminists can raise fresh questions about the legitimacy of state-sanctioned masculine privilege'. Nevertheless, patriarchy is not understood as a product of men's actions alone, but women are also held responsible for maintaining patriarchal structures and policing their femininity as well as those of other women. The war system entails and depends on the participation of women in a variety of ways, but most of all through what Enloe calls 'the militarisation of mothers'. To secure a regular supply of fresh soldiers the state machine 'militarises motherhood' by 'conceptualising the womb as a recruiting station' (Enloe 2000: 248).

In contrast to this perspective, differential feminists start from the standpoint that women and men are profoundly different creatures. Although they too see the pervasiveness of patriarchy as something that prevents the full realisation of women's potential, they are less focused on the moral and structural equality of the two genders and more on transforming the entire male-centric social order. They argue that the dominance of masculinism diminishes the value of unique feminine qualities such as greater nurturing abilities, better communicative skills, propensity towards non-violent resolution of conflicts and greater sociability. Gilligan (1982) argues that men and women utilise different moral psychologies: while men act and perceive others as individualists and on that basis tend to resolve their conflicts by advocating self-sufficiency and the 'ethics of justice', women are more sociable and responsible towards specific groups and hence oriented towards the 'ethics of care'. In this respect, differential feminists perceives men as more aggressive and war-prone than women and looks at warfare as being a masculine invention. As Cockburn (2007: 244) puts it, 'not only is patriarchy strengthened by militarism, militarism needs patriarchy'. Paradoxically, in this way differential feminism shares a great deal with biological and social masculinism as they all interpret warfare as men's domain. Nevertheless, whereas masculinists see this situation as normal and inevitable, differential feminists perceive it as an indicator of the dominance of patriarchy. Hence, for this perspective, the gendered character of warfare and the exclusion of women from combat is not an important issue since they see women as natural life-givers, not life-takers. For example, Ruddick (1989) sees the idea and practice of mothering as a distinctly feminine quality that stands asymmetrically opposed to violence and war. In this interpretation mothering is identified with life preservation, nurturing and peace, stemming from the different moral reasoning of men and women. Like Gilligan, Ruddick argues that whereas men construct their world around abstract, universalist notions, women understand social reality in a more particularist way that gives priority to particular contexts and particular group relationships (e.g. the unique sisterhood of women).

Post-essentialist feminism challenges the key starting positions of both rights-based and differential feminism. Rather than seeing men and women as very similar or very different corporal entities, post-essentialist feminists argue that gender itself is an arbitrary, fuzzy and contingent category. Haraway (1991: 155) states 'there is nothing about being "female" that naturally binds women. There is not even such a state as "being female", itself a highly complex category constructed in contested sexual scientific discourses and other social practices. Gender, race, or social consciousness is an achievement forced on us by the terrible historical experience of the contradictory social realities of patriarchy, colonialism and capitalism'. Post-essentialist feminists reject the notion of a single, true reality, arguing that all truth claims are fragmentary, provisional and discursive. Hence, instead of focusing on explaining gender inequalities or more specifically the exclusion of women from battlefields, post-essentialist researchers are committed to the deconstruction of all truth claims. In this perspective, concepts such as 'men' and 'women', commonly understood to imply essentialist, fixed and stable categories, are in fact products of specific discursive practices. Instead of such categories, post-essentialist feminists write about fractured identities and contingent and contextual forms of femininity and masculinity. What is considered to be important is not the substance of gender differences but the structurally and discursively created boundaries between masculinity and femininity. While both 'men' and women' are seen as being able to develop 'feminist subjectivities' (Harding 1998), it is the particular social contexts that determine the character and intensity of male–female dichotomies. The experience of warfare is especially identified as a terrain where power and knowledge blend into hegemonic discourses that reinforce singular and rigid gender identities. Post-essentialist analyses focus extensively on the use of language and how war discourses of masculinity depend on re-interpretations of femininity and vice versa. The extreme social situation that war represents, with its swiftly changing 'meta-narratives' of gender and violence, stands as the litmus paper of the apparent plasticity of gender roles. 'Just as we are fascinated by women terrorists, we are equally fascinated ... by male conscientious objectors. They are the exceptions to the supposed "rule" of how men and women are supposed to behave vis-à-vis violence' (Eager 2008: 20). To illustrate their arguments about the flexibility of gender roles in war, the post-essentialists single out individual cases of women warriors throughout history such as Deborah Samson, Franziska Scanagatta, Frances Day and Sarah Emma Edmonds, who all fought successfully in different wars (French Revolutionary Wars, American Civil War, etc.) disguised as men without their fellow soldiers noticing that they were women.

Despite providing such diverse accounts of gender and war, all feminist analyses share the understanding that the exclusion of women from combat roles and the male centricity of the war experience have deep historical roots in patriarchy. While rights-based feminists perceive this exclusion as a crucial obstacle in establishing gender equality, for differential and post-essentialist feminists this is just a symptom of the broader problem: the intrinsically violent nature of men and the dominance of the phallocentric social order or discursively constructed gender absolutism in war.

There is no doubt that patriarchal social conditions reinforce a strict gender division of labour, whereby fighting and warfare are for the most part identified with masculinity, while mothering and caring are synonymous with femininity. Militaristic discourses generally utilise the exclusivity of gender roles by invoking patriarchal imagery. Mussolini emphasised this vividly in his speeches: 'War is to man what maternity is to the woman. I do not believe in perpetual peace; not only do I not believe in it but I find it depressing and a negation of all the fundamental virtues of man' (Bollas 1993: 205). Furthermore, feminists are right that this male–female dualism is often deliberately perpetuated by state authorities, military establishments, propagandist mass media and other outlets with a view to controlling the actions of women, motivating men to fight, and obstructing the emergence of organised resistance to war. The sharp distinction between defenceless and weak 'womenandchildren' and brave and strong men on which much of militarist thought has been built has proven highly beneficial to states and military organisations. Not only has this gender dualism helped to demean femininity and deprive women of full citizenship rights, but it has also been used to provide a moral rationale for wars: a man's unwillingness to fight is not only linked to his lack of 'true masculinity' but also to his lack of morality, since cowardice on the battlefield supposedly leaves 'womenandchildren' in mortal danger.

Nevertheless, while patriarchy contributes to the gendering of war, it does not in itself explain the universal exclusion of women from combat roles. The simple fact is that the greater equality of women, the weakening of the patriarchal ethos and the reduction in sexist practices have not dramatically (or in many cases at all) altered the patterns of female participation on the battlefield. For example, in the social orders generally recognised as the least patriarchal, such as Canada, Denmark, Netherlands or Norway, where women have achieved greater levels of parity with men in many aspects of social, economic and political life, the number of female soldiers in combat roles still remains miniscule. Despite attempts towards greater gender integration in the military and the nominal opening up of all military positions for women, the 1993 figures indicate the there were only 168 women employed in ground combat units for all these countries combined. Although Canadian governments have pursued a policy of active recruitment of women for all military roles and have been, unlike most other Western states, highly successful in this regard with women making up 11 per cent of Canadian armed forces by 1998, only 1 per cent (165) of combat soldiers were female (Goldstein 2001: 10, 85). And even this small percentage has to be viewed in the context of available employment within militaries that have not been involved in warfare for a very long time. Hence with a

few exceptions involving UN-sponsored missions, none of these female soldiers had experience of actual combat. Furthermore, in states that have been
involved in periodic warfare and have also pursued active policies of gender
integration in the military, such as the USA and Israel, the participation of
women on the battlefield has not significantly increased. Despite the popular
perception that Israeli women are an integral part of the military machine
because they are required to undergo military training, very few of them
are involved in actual combat. As Van Creveld (1991: 184) points out: 'After
the 1948 War, Israeli women, though still subject to the draft, were confined to traditional occupations as secretaries, telephone operators, social
workers ... The weapons training that Israeli women are given in the army
is almost entirely symbolic' while the arms they train with mostly consist
of 'weapons that had previously been discarded by the men'.[6] Similarly, the
US military has made enormous efforts to open its doors to women soldiers
and they now represent 14 per cent of the total force. However, 'two-thirds
of US women soldiers are in administration, health care, communications
and service/supply occupations' and only 2.5 per cent are involved in combat related jobs, most of which are unlikely to ever see battlefield action
(Goldstein 2001: 93–105). In other words, the gradual deconstruction of
patriarchy has had little or no impact on perceptions or policies regarding
the exclusion of women from combat roles. Although patriarchy plays an
important part in gendering war, it in itself is no answer to the question of
why all wars are gendered.

The argument of differential feminists, that warfare is somehow a natural
prerequisite of men while women are inherently pacifist, is flawed on at least
two grounds. Not only do such essentialist views operate with empirically
unfounded notions of diametrically opposed sexes, but they also overlook
the historical significance of women's complicity in warfare. This perspective
shares a similar ontology with biological masculinism, an ontology that is
grounded in fiction not fact. As already demonstrated, physiological, cognitive and moral differences between the two genders are too slight to have
any significant impact on the exclusion of an entire gender from the battlefield. Warfare has little to do with individual physical aggression and much
more to do with one's ability to follow orders, be disciplined and work in

---

[6] As Goldstein (2001: 86) indicates, while military reserve duty for Israeli men is a lifelong responsibility, for Israeli women reserve duty stops at age 24 or upon becoming mothers. Furthermore more than
half of drafted women stay in the armed forces to serve in clerical and secretarial jobs. While only a
tiny number of those recruited are in combat units even they rarely experience real combat because
'as soon as actual combat looms, the women are immediately evacuated from the unit'.

small groups. Even if women do tend to employ different moral parameters than men this would not make them worse, but much better, soldiers, for 'the ethics of care' would make the small-group solidarity on which the internal cohesion of all militaries depend, an even more potent source of military efficiency. Furthermore, being a 'natural carer' and mother are not incompatible with providing vehement support for war. In fact, in many wars it was mothers who were responsible for reinforcing strict gender dualism, for teaching boys to be tough and strong, for encouraging them to volunteer for warfare and suicide missions (Yuval-Davis 1997; A. D. Smith 1998). For example, the mother of Palestinian suicide bomber Muhammad Fathi Farhat was videotaped with her son wishing him success before his suicide mission; after he blew himself up and killed five Israeli teenagers in Atzmona in March 2002, she organised a 'celebration' and 'reproached those who sobbed, asking them to leave because she would not accept tears on such a joyous occasion' (Hafez 2006: 46).

Post-essentialist feminists are right that gender cannot be reduced to one's physiognomy, but this does not imply that one can simply pick and choose between different 'gender narratives'. Although 'femininity' and 'masculinity' are social constructions created in particular historically and culturally contingent conditions, gender roles are never created in an arbitrary, ad hoc fashion. For if gender identities were so plastic and fuzzy, than it would be possible to change them at will with relative ease. Nevertheless, the experience of early women soldiers who had to hide their sex indicates not only that this was very difficult and demanding, with most women soldiers being quickly discovered, but more importantly, very few if any of these women were interested in changing their gender (Hall 1993). Instead, they were primarily interested in participating in combat, and as the patriarchal ethics did not allow their full involvement they were forced to adopt a male disguise. The post-essentialist stress on the plurality of truth claims and the discursive character of gender narratives is underpinned by a radical relativist epistemology that is unwilling and unable to distinguish between different 'regimes of truth' (Malešević 2004: 152–8). Such an approach, which consciously rejects analytical universality, cannot offer an adequate explanation for the gendered nature of war. Deconstructing gendered narratives might provide an insight into the workings of particular patriarchal discourses, but it cannot provide a coherent answer to the questions: Why is warfare so universally gender exclusive? And why are women nearly always excluded from the battlefields?

Gender, social organisation and ideology

Although physical differences between genders have regularly been used to justify women's exclusion from direct warfare, it is apparent that waging a successful war has nothing to do with the bodily strength or general biological make-up of individual soldiers. Similarly, while there is no doubt that patriarchal legacies, primary socialisation and 'cultural conditioning' play a significant part in reinforcing and reproducing the gendered character of war, none of these factors can provide a coherent account of why this is a universal phenomenon and why the general decrease in gender inequality had little or no bearing on women's participation in close combat. Even though this is a complex puzzle that involves a number of different variables, this chapter argues that the universal gendering of warfare stems principally from two inter-related processes – the cumulative bureaucratisation of violence and the centrifugal ideologisation of gender roles.

War and the cumulative bureaucratisation of gender roles

To understand the workings of these two processes it is necessary to remind ourselves that, as argued in Chapter 4, warfare is a recent historical development that emerged with the birth and expansion of civilisation, and its structural acceleration largely follows in the footsteps of expanding state power. For 99 per cent of their history, humans lived in small-scale nomadic foraging bands which had no organisational power, ability, interest or will to engage in large-scale protracted violent conflicts, that is, warfare. What was sociologically distinct about these nomadic groups was their highly egalitarian and, for the most part, non-violent character: they lacked clearly defined leadership and even rudimentary forms of social stratification, and they were flexible and fluctuating entities with individuals shifting easily from one band to another (Service 1978: 11–110; Fry 2007: 70). Although most bands relied on age and sex as markers of group divisions, neither one of those was used, or could be used, to enforce gender or age-specific forms of dominance. As Fry (2007: 199) points out: 'Contrary to the assumption that patrilineages of related males live together, most simple hunter-gatherer bands lack patrilineal descent groups … Contrary to the warring over women and territory assumption, disputes over women, when occurring between members of different bands, tend to be individual affairs.' In other words, before the emergence of sedentary social organisations, there was neither warfare nor gender stratification. Even later, more complex, formations such as kinship-based tribes, remained politically egalitarian with quite weak leadership whereby the right to lead was grounded in a person's exceptional achievements, commitment to the tribe, or ability to redistribute wealth (e.g. food, livestock, etc.), with the leaders lacking substantial coercive powers (Service 1978; De Waal 2005).

It is only much later, with the development of chiefdoms and pristine states, that the social order becomes visibly and distinctly hierarchical with pronounced gender segregation and stratification. Thus gender discrimination and the institutionalisation of the gendered division of labour came hand in hand with the birth and expansion of civilisation. To put it simply: warfare and gender polarisation, that is, the exclusion of women from the battlefield, appear on the historical stage together. Although it is difficult, if not impossible, to prove that one was the cause of the other, there is no doubt that their joint appearance was not coincidental. In this respect gender stratification is not unique, as the rise of complex social organisations such as chiefdoms, city-states and pristine empires was paralleled by an expansion of all forms of social hierarchy: religious, political, military and economic. As Tilly (1985) and Mann (1986) show, the process of 'social caging' and 'political racketeering' were decisive in securing the ascendancy of centralised political authorities in which individual mobility, liberty and autonomy was traded off for political and military security and relative economic wellbeing. Since civilisation was born through the imposition of coercive apparatuses, its very existence remains dependent on maintaining social hierarchies. In other words, centralised, large-scale, social organisations cannot operate without a hierarchical structure and elaborate division of labour. To create and sustain such chains of command and control, it is necessary to hierarchically organise social groups within a particular polity, as well as to justify such organisation. However, as social stratification is largely a structural, not voluntary, phenomenon, it could emerge (and has done so) only around the popularly self-evident markers: age, gender and whether or not a person was enslaved.

Because the backbone of the chiefdoms and pristine states was military power, and this power was dependent on a constant supply of new warriors, the warrior status inevitably rose high up on the prestige ladder. However, not everybody could become a warrior. Since the maintenance of warriors is generally expensive, and in some historical epochs such as the Bronze Age, early medieval period (and today) extremely costly, there is a need for extensive support systems involving the labour of huge numbers of slaves, peasants, merchants, miners and many others. The automatic exclusion of women from the warrior caste arose not because of their physical incompetence or supposed weaknesses but primarily because of their unique biological ability: they were the only gender able to conceive, carry, give birth to and initially feed newborn babies. Hence they were the only group capable of producing new warriors and new labourers, both essential for the preservation of chiefdoms and pristine states. It is this unique quality that relegated women almost exclusively to the domestic sphere and provided a ready-made rationale for keeping them away from the war zone. Therefore, the initial exclusion of women from combat had nothing to do with their physique or capacity to fight. Rather, their exclusion was a by-product of organisational demand: the gender whose involvement in human reproduction was negligible became the gender responsible for combat. Furthermore, as early forms of nascent warfare were often conflicts between the exogamous neighbouring tribes and chiefdoms from which spouses were obtained, the direct participation of women in warfare would imply fighting and killing their closest kin (fathers, brothers but also mothers and sisters). Hence, to prevent this situation, which would inevitably cause divided loyalties and thus undermine the organisational basis of warfare, women had to be excluded from combat zones (Adams 1983). When there was no such organisational obstacle the participation of women in early warfare was much greater. As Eckhardt (1992: 24) shows, in tribes and chiefdoms where endogamy was the dominant form of marriage 'women did fight as warriors at some time or another in about 25 per cent of such communities'.

Nevertheless, the gradual expansion and proliferation of warfare made sure that the status of warriors was dramatically enhanced at the expense of all civilians including those deemed responsible for society's procreation. Furthermore, the fact that warriors controlled all the means of coercion meant that what started off as an organisational necessity rooted in an ad hoc mechanism of the division of labour has gradually developed into a firm and stable gender hierarchy with men and women being institutionally confined to the two separate and mutually exclusive roles. In most respects, gender dominance in warfare developed as a form of, what Weber (1968: 43) termed, a monopolistic social closure.[7] Once established as a dominant social stratum, the warrior elite were in a position to monopolise its social prestige, material and political benefits by closing off access to all other groups and in particular to the entire other gender.

---

[7] Weber (1968: 43) distinguishes between open and closed social relationships whereby open relationships allow social mobility and relatively free access to group membership while closed relationships are 'closed against outsiders so far as, according to its subjective meaning and its binding rules, participation of certain persons is excluded, limited, or subject to conditions'. For more about Weber's theory of social closure see Parkin (1979), Rex (1986) and Malešević (2004:128–32).

This is best illustrated by comparing existing nomadic and semi-nomadic groups and organisationally highly advanced societies. For example, anthropological research on the Siriono of Bolivia, Paliyan of India, Netsilik Inuits of Canada, Semai of Malaysia, !Kung San of Namibia and Botswana and Australian Aborigines among others has demonstrated that the absence of organised violence is firmly linked with greater gender equality (Balikci 1970; Gardner 1972; Lee 1993; Fry 2007). Among the Siriono 'women have about the same privileges as men, and both sexes engage in about the same amount of work' while at the same time 'murder is almost unknown, as is sorcery, rape, and theft of non-food items'. When a conflict between individuals or families intensifies there is no violent struggle: the solution is found through one party joining another group (Fry 2007: 27). Similarly, Paliyan nomadic hunter-gatherers espouse sexual egalitarianism and value personal autonomy while utilising non-violent methods to settle in-group conflicts: polyandry is a common practice and neither one of the spouses has the right to dominate the other (Gardner 1972). The Semai of Malaysia are well known for their avoidance of violence, peaceful resolution of internal conflicts and refusal to fight even when attacked (preferring to retreat into the forest instead). What is less emphasised is their gender equality, with both men and women participating in fishing, horticulture and cooking; raising children is a communal responsibility while newly married couples often switch their residence patterns and can easily separate (De Waal 2005).

In contrast to this, most misogynist societies and those that practise gendered occupational segregation have an advanced social organisation and are involved in protracted warfare. For example, both Nazi Germany and Japan under the Imperial Rule Assistance Association insisted on clearly demarcated gender roles. Goebbels defined Nazism as a 'masculine movement by nature' and Hitler's speeches emphasised that a women's world is 'her husband, her family, her children, and her home' (Durham 1998: 16). The Nazi order fostered gender segregation with men associated with the supremacy of the warrior ethos and women confined to '*Kinder, Küche, Kirche*' (children, kitchen and church). Women were rigidly excluded from combat and even those few found in auxiliary roles were never trained or allowed to use any armaments (Goldstein 2001: 72). A large number of hardcore Nazis were distinctly misogynist, deeming all women who did not conform to the patriarchal image of mother or sister as prostitutes and enemy collaborators. While women who gave birth to four and more children were rewarded with the Cross of Honour of the German Mother, non-conformist women were loathed and often punished. WWII Japan was even more rigid in gender segregation and exclusion of women from military roles. The rulers introduced various policies to encourage greater fertility and conceptualised motherhood as an unquestioned national duty to the Japanese Empire. Moreover, Imperial Japanese Forces were involved in cultivating misogynist attitudes within the military and were responsible for organising the large-scale institutionalised system of sexual slavery through so called 'comfort women'. This organised system of mass rape involved between 100,000 to 200,000 mostly Korean teenage girls who were forced to have sex with up to 30 men per day (Hicks 1997). This is not to say that gender inequality stems directly from warfare: as various studies show, there is no conclusive evidence that frequent or protracted wars cause a decrease in the social standing of women. Instead, the war environment often enhances the position of women, with a substantial decline in domestic violence (Whyte 1978; Sanday 1981; Segal 1990). What is crucial here is the impact of social organisation: there seems to be a clear link between gender stratification, militarism and advanced social organisation. It is social organisation not culture that is the backbone of institutionalised gender difference and the exclusion of women from battlefields.

Enlightenment-infused modernist principles have created the conditions for the gradual emancipation of women and have slowly opened access to social realms previously monopolised by men. However, it is the transformation in the social organisation of warfare that made this emancipation possible. Despite all the demonstrations, activities and writings of the suffragettes and liberal and feminist intellectuals, the dramatic occupational changes in gender roles witnessed in the first half of the twentieth century owed nearly all to the two total wars. Although the labour of women has been indispensable for centuries, with 'camp followers' accompanying various armies as cooks, laundry workers, suppliers, medics etc.,[8] the organisational demands of WWI and II created an enormous shortage of civilian manpower in industry and agriculture, which could not be filled by any other group than women. The unprecedented scale of mobilisation of men combined with the development of large-scale armament industries meant that for the first time in modern history social organisations became dependent on the labour of women. More than 9 million US and 2 million British women were recruited during WWII to replace men in industrial workplaces. For

---

[8] As Goldstein (2001: 381) points out, 'camp followers' were often as numerous as the armies they accompanied and sometimes even much larger: 'One 40,000-soldier army during the Thirty Years War reportedly had 100,000 camp followers.'

example, in the UK 80 per cent of single women were employed in industry or military support roles; over 1 million women were involved in the production of munitions, and 40 per cent of those working in the aircraft industry were women (Enloe 1983; Costello 1985). What this example illustrates is that gendered occupational segregation is likely to change only in a situation where the old organisational model becomes unsustainable. In other words, the gender-specific division of labour is deeply rooted in social organisation and can only be transformed when the organisation itself is transformed. It is worth noting that all the rhetoric about women's physical or cultural inability to work in industry and the military auxiliary services instantly disappeared once their labour became indispensable for the very survival of the large-scale social organisation – the state.

The examples of the WWII Soviet Union and many guerrilla armies demonstrate that similarly dramatic shifts in attitudes and practices towards women's participation in combat are indeed possible. The unexpected and swift German invasion of 1941 coupled with huge military losses and widespread destruction forced the Soviet authorities to mobilise women for front-line roles. According to official figures nearly 1 million women were soldiers (800,000 in the Red Army and 200,000 in partisan units), out of which a staggering half a million served at the fronts (Griesse and Stites 1982). Although such official Soviet figures will always remain suspect and while there is no doubt that most of the women who served on the front line did not participate in direct combat, it is also clear that huge numbers of women have taken part in actual combat. Similarly, most guerrilla armies include large numbers of women soldiers many of whom are involved in battlefield action. The well-documented cases of Nicaragua, Vietnam, Iran, Eritrea, Sri Lanka, Italy, Argentina, Lebanon, Yugoslavia and Israel among others show that guerrilla resistance movements have relied heavily on women's participation in warfare. In Nicaragua's Sandinista guerrillas, one third of front-line soldiers were women; the Vietcong had so many women (at least 160,000 fighters) that the guerrilla force became known as the 'long-haired army'; in Israel's 1948 War of Independence 15 per cent of guerrillas were women; more than 10 per cent of Yugoslav partisan forces were female soldiers which by 1945 included no less than 100,000 women; in the Eritrean Civil War 25 per cent of the army consisted of female soldiers, while one third of the Sri Lankan Tamil Tigers were women (Dahn 1966; Jancar 1988; Jorgensen 1994; Jones 1997; Edgerton 2000). What these two unusual examples – the Soviet forces in WWII and guerrilla warfare experience – demonstrate is not only that when (exceptional) circumstances allow, women are readily accepted into military forces and they have no problems adjusting to combat roles, but also, and more importantly that the only real obstacle to women's full participation in warfare is the social organisation itself. It is only when the very existence of the social organisation is at stake that women's roles can be swiftly redefined.

However, as the social organisation of warfare is structurally and ideologically built on gender stratification, allowing the full participation of women in combat is bound to create a structural instability, organisational paralysis and possibly open the door for complete delegitimisation of the military activity. To put it simply, if both genders were fully included in the war enterprise this would profoundly undermine the nature of the enterprise. The cumulative coercive bureaucratisation of gender roles stems in part from the structural requirements of war: gender stratification is embedded in the division of labour and the social hierarchies necessary for the efficient waging of war. The existence and dominance of (male) soldiers in a war situation is dependent on the labour, support and 'incapacity' of (mostly female) non-soldiers. Permitting women to fight would not only disturb the starkly asymmetrical ratio of labourers and support workers to fighters, but would also undermine the gendered character of power relations within the social organisation and hence would undermine the social organisation itself. The WWII experience is a powerful indicator of what happens to social organisation when the gender barriers are shifted: once women were allowed to replace men in industry it was, as the 1960s demonstrated, practically impossible to turn the clock back. The outcome of WWII was not just a greater emancipation of women but also the drastic transformation of gender relations that made a direct contribution to the transformation of a variety of social organisations including the state itself. The fact that in both of these cases – guerrilla warfare and the WWII Soviet Union – most women were forced to leave their military roles as soon as the wars were over clearly suggests the importance of social organisation in maintaining gender stratification. Despite the visible efficiency of women as soldiers, once the militaries had recovered their strength in terms of numbers of male soldiers or guerrilla forces had been transformed into regular militaries, women almost automatically became excluded from combat roles. Therefore, although modernity has brought more gender equality within a variety of areas previously monopolised by men, the military sphere in general and combat in particular still remain the distinctive prerogative of men.

Although this war-induced bureaucratisation of gender roles is grounded in the working of the social organisation, it would not be able to operate effectively without a solid ideological foundation. Hence, to understand the almost universal exclusion of women from the battlefield it is also important to tackle the role of ideology.

War and the centrifugal ideologisation of gender roles

One of the most pronounced gender themes in warfare is the identification of violence, and even more so a person's ability to deal with violence, with masculinity. As culturalists emphasise, war is regularly interpreted as a test of manhood: 'warriors require intense socialisation and training in order to fight effectively' and in this context 'gender identity becomes a tool with which societies induce men to fight'; that is 'cultural norms force men to endure trauma and master fear, in order to claim the status of "manhood"' (Goldstein 2001: 252, 264). There is no doubt that most men are not 'natural born killers' and require a great deal of social incitement (and coercion) to participate in wars. There is also a great deal of evidence that most social orders use the masculinity card in propaganda to shame draft dodgers and motivate men to join the military. However, this in itself does not explain the gender exclusivity of warfare. It is far from being self-evident why the inducement to violence and in particularly the incitement to fight would be so tightly linked with masculinity. For one thing, concepts of masculinity vary through time and place: whereas a Semai man who fearlessly engages and fights enemy intruders would be ostracised from the group for his outrages and non-manly actions, the Japanese kamikaze pilot who returns home alive after an unsuccessful mission represented the epitome of male disgrace in WWII Japan.

More importantly, if one takes a closer look at the key themes and values of the 'warrior ethos' throughout history, it is clear that anybody, regardless of their gender, can emulate and live by these principles. For example, following a wide survey of different social orders, McCarthy (1994: 106) identifies the following four ideal types as central to the 'warrior ethos':

1. Physical courage, which includes enjoyment of fight and bravery in facing death;
2. Endurance, which refers to one's ability to withstand intensive pain, hunger and thirst and severe climatic conditions without ever being demoralised;
3. Strength and skill, which suggest the warrior's physical robustness, bodily fitness and knowledge of tactics, planning and effective use of weaponry;
4. Honour, which consists of honourable behaviour on the battlefield, loyalty to leaders and comrades, eagerness to protect the weak and vulnerable as well as extreme protectiveness of one's reputation.

What is remarkable here is that none of these principles are gender exclusive. Women just as men can enjoy fighting, show courage, endure pain and hunger, be fit, know about tactics, learn to handle weapons skilfully and be loyal and honourable on the battlefield. There is nothing inherently masculine about these warrior ideals nor does one require a penis or any other biological entailment to acquire these skills and qualities. In other words, the physical attributes of masculinity remain largely irrelevant for gender segregation in warfare. Yet in many social contexts masculinity has become wedded to combat experience. While feminists might be right that this link between masculinity and warfare has proved to be beneficial for the preservation of patriarchy, it is not clear why values such as bravery, endurance or honour are associated almost exclusively with masculinity. To unravel this puzzle it is necessary not only to focus on the role of social organisation, which remains crucial in institutionalising and perpetuating gendered stratification in warfare, but also the look at the process of centrifugal ideologisation.

Nevertheless, it is important to emphasise that ideology is not culture. Culture is a particular way of collective living, expressed in the symbolic articulation, classification and communication of common experience, but ideology is only a small part of culture. More specifically, as outlined in the introductory chapter, I define ideology as a relatively universal and multifaceted social process through which individual and social actors articulate their beliefs and behaviour. It is a form of 'thought-action' that penetrates most social practice and which is conveyed through the distinct conjectural arrangements of a particular social order. Its contents often surpass experience, as they are, for the most part, non-testable, offering a transcendent grand vista of collective authority. Ideological messages are constructed to make potent appeals to advanced ethical norms, superior knowledge claims, to individual or group interests or to popular emotions in order to justify actual or potential social action (Malešević 2002; 2006). Hence the view that cultural norms force men to fight in order to claim their masculinity is wrong. Rather than initiating a particular form of behaviour, cultural norms mostly serve to reinforce what is already popularly understood to be the appropriate course of action. Hence to understand why and how participation in warfare is linked to manhood, it is crucial to look at the broader picture. In other words, the willingness of men to take part in combat so as to prove their masculinity is really a symptom of a broader sociological phenomenon: a group morality.

The key reason why large numbers of men accept war as a measure of their manhood is not cultural: it is social, and more specifically ideological. As Durkheim (1986: 202–3) was aware, human beings always operate within, and are guided by, a particular moral universe: 'morals are what the society is' whereas 'man is a moral being only because he lives within established societies'. Since morality is a communal affair, to be a moral individual implies sharing a particular ethical universe and hence behaving within the set normative parameters of this universe. Therefore, not conforming to an ideal of masculinity in times of war inevitably suggests a substantial degree of moral erosion. A man who does not fight is perceived as someone who lacks moral fibre: selfishly saving his own life at the expense of the lives of those closest and dearest to him (his children, wife, girlfriend, mother or father). In this sense, by not taking part in combat, a man undermines the moral universe and hence the social solidarity of the group he belongs to. When the state propaganda machine invokes the imagery of male cowardice it directly makes an appeal to group morality rather than to the individual's self-interest or even sense of self-worth.

Nevertheless, what Durkheim largely ignored is the ideological potency of such group feelings and in particular the ideological processes that underpin war rhetoric. It is through the centrifugal ideologisation of gender roles that the boundaries of group morality are firmly delineated. It is ideology that establishes the ethical parameters of collective action and articulates the link between masculinity and warfare. Whereas war-induced bureaucratisation establishes gender hierarchies that make war possible, ideologisation provides justification for the existence of these hierarchies. The mutually exclusive categories of masculinity and femininity do not stand on their own; rather, they are deduced from a broader dichotomy that permeates the entire social order, a dichotomy that is perpetuated and reinforced over a long period of time in ordinary and banal ways. This dichotomy is a clear distinction between the civilian and military spheres. This dichotomy simultaneously constitutes and legitimises the moral universe of war. As argued previously (see introduction and Chapter 7), centrifugal ideologisation is a continuous process geared towards making the artificial and external entities that are social organisations into natural, kinship-like, hubs of solidarity. This process essentially works in two ways: through the institutional enhabitation of routine practices and through the subjective disciplining and internalisation of ideological discourses. Since the principal purpose of large-scale social organisations, such as the nation-state, in war is military success, its primary imperative is to galvanise society-wide popular support for war and in particular to mobilise large groups of soldiers. However, no state can afford to turn all citizens into bloodthirsty killers. Instead the firm distinction between the civilian realm, characterised by order, peace, gentleness, compassion and benevolence, has to be counterpoised to the military realm of violence, cruelty, resilience and strength. Not only is this dichotomy crucial in preserving order, stability and the status quo in times of peace, whereby violence, killing and cruelty are externalised and kept in check by the social organisation itself, but more importantly the presence of this dichotomy allows the justification of extreme forms of behaviour when war comes.

Whereas during times of peace, the values of civility are institutionally held in much higher regard than those of 'warrior ethics', the exceptionality of the war situation quickly reverses their relative positions. Since in times of war social organisations have different priorities, it becomes paramount to redefine 'civilian' as weak, passive, dependent and in need of protection while 'military' acquires the attributes of strength, leadership, determination and assertiveness. And since this change is grounded in already familiar and institutionalised dichotomies it often resonates well with the larger population. It often seems normal and natural that the people, who have already internalised this distinction, should make this switch of values in an extremely adverse situation. At the same time, military organisations do not have to make this mental switch at all as they are ideologically built on war-based dichotomies of the civilian and the non-civilian, whereby civilian life is regularly conceptualised as inferior in most respects. What happens in times of war is just that the entire society embraces the military version of this dichotomy by accepting the primacy of the military over the civilian sphere. The key point here is that gender stratification is a direct outcome of this broader dichotomy in which the 'inherent weakness' of femininity is derived from the secondary role of 'civility' under war conditions, while 'masculinity' becomes synonymous with military action. In other words, the social organisation requires and perpetuates these dichotomies in order to fulfil its central goal: to defeat the other social organisation (i.e. the enemy state). In order to succeed in this goal it needs to maintain the sharp distinction between the two realms so as to motivate men to fight, and women, as well as the non-fighting males, to support their fight. The role of ideology is central in this process as it is through ideologisation that the actions of men soldiers are articulated, not as the fulfilment of organisational goals, but as the defence of innocent and vulnerable 'womenandchildren'. In other words, by invoking the language of moral responsibility and kinship ties, social organisations are able to make such unprecedented acts as killing, destruction and self-sacrifice possible. In this context group morality is ideologically utilised in circular form. Both men as soldiers and women as civilians are emotionally blackmailed: if you as a soldier do not fight, kill and die on the battlefield you expose your mother, sister, wife, etc. to mortal danger resulting from the enemy's invasion; if you as a woman oppose the war effort, or do not perform your civilian duties, you expose your father, husband, brother etc. who bravely serves on the battlefield to the mortal danger of being overpowered by the enemy. The fact that the idioms of masculinity and femininity are derived from the civilian vs. military dichotomy indicates that they are not dependent on the biological differences between two sexes. Instead they are both used as normative parameters of group morality, that is, as a measurement of how well an individual performs the role created by the social organisation. Calling a soldier a wimp or sissy does not denote that the particular individual has become a woman in any form, but only that his performance on the front line does not measure well according to the (organisationally) set standards of group morality. The soldier who openly cries or visibly shows other emotions brings 'civilian' ethics to the battlefield, where there is no place for them. This act is understood as an attempt to 'pollute' and thus undermine the foundations of the military sphere, where suppression of emotions, strength, resilience and determination are identified as essential ingredients for survival on the battlefield. The fact that women soldiers use the same masculinist rhetoric when on the front line clearly indicates that this dichotomy has little to do with gender and a great deal to do with position in the social organisation.[9] Thus, the exclusion of women from combat roles is not grounded in biology, culture or patriarchy, although all three of these have contributed to this process; it is a product of bureaucratisation and ideologisation. Keeping the two genders apart is an organisational device that keeps war going and, as the prison system clearly demonstrates, coercively induced gender division regularly creates aggressive genderisation of social roles. Fronts, just as prisons, are 'abnormal' and extreme situations where regular gender interaction is drastically and dramatically curtailed, the outcome of which is emotional and social deprivation. It is this organisationally produced deprivation that fosters gender polarisation, stratification and exclusion. The dichotomisation of the world into civilian/female and military/male makes war both possible and justified.

[9] For illustrative examples see Addis *et al.* (1994); Edgerton (2000) and Goldstein (2001).

Conclusion

Warfare seems to be the last bastion of male dominance. Although the gradual dismantling of patriarchy has penetrated most social spheres previously monopolised by men, participation in combat remains firmly gender exclusive with women being formally or informally banned from the battlefields. This puzzle has been tackled by three distinct explanatory perspectives which I have called masculinist, culturalist and feminist. The chapter has challenged all three of these accounts by stressing that biological differences play a marginal role in the conduct of war, that the cultural functionality of the gender division does not explain either its origin or its universality and that the patriarchal character of this division cannot account for the exclusivity of gender stratification in combat present even in the least patriarchal contexts. Instead, the argument focuses on the role of social organisation and ideology in initiating, reproducing, reinforcing and perpetuating the genderisation of warfare. In other words, gendering of war roles tells us as much about gender as it does about war. Since warfare is a product of social organisation, its structural proliferation is closely linked to that of the organisation itself. The conduct of warfare depends on the existence of social hierarchy, the division of labour and institutional and organisational complexity, in which gender plays a central role. War-induced bureaucratisation and the ideologisation of gender roles simultaneously generate reasons for war as well as the justifications for it. The ever-increasing complexity of social organisations and their ideological powers have fostered greater gender stratification in the military and have also increased the destructive potential of warfare. Not only is gender separation functional for warfare; more importantly, this separation makes war possible and socially meaningful.

Part V

Organised violence in the twenty-first century

New wars?

Any dramatic historical change is bound to challenge the existing sociological comprehension of reality. Ultimately this can lead to the articulation of new analytical models and new conceptual apparatuses devised to come to terms with these unprecedented changes. Social transformations of any magnitude necessitate new interpretative horizons and new explanatory paradigms. However, macro-level sociologists rarely encounter such unique, earth-shattering, historical moments of rupture. As most *longue durée* research clearly shows, the trajectories of human development are usually shaped by, and measured in, centuries and millennia rather than decades and years. Hence, it is hard to assess whether the times we live in constitute such a rare and historically transformative episode. Although the collapse of communism, the end of a bipolar world, economic globalisation and the spectacular rise of religiously framed violence are obviously good candidates, there is no certainty that twenty-fourth-century historical sociology will judge them as momentous events and processes in the way we are prone to do. Not only do we tend towards chronocentrism (Fowles 1974), and what Peel (1989) calls 'blocking presentism', that is, an overemphasis on present events and our own depiction of the past, but we are not immune to a presentist interpretation of the future either. This chapter attempts to critically engage with recent developments in the study of war and violence and in particular with an emerging research paradigm that claims fundamental historical novelty – the theory of new wars. More specifically, the focus is on the highly influential but rarely scrutinised macro-level sociological accounts of the new-wars paradigm and their claims about the unprecedented causes of recent violent conflicts and the qualitative transformation in the objectives and goals of these wars.

Firstly, I briefly summarise the central tenets and existing criticisms of the new-wars paradigm. Secondly, I explore the sociological theories of new wars by identifying their distinctive features and commonalities. The focus is in particular on the causes and changing objectives of contemporary warfare. Finally, I assess the explanatory strength of the new-wars paradigm in sociology, arguing that the paradigm fails on both accounts, since current wars exhibit more similarity than difference with conventional nineteenth and twentieth century wars. Instead of historically novel forms of violence, one encounters processes that have been intensifying since the birth of the modern era: the cumulative bureaucratisation of coercion and centrifugal ideologisation. However, this is not to argue that nothing has changed in the relationship between warfare and society. What has significantly changed is the level of social reliance on technology and, most of all, the social, geopolitical and ideological context in which recent wars have been fought.

The new-wars paradigm

A variety of influential scholars from across a range of disciplines as diverse as security studies (Snow 1996; Duffield 2001), political economy (Collier 2000; Jung 2003), international relations (Gray 1997; Keen 1998) and political theory (Munkler 2004) have embraced the new-wars paradigm. They all argue that violent conflicts since the end of the twentieth century are utterly different from their predecessors. The argument is that these new wars differ in terms of scope (civil rather than inter-state conflicts), methods, and models of financing (external rather than internal), and are characterised by low intensity coupled with high levels of brutality, with the deliberate targeting of civilians. These wars are seen to be on the increase, less restrained and more atrocious, hence dramatically increasing the number of civilians both killed and displaced. Furthermore, unlike the 'old wars' these new violent conflicts are premised on different fighting tactics (terror and guerrilla actions instead of conventional battlefields), different military strategies (population control rather than territory capture), utilise different combatants (private armies, criminal gangs and warlords instead of professional soldiers or conscripts) and are highly decentralised. The new wars are also seen as chaotic since they blur traditional divisions (legal vs. illegal, private vs. public, civilian vs. military, internal vs. external and local vs. global).

While the research emanating from the new-wars paradigm has proved highly beneficial in highlighting some distinctive features of civil wars during the 1990s, the subsequent cross-discipline empirical research has seriously challenged many of their claims. Firstly, although in recent times intra-state warfare has been more frequent than inter-state warfare, there is no causal relationship between the two. Not only do some wars start off as civil wars and, if successful for the warring side claiming independence, quickly become redefined as inter-state wars (from the American War of Independence to the Wars of Yugoslav Succession), but also many wars have elements of both, as most civil wars are fought with direct economic, political and military support from neighbouring states and global powers.[1] A typical example here is the so called Second Congo War (1998–2003), which involved eight African states and over twenty-five armed groups. However, much more damaging to the new-wars paradigm is the well-documented fact that both civil and inter-state wars have been in decline since the early 1990s (Gleditsch *et al.* 2002; Newman 2004; Harbom and Wallensteen 2005; Mack 2005). Thus, there is no evidence for the claimed proliferation of 'new' wars.

Secondly, there is no empirical foundation for the claim that recent conflicts are more violent either in terms of human casualties or levels of atrocity. As Lacina and Gleditsch (2005) demonstrate, there has actually been a significant decline in the number of battle deaths in the context of recent wars. Post-WWII conflicts reached their peak in the early 1950s, with almost 700,000 deaths per year, while the 1990s and the beginning of this century rarely witnessed wars accounting for more than 100,000 human casualties. Furthermore, the ratio of military and civilian deaths has not significantly changed in recent conflicts. The research of Melander *et al.* (2007) and Sollenberg (2007) clearly shows that in most recent wars, just as in their historical predecessors such as WWI and WWII, the civilian military death ratio rarely exceeded the 50/50 figure.[2] As for the intensity of atrocities, Melander *et al.* (2007: 33) have calculated that 'the post-Cold War era [is] significantly less atrocious than the Cold War era'. Although there was some increase in population displacement during the early 1990s, the magnitude of violence against civilians was significantly lower then in previous periods.

Thirdly, the uniqueness of the deliberate targeting of civilians and the use of terrorist and guerrilla tactics is also questionable. Newman (2004: 182) points out that earlier civil conflicts such as those of the Mexican Revolution (1910–1920) and the Congo Free State (1886–1908) were typical examples of wars where civilians were the primary target of violence. With the exception

---

[1] As Kalyvas (2006: 17) points out, this semantic conflict about how to term particular wars is part of war itself, as the use of terms such as civil or inter-state war are deeply contested by the parties involved, because they confer or deny legitimacy to their actions.

[2] For example the Bosnian War of 1992–1995 is singled out as typical of the new wars because civilian deaths were often seen as being highly disproportionate to those of the military. However as the most recent data collection indicates (Tokača 2007) the human casualties were not far off the standard 50/50 ratio with a slight majority of casualties on the military side (59 per cent vs. 41 per cent).

of the Rwandan genocide,[3] the 'new wars' have never reached the enormity of civilian bloodshed registered in the genocides of Herreros, Namaquas, Native Americans, Armenians or Jews in the Holocaust. Similarly, there is nothing new and exceptional in the reliance on terror threats and guerrilla warfare, as this was and remains an essential tactic of all civil wars – old and new (Kalyvas, 2001; 2006: 83).

What is evident from this brief summary is that cross-discipline research has demonstrated serious weaknesses in the new-wars paradigm. The critics have successfully challenged claims about the novelty of means, methods, strategies, tactics and the level of brutality of the 'new wars'. They have also convincingly demonstrated that recent conflicts do not significantly differ from conventional warfare in terms of human casualties or the civilian involvement ratio. However, what has rarely been challenged or carefully explored are the macro-level structural causes and the alleged transformation of the central goals of the 'new' warfare.[4] Even if specialist studies are able to demonstrate the empirical untenability of the new-wars paradigm through meticulous quantitative research, this still would not be enough to undermine the heuristic and interpretative potential of the paradigm. As Kuhn (1962) rightly argues, paradigms are conceptual worlds which allow us to think differently about the same research problem. They are non-cumulative and as such often incommensurable with previous or existing knowledge claims. Rather than complementing or falsifying each other, paradigms provide competing understandings of reality, which, if successful, reduce the old paradigms to a special case of a new paradigm. Replacing one paradigm by another often requires a scientific revolution. New paradigms are valuable as they open novel avenues of thinking, research and analysis and question the established canons. Moreover, conceptual models and theoretical approaches cannot be rebuffed simply on how well they meet the criteria of positivist science (Giddens 1976). All of this suggests that in order to explore the causes and the central objectives of the 'new wars', one has to engage with the stronger theoretical and explanatory models, that is, with the sociological articulations of the new-wars paradigm. The focus of an analysis should include both: how well the new-wars paradigm works as a novel interpretative frame but also how sound are the empirical claims on which this new interpretative frame is built.

---

[3] It is also highly debatable whether the Rwandan genocide of 1994 took place within or outside of war conditions.

[4] Kalyvas (2001) is a partial exception here, as his analysis is also focused on the causes and motivation of 'new wars'. However he only explores the arguments about civil wars and does not engage with high-tech warfare. Furthermore, his study is distinctly oriented towards the micro level and largely ignores the analysis of the macro-level structural causes and goals.

The sociology of new warfare

Although war has been and remains a largely neglected topic of contemporary sociological research, there have been a few recent conceptual, theoretical and empirical analyses most of which problematise the nature of contemporary conflicts. Political sociologists such as Martin Shaw (2002, 2003, 2005) and Mary Kaldor (2001, 2007) and Kaldor and Vashee (1997), and social theorists such as Zygmunt Bauman (2001, 2002a, 2002b) have been at the forefront of work on the new-wars paradigm. They too see these violent conflicts as historically novel in terms of methods, strategies, tactics and level of human sacrifice. However, they also differ from typical representatives of the new-wars paradigm in their focus on the broader macro-level sociological picture whereby the transformation in warfare is seen as a symptom of larger societal changes. The underlining causal factor in most of these accounts is the transformative power of economic globalisation. They distinguish between two typical forms that the new warfare takes: parasitic or predatory wars and technologically advanced Western-style warfare. Predatory wars emerge in the context of rampant economic liberalisation which undermines already weakened states, thus resulting in their virtual collapse. It is on the ruins of these failed states that the new parasitic wars emerge. In other words, inability to compete at the global level weakens the state's economy and simultaneously its capacity to extract revenue, thus opening the door to systematic corruption, criminality and, consequently, the general privatisation of violence. State failure creates a new Hobbesian environment where armed warlords control the remnants of state structures, and, relying on foreign remittances and international aid, invoke identity politics to spread terror among those deemed a threat to their religious or ethnic group.

The new technologically advanced Western-style wars have developed gradually but most of all through the recent revolution in military affairs (RMA), with the maturation of new technologies and novel military systems relying heavily on air power, the routinisation of precision and the ability to fight an adversary from a distance without suffering significant casualties. They too are seen as being principally linked to the global forces of economic liberalisation, as they are used to open up global markets and coerce opponents of the neo-liberal model of development.[5]

[5] While much of the non-sociological literature on the 'new wars' tends to treat these two forms of violent conflict (i.e. 'predatory wars' and 'high tech warfare') as highly distinct and even unrelated phenomena, most macro-level sociologists, including the authors discussed here, start from the proposition that they are deeply interlinked, being a part of the same processes of globalisation.

Hence, Zygmunt Bauman's (2000, 2002a, 2002b) analysis of the 'new wars' is situated in the context of a transition from the stable, solid and for the most part regulated modern order, towards an unregulated and principally chaotic liquid modernity. In his view, modernity was built on the Enlightenment's ideas of an ordered totality, favouring the elimination of randomness and ambivalence, and the privileging of compact territorial administrative organisation. In contrast to this, liquid modernity is extra-territorial, with the speed and mobility of global capital dissolving state borders as power shifts from the nation-state to global corporations. In this highly fluid world, as Bauman argues, most human beings operate as individualised consumers rather than citizens of their respective polities. Such a structural alteration generates two distinct but deeply interlinked forms of new warfare: globalising wars fought at a distance through technologically advanced weaponry, and globalisation-induced wars conducted in the void left by the collapse of old state structures (Bauman 2001). These two types of war erupt in the empty space that separates the co-ordinated machinery of global markets from the incoherent and disconnected forms of localised politics. As the era of liquid modernity advantages mobility over spatial control, the new wars are, in Bauman's view, not aimed at territorial conquest or ideological conversion, as was the case with the conflicts of the nineteenth and early twentieth century; instead, their goals stem from the economic logic of liquid modernity. For the globalising wars the central goal becomes 'the abolition of state sovereignty or neutralising its resistance potential' to accommodate the integration and co-ordination of the accelerated flow of global markets, whereas for the globalisation-induced warfare the aim is to reactively 'reassert the lost meaning of space' (Bauman 2001: 11).

The central argument is that liquid modernity generates new forms of insecurity, fear and threat that are extra-territorial and cannot be contained or resolved within the framework of nation-states (Bauman 2000; 2006). Rather, the space within which conflict is staged is open and fluid, with adversaries in a state of permanent mobility and with military coalitions floating and provisional. In Bauman's (2002a: 88, 2002b: 94–8) view, the most common form of fighting in this unregulated environment of the global frontier-land are reconnaissance battles, where soldiers are not ordered to capture the adversary's territory but 'to explore the enemy's determination and endurance, the resources the enemy can command and the speed with which such resources may be brought to the battlefield.' In other words, the new wars are hit-and-run affairs. Furthermore, the new globalising wars rely solely on professional, well-trained, armies of technical experts whose individualised service is treated similarly to other paid occupations and who perform their tasks with detached professionalism. For Bauman, (2001: 27) 'the times of mass conscript armies are over and so is the time of ideological mobilisation, patriotic ecstasies and 'dedication to the cause'.

Martin Shaw (2000, 2005) shares this view that globalisation has changed the nature of warfare for good. He also links the two forms of war by seeing them not as separate types but as asymmetrical products of the same globalising tendencies, together transforming the entire mode of warfare from the industrialised total war of the early twentieth century into a global surveillance mode of warfare. As does Bauman, he argues that these new wars no longer require mass armies or direct mass mobilisation. Whereas 'total warfare had the capacity to dominate society: it could override market relations, suppress democratic politics and capture media', global surveillance warfare is 'generally subordinate to economy, polity and culture' (Shaw 2005: 55). Although there are remnants of industrialised total warfare in all of this, such as 'national-militarist' (e.g. Russia, China and India) and 'ethnic-nationalist' states (e.g. some Balkan and African states), with conscript armies and mass-produced weapons, their actions are nonetheless constrained by global forces and local elites committed to 'integration into global markets and institutions' (Shaw 2005: 64). Shaw sees the new mode of Western warfare developing in reaction to the 'degeneracy of the twentieth century Western way of war' with its systematic killing of civilians and its genocidal projects (Shaw 2003: 4). The new wars emerge as the logic of nuclear proliferation weakened 'war-induced statism' and economic liberalisation spread around the globe.

In this context, he concentrates primarily on the 'new Western way of warfare' where the central issue is the transfer of risk. Drawing in part on Ulrich Beck's (1992, 1999) concept of the risk society as 'an inescapable structural condition of advanced industrialisation', Shaw (2005: 97) argues that risk exposure has replaced class as a central form of inequality in the late modern era and that this has profound implications on the theory and practice of contemporary warfare. According to Shaw these new risk-transfer wars are waged by the most technologically advanced states, which have undergone a successful revolution in military affairs (RMA) such as the USA and the UK. Their key war aim is minimising life-risks to Western military personnel and consequently minimising electoral and political risks to the state leadership, which is accomplished by transferring these risks directly to the weaker enemy.[6] From the Falklands War to the Gulf, Kosovo, Afghanistan and Iraq

---

[6] Heng (2006) develops a similar argument by linking Beck's concept of 'world risk society' with the recent international relations literature on the 'new wars'. He contends that the new 'high tech' wars are primarily concerned with the management of globalised systematic risks. Seeing globalisation as a

Wars, the reliance on technologically sophisticated weapons helps create the systematic transfer of risks from elected politicians to the military personnel and from them to the enemy combatants and their civilians. When the choice is between (foreign) civilian lives and the lives of Western soldiers, then the Western soldiers always have priority. The militarism of new wars does not require direct popular mobilisation, rather it aims to indirectly acquire passive support by relying on the media as a neutraliser of electoral surveillance. In his view the goals of new wars are rarely ideological or nationalist but are principally policy-driven and instrumental – 'war is justified only as a response to a manifest threat', that is when there is a 'plausible perceptions of risk to Western interests, norms and values' (Shaw 2003: 71–2). As such, new wars acquire electoral legitimacy only when they are limited, sanitised, quick-fix affairs taking place in distant parts of the world.

Like Bauman and Shaw, Mary Kaldor (2001, 2004, 2007) posits globalisation as a key cause of new wars. In her understanding, the 'globalisation of the 1980s and 1990s is a qualitatively new phenomenon' that emerged as 'a consequence of the revolution in information technologies and dramatic improvements in communication and data-processing'. This has revolutionised military technology but even more importantly has produced 'a revolution in the social relations of warfare' (Kaldor 2001: 3). Although Kaldor shares Bauman's and Shaw's belief that there are two dominant forms of new warfare, the focal point of her analysis is predatory wars, rather than what she calls 'American high tech wars'. These new wars arise as the autonomy of the state, especially its economy, is eroded by the global forces of economic neo-liberalism. As the revenues of the weakened states decline, they experience gradual or total erosion of their monopoly on the legitimate use of coercion, with the result that the means of violence is privatised and acquired by criminal warlords. Using paramilitaries and the remnants of collapsing state structures, they politicise cultural differences and wage genocidal wars on civilians while at the same time acquiring personal wealth and maintaining a hold on power. As one of the pioneers of this paradigm, Kaldor articulates an exceptionally strong version of the new-war thesis whereby the recent violent conflicts differ in every respect from conventional warfare – from their strategy, tactics, methods of fighting, the increased levels of bloodshed, the chaotic nature of the conflicts to rampant asymmetry in the civil–military

key driver of global economic and security developments, Heng argues that recent 'Anglo-American' wars, from Kosovo to Afganistan and Iraq, were all 'driven by a perceived globalisation of risks' (2006: 70–2).

ratio of human casualties. She also emphasises the facts that new wars are highly decentralised, thrive on the availability of cheap light weaponry and are heavily dependent on external financial resources such as diaspora remittances and international humanitarian aid, which often help create or reinforce the new globalised war economy. Nevertheless, what is central in her argument is the view that new wars are fought for very different reasons than previous conflicts. As she puts it: 'the goals of the new wars are about identity politics in contrast to the geopolitical or ideological goals of earlier wars' (Kaldor 2001: 6). In this view, 'identity politics' differs from ideology, as it makes power claims on the basis of mutually exclusive group labels rather than coherent systems of ideas. Kaldor (2001: 7) views these label claims as parasitic and fragmentary: 'Unlike the politics of ideas which are open to all and therefore tend to be integrative, this type of identity politics is inherently exclusive and therefore tends to fragmentation.' Just as Bauman, she argues that geopolitical motives play no part, as territory loses its previous significance. Instead, the new wars tend towards the expulsion of the civilian population: 'the aim is to control the population by getting rid of everyone of a different identity' (Kaldor 2001: 8).

Warfare between the nation-state and globalisation

Sociological accounts of the new-wars paradigm provide a more potent and theoretically coherent understanding and interpretation of recent violent conflicts. Instead of adopting a narrow and particularist view, abstracting recent wars from the broader social and historical context, these sociological analyses successfully situate these conflicts within macro-level structural changes. New wars do not emerge in a social and historical vacuum but are integral to the wider transformations of modernity, and in particular to the worldwide expansion of globalisation. What one encounters here is truly an attempt at a paradigm shift in a classical Kuhnian sense: to understand recent conflicts it is not enough to account for precise factual variations. Rather, this paradigm shift entails a new understanding of social reality. In this context Bauman, Shaw and Kaldor engage more thoroughly with the central questions, such as: What are the social causes of new wars? And why and how have the central goals of warfare changed? It is primarily in the answers to these questions that one can assess the explanatory strength and weaknesses of the new-wars paradigm.

However, despite the illuminative and elegant responses that these sociological theories offer, their central arguments are built on shaky foundations.

Even if the earlier criticisms that centred on tactics, strategy, human casualties, financing or methods of fighting are completely discounted in favour of assessing the paradigm as a heuristic model on its own terms, the theory of new wars fails to convince.

Firstly, linking recent wars so tightly to the forces of economic globalisation is a form of structuralist economic reductionism which attributes too much power to market forces. Historically, wars were initiated and fought for a variety of reasons – ideological, geopolitical, economic or ecological – and have had origins in both human agency and social structure (Howard 1976; McNeill 1982; Keegan 1994; Joas 2003). This is as much the case with contemporary wars which also depend on historical contingencies and a confluence of different factors. Not all groups, organisations and individuals involved directly or indirectly in these violent conflicts are motivated by the maximisation of economic resources (P. Smith 2005; Gat 2006). Similarly, structural transformations in the world economy do not affect weaker states equally, and some not at all. This economistic argument cannot explain why some states such as Somalia, Bosnia and Georgia found themselves on the verge of collapse in the context of brutal civil wars, while others, whose economies have been undermined by global trade to a greater extent such as many Asian, African and Latin American states, have avoided excessively violent conflicts.

Furthermore, the perception that the expansion of liberalised markets automatically means less regulation and more chaotic arrangements is a common misperception. As Steven Vogel's (1996) important study of economic reform patterns in such sectors as telecommunications, finance, broadcasting, transport and utilities in the USA, UK, Japan, France and Germany shows, freer markets have actually led to more administrative regulation. Despite loud proclamations to the contrary, in most cases liberalisation does not mean the loss of state autonomy. Instead, most states combine the opening-up of markets with tighter regulation. As Vogel (1996: 5) puts it, 'there is no logical contradiction between more competition and greater government control ... a movement aimed at reducing regulation has only increased it; a movement propelled by global forces has reinforced national differences; and a movement purported to push back the state has been led by the state itself'. What this tells us is that economic forces and markets do not work on their own. Instead, powerful states release economic forces, and even in such tight economic and monetary associations as the European Union, the calculations of leading states in negotiating political and economic deals still remain central to the decision-making process (Hall 2006). Hence, we may live in liquid modernity but this is still a fairly regulated environment.

Consequently, the milieu of contemporary wars is no more chaotic than that of their predecessors.

Secondly, to establish a causal link between contemporary wars and growing economic liberalisation one would have to prove that the patterns and dynamics of world trade have dramatically changed, and that this change has affected transformations in warfare. However both of these claims are untenable.

The argument that economic globalisation is a historically unprecedented phenomenon has been challenged by many historical sociologists. For example Hirst and Thompson (1999), Mann (1997, 2003) and Hall (2000, 2002) among others have demonstrated that the existing levels of trade for North America, Japan and the European Union of 12 per cent of their GDP are almost the same as the levels reached before WWI. Over 80 per cent of the world's total production remains traded within the borders of nation-states (Mann 2001). Most so called transnational corporations are really national companies whose ownership, assets, sales and profits remain within nation-states. They chiefly rely on the domestic human capital generated through their own educational systems, existing national communications infrastructure and a substantial deal of state protectionism for externally vulnerable economic sectors (Carnoy 1993; Wade 1996). The technology is also mostly produced on the national level while an overwhelming majority of companies remain traded solely on national stock markets. Rather than being global, world trade is distinctly 'trilateral' with the US, Japan and Europe producing and consuming more than 85 per cent of world trade (Mann 1997; Hall 2000). In other words, contrary to the arguments of the new-wars paradigm, economic globalisation does not diminish the influence of the nation-states. Instead, it is the most powerful nation-states that are the backbone of world trade. As Mann (1997: 48) puts it: 'capitalism retains a geo-economic order, dominated by the economies of the advanced nation-states. Clusters of nation-states provide the stratification order of globalism'. In addition, nation-states remain in full control of their population, since human beings are much less mobile than goods, money and services, and despite the expansion of international law the nation-state preserves a monopoly of law over its territory (Hirst and Thompson 1999).[7]

The second claim is yet more problematic. Even if one disregards the fact that there is no direct evidence that economic globalisation causes an

---

[7] As Hirst and Thompson (1999: 277) conclude: 'nation-states as sources of the rule of law are essential prerequisites for regulation through international law, and as overarching public powers they are essential to the survival of pluralistic 'national' societies with diversified forms of administration and community standards'.

increase in violent intra-state conflicts, thus concentrating solely on indirect influence, it is not difficult to show the obvious flaws in this argument. Not only does the empirical research prove civil warfare to be in decline, so that if globalisation has any effect this could only be interpreted as a factor that diminishes violence, but more importantly, the privatisation of violence existed as much in the pre-global era as it does now. As Kalyvas (2006: 333) and Newman (2004: 183–4) rightly point out, a similar pattern of chaotic war-lordism, criminality and privatised violence was witnessed long before the current era in, for example, the Greek Civil War of 1943–1949, the Nigeria-Biafra Civil War and the Congo Civil War of the early 1960s. Not only does the 'globalised war economy' fail to explain more protracted conflicts such as those in Chechnya, Sri Lanka, the Basque country and Indonesia, but even the conflicts that are seen to epitomise the new wars, such as those in the Balkans, the Horn of Africa and the Caucasus, in many respects predate or have developed outside of the forces of economic liberalism. The origins of the Yugoslav Wars of Succession had very little, if anything, to do with economic globalisation. They started off not as economic but as political conflicts, created in part by party elites attempting to avoid genuine democratisation through decentralisation, and in part by the idiosyncratic federal organisation of the communist state (Malešević 2002; 2006: 157–84).

The views expressed by Bauman and Kaldor, that the new wars have lost geopolitical significance as 'the era of space' is over, and that territory has little meaning in the new globalised wars, is equally untenable. Firstly, this argument is built on an overstretched and stark comparison between early modern nation-states and late modern and post-modern polities, where the former are depicted as tightly bound, highly centralised and bureaucratic, in full control of their territory, economy and population, whereas the latter are presented as the exact opposite. In this view, early modernity is associated exclusively with economically and politically autarchic nation-states obsessed with territorial expansion, while the contemporary era is seen as one of global economic interdependence and integration. However, as Tilly (1975), Downing (1992), Ertman (1997), Mann (1986, 1993) and many other historical sociologists have shown, the post-Westphalian nation-states have emerged and developed in the context of two rival forces: international trade and political and military competition. Rather than being isolated autarchies, nation-states have grown in response to the changing geopolitical environment by tightening fiscal control and by extending citizenship rights. Commercial developments and increased trade have strengthened the capacity of the state, making it in this process a more powerful military machine. In other words, transnational economic space is neither novel nor unconnected to the birth of the nation-state. The administrative and territorial boundness of the early nation-states had always more to do with the rulers' projected ideals than actual reality. In most respects the rise in infrastructural and surveillance powers is something more associated with contemporary nation-states, as they have only recently been able to fully police their borders, tax at source, gather intelligence on all of their citizens and successfully control their territories.

Furthermore, military might still remains the only reliable guarantor of economic wellbeing in the long term, as all three economic powerhouses – the USA, European Union and Japan – have developed and continue to prosper economically on the back of American military supremacy, which provides geopolitical stability and security in the North. Although most Northern states have moved away from what Mann (1997) calls 'hard geopolitics' to 'soft geopolitics' this is not the case for the rest of the world. Universal conscription is still the order of the day in the great majority of states with most states in Africa, Latin America, Eastern Europe and Asia (including the two superpowers: China and Russia) having compulsory military service.[8] Indeed, it would be highly premature to see it as a thing of the past in the West either, as the proponents of the new-wars paradigm claim. Nearly all states reserve the right to reintroduce conscription in the case of major war. Historically speaking, we have been here before: the so-called long peace of 1870–1914 witnessed the dominance of similar 'pacifist' theories which saw economics replacing geopolitics (J. A. Hobson (1901); Angel 2007 [1909]; Lenin 1939 [1916]). However, even if the militaries of most Western and Westernising states have been reduced in size, the state's monopoly on the legitimate use of violence has been strengthened even further with the continuous expansion of police forces, surveillance apparatuses and a variety of private and state-controlled security agencies (Dandeker 1990; Lyon 2001).

What has changed in the post-colonial era is not the alleged unimportance of space but the illegitimacy of territorial conquest. In fact, space is now more important than ever before as it is institutionalised and taken for granted by nearly everybody that state borders cannot be changed at will. As US soldiers quickly realised when they initially placed the Star Spangled Banner on Saddam Hussein's statue, and then had to promptly replace it with the Iraqi flag, it is impossible to legitimately capture the territory of another sovereign nation-state. This is a powerful reminder that the internal spatial monopoly

---

[8] Although the abolition of the military draft has dramatically increased in the last two decades there are still only thirty-two states in the world without mandatory military service.

on the use of violence defined through the idea of territorial sovereignty remains the indisputable norm of international relations. While initially this principle was understood as a prerogative of statesmen and political elites, the cumulative bureaucratisation of coercion and centrifugal ideologisation have transformed it over the last two centuries into a mass phenomenon. In other words, the inviolability of territorial integrity has become ideologically and organisationally so ingrained that any attempt to break this rule is swiftly and widely delegitimised and sanctioned. If late, or in Bauman's words liquid, modernity is an era where one can transcend space – a view deeply contested here – this cannot happen through the simplified globalist formula of 'geography becoming history' but only when territorial sovereignty becomes so institutionalised, routinised and taken for granted that it becomes an unalienable right that few would dare to challenge. The obvious sacredness of state territory is clearly evident in numerous cases, including the Falklands episode when Britain quickly went to war over a faraway depopulated island, the Gulf War where the Iraqi infringement of Kuwaiti sovereignty provoked almost unanimous outrage, the devastating Chechen wars, and the still unresolved disputes between Russia and Japan over the Kuril Islands, Britain and Spain over Gibraltar, and Greece and Turkey over Cyprus and many uninhabited rocks of the Aegean Sea. No state authority, democratic or autocratic, huge or small, developed or underdeveloped is likely ever to give up lightly even a tiny stretch of its territory. From medieval times, when waging war was the sole privilege of kings and aristocrats, through to the mid nineteenth century, when Russian Tsar Alexander II sold Alaska to the USA in 1867 for 7.2 million dollars (Jensen 1975), rulers could divide, trade and cede territory without much popular resistance. Today, the success of the two historical processes, the cumulative bureaucratisation of coercion and centrifugal ideologisation, have made such bargains nearly impossible. Neither the social organisation of the modern nation-state nor the ideological potency of nationalism, widespread and ingrained throughout the social order, permits territorial concessions without public humiliation. And this leads us directly to the second issue – the supposedly changed goals of contemporary warfare.

The objectives of contemporary wars

The proponents of the new-war paradigm are adamant that what sets contemporary wars apart from their predecessors is the unequivocal transformation of objectives and goals. The new violent conflicts are no longer about ideology, or nationalism in particular, but about identity (Kaldor), the economic logic of globalisation (Bauman) or perceptions of risk to Western interests and norms (Shaw). In their own words: 'nation-building coupled with patriotic mobilisation has ceased to be the principal instrument of social integration and states' self-assertion' (Bauman 2002a: 84); 'in the context of globalisation, ideological and/or territorial cleavages of an earlier era have increasingly been supplanted by an emerging cleavage between … cosmopolitanism, based on inclusive, universalist multicultural values, and the politics of particularist identities' (Kaldor 2001: 6); and it is 'a specifically late-modern, Western perception' that 'war is justified only as a response to a manifest threat' (Shaw 2005: 71–2).

Kaldor's strict distinction between identity and ideology is untenable, as the discourse of identity is nearly always embedded in the rhetoric of a specific ideology. In other words, claims to a particular or universal identity such as German, Sikh, policewoman, Maori, gay or cosmopolitan are premised on distinctive political projects of what it means to be a particular German, Sikh, policewoman, Maori, gay or cosmopolitan individual. As there is never just one way of how somebody can be a member of a particular group, the identitarian language of collective solidarity is inherently political: it speaks in the terms of cultural authenticity but it acts through political projects (Brubaker 2004; Malešević 2006). The argument that, unlike ideology, which espouses systematic ideas, identity is only about group labels, equally does not stand. From Barthes (1993) and Althusser (1994) we know only too well that ideology works best through hailing or interpellation of group labels, by caging individuals in particular 'identities'. More importantly, group labels can have popular resonance only if seen as integral to a specific political project. Despite evident diversities in the content of normative ideologies throughout the world, the process of centrifugal ideologisation operates similarly: the ideological message radiates from the centre and back by adopting and constantly re-articulating its key principles. In this sense, there is no significant difference here between today's depictions of the citizens of Iraq as mutually exclusive Shia, Sunni and Kurds, and yesteryears' socialist rhetoric of proletariat and bourgeoisie locked together in an uncompromising class war. They both invoke group labels as a part of a concrete ideological project to justify a specific political course of action, including warfare, and to mobilise popular support. Ethnic, religious and nationalist ideologies are grounded in systematic programmes just as much as the 'old' ideologies of socialism, liberalism and conservatism. There is no substantial ontological difference between those political projects that aim to implement a blueprint of a classless social order and those bent on setting up an ethno-nationally pure society. In other words, there is no identity without ideology and no ideology can successfully mobilise mass support without constructing meaningful group labels. In this respect, the objectives and rhetoric of new wars have not significantly changed, as they all have to rely on nationalist imagery to foster mass support. The historically ongoing process of centrifugal mass, ideologisation does not stop with economic globalisation.

The problem is that in Kaldor's economistic view, nationalism is never seen as an original generator of social action, but always as a second-order reality, a reactive force to some other supposedly primary cause such as globalisation (Kaldor 2001: 76, 78–9). Analysing the Bosnian War of 1992–1995 as the epitome of new war, she argues that the central aims were not ideological or geopolitical but identity-based – to ethnically cleanse a population of the 'other identity'. This view confuses means and ends, since ethnic cleansing and genocide are rarely, if ever, ends in themselves, but are rather means through which particular ideological projects are implemented. The ethnic cleansing in Bosnia was definitely not a chaotic, decentralised and spontaneous reaction of local warlords. Instead, as recent research clearly shows (Čekić 1999; Oberschall 2000; Ron 2003), it was a highly structured, well-organised, meticulously documented process that relied on existing centralised state structures, from the top political and military leadership in Serbia and Croatia to the municipal executive committees, mayors' offices, local police, the municipal territorial defence organisation and the so-called crisis committees that acted as the principal tools of the euphemistically termed 'population exchange'. In the Bosnian case, just as in other recent wars, the 'old', geopolitical, organisational and ideological motives predominated, that is, the key goals were the capture of a particular territory in order to implement distinct political goals by establishing a Greater Serbia and Croatia. The fact that the post-WWII international order does not tolerate territorial conquests any more is one of the principal reasons why the Yugoslav conflict was externally seen as a throwback to the past, an irrational attachment to primordial 'labels' rather than what it actually was – an organised seizing of territory in order to fulfil a specific ideological project. In this context, as Kalyvas (2001), Newman (2004) and Berdal (2003) rightly argue, what has changed is not the nature of warfare itself but the Western perception of war.

Similarly, Bauman's view of liquid modernity as an era that transcends the bounded space, where global capital dominates nation-states, and where consumerism overpowers nationalism, is misplaced. The interests of global corporations can sometimes overlap with the ideology and the geopolitical motives of powerful states but the two are not causally linked. The so-called 'globalising' wars are almost exclusively fought by a single state, the USA, which, as much as any social organisation or nation-state in modern history, pursues its own geopolitical and ideological goals. As Mann (2001b, 2003) rightly emphasises, unlike US military might, US economic power is not hegemonic over its European and Japanese rivals, as they are all 'back-seat drivers' of the contingencies and fluctuations rooted in worldwide capitalist development. While the Gulf War of 1991 was fought to restore the status quo, thus potentially benefitting the further spread or dominance of Western-based global corporations, all other 'globalising' wars such as Kosovo, Afghanistan and Iraq were initiated and fought much more for ideological and geopolitical reasons than for reasons arising from global economic logic. Obviously, neither impoverished and desolate Afghanistan nor small and remote Serbia were ideal new markets worth fighting over. In both cases there was a central motive for war that originated in a sense of wounded national pride (hence nationalism) either because a superpower was attacked on its own soil (9/11), or because some minor autocrat dared to resist the will of the powerful Western states. Both of these wars were motivated by the desire to achieve ideological conversion and in fact they have succeeded in this by managing to replace the rigid Islamists of the Taliban and the autocratic nationalists around Milošević with more moderate political regimes. The motivation behind the Iraq War is perhaps more complicated, as it also involved economic motives (the control of oil reserves) which could have benefitted global corporations, but even this motive had more to do with the requirements of a particular social organisation or nation-state rooted in its ambition of geopolitical control of resources (and security) rather than in the opening-up of new markets for the global economy. Furthermore, ideological motives loomed large too, as the war was in part an attempt to implement a specific neo-conservative blueprint (including 'Rebuilding America's Defenses' and other proposals developed by the highly influential think tank the Project for the New American Century) (Mann 2003: 3; P. Smith 2005: 164). In all three cases the wars relied on strong popular support. While in Kosovo and Afghanistan, nationalism was supplemented with the broader international 'humanitarian' and 'just cause' rhetoric, thus extending the wars' national support bases, the war in Iraq was politically divisive in the international arena, thus reinforcing US nationalism and having to rely almost exclusively on it. To put it simply, the aims of 'globalising' wars have not substantially changed, since ideology and the geopolitical motives of the specific social organisations remain as important as ever.

Although Shaw provides a more compelling account that recognises the importance of territorial organisation and geopolitics, he too sees new wars as being subordinate to economic and other global forces. In his account of risk transfer, the distinction between the Western and non-Western worlds and the corresponding forms of warfare is overstretched. Albeit technological sophistication and dependence on precision targeting and air power is obviously a historical novelty, it is not a global development but something that symbolises the strength of a particular nation-state – the USA. In his analysis of recent 'global surveillance wars' nearly all conflicts, with the exception of the short, small and rather atypical Falklands War, were fought principally if not exclusively by US military power. In other words, the transfer of risks is not that much of a Western phenomenon (although it has some resonance in the UK and a few other European states) as it is a phenomenon of a distinct social organisation or nation-state – the USA. In this sense the USA is a true military empire, as it is the only state that has a military presence in 153 countries of the world, and has the technical know-how, re-fuelling facilities, laser-guided missiles, aircraft-carrier ships, etc. to impose its military hegemony throughout the world. As Mann (2001b: 6) puts it: 'No state would rationally seek war with the US, and few could survive it … this is American, not Northern, military hegemony. It is not at the service of Northern economic imperialism. It is only at the service of interests defined by American governments.' This is important in the context of popular support, as Shaw argues that Western-style global warfare no longer requires direct mass mobilisation, preferring instead the media-induced mobilisation of passivity. However, this is another case of chronocentrism, as it attempts to generalise on the basis of a very short historical period. Whereas an enormous superpower such as the USA can rely on a professional army to fight small wars with relatively few casualties, paying little attention to internal dissent, major wars with potential for substantial casualties still require the same level of direct mobilisation as before. Both the Vietnam War and the Iraq War illustrate this only too well. To fight a protracted large conflict, even the most powerful states have to contemplate reintroducing conscription and if necessary overriding economics, domestic politics and cultural life. The so-called 'war on terror' clearly indicates how 'economy, polity and culture' can easily become subordinated to war aims and how banal nationalism can quickly transform into a virulent battle cry and crusade against the Other. The speed and congressional unanimity with which the Patriot Act was passed, with little if any popular dissent in the aftermath of 9/11, is a potent reminder of how quickly the social organisation or nation-state can assume firm control over society. Hence, it is not the perception of a threat to 'Western interests and values' that motivates public support, it is primarily the ideology of nationalism in all its guises that secures popular mobilisation and it is a geopolitical logic that dictates the conduct of nation-states. The USA is no exception here; it is just a much bigger and more powerful social organisation than has ever inhabited this planet.

What is old and what is new?

Despite its explanatory pitfalls, the sociology of 'new wars' has opened up an important area of research and has raised novel questions about the nature of recent violent conflicts. Most of all, these sociological accounts place the new-wars debate in the wider social and historical context, thus attempting to link the changing forms of violence with the transformations of modernity. To argue that the causes and objectives of contemporary warfare do not significantly differ from their pre-global era predecessors does not automatically imply that nothing has changed. On the contrary, the historical setting of the post-WWII world has been substantially transformed, as the traditional geopolitical goals of nation-states, such as territorial expansion, colonial domination and imperial conquest, have lost their legitimacy, both at the national and especially at the international level. This is even more the case with some of the principal normative ideologies of the twentieth such as state socialism, eugenics and scientific racism, fascist corporatism and the imperial civilising mission. Contemporary warfare clearly emerges in a different historical milieu and as such its goals and aims are shaped and restricted by these macro-level structural forces. Regardless of its military or economic might, no state can legitimately invade the territories of other states or treat the citizens of those states as a culturally or racially inferior species. Furthermore, the revolution in military affairs is a novel development that allows a military superpower, such as the USA, to rely extensively on sophisticated technology to put coercive pressure on unco-operative governments and to fight small and medium-range hit-and-run wars. However, neither of these two new developments has substantially changed the causes and objectives of warfare. While new technology has to some extent transformed the means of fighting, such as minimising military casualties by relying on the relative precision of airpower and missile navigation in short and limited wars, it has not changed the ends of warfare.[9]

Similarly, the new social and historical context has constrained the actions of, particularly Northern, nation-states by forcing them to adopt the soft geopolitics of bargaining, enticement and occasional coercive pressure and give up the hard geopolitics of spatial conquest, but it has not dented the 'old' multiple causes of violent conflicts. Just as in the nineteenth and twentieth centuries, wars are initiated and fought for ecological, economic, political but most of all for ideological and organisational or geopolitical reasons. An acceleration of economic globalisation perhaps adds another layer of complexity and constraint to the 'old' ideological and geopolitical motives of nation-states, but it could not possible obliterate either these motives or the nation-states themselves. Not only is it the case that more extensive economic integration requires more administrative state regulation, but it is also true that, without the powerful nation-states that provide geopolitical stability, global economic expansion and incorporation would evaporate in a quasi-Darwinian world of anarchic brutality.

Finally, the popular support on which modern conflicts have to build if they are to have any chance of success is still largely derived from the same ideological, nationalist sources as before. Since the birth of modernity in the French and American Revolutions, the Enlightenment and Romanticism, nationalism has been and remains the principal glue of legitimate rule (Gellner 1983; A. D. Smith 2003; Malešević 2006; 2007). Having powerful protean capacity, nationalism is able to accommodate modern political formations as diverse as liberal democracies, state socialist orders, contemporary monarchies and military juntas as well as the theocratic states. No state authority is likely to generate a significant support base without invoking the solidaristic images of 'our glorious nation'. Even though nationalism has become less virulent in the North when compared to the early twentieth century, no political leader or political party can survive long in office if deemed to be insufficiently patriotic. The fact that the aggressive, militarist and jingoistic nationalisms of the two world wars have given way to banal and softer

---

[9] However even the impact of superior technology is relative in the historical context. As Biddle (2004: 23, 58–9) shows, the astonishing technological developments in the military sector have had little or no impact on success in wars throughout the twentieth century: 'From 1900 to 1990, weapon platforms' nominal speed increased by more than a factor of ten, yet armies' average rate of advance remained virtually at levels little changed since Napoleon's day … None of the major lethality increases since 1918, whether direct fire, artillery, or air-delivered weapons, has been as effective against covered as exposed targets … the principles today's armies must use to survive are the same as 1918s.'

counterparts, does not suggest, as proponents of the new-wars paradigm argue, that nationalism as such is on the wane. Rather, as the infrastructural capacities of modern nation-states expand further, the habitual character and routinised nature of its reproduction ensures that the nation-centric view of the world is perpetually normalised and naturalised in the mass media, educational systems, the institutions of 'high' culture, the state administration systems, outlets of popular culture, youth organisations, civil society groups and even internet websites. All of these make nationalism a powerful ideological force of everyday life; a force available for swift mobilisation in times of major conflict. As Billig (1995) tellingly observes, banality does not equal lenience. On the contrary, in reproducing state structures and institutions that possess immense armaments which can be rapidly utilised, banal nationalism can easily and quickly be transformed into a baby-faced killer.

Conclusion

Despite the popular perception that organised violence is as old as the human species, in historical terms, warfare is a relatively recent phenomenon. Once we conceptually decouple individual aggression from the sociological processes of war and collective violence, it is possible to realise that a great majority of our predecessors were not involved in these brutal practices. Since for 99 per cent of their history, *Homines sapientes* have lived in tiny, egalitarian, nomadic hunting and gathering bands that lacked social organisation and normative cohesion, they had neither the means nor the interest or will to engage in protracted violent conflicts. Hence, rather than being a throwback to the primitive past, organised violence is a direct product of social development. As Eckhardt's (1992: 3) comprehensive data sets demonstrate well, civilisation and warfare emerged together and the 'later civilisations have been more militaristic than earlier civilisations, regardless of population'. In contrast to Elias's (2000 [1939]) diagnosis, rather than taming our supposedly innate aggressiveness, the civilising process in fact creates institutional conditions for the proliferation of violence on a much grander scale. Since neither biological composition nor cultural upbringing prepare human beings for violent acts, the only reliable way to make men and women engage or support fighting, killing and dying is to utilise the mobilising and justifying powers of social organisations and ideologies. Without organised action and the doctrines that legitimise such action there would be no warfare.

This is not to say that either social organisations or ideologies are superhuman forces that determine how we think or act. Rather, they are both creations of the ongoing social actions of thousands and millions of individuals and, as such, they remain dependent on human agency. The point is that the cumulative character of these powers puts severe constraint on their possible transformation: while one can work towards overthrowing a despotic government, replacing one political order with another or splitting the existing social formation into two or more, it is much more difficult, and often nearly impossible, to dismantle entire social organisations such as nation-states, militaries, mega corporations and police forces. However, even when this is possible, as contemporary Somalia or the Democratic Republic of Congo illustrate so well, it is not something that most people would desire, as the loss of monopoly on the legitimate use of violence over a particular territory only leads to incessant warfare with violent attempts to re-establish that monopoly. As in Plato's allegory of the cave, once you see the actual sun and understand that human shadows do not constitute real beings there is no turning back. Any attempt to dispense with warfare and organised violence has to start from the fact that we cannot recreate the world of early hunters and gatherers, nor can we abolish existing organisational and ideological powers. For one thing, these are the very same powers that provide security and safety, economic growth and social wellbeing for millions of individuals worldwide. For another, coercive power operates in a similar way to accumulated energy: it can be confined, controlled, concealed, removed from one place to another and transformed into a completely different form but it can never be obliterated. Any attempt to disperse already accumulated coercive powers would itself depend on the very use of these same powers, thus inevitably creating conditions for even greater bloodshed. As the Jacobin Reign of Terror, the October Revolution and the Khmer Rouge's regime illustrate so well, the movements and social organisations armed with ideologies that loudly advocate radical egalitarianism, absolute justice and the dispersion of coercive powers are likely to end up as the most violent of all.

Similarly, once in (historical) motion there is no escape from centrifugal ideologisation either. In secularised, though not necessarily secular, modernity, where everyday life is dependent on the regular use of different and often mutually exclusive semantic discourses and where literacy is a norm, all interpretations of social and political reality are necessarily ideological. Furthermore, since ideological messages are constantly disseminated from diverse sources in different ways and target a variety of audiences, there is an ideological cacophony in modernity that persistently creates popular 'ideological dilemmas' and 'contradictions of common sense' (Billig *et al.* 1988), which are often resolved violently. However, since living in the predominately semantic world of modern times implies a substantial degree of political literacy too, every social and political act presumes the existence of a particular ideological coating. In other words, since no social and political events and processes speak for themselves, there is a need to use particular ideological matrices to interpret such situations. Here too, just as with the bureaucratisation of coercion, those people that fiercely invoke ideological neutrality and cold objectivity are often the most ideological of all. As the Frankfurt School sociologists (Marcuse 1964; Adorno and Horkheimer 1972) noticed long ago, precisely because science and technology have acquired a nearly indisputable position in modernity, and in this process have managed to delegitimise other discourses by establishing themselves as the principal sources of legitimate authority, they have acquired unprecedented ideological powers. A mother wrongly accused of killing her own baby ends up publicly ostracised, imprisoned and emotionally broken on the basis of a single testimony by an 'expert witness'. In addition, as Barthes (1977, 1993) demonstrates in many of his studies, ideological power increases with invisibility: the things, meanings and processes that are deemed normal, natural and ordinary are rarely questioned. Hence, rather than fabricating reality, centrifugal ideologisation is a process that purifies meanings by making them innocent and obvious. We don't question what we see as normal and natural. And this is the ultimate ambition of every ideological discourse: to become invisible through normalisation and habitual acts.

Hence, the most realistic way to contain bureaucratic and ideological power is not to try to dismantle social organisations or to suppress ideological discourses but to work on their proliferation with a view to keeping a balance between the different organisational layers and ideological movements. Instead of less bureaucracy and fewer ideologies, it seems reasonable to have more competing social organisations and ideological doctrines of equal or similar strength that can counterbalance and challenge each other without allowing either the emergence of a single hegemonic entity or an anarchic dissolution into war-lordism. The example of the European Union shows how adding another organisational layer can help prevent the dominance of a single, historically war-prone social organisation that is the nation-state. Thus, instead of working towards replacing nation-states with global entities or opposing the existence of such supranational entities, it seems more reasonable to stimulate the proliferation of stable and durable social organisations on various levels: from the local, regional, national, continental to global and beyond.

Living in twenty-first century Europe or North America can give a person a sense that organised violence and ideology are less relevant today than in previous epochs. However this is only an illusion. In fact this perception is a direct outcome of the processes that have been unfolding over the last several millennia: the cumulative bureaucratisation of coercion and centrifugal ideologisation. The fact that the northern part of the globe enjoys such stability, prosperity and peacefulness has nothing to do with the alleged gradual and widespread realisation that war and violence are barbaric practices not worthy of advanced modernity; since historical processes rarely change through popular perceptions alone, this outcome is no different. If it were not for the cumulative bureaucratisation of coercion and centrifugal ideologisation, we would not be where we are now. The illusion that we live in a less barbaric and less ideology-ridden world stems from the chronocentric perception of social reality that pays little attention to the fact that this peaceful state is historically specific and hence a temporary condition. It is a condition grounded in the peculiar geopolitical reality whereby the organisational monopoly on violence coupled with the soft ideological hegemony (and the political and economic dominance) of the victors in the WWII have helped pacify the northern part of the globe. The rest of the world – where the ideological and organisational struggle is still very visible – cannot afford such illusory perceptions.

Hence, when mainstream sociologists study gender, stratification, nationalism and solidarity without making any reference to organised coercion or warfare, such analyses are bound not only to remain reductionist and incomplete, but are also likely to produce inaccurate explanations of social reality. As repeatedly argued in this book, neither organised coercion nor the social can be properly explained without the careful study of their interaction. Just as warfare and violence are first and foremost sociological phenomena and cannot be adequately addressed without the use of sociological tools, the same applies to human subjectivity, which can never be properly understood without engaging with one of its key historical constituents – organised violence. Although the links between the two are not always easily discernible, it is our job as sociologists to find these connections and explain why they are important. The fact that something is not obvious should make it even more relevant for our analysis, since sociology is primarily the study of the non-obvious. As Collins (1992: 188) puts it: 'The best sociology is like a hidden treasure chest. Most people don't know much sociology beyond the most obvious … Non-obvious sociology pulls some insights out of the treasure chest, letting us see the underlying conditions that are moving us, and giving us the chance to steer our course instead of just blindly drifting.' It is precisely this non-obviousness that makes the bureaucratisation of coercion and centrifugal ideologisation so invisible yet so pervasive.

References

Adams, D. B. 1983. 'Why There are so Few Women Warriors', *Behaviour Science Research*, **18**(3): 1–13.

Addis, E., Russo, V. and Sebesta, L. (eds.) 1994. *Women Soldiers: Images and Realities*. New York: St. Martin's Press.

Adorno, T. and Horkheimer, M. 1972. *Dialectic of Enlightenment*. New York: Herder and Herder.

Adshead, S. A. M. 1995. *China in World History*. New York: St. Martin's Press.

Ahmad, A. and Wilke, A. S. 1973. 'Peace and War Themes in Social Science Periodicals: 1946 to Present', *Journal of Political and Military Sociology*, **1**: 39–56.

Aho, J. A . 1975. *German Realpolitik and American Sociology*. London: Associated University Presses.

1979. 'The Protestant Ethic and the Spirit of Violence', *Journal of Political and Military Sociology* **7**: 103–19

Ajangiz, R. 2002. 'The European Farewell to Conscription?' In L. Mjøset and S. van Holde (eds.), *The Comparative Study of Conscription in the Armed Forces*. Bingley, UK: Emerald, pp. 307–33.

Alexander, J. 1987. 'The Centrality of the Classics'. In: A. Giddens and J. H. Turner (eds.), *Social Theory Today*. Cambridge: Polity Press, pp. 11–57.

2003. *The Meanings of Social Life: A Cultural Sociology*. New York: Oxford University Press.

2004. 'Toward a Theory of Cultural Trauma'. In J. C. Alexander, R. Eyerman, B. Giesen, N. J. Smelser and P. Sztompka (eds.), *Cultural Trauma and Collective Identity*. Berkeley: University of California Press, pp. 1–30.

Alpern, S. 1998. *Amazons of Black Sparta: The Women Warriors of Dahomey*. New York University Press.

Alperovitz, G. 1995. *The Decision to Use the Atomic Bomb*. New York: Knopf.

Althusser, L. 1994. 'Ideology and Ideological State Apparatuses (Notes Towards an Investigation)'. In S. Žižek (ed.), *Mapping Ideology*. London: Verso, pp. 100–41.

Anderson, B. 1983. *Imagined Communities: Reflections on the Origin and Spread of Nationalism*. London: Verso

Anderson, F. and Cayton, A. 2005. *The Dominion of War: Empire and Liberty in North America, 1500-2000*. New York: Viking.

Andren, A. and Crozier A. 1998. *Between Artifacts and Texts: Historical Archaeology in Global Perspective*. New York: Springer.

Andreski, S. 1968. *Military Organization and Society*. London: Routledge & Kegan Paul.

Angel, N. 2007 [1909]. *The Great Illusion*. New York: Cosimo.

Angier, N. 1995. 'Does Testosterone Equal Aggression? Maybe Not', *The New York Times*, 20 June 1995, p. 3.

Angle, J. 1986. 'The Surplus Theory of Social Stratification and the Size Distribution of Personal Wealth', *Social Forces*, **65**: 293–326.

Angold, M. 2001. *Byzantium: The Bridge from Antiquity to the Middle Ages*. London: Phoenix Press.

Antonucci, M. 1993. 'War by Other Means: The Legacy of Byzantium', *History Today* **43**(2): 11–13.

Arendt, H. 1951. *The Origins of Totalitarianism*. New York: Harcourt.

Aristotle 2004. *Politics*. New York: NuVision Publications.

Aron, R. 1958. *War and Industrial Society*. Oxford University Press.

　　1966. *Peace and War: A Theory of International Relations*. Garden City, NY: Doubleday & Company.

Ashworth, C. and Dandeker, C. 1987. 'Warfare, Social Theory, and West European Development', *Sociological Review*, **35**: 1–18.

Ashworth, T. 1968. 'The Sociology of Trench Warfare 1914–1918', *British Journal of Sociology*, **19**: 407–23.

　　1980. *Trench Warfare, 1914–1918: The Live and Let Live System*. London: Macmillan.

Atkinson, T. 2002. 'Is Rising Income Inequality Inevitable? A Critique of the 'Transatlantic Consensus'. In P. Townsend and D. Gordon (eds.), *World Poverty: New Policies to Defeat an Old Enemy*. Bristol: Policy Press, pp. 251–70.

Ayton, A. and Price, J. L. (eds.) 1995. *The Medieval Military Revolution. State, Society and Military Change in Medieval and Early Modern Europe*. London: I.B.Tauris.

Ayubi, N. 1991. *Political Islam: Religion and Politics in the Arab World*. London: Routledge.

Baker, M. 1982. *Nam: The Vietnam War in the Words of the Men and Women Who Fought There*. New York: Morrow.

Balikci, A. 1970. *The Netsilik Eskimo*. Garden City, NY: Natural History Press.

Banton, M. 1983. *Racial and Ethnic Competition*. Cambridge University Press.

Bar-Tal, D. 1989. 'Delegitimization: The Extreme Case of Stereotyping and Prejudice'. In D. Bar-Tal, C. F. Graumann, A. W. Kruglanski and W. Stroebe (eds.), *Stereotyping and Prejudice: Changing Conceptions*. New York: Springer, pp. 169–88.

Bar-Yosef, O. 1986. 'The Walls of Jericho: An Alternative Interpretation', *Current Anthropology*, **27**: 157–62.

Baron, J. N. 1994. 'Reflections on Recent Generations of Mobility Research'. In D. B. Grusky (ed.), *Social Stratification: Class, Race, and Gender in Sociological Perspective*. Boulder, CO: Westview Press, pp. 542–52.

Baron, R. and Richardson, D. 1994. *Human Aggression*. New York: Plenum.

Barthes, R. 1977. *Roland Barthes*. Basingstoke: Macmillan.

　　1993. *Mythologies*. London: Vintage.

Bataille, G. 1986. *Eroticism: Death and Sensuality*. San Francisco: City Lights Books.

Bauman, Z. 1987. *Legislators and Interpreters*. Cambridge: Polity Press.

　　1989. *Modernity and the Holocaust*. Cambridge: Polity Press.

　　1991. *Modernity and Ambivalence*. Cambridge: Polity Press.

　　1998. *Globalisation: Human Consequences*. Cambridge: Polity Press.

2000. *Liquid Modernity*. Cambridge: Polity Press.

2001. 'Wars of the Globalisation Era', *European Journal of Social Theory*, **4**(1): 11–28.

2002a. 'Reconnaissance Wars of the Planetary Frontierland', *Theory, Culture and Society*, **19**(4): 81–90.

2002b. *Society under Siege*. Cambridge: Polity Press.

2006. *Liquid Fear*. Cambridge: Polity Press.

Beck, U. 1992. *Risk Society*. Cambridge: Polity Press.

1999. *World Risk Society*. Cambridge: Polity Press.

2002. 'The Cosmopolitan Society and its Enemies', *Theory, Culture and Society*, **19**(1–2), pp. 17–44.

Beeler, J. 1971. *Warfare in Feudal Europe, 730–1200*. Ithaca NY: Cornell University Press.

Bell, D. 1973. *The Coming Crisis of Post-Industrial Society*. New York: Basic Books.

Bentley, A. 1926. 'Simmel, Durkheim and Ratzenhofer', *American Journal of Sociology*, **32**: 250–6.

Berdal, M. 2003. 'How New are 'New Wars'? Global Economic Change and the Study of Civil Wars', *Global Governance*, **9**(4): 477–502.

Berkun, M. 1958. *Inferred Correlation Between Combat Performance and Some Field Laboratory Stresses*. Arlington, VA.: Human Resources Research Office.

Biddle, S. 2004. *Military Power: Explaining Victory and Defeat in Modern Battle*. Princeton University Press.

Billig, M. 1995. *Banal Nationalism*. London: Sage.

2002. 'Ideology, Language and Discursive Psychology'. In S. Malešević and I. Mackenzie (eds.), *Ideology after Poststructuralism*. London: Pluto, pp. 134–56.

Billig, M., Condor, S., Edwards, D., Gane, M., Middleton, D. and Radley, A. R. 1988. *Ideological Dilemmas: A Social Psychology of Everyday Thinking*. London: Sage.

Binford, L. 1987. 'The Hunting Hypothesis: Archeological Methods and the Past', *American Journal of Physical Anthropology*, **8**: 1–9.

Black, J. 1991. *A Military Revolution?: Military Change and European Society, 1550–1800*. London: Macmillan.

Black, P. 1972. *The Biggest Aspidistra in the World*. London: BBC.

Blanchard, I. 1989. *Russia's Age of Silver Precious-Metal Production and Economic Growth in the Eighteenth Century*. London: Routledge.

Boehm, C. 1999. *Hierarchy in the Forest: The Evolution of Egalitarian Behaviour*. Cambridge, MA: Harvard University Press.

Bollas C. 1993. *Being a Character. Psychoanalysis and Self Experience*. Routledge: London.

Boothby, N. and Knudsen, C. 2000. 'Children of the Gun', *Scientific American*, **282**(6): 60–5.

Boudon, R. 1973. *Education, Opportunity and Social Inequality*. New York: Wiley.

1989. *The Analysis of Ideology*. Cambridge: Polity Press.

2003. 'Beyond Rational Choice Theory', *Annual Review of Sociology*, **29**: 1–21.

Bourdieu, P. 1984. *Distinction: A Social Critique of the Judgment of Taste*. Cambridge, MA: Harvard University Press.

1990. *Language and Symbolic Power*. Cambridge, MA: Harvard University Press.

1996. *The State Nobility: Elite Schools in the Field of Power*. Cambridge: Polity Press.

Bourdieu, P. and Passeron, J.-C. 1977. *Reproduction in Education, Society, and Culture*. Beverly Hills: Sage.

Bourke, J. 2000. *An Intimate History of Killing*. London: Granta.

Bourne, J. 2005. 'Total War I: The Great War'. In: C. Townshend (ed.), *The Oxford History of Modern War*. Oxford University Press, pp. 117–37.

Bowlby, J. 1953. *Child Care and the Growth of Love*. Harmondsworth: Penguin.

Braverman, H. 1974. *Labor and Monopoly Capital*. New York: Monthly Review Press.

Breuilly, J. 1993. *Nationalism and the State*. Manchester University Press.

Breuilly, J., Ceserani, D., Malešević, S., Neuberger, B. and Mann, M. 2006. 'Debate on Michael Mann's *The Dark Side of Democracy: Explaining Ethnic Cleansing*', *Nations and Nationalism*, **12**(3): 389–412.

Browning, C. R. 1992. *Ordinary Men: Reserve Police Battalion 101 and the Final Solution in Poland*. New York: HarperCollins.

Brubaker, R. 1992. *Citizenship and Nationhood in France and Germany*. Cambridge, MA: Harvard University Press.

  1996. *Nationalism Reframed*. Cambridge University Press.

  2004. *Ethnicity without Groups*. Cambridge, MA: Harvard University Press.

Brubaker, R. and Laitin, D. 1998. 'Ethnic and Nationalist Violence', *Annual Review of Sociology*, **24**: 423–52.

Burk, J. 1998. *The Adaptive Military: Armed Forces in the Turbulent World*. New Brunswick, NJ: Transaction.

Campbell, A. 1993. *Men, Women and Aggression*. New York: Basic Books.

Caputo, P. 1977. *A Rumor of War*. New York: Ballantine.

Carnoy, M. 1993. 'Multinationals in a Changing World Economy: Whither the Nation-State?' In M. Carnoy (ed.), *The New Global Economy in the Information Age*. College Park: Pennsylvania State University Press, pp. 45–96.

Carr, L. J. and Stermer, J. E. 1952. *Willow Run: A Study of Industrialization and Cultural Inadequacy*. New York: Harper & Brothers.

Cartledge, P. 1979. *Sparta and Lakonia: a Regional History, 1300–362 BC*. London: Routledge & Kegan Paul.

Cartmill, M. 1993. *A View to a Death in the Morning: Hunting and Nature Through History*. Cambridge, MA: Harvard University Press.

Cashdan, E. A. 1980. 'Egalitarianism Among Hunter-Gatherers', *American Anthropologist*, **82**: 116–20.

Čekić, S. (ed.) 1999. *Srebrenica 1995: Dokumenti i svjedočenja I*. Sarajevo: Institut za istraživanje zločina protiv čovječnosti i medjunarodnog prava.

Centeno, M. A. 2002. *Blood and Debt: War and the Nation-State in Latin America*. University Park: Penn State University Press.

Childe, V. G. 1950. 'The Urban Revolution', *Town Planning Review*, **XXI**(1): 3–17.

Childs, J. 2005. 'The Military Revolution I: The Transition to Modern Warfare'. In: C. Townshend (ed.), *The Oxford History of Modern Warfare*. Oxford University Press, pp. 20–39.

Chomsky, N. 2002. *Media Control: The Spectacular Achievements of Propaganda*. New York: Seven Stories Press.

Clausevitz, C. von 1997. *On War*. Ware, UK: Wordsworth.

Clodfelter, M. 1992. *Warfare and Armed Conflicts: A Statistical Reference*. Vol I. Jefferson, NC: McFarland and Company.

Cockburn, C. 2007. *From Where We Stand: War, Women's Activism and Feminist Analysis.* London: Zed Books.

Coie, J. and Dodge, K. 1998. 'Aggression and Antisocial Behavior'. In W. Damon and N. Eisenberg (eds.), *Handbook of Child Psychology.* New York: Wiley, pp. 779–862.

Cole, A. and Campbell, P. 1989. *French Electoral Systems and Elections since 1789.* Aldershot, UK: Gower.

Collier, P. 2000. 'Rebellion as a Quasi-Criminal Activity', *Journal of Conflict Resolution,* **44**(6): 839–53.

Collins, Randall 1974. 'Three Faces of Cruelty: Towards a Comparative Sociology of Violence', *Theory and Society,* **1**: 415–40.

    1975. *Conflict Sociology.* New York: Academic Press.

    1979. *Credential Society.* New York: Academic Press.

    1981. *Sociology Since Mid-Century: Essays in Theory Cumulation.* New York: Academic Press.

    1985. *Four Sociological Traditions.* Oxford University Press.

    1986. *Weberian Sociological Theory.* Cambridge University Press.

    1988. *Theoretical Sociology.* San Diego: Harcourt Brace Jovanovich.

    1989. 'Sociological Theory, Disaster Research and War'. In G. Krebs (ed.), *Social Structure and Disaster.* Newark: University of Delaware Press, pp. 365–85.

    1992. *The Sociological Insight.* Oxford University Press.

    1999. *Macro History: Essays in Sociology of the Long Run.* Stanford University Press.

    2004. *Interaction Ritual Chains.* Princeton University Press.

    2008. *Violence: A Micro-Sociological Theory.* Princeton University Press.

Collins, Roger. 2005. 'Charlemagne's Imperial Coronation and the Annals of Lorch'. In: J. Story (ed.), *Charlemagne: Empire and Society.* Manchester University Press, pp. 52–70.

Čolović, I. 1999. *Kad kazem novine.* Belgrade: Samizdat B92.

Cordesman, A. H. and Kleiber, M. 2007. *Iran's Military Forces and Warfighting Capabilities: The Threat in the Northern Gulf.* New York: Greenwood Press.

Costello, J. 1985. *Virtue Under Fire: How World War II Changed Our Social and Sexual Attitudes.* Boston: Little and Brown.

Cottam, K. J. 1983. *Soviet Airwomen in Combat in World War II.* Manhattan, KS: Sunflower University Press.

Coupland, S. 2005. 'Charlemagne's Coinage: Ideology and Economy'. In: J. Story (ed.), *Charlemagne: Empire and Society.* Manchester University Press, pp. 211–29.

Crompton, R. 1993. *Class and Stratification: an Introduction to Current Debates.* Cambridge: Polity Press.

Curtin, P. D. 1969. *The Atlantic Slave Trade: a Census.* Madison: University of Wisconsin Press.

Dahn, L. H. 1966. 'The Long-Haired Army', *Vietnamese Studies,* **10**: 61–7.

Dahrendorf, R. 1959. *Class and Class Conflict in Industrial Society.* Stanford University Press.

Dandeker, C. 1990. *Surveillance, Power and Modernity: Bureaucracy and Discipline from 1700 to the Present Day.* New York: St Martin's Press.

Dart, R. A. 1953. 'The Predatory Transition from Ape to Man', *International Anthropological and Linguistic Review,* **1**: 201–18.

Darwin, J. 2008. *After Tamerlane: The Rise and Fall of Global Empires, 1400–2000,* London: Penguin.

Davies, J. B., Sandstrom, S., Horrocks, A. and Wolff, E. N. 2006. *The World Distribution of Household Wealth*. World Institute for Development Economics Research of the United Nations University.

Davis, H. W. C. 1915. *The Political Thought of H. von Treitschke*. New York: Charles Scribner's Sons.

Dawkins, R. 1986. *The Blind Watchmaker*. New York: W. W. Norton.

    1989. *The Selfish Gene*. Oxford University Press.

De Waal, F. 2005. *Our Inner Ape: A Leading Primatologist Explains Why We Are Who We Are*. New York: Riverhead Books.

Dickens, A. G. 1968. *Reformation and Society in Sixteenth Century Europe*. New York: Harcourt Brace Yovanovich.

DiMaggio, P. 1987. 'Classification in Art', *American Sociological Review,* **52**: 440–55.

    1991. 'Social Structure, Institutions and Cultural Goods: the Case of the United States'. In: P. Bourdieu and J. S. Coleman (eds.), *Social Theory for a Changing Society*. Boulder, CO: Westview Press. pp. 133–55.

Dollard, J. 1977. *Fear in Battle*. Westport, CT: Greenwood Press.

Downing, B. 1992. *The Military Revolution and Political Change*. Princeton University Press.

Drake, R. 2003. *Apostles and Agitators: Italian Marxist Revolutionary Tradition*. Cambridge, MA: Harvard University Press.

Duffield, M. 2001. *Global Governance and the New Wars: The Merger of Development and Security*. London: Zed.

Dunn, S. 2004. *Jefferson's Second Revolution: The Election Crisis of 1800 and the Triumph of Republicanism*. Boston: Houghton Mifflin.

Dupuy, E. and Dupuy, T. 1986. *The Encyclopedia of Military History from 3500 BC to the Present*. New York: Harper and Row.

Durham, M. 1998. *Women and Fascism*. London: Routledge.

Durkheim, E. 1915. *Germany Above All: German Mentality and War*. Paris: Armand Colin.

    1933. *The Division of Labour in Society*. New York: Macmillan.

    1952. *Suicide*. London: Routledge & Kegan Paul.

    1959. *Socialism and Saint-Simon*. London: Routledge & Kegan Paul.

    1973. 'Pacifism and Patriotism', translated and introduced by N. Layne, *Sociological Inquiry,* **43**(2): 99–103.

    1986. *Durkheim on the Politics and the State*. Cambridge: Polity Press.

    1992. *Professional Ethics and Civic Morals*. London: Routledge & Kegan Paul.

    2001 [1915]. *The Elementary Forms of Religious Life*. New York: Oxford University Press.

Durkheim E. and Denis, E. 1915. *Who Wanted War? The Origin of the War According to Diplomatic Documents*. Paris: Armand Colin.

Dyer, G. 1985. *War*. London: Guild.

Eager, P. W. 2008. *From Freedom Fighters to Terrorists: Women and Political Violence*. Aldershot, UK: Ashgate.

Eagly, A. and Steffen, V. 1986. 'Gender and Aggressive Behaviour: A Meta-Analytic Review of the Social Psychological Literature', *Psychological Bulletin,* **100**, 3: 309–30.

Eckhardt, W. 1990. 'Civilizations, Empires and Wars', *Journal of Peace Research,* **27**(1): 9–24.

1992. *Civilizations, Empires and Wars: A Quantitative History of War.* Jefferson, NC: McFarland.

Edensor, T. 2002. *National Identity, Popular Culture and Everyday Life.* Oxford: Berg.

Edgerton, R. B. 2000. *Warrior Women: The Amazons of Dahomey and the Nature of War.* Boulder, CO: Westview Press.

Ehrenreich, B. 1997. *Blood Rites: Origins and History of the Passions of War.* New York: Henry Holt and Company.

Eibl-Eibesfeldt, I. 1971. *Love and Hate: The Natural History of Behavior Patterns.* New York: Holt, Rinehart and Winston.

1979. *The Biology of Peace and War: Men, Animals, and Aggression.* New York: Viking.

Eibl-Eibesfeldt, I. and Salter, F. K. 1998. 'Introduction'. In I. Eibl-Eibesfeldt and F. K. Salter (eds.), *Indoctrinability, Ideology, and Warfare: Evolutionary Perspectives.* New York: Berghahn Books, pp. 1–20.

Elias, N. 2000 [1939]. *The Civilizing Process: Sociogenetic and Psychogenetic Investigations.* London: Blackwell.

Eller, J. and Coughlan, R. 1993. 'The Poverty of Primordialism: the Demystification of Ethnic Attachments', *Ethnic and Racial Studies,* **16**(2): 183–202.

Ellul, J. 1965. *Propaganda: The Formation of Men's Attitudes.* Trans. Konrad Kellen and Jean Lerner. New York: Knopf.

Elster, J. 1985. *Making Sense of Marx.* Cambridge University Press.

Eltis, D. 1995. *The Military Revolution in Sixteenth Century Europe.* London: Tauris.

Ender, M. G. and Gibson, A. A. 2005. 'Invisible Institution: The Military, War, and Peace in pre 9/11 Introductory Sociology Textbooks', *Journal of Political and Military Sociology,* **33**(2): 249–66.

Engels. F. 1962. *Anti-Duhring.* Moscow: Foreign Languages Publishing House.

Enloe, C. 1983. *Does Khaki Become You? The Militarisation of Women's Lives.* Berkeley: University of California Press.

1990. 'Womenandchildren: Making Feminist Sense of the Persian Gulf Crisis', *The Village Voice,* 25 September 1990.

2000. *Maneuvers: The International Politics of Militarizing Women's Lives.* Berkeley: University of California Press.

Ertman, T. 1997. *Birth of the Leviathan.* Cambridge University Press.

Fearon, J. 1994. 'Signaling versus the Balance of Power and Interests: An Empirical Test of a Crisis Bargaining Model', *Journal of Conflict Resolution,* **38**: 236–69.

1995. 'Rationalist Explanations for War', *International Organisation,* **49**: 379–414.

Fearon, J. and Laitin, D. 1996. 'Explaining Interethnic Cooperation', *American Political Science Review,* **90**(4): 715–35.

Ferrill, A. 1985. *The Origins of War: From the Stone Age to Alexander the Great.* London: Thames & Hudson.

Festinger, L. 1957. *A Theory of Cognitive Dissonance.* Stanford University Press.

Fletcher, C. R. L. 1890. *Gustavus Adophus and the Struggle of Protestantism for Existence.* London: Kessinger Publishing.

Floud, R., Wachter, K. and Gregory, A. 1990. *Height, Health and History: Nutritional Status in the United Kingdom, 1750–1980.* Cambridge University Press.

Frank, Jill. 2007. 'Wages of War: On Judgement in Plato's Republic', *Political Theory,* **35**(4): 443–67.

Frank, Joseph. 1961. *The Beginnings of the English Newspaper; 1620–1660*. Cambridge, MA: Harvard University Press.

Freeden, M. 1996. *Ideologies and Political Theory: A Conceptual Approach*. Oxford: Clarendon Press.

2003. *Ideology: A Very Short Introduction*. Oxford University Press.

French, D. 2005. 'The Nation in Arms II: The Nineteenth Century'. In: C. Townshend (ed.), *The Oxford History of Modern Warfare*. Oxford University Press.

Frisby, D. 1984. *Georg Simmel*. London: Tavistock.

Forrest, A. 2005. 'The Nation in Arms I: The French Wars'. In: C. Townshend (ed.), *The Oxford History of Modern Warfare*. Oxford University Press, pp. 55–73.

Forrest, W. G. 1963. *A History of Sparta 950–192 BC*. New York: W. W. Norton.

Foucault, M. 1980. 'Truth and Power'. In C. Gordon (ed.), *Michael Foucault, Power/Knowledge*. Brighton: Harvester Press, pp. 109–33.

Fowles, J. 1974. 'Chronocentrism', *Features*, **6**: 65–8.

Fry, D. S. 2007. *Beyond War: The Human Potential for Peace*. Oxford University Press.

Gabriel, R. A. 1987. *No More Heroes: Madness and Psychiatry in War*. New York: Hill and Wang.

Gabriel, R. A. and Savage, P. L. 1979. 'Crisis in Command: Mismanagement in the Army', *Journal of Applied Behavioural Science*, **3**: 393–405.

Gafar, J. 2003. 'Poverty Estimates and Poverty Reducing Strategies for the Developing Economy'. In J. Baffoe-Bonnie and M. Khayum (eds.), *Contemporary Economic Issues in Developing Countries*. New York: Greenwood Publishing, pp. 75–96.

Galanter, M. 1989. *Cults: Faith, Healing, and Coercion*. New York: Oxford University Press.

Galtung, J. and Ruge, M. H. 1965. 'The Structure of Foreign News. The Presentation of the Congo, Cuba and Cyprus Crises in Four Norwegian Newspapers', *Journal of Peace Research* vol. **2**, pp. 64–91.

Gambetta, D. 2006 (ed.). *Making Sense of Suicide Missions*. Oxford University Press.

Gamson, W. 1995. 'Hiroshima, the Holocaust, and Politics of Exclusion', *American Sociological Review*, **60**: 1–20.

Gardner, J. 1974. *Leadership and the Cult of Personality*. University of Michigan Press.

Gardner, P. M. 1972. 'The Paliyans'. In M. G. Bicchieri (ed.), *Hunters and Gatherers Today: A Socioeconomic Study of Eleven Such Cultures in the Twentieth Century*. New York: Holt, Rinehart and Winston, pp. 404–47.

Gardner, S. and Resnick, H. 1996. 'Violence among Youth. Origins and a Framework for Prevention'. In R. L. Hampton, P. Jenkins and T. P. Gullotta (eds.), *Preventing Violence in America*. Thousand Oaks, CA: Sage, pp. 157–77.

Garrett, S. A. 1993. *Ethics and Air Power in World War II: The British Bombing of German Cities*. London: Palgrave Macmillan.

Gat, A. 2006. *War in Human Civilization*. Oxford University Press.

Gellner, E. 1964. *Thought and Change*. London: Weidenfeld and Nicolson.

1983. *Nations and Nationalism*. Oxford: Blackwell.

1988a. 'Introduction'. In J. Baechler, J.A. Hall and M. Mann (eds.), *Europe and the Rise of Capitalism*. Oxford: Blackwell, pp. 1–5.

1988b. *Plough, Sword and the Book: The Structure of Human History*. London: Collins Harvill.

1997. *Nationalism*. London: Phoenix.

Genovese, E. D. 1965. *The Political Economy of Slavery*. New York: Pantheon.

Giddens, A. 1976. *New Rules of Sociological Method*. London: Hutchinson.

1985. *The Nation-State and Violence*. Cambridge: Polity Press.

1991. *Modernity and Self-Identity*. Cambridge: Polity Press.

2009. *Sociology*. 6th edition. Cambridge: Polity Press.

Giesen, B. 1998. *The Intellectuals and the Nation: Collective Identity in a German Axial Age*. Cambridge University Press.

2004. 'The Trauma of Perpetuators: The Holocaust as the Traumatic Reference in the German National Identity'. In J. C. Alexander, R. Eyerman, B. Giesen, N. J. Smelser and P. Sztompka, *Cultural Trauma and Collective Identity*. Berkeley: University of California Press, pp. 112–54.

Gilbert F. 1975. 'Introduction'. In F. Gilbert (ed.), *The Historical Essays of Otto Hintze*. New York: Oxford University Press, pp. 3–32.

Gilligan, C. 1982. *In a Different Voice: Psychological Theory and Women's Development*. Cambridge, MA: Harvard University Press.

Girard, R. 1977. *Violence and the Sacred*. Translated by Patrick Gregory. Baltimore, MD: Johns Hopkins University Press.

Gleditsch, N. P., Wallensteen, P., Eriksson, M., Sollenberg, M. and Strand, H. 2002. 'Armed Conflict 1946–2001: A New Data Set', *Journal of Peace Research*, **39**(5): 615–37.

Gochman, C. and Maoz, Z. 1990. 'Militarized Interstate Disputes, 1816–1976: Procedures, Patterns, and Insights'. In J. D. Singer and P. Diehl (eds.), *Measuring the Correlates of War*. Ann Arbor: University of Michigan Press, pp.193–221.

Goebbels, J. 1941. *Die Zeit ohne Beispiel*. Munich: Zentralverlag der NSDAP.

Goldsmith, R. W. 1946. 'The Power of Victory: Munitions Output in World War II', *Military Affairs*, **10**: 69–80.

Goldstein, R. J. 1978. *Political Repression in Modern America*. Cambridge, MA: Schenkman.

1983. *Political Repression in Nineteen Century Europe*. London: CroomHelm.

2001. *War and Gender: How Gender Shapes the War System and Vice Versa*. Cambridge University Press.

Goldstone, J. 1991. *Revolution and Rebellion in the Early Modern World*. Berkeley: University of California Press.

2002. 'Efflorescence and Economic Growth in World History: Rethinking the 'Rise of the West' and the Industrial Revolution', *Journal of World History*, **13**:1: 67–138.

Goldsworthy, A. K. 1997. 'The Othismos, Myths and Heresies: The Nature of Hoplite Battle', *War in History*, **4**(1): 1–26.

Goldthorpe, J. H. 1987. *Social Mobility and Class Structure in Modern Britain*. Oxford: Calderon Press.

Goodall, J. 1986. *The Chimpanzees of Gombe: Patterns of Behavior*. Cambridge, MA: Harvard University Press.

Gorski. P. 2006. 'Mann's Theory of Ideological Power: Sources, Applications and Elaborations'. In J. A. Hall and R. Schroeder (eds.), *An Anatomy of Power: The Social Theory of Michael Mann*. Cambridge University Press, pp. 101–34.

Gouldner, A. 1970. *The Coming Crisis of Western Sociology*. New York: Basic Books.

1976. *The Dialectic of Ideology and Technology: The Origins, Grammar and Future of Ideology*. London: Macmillan.

Graves, R. 1957. *Goodbye to All That*. New York: Doubleday.

Gray, C. H. 1997. *Postmodern War: The New Politics of Conflict*. New York: Guilford Press.

Griesse, A., Eliot, A. and Stites, R. 1982. 'Russia: Revolution and War. In N. Goldman (ed.), *Female Soldiers – Combatants or Noncombatants? Historical and Contemporary Perspectives*. Westport, CT: Greenwood, pp. 61–84.

Griffith, P. 1989. *Battle Tactics of the Civil War*. New Haven, CT: Yale University Press.

Grossman, D. 1996. *On Killing: The Psychological Cost of Learning to Kill in War and Society*. Boston: Little, Brown and Company.

Grusky, D. B. 1994. 'The Contours of Social Stratification'. In D. B. Grusky (ed.), *Social Stratification: Class, Race, and Gender in Sociological Perspective*. Boulder, CO: Westview Press, pp. 3–35.

Guilaine, J. and Zammit, J. 2005. *Origins of War: Violence in Prehistory*. Oxford: Blackwell.

Gumplowicz, L. 1899. *The Outlines of Sociology*. Philadelphia, PA: American Academy of Political and Social Science.

    2007 [1883]. *Der Rassenkampf: Soziologishe Untersuchungen*. Saarbrücken: VDM Verlag.

Gurney, G. 1958. *Five Down and Glory*. New York: Random House.

Hafez. M. M. 2006. *Manufacturing Human Bombs: The Making of Palestinian Suicide Bombers*. Washington, DC: United States Institute of Peace.

Hall, J. A. 1985. *Powers and Liberties: The Causes and Consequences of the Rise of the West*. London: Blackwell.

    1987. 'War and the Rise of the West'. In: C. Creighton and M. Shaw (eds.), *The Sociology of War and Peace*. London: Macmillan, pp. 37–53.

    1988. 'States and Societies: the Miracle in Comparative Perspective'. In J. Baechler, J. A. Hall and M. Mann (eds.), *Europe and the Rise of Capitalism*. Oxford: Blackwell, pp. 20–38.

    2000. 'Globalisation and Nationalism'. *Thesis Eleven*, **63**: 63–79

    2002. 'A Disagreement about Difference'. In S. Malešević and M. Haugaard (eds.), *Making Sense of Collectivity: Ethnicity, Nationalism and Globalisation*. London: Pluto, pp. 181–94.

    2006. 'L'Europe des Patries, or Megalomania Breeds Ruritanians'. In R. Rogowski and C. Turner (eds.), *The Shape of the New Europe*. Cambridge University Press.

Hall, J. A. and Schroeder, R. (eds.) 2006. *An Anatomy of Power: The Social Theory of Michael Mann*. Cambridge University Press.

Hall, R. 1993. *Patriots in Disguise: Women Warriors of the Civil War*. New York: Paragon House.

Halperin, S. 2004. *War and Social Change in Modern Europe: The Great Transformation Revisited*. Cambridge University Press.

Hampson, E. and Kimura, D. 1992. 'Sex Differences and Hormonal Influences on Cognitive Function in Humans'. In. J. Becker, M. Breedlove, and D. Crews (eds.), *Behavioral Endocrinology*. Cambridge, MA: MIT Press, pp. 357–98.

Hanley, W. 2005. *The Genesis of Napoleonic Propaganda, 1796–1799*. New York: Columbia University Press.

Hanson, V. D. 1989. *The Western Way of War: Infantry Battle in Classical Greece*. New York: Knopf.

    2001. *The Soul of Battle: From Ancient Times to the Present Day, How Three Great Liberators Vanquished Tyranny*. New York: Anchor Books.

Haraway, D. 1991. *Simians, Cyborgs, and Women: The Reinvention of Nature*. London: Free Association Books.

Harbom, L. and Wallensteen, P. 2005. 'Armed Conflict and its International Dimensions 1946–2004', *Journal of Peace Research*, **42**(5): 623–35.

Harding, S. 1998. *Postcolonialism, Feminisms and Epistemologies*. Bloomington: Indiana University Press.

Hartup, W. 1983. 'Peer Relations'. In P. Mussen (ed.), *Handbook of Child Psychology*. New York: Wiley, pp. 103–96.

Hauser R. M. and Featherman, D. L. 1976. 'Equality of Schooling: Trends and Prospects', *Sociology of Education*, **49**: 99–120.

Hayden, B. 1995. 'Pathways to Power: Principles for Creating Socioeconomic Inequalities'. In T. D. Price and G. M. Feinman (eds.), *Foundations of Social Inequality*. New York: Plenum Press, pp. 15–85.

Hechter, M. 1995. 'Explaining Nationalist Violence', *Nations and Nationalism*, **1**(1): 53–68.

Hellie, R. 1971. *Enserfment and Military Change in Muscovy*. University of Chicago Press.

Henderson. W. D. 1979. *Why the Vietcong Fought: A Study of Motivation and Control in a Modern Army in Combat*. Westport, CT: Greenwood Press.

Heng, Y. 2006. 'The 'Transformation of War' Debate: Through the Looking Glass of Ulrich Beck's World Risk Society', *International Relations*, **20**(1): 69–91.

Herbst, J. 1990. 'War and the State in Africa', *International Security*, **14**(4):117–39.

    2000. *States and Power in Africa: Comparative Lessons in Authority and Control*. Princeton University Press.

Herodotus 1985. *The Histories*. University of Chicago Press.

Herwig, H., Archer, C., Travers, T. and Ferris, J. 2003. *Cassell's World History of Warfare*. London: Cassel.

Heuer, R. J. 1999. *Psychology of Intelligence Analysis*. Washington, DC: Centre for the Study of Intelligence.

Hicks, G. 1997. *The Comfort Women. Japan's Brutal Regime of Enforced Prostitution in the Second World War*. New York: W. W. Norton.

Hintze, O. 1975. *The Historical Essays of Otto Hintze*. New York: Oxford University Press.

Hirst, P. 2001. *War and Power in the Twenty-First Century*. Cambridge: Polity Press.

Hirst, P. and Thompson, G. 1999. *Globalisation in Question*. Cambridge: Polity Press.

Hitler, A. 2001 [1925]. *Mein Kampf*. London: Pimlico.

Hobbes, T. 1998 [1651]. *Leviathan*. Oxford University Press.

Hobsbawm, E. 1990. *Nations and Nationalism since 1780*. Cambridge University Press.

Hobson, J. A. 1901. *The Psychology of Jingoism*. London: Grant Richards.

Hobson, J. M. 2004. *The Eastern Origins of Western Civilisation*. Cambridge University Press.

Hodgson, M. G. S. 1974. *The Venture of Islam*. Vol. III. University of Chicago Press.

Holmes, R. 1985. *Acts of War*. New York: Free Press.

Holmes, L. 1997. *Post-Communism: An Introduction*. Cambridge: Polity Press.

Holsti, K. 1991. *Peace and War: Armed Conflicts and International Order 1648-1989*. Cambridge University Press.

Hopkins, K. 1978. *Conquerors and Slaves*. Cambridge University Press.

Howard, M. 1976. *War in European History*. Oxford University Press.

    1991. *Lessons of History*. New Haven, CT: Yale University Press.

    2002. *The First World War*. Oxford University Press.

Human Rights Watch 2008. *Child Soldiers Global Report.* New York: HRW.

Huntington, S. 1993. 'The Clash of Civilizations?', *Foreign Affairs,* **72**(3): 22–50.

1996. *The Clash of Civilizations and the Remaking of the World Order.* University of Chicago Press.

Hurtado, A. L. 1988. *Indian Survival on the California Frontier.* New Haven, CT: Yale University Press.

Hutchinson, J. 2005. *Nations as Zones of Conflict.* London: Sage.

2007. 'Warfare, Remembrance and National Identity'. In A. Leoussi and S. Grosby (eds.), *Nationalism and Ethnosymbolism.* Edinburgh University Press, pp. 42–54.

Hyde, J. 1986. 'Gender Differences in Aggression'. In J. Hyde and M. C. Linn (eds.), *The Psychology of Gender: Advances through Meta-Analysis.* Baltimore, MD: John Hopkins University Press, pp. 159–77.

Inalcik, H. 1994. 'The Ottoman State: Economy and Society 1300–1600'. In H. Inalcik and D. Quataert (eds.), *An Economic and Social History of the Ottoman Empire 1300–1914.* Cambridge University Press, pp. 9–43.

Insoll, T. 1996. *Islam, Archaeology and History: Gao Region (Mali) ca. AD 900–1250.* Ann Arbor: University of Michigan Press.

Jančar, B. 1988. 'Women Soldiers in Yugoslavia's National Liberation Struggle 1941–1945'. In E. Isaksson (ed.), *Women and the Military System.* New York: Harvester, pp. 47–67.

Janowitz, M. 1953. *The Professional Soldier and Political Power.* University Of Michigan Institute of Public Administration.

1957. 'Military Elites and the Study of War', *Journal of Conflict Resolution,* **1**: 9–18.

Jansen, M. B. 1992. *China in the Tokugawa World.* Cambridge: Harvard University Press.

Jenkins, R. 2002. 'Different Societies? Different Cultures? What are Human Collectivities?' In S. Malešević and M. Haugaard (eds.), *Making Sense of Collectivities: Ethnicity, Nationalism and Globalisation.* London: Pluto, pp. 12–32.

2008. *Social Identity.* 3rd edition. London: Routledge.

Jensen, R. J. 1975. *The Alaska Purchase and Russian-American Relations.* Seattle: University of Washington Press.

Jervis, R. 1978. 'Cooperation under the Security Dilemma', *World. Politics,* **30**(2): 167–214.

Joas, H. 2003. *War and Modernity.* Cambridge: Polity Press.

Jones, D. 1997. *Women Warriors: A History.* Washington, DC: Brassey's.

Jones, E. 1987. *The European Miracle.* Cambridge University Press.

Jorgensen, C. 1994. 'Women, Revolution, and Israel'. In M. A. Tetrault (ed.), *Women and Revolution in Africa, Asia, and the New World.* Columbia: University of South Carolina Press, pp. 272–96.

Jowett G. S. and O'Donnell, V. 2006. *Propaganda and Persuasion.* London: Sage.

Jung, D. 2003. 'A Political Economy of Intra-State War: Confronting a Paradox'. In D. Jung (ed.), *Shadow Globalization, Ethnic Conflicts and New Wars: A Political Economy of Intra-State War.* London: Routledge. pp. 9–26.

Kagan, D. 1995. *On the Origins of War.* London: Hutchinson.

Kaldor, M. 2001. *New and Old Wars: Organised Violence in a Global Era.* Cambridge: Polity Press.

2004. 'Nationalism and Globalisation', *Nations and Nationalism,* **10**(1–2): 161–77.

2007. 'Oil and Conflict: the Case of Nagorno Karabakh'. In M. Kaldor, T. Karl and Y. Said (eds.), *Oil Wars.* London: Pluto, pp 157–83.

Kaldor, M. and Vashee, B. (eds.) 1997. *New Wars*. London. Continuum.

Kalyvas, S. 2001. "'New' and 'Old' Civil Wars: A Valid Distinction?', *World Politics*, **54**: 99–118.

2003. 'The Ontology of 'Political Violence': Action and Identity in Civil Wars', *Perspectives on Politics*, **1**:3, 475–94.

2005. 'Warfare in Civil Wars'. In I. Duyvesteyn and J. Angstrom (eds.), *Rethinking the Nature of War*. Abingdon, UK: Frank Cass, pp. 88–108.

2006. *The Logic of Violence in Civil War*. Cambridge University Press.

2007. 'Civil Wars'. In C. Boix and S. Stokes (eds.), *Handbook of Political Science*. New York: Oxford University Press, pp. 416–34.

2008. 'Ethnic Defection in Civil Wars', *Comparative Political Studies*, **41**:8, 1043–68.

Kant, I. 1991 [1784]. *Political Writings*. Cambridge University Press.

Kaplan, R. 1993. *Balkan Ghosts: A Journey through History*. New York: St. Martin's Press.

Kardin, N. N. 2002. 'Nomadism, Evolution, and World-Systems: Pastoral Societies in Theories of Historical Development', *Journal of World-System Research*, **8**: 368–88.

2004. 'Nomadic Empires in Evolutionary Perspective'. In L. Grinin (ed.), *The Early State: Its Alternatives and Analogues*. Volgograd: Uchitel, pp. 501–24.

Karve I. 1961. *Hindu Society – An Interpretation*. Deshmukh Prakashan, Poona.

Keegan, J. 1976. *The Face of Battle: A Study of Agincourt, Waterloo, and the Somme*. New York: Random House.

1994. *A History of Warfare*. New York: Vintage.

Keeley, L. H. 1996. *War before Civilization: The Myth of the Peaceful Savage*. Oxford University Press.

Keen, D. 1998. *The Economic Functions of Violence in Civil Wars*. Adelphi Paper 320. Oxford: IISS.

Kelly, R. 1995. *The Foraging Spectrum: Diversity In Hunter-Gatherer Lifeways*. Washington DC: Smithsonian Institution Press.

Khazanov, A.M. 1993. 'Muhammad and Jenghiz Khan Compared: The Religious Factor in World Empire Building', *Comparative Studies in Society and History*, **35**: 461–79.

Kidd, B. 1894. *Social Evolution*. London: Macmillan.

Kimura, D. 1992. 'Sex Differences in the Brain', *Scientific American*, **267**(3): 118–25.

Knightley, P. 2002. *The First Casualty: The War Correspondent as Hero*. Baltimore, MD: John Hopkins University Press.

Kohn, G. C. 1987. *Dictionary of Wars*. Garden City, NY: Anchor.

Komlos, J. (ed.) 1994. *Stature, Living Standards, and Economic Development: Essays in Anthropometric History*. Chicago University Press.

Konner, M. 1988. 'The Aggressors', *The New York Times Magazine*, 14 August 1988, p. 33.

Kuhn, T. 1962. *The Structure of Scientific Revolutions*. University of Chicago Press.

Lacina, B. and Gleditsch, N. P. 2005. 'Monitoring Trends in Global Combat: A New Dataset of Battle Deaths', *European Journal of Population*, **21**(2–3): 145–66.

Laitin, D. 1995. 'National Revivals and Violence', *European Journal of Sociology*, **36**: 3–43.

2000. 'Language Conflict and Violence: the Straw that Strengthens the Camel's Back', *European Journal of Sociology*, **XLI**(1): 97–137.

2007. *Nations, States, and Violence*. Oxford University Press.

Lamont, M. 1992. *Money, Morals and Manners: The Culture of the French and the American Upper-Middle Class*. University of Chicago Press.

2002. *The Dignity of Working Men: Morality and the Boundaries of Race, Class, and Immigration*. Cambridge, MA: Harvard University Press

Lash, S. and Urry, J. 1987. *The End of Organized Capitalism*. Cambridge: Polity Press.

Lawrence, T. E. 1935. *Seven Pillars of Wisdom: A Triumph*. London: Jonathan Cape.

Lee, R. B. 1993. *The Dobe Ju/'hoansi*. Fort Worth, TX: Harcourt Brace College Publishers.

Lee, S. 1988. *Aspects of European History 1789–1980*. London: Routledge.

1991. *The Thirty Years War*. London: Routledge.

Lenin, V. I. 1939 [1916]. *Imperialism, the Highest Stage of Capitalism: A Popular Outline*. New York: International Publishers.

Lenski, G. 1966. *Power and Privilege*. New York: McGraw-Hill.

Lentner, C. (ed.) 1984. *Geigy Scientific Tables, Vol III: Physical Chemistry, Composition of Blood, Hematology, Somatometric Data*. Basle: Ciba-Geigy.

Lerner, D. 1972. *Propaganda in War and Crisis: Materials for American Policy*. New York: Arno Press.

Letiche, M. and Dmytryshyn, B. 1985. *Russian Statecraft*. New York: Basil Blackwell.

Lever, J. 1978. 'Sex Differences in the Complexity of Children's Play and Games', *American Sociological Review*, **43**: 471–83.

Levy, J. 1978. 'Lateral Differences in the Human Brain in Cognition and Behavioral Control'. In P. Buser and A. Rougeul-Buser (eds.), *Cerebral Correlates of Conscious Experience*. New York: North-Holland, pp. 215–32.

Lewis, M. 1957. *The History of the British Navy*. Harmondsworth: Penguin.

Linn, M. C. and Petersen, A. C. 1986. 'A Meta-Analysis of Gender Differences in Spatial Ability: Implications for Mathematics and Science Achievement'. In J. Hyde and M. C. Linn (eds.), *The Psychology of Gender: Advances through Meta-Analysis*. Baltimore, MD: John Hopkins University Press, pp. 67–101.

Lockwood, D. 1989. *The Black Coated Worker*. London: Allen and Unwin.

Lord, J. 1972. *The Maharajahs*. London: Hutchinson.

Lorenz, K. 1966. *On Aggression*. New York: Harcourt Brace Jovanovich.

Low, B. 1993. 'An Evolutionary Perspective on War'. In L. W. Zimmerman and H. Jacobsen (eds.), *Behavior, Culture and Conflict in World Politics*. Ann Arbor: University of Michigan Press, pp. 13–55.

Lukacs, G. 1971. *History and Class Consciousness*. London: Merlin Press.

Luther, M. 1974. *Luther's Works*, edited by H. C. Oswald. St. Louis, MO: Concordia Publishing House.

Lynn, J. A. 1990. *Tools of War*. Urbana: University of Illinois Press.

2003. *Battle: A History of Combat and Culture*. Boulder, CO: Westview Press.

Lyon, D. 2001. *Surveillance Society: Monitoring Everyday Life*. London: Open University Press.

Maccoby, E. 1998. *The Two Sexes: Growing Up Apart, Coming Together*. Cambridge, MA: Harvard University Press.

Machiavelli, N. 1997 [1532]. *The Prince*. Ware, Hertfordshire: Wordsworth.

Mack, A. 2005. *Human Security Report*. Oxford University Press.

Mackenzie, J. 1984. *Propaganda and Empire: The Manipulation of British Public Opinion, 1880–1960*. Manchester University Press.

Maddison, A. 1971. *Class Structure and Economic Growth: India and Pakistan since the Moghuls*. New York: W. W. Norton.

Malešević, S. 1998. 'Chetniks and Ustashas: Delegitimisation of an Ethnic Enemy in the Serbian and Croatian War-Time Cartoons'. In C. W. Lowney (ed.), *Identities: Theoretical Considerations and Case Studies*. Vienna: IWM, pp. 223–64.

   2002. *Ideology, Legitimacy and the New State: Yugoslavia, Serbia and Croatia.* London: Routledge.

   2004. *The Sociology of Ethnicity.* London: Sage.

   2006. *Identity as Ideology: Understanding Ethnicity and Nationalism.* New York: Palgrave Macmillan.

   2007. 'Between the Book and the New Sword: Gellner, Violence and Ideology'. In S. Malešević and M. Haugaard (eds.), *Ernest Gellner and Contemporary Social Thought.* Cambridge University Press, pp. 140–67.

   2008a. 'Solidary Killers and Egoistic Pacifists: Violence, War and Social Action', *Journal of Power,* **1**(2): 207–16.

   2008b. 'The Sociology of New Wars?: Assessing the Causes and Objectives of Contemporary Violent Conflicts', *International Political Sociology,* **2**(2): 97–112.

   2009a. 'Collective Violence and Power'. In S. Clegg and M. Hugaard (eds.), *Sage Handbook of Power.* London: Sage. pp. 274–90.

   2010. 'How Pacifist were the Founding Fathers?', *European Journal of Social Theory,* **13**(2).

Malešević, S. and Uzelac, G. 1997. 'Ethnic Distance, Power and War: the Case of Croatian Students', *Nations and Nationalism,* **3**(2): 291–98.

Mandel, E. 1968. *Marxist Economic Theory.* London: Merlin Press.

Mango, C. 2005. *Byzantium: The Empire of the New Rome.* London: Phoenix.

Mann, M. 1986. *The Sources of Social Power I: A History of Power from the Beginning to AD 1760.* Cambridge University Press.

   1988. *States, War and Capitalism: Studies in Political Sociology.* Oxford: Blackwell.

   1993. *The Sources of Social Power II: The Rise of Classes and Nation-States, 1760–1914.* Cambridge University Press.

   1997. 'Has Globalization Ended the Rise and Rise of the Nation-state?', *Review of International Political Economy,* **4**(3): 472–96.

   2001a. 'Explaining Murderous Ethnic Cleansing: The Macro-Level'. In M. Guibernau and J. Hutchinson   (eds.), *Understanding Nationalism.* Cambridge: Polity Press, pp. 207–41.

   2001b. 'Globalisation and September 11', *New Left Review,* **12**: 51–72.

   2003. *Incoherent Empire.* London: Verso.

   2004. *Fascists.* Cambridge University Press.

   2005. *The Dark Side of Democracy: Explaining Ethnic Cleansing.* Cambridge University Press.

   2006. 'The Sources of Social Power Revisited: A Response to Criticism'. In J. A. Hall and R. Schroeder (eds.), *An Anatomy of Power: The Social Theory of Michael Mann.* Cambridge University Press, pp. 343–96.

   2007. 'Predation and Production in European Imperialism'. In S. Malešević and M. Haugaard (eds.), *Ernest Gellner and Contemporary Social Thought.* Cambridge University Press, pp. 50–74.

Mannheim, K. 1966 [1936]. *Ideology and Utopia*, London: Routledge & Kegan Paul.

Marcuse, H. 1964. *One-Dimensional Man.* Boston, MA: Beacon Press

Marlin, R. 2002. *Propaganda and the Ethics of Persuasion*. Orchard Park, NY: Broadview Press.

Marshall, S. L. A. 1947. *Men against Fire: The Problem of Battle Command*. New York: Morrow.

Marsland, D. 1986. *Neglect and Betrayal*. London: Institute for European Defence and Strategic Studies.

Martin, J. L. 2005. The Objective and Subjective Rationalization of War. *Theory and Society*. **34**: 229–57.

Martins, H. 1974. 'Time and Theory in Sociology'. In J. Rex (ed.), *Approaches to Sociology*. London: Routledge & Kegan Paul, pp. 246–94.

Marvin, C. and Ingle, D. 1999. *Blood Sacrifice and the Flag*. Cambridge University Press.

Marwick, A. 1981. *Class: Image and Reality in Britain, France and the USA since 1930*. London: Fontana.

Marx, K. 1972 [1894]. *Capital*. 3 vols. London: Lawrence and Wishart.

    1988. *The Civil War in France: The Paris Commune*. New York: International Publishers.

    1999. *Capital: An Abridged Edition*. Oxford University Press.

Marx, K. and Engels, F. 1998. *The Communist Manifesto*. London: Verso.

Mazur, A. and Booth, A. 1998. 'Testosterone and Dominance in Men', *Behavioral and Brain Sciences*, **21**(3): 353–63.

McCarthy, B. 1994. 'Warrior Values: A Socio-Historical Survey'. In J. Archer (ed.), *Male Violence*. London: Routledge, pp. 105–20.

McDougall, W. 1915. *An Introduction to Social Psychology*. London: Methuen.

McLuhan, M. 2001. *Understanding Media: The Extension of Man*. London: Routledge.

McNeill, W. 1982. *The Pursuit of Power*. University of Chicago Press.

    1991. *Keeping Together in Time. Dance and Drill in Human History*. Cambridge, MA: Harvard University Press.

Melander, E., Oberg, M. and Hall, J. 2007. 'The 'New Wars' Debate Revisited: An Empirical Evaluation of the Atrociousness of 'New Wars'', *Uppsala Peace Research Papers*, **9**: 1–42.

Mellaart, J. 1975. *The Neolithic Of the Near East*. London: Thames & Hudson.

Merleau-Ponty, M. 1969. *On Humanism and Terror*. Boston, MA: Beacon Press.

Merton, R. K. 1952. 'Bureaucratic Structure and Personality', *Social Forces*, **17**: 560–8.

Milanović, B. 1998. *Income, Inequality, and Poverty During the Transformation from Planned to Market Economy*. Washington DC: The World Bank.

Miles, R. 1984. 'Marxism Versus the Sociology of 'Race Relations'', *Ethnic and Racial Studies*, **7**(2): 217–37.

    1988. 'Racism, Marxism and British Politics', *Economy and Society*, **17**(3): 428–60.

Miller, W. I. 2000. *The Mystery of Courage*. Cambridge, MA: Harvard University Press.

Mills, C. W. 1958. *The Causes of World War Three*. New York: Simon and Schuster.

Monaghan, E. and Glickman, S. 1992. 'Hormones and Aggressive Behavior'. In J. Becker, M. Breedlove and D. Crews (eds.), *Behavioral Endocrinology*. Cambridge, MA: MIT Press, pp. 262–86.

Montagu, L. 1970. *More Equal than Others: The Changing Fortunes of the British and European Aristocrats*. London: Michael Joseph.

Monter, E. W. 2003. *Frontiers of Heresy: The Spanish Inquisition from the Basque Lands to Sicily*. Cambridge University Press.

Montgomery, B. 1968. *A Concise History of Warfare*. London: Collins.

Moore, B. 1966. *Social Origins of Dictatorship and Democracy.* Boston, MA: Beacon Press.

Moore, R. L. 1994. *Selling God: American Religion in the Marketplace of Culture.* Oxford University Press.

Morris, Desmond. 1967. *The Naked Ape.* London: Jonathan Cape.

Morris, Donald. 1965. *The Washing of the Spears: The Rise and Fall of the Zulu Nation.* New York: Simon and Schuster.

Mosca, G. 1939. *The Ruling Class.* New York: McGraw Hill.

Moscovici, S. 1986. 'The Conspiracy Mentality'. In C. F. Graumann, and S. Moscovici (eds.), *Changing Concepts of Conspiracy.* New York: Springer, pp. 151–69.

Mosse, G. 1991. *Nationalization of the Masses.* Ithaca, NY: Cornell University Press.

Mouzelis, N. 1995. 'In Defence of the Sociological Canon: A Reply to David Parker', *Sociological Review,* **45**(2): 244–53.

Munkler, H. 2004. *The New Wars.* Cambridge: Polity Press.

Nairn, T. 1977. *The Break-up of Britain.* London: New Left Books.

Neville, L. 2004. *Authority in Byzantine Provincial Society, 950–1100.* Cambridge University Press.

Newman, E. 2004. 'The 'New Wars' Debate: A Historical Perspective is Needed', *Security Dialogue,* **35**(2): 173–89.

Nissen, H. J. 1988. *The Early History of the Ancient Near East, 9000–2000 BC.* University of Chicago Press.

Norman, A. W. and Litwack, G. 1987. *Hormones.* Orlando, FL: Academic Press.

O'Connor, D. 1993. 'Urbanism in Bronze Age Egypt and Northern Africa'. In T. Shaw, P. Sinclair, A. Bassey and A. Okpoko (eds.), *The Archeology of Africa: Food, Metals and Towns.* London: Routledge, pp. 570–86.

O'Shaughnessy, N. J. 2004. *Politics and Propaganda: Weapons of Mass Seduction.* Manchester University Press.

Oberschall, A. 2000. 'The Manipulation of Ethnicity: From Ethnic Cooperation to Violence and War in Yugoslavia', *Ethnic and Racial Studies,* **23**(6): 982–1001.

Oman, C. W. C. 1968. *The Art of War in the Middle Ages.* Ithaca, NY: Cornell University Press.

Oppenheimer, F. 2007 [1914]. *The State.* Montreal: Black Rose Books.

Otterbein, K. F. 2004. *How War Began.* College Station: Texas A&M University Press.

Overy, R. 2005. 'Total War II: The Second World War'. In C. Townshend (ed.), *The Oxford History of Modern Warfare.* Oxford University Press, pp. 138–57.

Pape, R. A. 2006. *Dying to Win: Why Suicide Terrorists Do it.* London: Gibson Square Books.

Pareto, V. 1935. *The Mind and Society.* New York: Harcourt, Brace & Co.

   1966. *Sociological Writings.* Oxford: Blackwell.

   1973 [1902]. 'Extracts from Les Systemes Socialistes'. In A. Lyttelton (ed.), *Italian Fascisms.* New York: Harper and Row, pp. 71–90.

Parker, G. 1976. 'The Military Revolution, 1560–1660 – A Myth?' *Journal of Modern History,* **48**: 195–214.

   1996. *The Military Revolution, 1500–1800: Military Innovation and the Rise of the West.* Cambridge University Press.

Parkin, F. 1979. *Marxism and Class Theory: A Bourgeois Critique.* London: Tavistock.

Parsons, T. and Bales, R. 1956. *Family, Socialization and Interaction Process*. London: Routledge & Kegan Paul.

Peel, J. 1989. 'The Cultural Work of Yoruba Ethno-genesis'. In El Tonkin, M. McDonald and M. Chapman (eds.), *History and Ethnicity*. London and New York: Routledge, pp. 198–215.

Perry, W. 2004. *Network Based Operations for the Swedish Defence Forces: An Assessment Methodology*. New York: Rand Corporation.

Peters, E. 1989. *Inquisition*. Berkeley: University of California Press.

Pickles, J. and Smith, A. 1998. 'Introduction: Theorising Transition and the Political Economy of Transformation'. In J. Pickles and A. Smith (eds.), *Theorising Transition: The Political Economy of Post-Communist Transformations*. London: Routledge, pp. 1–24.

Picq, Ardant du 2006 [1921]. *Battle Studies*. Charleston, SC: BiblioBazaar.

Plato 1996. *The Republic*. New York: W.W. Norton.

Porch, D. 2005. 'Imperial Wars: From the Seven Years War to the First World War'. In C. Townshend (ed.), *The Oxford History of Modern Warfare*. Oxford University Press, pp. 94–116.

Poggi, G. 1978. *The Development of the Modern State*. Stanford University Press.
    2001. *Forms of Power*. Cambridge: Polity Press.
    2004. 'Theories of State Formation'. In K. Nash and A. Scott (eds.), *The Blackwell Companion to Political Sociology*. Oxford: Blackwell, pp. 95–106.
    2006. 'Political Power Un-Manned: A Defence of the Holy Trinity from Mann's Attack'. In J. A. Hall and R. Schroeder (eds.), *An Anatomy of Power: The Social Theory of Michael Mann*. Cambridge University Press, pp. 135–49.

Pomeranz, K. 2000. *The Great Divergence: China, Europe, and the Making of the Modern World Economy*. Princeton University Press.

Ponsonby, A. 2005 [1928]. *Falsehood in Wartime*. London: Kimble and Bradford.

Posen, B. 1993. 'Nationalism, the Mass Army, and Military Power', *International Security*, **18**(2): 80–124.

Postgate, N. 1994. *Early Mesopotamia: Society and Economy at the Dawn of History*. London: Routledge.

Poulanzas, N. 1974. *Classes in Contemporary Capitalism*. London: Verso.

Ratzenhofer, G. 1881. *Die Staatswehr*. Stuttgart: Cottasche Buchhandlung.
    1904. 'The Problems of Sociology', *American Journal of Sociology*, **10**: 177–88.

Reid, W. 1976. *Arms Through the Ages*. New York: Harper and Row.

Rex, J. 1986. *Race and Ethnicity*. London: Open University Press.

Ridley, M. 1997. *The Origins of Virtue: Human Instincts and the Evolution of Cooperation*. New York: Viking.

Risjord, N. K. 2005. *Populists and Progressives*. Lanham, MD: Rowman and Littlefield.

Roberts, M. 1955. 'The Military Revolution, 1560–1660'. In M. Roberts (ed.), *Essays in Swedish History*. Minneapolis: University of Minnesota Press, pp. 195–225.

Ron, J. 2003. *Frontiers and Ghettos: State Violence in Serbia and Israel*. Berkeley: University of California Press.

Rousseau, J.-J. 2004 [1755]. *Discourse on the Origin of Inequality*. New York: Dover Publications.

Ruane, K. 2000. *The Vietnam Wars*. Manchester University Press.

Ruddick, S. 1989. *Maternal Thinking: Towards a Politics of Peace*. London: The Women's Press.

Russell, J. 1972. *Medieval Regions and their Cities*. Newton Abbot, UK: David and Charles.
    1984. *Witchcraft in the Middle Ages*. Ithaca, NY: Cornell University Press.
Rustow, A. 1980. *Freedom and Domination*. Princeton University Press.
Sahlins, M. 1972. *Stone Age Economics*. Chicago: Aidine Atherton.
Sakwa, R. 1999. *Postcommunism*. Buckingham: Open University Press.
Sanday, P. R. 1981 *Female Power and Male Dominance: On the Origins of Sexual Inequality*.
    Cambridge University Press.
Santosuosso, A. 2001. *Storming the Heavens: Soldiers, Emperors, and Civilians in the Roman
    Empire*. Boulder, CO. Westview Press.
Sassen, S. 2006. *Territory, Authority, Rights: From Medieval to Global Assemblages*. Princeton
    University Press.
Schmitt, C. 1996. *The Concept of the Political*. Chicago University Press.
Scholtz, P. 2001. *Eunuchs and Castrati: A Cultural History*. New York: Markus Wiener
    Publishers.
Scruton, R. 1987a. 'Left and Right: War and Peace', *British Journal of Sociology*, **38**(2): 281–5.
    1987b. 'Notes on the Sociology of War', *British Journal of Sociology*, **38**(3): 295–309.
Segal, D. 1989. *Recruiting for Uncle Sam: Citizenship and Military Manpower*. Lawrence: Kansas
    University Press.
Segal, L. 1990. *Slow Motion: Changing Masculinities, Changing Men*. New Brunswick, NJ:
    Rutgers University Press.
Semmel, B. 1981. *Marxism and the Science of War*. Oxford University Press.
Service, E. R. 1978. *Profiles in Ethnology*. New York: Harper and Row.
Shalit, B. 1988. *The Psychology of Conflict and Combat*. New York: Praeger Publishers.
Shaw, M. 1984. 'War and Social Theory'. In M. Shaw (ed.), *War, State and Society*.
    London: Macmillan, pp. 1–24.
    2000. *The Theory of the Global State*. Cambridge University Press.
    2002. 'Risk-Transfer Militarism, Small Massacres and the Historic Legitimacy of War',
    International Relations, **17**(3): 343–60.
    2003. *War and Genocide: Organized Killing in Modern Society*. Cambridge: Polity Press.
    2005. *The New Western Way of War: Risk-Transfer War and Its Crisis in Iraq*
    Cambridge: Polity Press.
Shaw, R. and Wang, Y. 1989. *The Genetic Seeds of Warfare*. London: Routledge.
Shils, E. and Janowitz, M. 1948. 'Cohesion and Disintegration in the Wehrmacht in World
    War II', *Public Opinion Quarterly*, **12**: 280–315.
Sidebottom, H. 2004. *Ancient Warfare: A Very Short Introduction*. Oxford University
    Press.
Sifry, M. and Cerf, C. 1991. *The Gulf War Reader*. New York: Random House.
Simmel, G. 1917. *Der Krieg und die geistigen Entscheidungen*. Munich: Duncker and
    Humblot.
    1955 [1908]. *Conflict and the Web of Group Affiliations*. Glencoe: Free Press.
Singh, J. 2001. '"Medieval' Taliban lashed over Buddhist Demolition', *APF News*, 2 March
    2001.
Sklair, L. 1991. *Sociology of the Global System*. London: Harvester.
    2001. *The Transnational Capitalist Class*. Oxford: Blackwell.
    2002. *Globalization: Capitalism and Its Alternatives*. Oxford University Press.

Skocpol, T. 1979. *States and Social Revolutions: A Comparative Analysis of France, Russia, and China*. Cambridge University Press.

Smaldone, J. P. 1977. *Warfare in the Sokoto Caliphate: Historical and Sociological Perspectives*. Cambridge University Press.

Small, A. 1905. *General Sociology*. University of Chicago Press.

Smelser, N. J. 2004. 'Psychological Trauma and Cultural Trauma'. In J. C. Alexander, R. Eyerman, B. Giesen, N. J. Smelser and P. Sztompka, *Cultural Trauma and Collective Identity*. Berkeley: University of California Press, pp. 31–59.

Smith, A. D. 1981. 'War and Ethnicity: The Role of Warfare in the Formation, Self-Images, and Cohesion of Ethnic Communities', *Ethnic and Racial Studies*, **4**: 375–97.

  1986. *The Ethnic Origins of Nations*. Oxford: Blackwell.

  1991. *National Identity*. Harmondsworth: Penguin.

  1998. *Nationalism and Modernism*. London: Routledge.

  1999. *Myths and Memories of the Nations*. Oxford University Press.

  2003. *Chosen Peoples: Sacred Sources of National Identity*. Oxford University Press.

  2009. *Ethnosymbolism and Nationalism: A Cultural Approach*. London: Routledge.

Smith, P. 1991. 'Codes and Conflict: Towards a Theory of War as Ritual', *Theory and Society*, **21**: 103–38.

  1994. 'The Semiotic Foundations of Media Narratives: Saddam and Nasser in the American Mass Media', *Journal of Narrative and Life History*, **4**(1&2): 89–118.

  2005. *Why War?: The Cultural Logic of Iraq, the Gulf War, and Suez*. Chicago University Press.

  2008. 'Meaning and Military Power: Moving on from Foucault', *Journal of Power*, **1**(3): 275–93.

Snow, D. (1996). *Uncivil Wars: International Security and the New Internal Conflicts*. Boulder, CO: Lynne Rienner.

Sollenberg, M. 2007. 'From Bullets to Ballots: Using the People as Arbitrators to Settle Civil Wars'. In M. Öberg and S. Kaare (eds.), *Governance, Resources and Civil Conflict*. London: Routledge, pp. 178–204.

Sombart, W. 1913. *Krieg und Kapitalismus*. Munich: Duncker & Humblot.

Sorel, G. 1950 [1908]. *Reflections on Violence*. Glencoe: Free Press.

Sorokin, P. 1957. *Social and Cultural Dynamics*. Boston, MA: Porter Sargent.

Spencer, H. 1971. *Herbert Spencer: Structure, Function and Evolution*. Edited by S. Andreski. London: Nelson.

Spengler, O. 1991 [1918]. *The Decline of the West*. New York: Oxford University Press.

Stannard, D. 1992. *American Holocaust*. Oxford University Press.

Stein, G. 1994. 'Economy, Ritual, and Power in Ubaid Mesopotamia'. In G. Stein and M. Rothman (eds.), *Chiefdoms and Early States in the Near East*. Madison: Prehistory Press, pp. 34–46.

Stepper, R. 2001. 'Roman–Carthaginian Relations: From Co-operation to Anihilation'. In A. V. Hartmann and B. Heuser (eds.), *War, Peace and World Orders in European History*. London: Routledge, pp. 72–83.

Stiehm, J. H. 1989. *Arms and the Enlisted Woman*. Philadelphia, PA: Temple University Press.

Stone, N. 1983. *Europe Transformed, 1878–1919*. London: Fontana.

Stouffer, S. A., Suchman, E. A., DeVinney, L. C., Star, S. A. and Williams, R M. (eds.) 1949. *The American Soldier: Combat and its Aftermath*. Princeton University Press.

Strauss, B. 1987. *Athens After the Peloponnesian War: Class, Faction and Policy, 403–386 BC*. Ithaca, NY: Cornell University Press.

Sumner, W.G. 1906. *Folkways*. Boston, MA. Ginn and Company.

1911. *War and Other Essays*. New Haven, CT: Yale University Press.

Taagepera, R. 1997. 'Expansion and Contraction Patterns of Large Polities: Context for Russia', *International Studies Quarterly*, **41**(3): 475–504.

Taylor, F. 2004. *Dresden: Tuesday, February 13, 1945*. New York: HarperCollins.

Taylor. P. M. 2003. *Munitions of the Mind: A History of Propaganda from the Ancient World to the Present Day*. Manchester University Press.

Taylor, T. 1996. *The Prehistory of Sex: Four Million Years of Human Sexual Culture*. New York: Bantam.

Textor, R. B. 1967. *A Cross-Cultural Summary*. New Haven, CT: Human Relations Area Files Press.

Thomas, J. A. 1939. *The House of Commons: 1832–1901: A Study of its Economic and Functional Character*. Cardiff: University of Wales Press.

Tiger, L. 1969. *Men in Groups*. New York: Viking.

Tiger, L. and Fox, R. 1971. *The Imperial Animal*. New York: Holt, Rinehart and Winston.

Tilly, C. (ed.) 1975. *The Formation of National States in Western Europe*. Princeton University Press.

1978. *From Mobilization to Revolution*. Reading MA: Addison Wesley.

1985. 'War Making and State Making as Organized Crime'. In P. Evans, D. Rueschemeyer and T. Skocpol (eds.), *Bringing the State Back In*. Cambridge University Press, pp. 169–91.

1986. *The Contentious French: Four Centuries of Popular Struggle*. Cambridge, MA: Harvard University Press.

1992a. 'War in History', *Sociological Forum*, **7**(1): 187–95.

1992b. *Coercion, Capital and European States*. Oxford: Blackwell.

1999. 'Power: Top Down and Bottom Up', *The Journal of Political Philosophy*, **7**(3): 330–52.

2003. *The Politics of Collective Violence*. Cambridge University Press.

2007. *Democracy*. Cambridge University Press.

Tinbergen, N. 1951. *The Study of Instinct*. Oxford University Press.

Tiryakian, E. A. 1999. 'War: The Covered Side of Modernity', *International Sociology*, **14**(4): 473–89.

Tokača, M. 2007. 'Istrazivacko-dokumentacijski centar: Od '91 do '95 u BiH ubijeno 97 tisuca ljudi', *Jutarnji List*, 21 June 14, p. 3.

Totman, C. 1993. *Early Modern Japan*. Berkeley: University of California Press.

Townshend, C. 2005. 'People's War'. In C. Townshend (ed.), *The Oxford History of Modern Warfare*. Oxford University Press, pp. 177–97.

Toynbee, A. J. 1950. *War and Civilization, Selections from A Study of History*. New York: Oxford University Press.

Treitschke, H. von 1914. *Selections from Treitschke's Lectures on Politics*. London: Gowans & Gray.

Truman Library 1945. 'Draft Statement on Dropping of the Bomb. President's Secretary's File', *Truman Papers*. www.trumanlibrary.org/index.php.

Turner, B. S. 1986. *Citizenship and Capitalism*. London: Allen and Unwin.

1988. *Status*. Minneapolis: University of Minnesota Press.

Tyerman C. 2004. *Fighting for Christendom: Holy War and the Crusades*. Oxford University Press.

Van den Berghe, P. 1981. *The Ethnic Phenomenon*. New York: Elsevier.

1995. 'Does Race Matter?', *Nations and Nationalism*, **1**(3): 357–68.

Van Creveld, M. 1991. *The Transformation of War*. New York: Free Press.

Van der Dennen, J. 1995. *The Origin of War*. Groningen: Origin Press.

1999. 'Of Badges, Bonds and Boundaries: In-Group/Out-Group Differentiation and Ethnocentrism Revisited'. In K. Thienpont and R. Cliquet (eds.), *In-Group/Out-Group Behaviour in Modern Societies: An Evolutionary Perspective*. Brussels: NIDI CBGS Publications, pp. 37–74.

Van Hooff, J. 1990. 'Intergroup Competition and Conflict in Animals and Man'. In J. van der Dennen and V. Falger (eds.), *Sociobiology and Conflict: Evolutionary Perspectives on Competition, Cooperation, Violence and Warfare*. New York: Chapman and Hall, pp. 23–54.

Vogel, S. 1996. *Freer Markets, More Rules: Regulatory Reform in Advanced Industrial Countries*. Ithaca, NY: Cornell University Press.

Wade, R. 1996. 'Globalisation and its Limits: Reports of the Death of the National Economy are Greatly Exaggerated'. In S. Berger and R. Dore (eds.), *National Diversity and Global Capitalism*. Ithaca, NY: Cornell University Press, pp. 60–88.

Wallerstein, I. 2000. *The Essential Wallerstein*. New York: New Press.

Walter, B. 2002 *Committing to Peace: The Successful Settlement of Civil Wars*. Princeton University Press.

Walzer, M. 1965. *The Revolution of the Saints: A Study in the Origins of Radical Politics*. Cambridge, MA: Harvard University Press.

Ward, L. F. 1907. 'Social and Biological Struggles', *American Journal of Sociology*, **13**(3): 289–99.

1913. *Dynamic Sociology*. New York: Appleton.

1914. *Pure Sociology*. London: Macmillan.

Watier, P. 1991. 'The War Writings of Georg Simmel', *Theory, Culture and Society*, **8**: 219–33.

Weber, E. 1976. *Peasants into Frenchmen*. Stanford University Press.

Weber, M. 1930. *The Protestant Ethic and the Spirit of Capitalism*. New York: The Citadel Press.

1946. *From Max Weber: Essays in Sociology*. Translated and edited by H. H. Gerth and C. Wright Mills. New York: Galaxy.

1963. *The Sociology of Religion*. Boston, MA: Beacon Press.

1976. *The Agrarian Sociology of Ancient Civilizations*. London: New Left Books.

1968. *Economy and Society*. New York: Bedminster Press.

1994. *Weber: Political Writings*. Cambridge University Press.

2004. *The Essential Weber: A Reader*. London: Routledge.

Webster, D. L. 1976. 'Lowland Maya Fortifications', *Proceedings of the American Philosophical Society*, **120**: 361–71.

Wegener, B. 1991. 'Relative Deprivation and Social Mobility: Structural Constraints on Distributive Justice Judgments', *European Sociological Review*, 7: 3–18.

Weingast, B. 1998. 'Constructing Trust: The Political and Economic Roots of Ethnic and Regional Conflict'. In K. Soltan, E. M. Uslaner and V. Haufler (eds.), *Where is the New Institutionalism Now?* Ann Arbor: University of Michigan Press, pp. 163–200.

Weintraub, S. 1988. *Annual Summary of Investigations Relating to Reading*. Berkeley: University of California Press.

Welchman, 1982. *The Hut Six Story*. New York: McGraw Hill.

Wheeler, E. 1991. 'The General as Hoplite'. In V. Hanson (ed.), *Hoplites: The Classical Greek Battle Experience*. London: Routledge, pp. 121–70.

Whiting, B. and Edwards, C. 1988. *Children of Different Worlds: The Formation of Social Behaviour*. Cambridge, MA: Harvard University Press.

Whyte, M. K. 1978. *The Status of Women in Preindustrial Societies*. Princeton University Press.

Wilson, E. O. 1975. *Sociobiology: The New Synthesis*. Cambridge, MA: Harvard University Press.

1978. *On Human Nature*. Cambridge MA: Harvard University Press.

Wimmer, A. 2008. 'The Making and Unmaking of Ethnic Boundaries: A Multilevel Process Theory', *American Journal of Sociology*, 113(4): 970–1022.

Wimmer, A. and Glick-Schiller, N. 2002. 'Methodological nationalism and beyond: Nation-state building, migration and the social sciences', *Global Networks*, 2(4): 301–34.

Wimmer, A. and Min, B. 2006. 'From Empire to Nation-States. Explaining Wars in the. Modern World', *American Sociological Review*, 71(6): 867–97.

Winter, J. 1995. *Sites of Memory, Sites of Mourning: the Great War in European Cultural History*. Cambridge University Press.

Winterhalder, B. 2001. 'The Behavioral Ecology of Hunter-Gatherers'. In C. Panter-Brick, R. H. Layton and P. A. Rowley-Conwy (eds.), *Hunter-Gatherers: An Interdisciplineary Perspective*. Cambridge University Press, pp. 12–38.

Wintrobe, R. 2006. *Rational Extremism*. Cambridge University Press.

Wittfogel, K. 1957. *Oriental Despotism: A Comparative Study of Total Power*. New Haven, CT: Yale University Press.

Wright, E.O. 1979. *Class Structure and Income Distribution*. New York: Academic Press.

1989. *The Debate on Classes*. London: Verso.

Wright, Q . 1965. *A Study of War*. Chicago University Press.

Xenophon, 2009. *Hellenica*. http://ebooks.adelaide.edu.au/x/xenophon/

Yuval-Davis, N. 1997. *Gender and Nation*. London: Sage.

Index